CW01023329

THE LIFE AND TIMES OF ARTHUR BROWNE IN IRELAND AND
AMERICA, 1756–1805

The Life and Times of Arthur Browne in Ireland and America, 1756–1805

Civil Law and Civil Liberties

JOSEPH C. SWEENEY

FOUR COURTS PRESS

in association with

THE IRISH LEGAL HISTORY SOCIETY

Typeset in 10.5pt on 12.5pt EhrhardtMt by
Carrigboy Typesetting Services for
FOUR COURTS PRESS LTD
7 Malpas Street, Dublin 8, Ireland
www.fourcourtspress.ie
and in North America for
FOUR COURTS PRESS
c/o ISBS, 920 N.E. 58th Avenue, Suite 300, Portland, OR 97213.

© Joseph C. Sweeney and Four Courts Press 2017

A catalogue record for this title is available
from the British Library.

ISBN 978–1–84682–622–1

All rights reserved.
No part of this publication may be
reproduced, stored in or introduced into a retrieval system,
or transmitted, in any form or by any means (electronic, mechanical,
photocopying, recording or otherwise), without the prior
written permission of both the copyright owner and
publisher of this book.

Printed in England,
by CPI Antony Rowe, Chippenham, Wilts.

For my wife, Alice,
and her sister, Joan M. Quill

Contents

Illustrations

Foreword

by Patrick Geoghegan

ARTHUR BROWNE WAS A REMARKABLE public figure and intellectual, a legal scholar, politician and academic who made a significant contribution to Irish politics in the late eighteenth century and whose legal works continue to be used and cited. According to Seán Patrick Donlan, a distinguished academic, and for many years a council member of the Irish Legal History Society, he was 'among the most gifted jurists of eighteenth-century Ireland'.[1] F.E. Ball, in his definitive study of the judges in Ireland, hailed him as one of the three greatest teachers of law at Trinity College Dublin.[2] R.B. McDowell called him an 'intelligent and influential don' and praised him for being 'conspicuously active in rather different spheres of public life' and for being 'a strenuous defender of civil liberties'.[3] Anne Crookshank and David Webb described him as someone who was 'widely respected as a man of integrity and honesty, though without the severity that too often accompanies these virtues'.[4]

Today Browne's legal contributions are recognized and honoured. In 2010 a prize was instituted at the King's Inns in Dublin, and named the Arthur Browne Prize, awarded for the highest grade in the entrance examination to the course leading to the degree of barrister-at-law. In its account of Browne in the prize description, the King's Inns notes that the United States Supreme Court has cited Browne in over forty judgments, and that through his work Browne 'has a claim on being the father of American Admiralty Law'.[5] In 2016 the School of Law in Trinity College Dublin named a prestigious new annual lecture series after Browne. The inaugural Arthur Browne lecture was delivered by Professor Gráinne de Búrca of the NYU School of Law on 13 May 2016 on the question of whether EU anti-discrimination law is in decline. It is a nice coincidence that Professor de Búrca worked alongside Professor Sweeney for four years in the Fordham law faculty before moving to NYU.

1   Seán Patrick Donlan, '"Regular obedience to the laws": Arthur Browne's prelude to union', in Michael Brown and Seán Patrick Donlan (eds), *The law and other legalities of Ireland* (London, 2016), p. 255.
2   F.E. Ball, *The judges in Ireland*, 2 vols (London, 1926), i, xx.
3   R.B. McDowell, *Historical esssays, 1938–2001* (Dublin, 2003), pp 63–4.
4   Anne Crookshank and David Webb, *The paintings and sculptures in Trinity College Dublin* (Dublin, 1990), p. 26.
5   www.kingsinns.ie.

This recent recognition of Browne marks a big change. For many years he was shunned, deliberately ignored because of his conduct during the debates over the Act of Union, and it has taken the passing of considerable time for his remarkable achievements and accomplishments to be honoured. Because Browne switched sides on the issue, voting against the union in 1799 and for it in 1800, he was accused of inconsistency and, worse, dishonesty. In Jonah Barrington's hugely influential account of what happened, Browne was condemned for 'one of the most unexpected and flagitious acts of public corruption'.[6] According to this version he was haunted by shame afterwards, and 'he hated himself'. Dismissed as 'an amiable man [who] fell a victim to corruption', it is claimed that 'he rankled and pined' and his death in 1805 is attributed to 'a wretched mind and a broken constitution'. In the memoir of this period by Henry Grattan's son, Browne is separated from the 'mercenaries, soldiers, bravoes or bullies', who supported the union, but he is still criticized for 'his loss of honour'.[7] It is noted that he 'repented his conduct, but his regret came too late, and he died of a broken heart'.

The union controversy overshadowed what had been a glittering career until then as a leading academic and as a champion of civil liberties. Born in America and orphaned at the age of 16, Browne turned down an opportunity to go to Harvard and instead came to Ireland in 1772 to study at Trinity College Dublin, and in doing so followed in the footsteps of his father and grandfather. He was an international student long before the days when such things were fiercely prized by universities. Academic achievements followed quickly. He became a scholar in 1774 and graduated BA in 1776, MA in 1779, LLB in 1780 and LLD in 1784. A good indication of his academic prowess is the fact that he was elected to fellowship in 1777, following a rigorous examination, just one year after taking his BA degree. Appointed to the Regius professorship of civil and canon law in 1785, Browne has been described in the *Irish Jurist* as 'the most distinguished of the early professors' in Trinity in terms of legal scholarship.[8] James Quinn, in the Royal Irish Academy's *Dictionary of Irish biography*, has noted that 'he was popular with students and, unlike many of his predecessors, he took his academic duties seriously'.[9] Possessing a detailed knowledge of international law, he pioneered its teaching in Trinity and he 'is generally recognized as one of the most able and learned academic lawyers ever to teach there'. With his aptitude for Greek (he could also read Latin, French, Italian and Spanish, and had a working knowledge of German, Hebrew and Persian), he was invited to serve as Regius professor of Greek on three occasions. Because of his seniority he became a senior fellow in 1795. This gave him considerable clout in Trinity, and he became a member of the governing body.

6   Jonah Barrington, *Historic records and secret memoirs of the legislative union* (London, 1844), p. 460.
7   Henry Grattan, *Memoirs of the life and times of the Rt Hon. Henry Grattan*, 5 vols (London, 1842), v, 164.
8   *Irish Jurist*, 18 (1983), 188.
9   James Quinn, 'Browne, Arthur', in James McGuire and James Quinn (eds), *Dictionary of Irish biography* (Cambridge, 2009).

We know the quality of Browne's lectures on admiralty law because he put them together for a book in the 1790s. Browne's *A compendious view of the civil law and of the law of admiralty*, published in two volumes in 1797–9, has been hailed as 'the first treatise to deal comprehensively with admiralty law in the English language'.[10] It became a key text for legal scholars in Canada and the United States, and John Gage Marvin's famous and hugely influential *Legal bibliography*, first published in 1847, called it simply, 'the best book in the language showing the connexion between the common and the Civil Law'.[11] When a library was created in the White House during the presidency of Millard Fillmore in the early 1850s, it was one of the works that was purchased for inclusion, and Catherine M. Parisian, the historian of the first White House library, has noted that the second volume, on admiralty law, 'would have been of particular interest to Fillmore at this time'.[12] As Professor Sweeney's scholarship on this area has shown, Fillmore, who was in the middle of a major constitutional crisis about the extension of slavery, signed the first federal statute on admiralty liability in disasters at this time.[13]

Aside from academic life, Browne also excelled in the courts and in parliament. Called to the bar in 1779, he was a skilled advocate in the courtroom and was much in demand for civil law cases. He became a king's counsel in 1795. One of his most famous cases was in 1789–90, when he represented John Magee, the editor of the *Dublin Evening Post*, who was being sued by Richard Daly, the theatre manager. Browne lost the case, but by drawing attention to the use of judicial fiats he raised so many concerns that they were never used against the press again.

Elected as MP for the University of Dublin in 1783, Browne represented Trinity in the Irish House of Commons until 1800. He once told parliament that he was 'no party man', but he was broadly in agreement with the Whigs and supported civil liberties, the reform of parliament, and Roman Catholic relief, and opposed authoritarian government. Described by one contemporary as an 'acute, strong and forcible' debater, he was considered one of the best speakers in the Irish House of Commons.[14] Henry Grattan Jnr considered him 'the most gentlemanlike' of the liberal MPs, with 'a degree of ease and elegance of manner as well as mind'.[15] During the infamous visitation of Trinity in 1798, Browne was criticized by the lord chancellor, the earl of Clare, for defending two scholars who had been expelled.

By supporting the union in 1800, Browne went against the wishes of his electors (the fellows and scholars of the university), who had published an address the previous year calling on its members to oppose it. His change of mind on the union

---

10 Philip Girard, *Lawyers and legal culture in British North America* (Toronto, 2011), p. 41.
11 Catherine M. Parisian, *The first White House library: a history and annotated catalogue* (University Park, PA, 2010), p. 125.
12 Ibid.
13 Joseph Sweeney, 'Limitation of ship-owner liability: its American roots and some problems particular to collision', *Journal of Maritime Law and Commerce*, 32:2 (2001), 241–77.
14 Quinn, 'Browne, Arthur', in *Dictionary of Irish biography*.
15 Grattan, *Memoirs*, v, p. 163.

ensured that he was denounced by those who had previously been closest to him, including Henry Grattan and William Plunket. As compensation (to his enemies it was a reward), he was appointed to the board of accounts in 1801, and was made prime serjeant on 29 December 1802 (becoming the last person to hold that office), a privy counsellor in 1802, and a bencher of King's Inns in 1803, but it was little consolation. In early 1805 he attempted to make a political comeback, standing in the by-election for the University of Dublin, but he only secured eleven votes (out of ninety-two cast) and came third in the contest.[16] He died suddenly in June 1805 after a bout of 'dropsy'. At the auction after his death, Trinity College Dublin purchased a Shakespeare first folio that he had owned, for 22½ guineas, and it became one of the treasures of the library.[17] For many years afterwards it was considered his only positive legacy. Browne's reputation was damaged by question marks over why he had switched sides over the union, his name appearing on lists of those who changed sides between 1799 and 1800.

Given the controversy that has tainted Browne's legacy, it is time for a re-evaluation of his life and career. Therefore, the Irish Legal History Society was delighted to be approached by Professor Joseph Sweeney to publish this book, the first full-length biography of Browne. It is a significant contribution to our understanding of Browne and the context in which he lived and acted, and provides a new perspective on his legal career, his academic career and his role as a politician. Given that Browne was by birth an American, it is perhaps appropriate that this task has been undertaken by a fellow American and, not only that, someone who has been hailed as 'the pre-eminent American scholar in admiralty and maritime law, a rare expert in aviation law, and respected author in public international law'.[18]

Over a long and impressive career, Joseph Sweeney served in the United States Navy's Judge Advocate General's Corps in Rhode Island and overseas, and then worked in a New York admiralty firm, before joining the faculty of the Fordham School of Law, where he taught with distinction for forty-seven years. There he held the John D. Calamari Distinguished Professorship at Fordham University, and was hailed as a 'scholar, teacher [and] pillar of the Fordham Law School Community'.[19] The author of over fifty law-review articles, he co-authored the acclaimed treatise, *The law of marine collision*, as well as a text on aviation law, and edited volumes on international project finance and on the regulation of maritime transport. In 2008, on the occasion of his seventy-fifth birthday, an issue of the *Fordham International Law Journal* was dedicated in his honour, and it was recognized that 'some professors are leading scholars but are not particularly interested in teaching; others are dynamic teachers but only minimally involved in writing; but

16 R.G. Thorne (ed.), *The House of Commons: survey* (London, 1986), p. 652.
17 Peter Fox, *Trinity College Library Dublin: a history* (Cambridge, 2014), p. 139.
18 Roger J. Goebel, 'Joseph Sweeney: scholar, teacher, pillar of the Fordham law school community', *Fordham International Law Journal*, 32:4 (2008), 1133.
19 Ibid.

Professor Sweeney is extraordinarily able as both a scholar and a teacher'.[20] In his honour, the new office of the *Fordham International Law Journal* was named after him. The leading expert on the life and career of Arthur Browne, Sweeney has published groundbreaking articles on his work on admiralty law, and was invited by the *Oxford dictionary of national biography* to contribute its entry on Browne.

Seán Patrick Donlan has shrewdly recognized that 'we have little more than the public record on which to judge' Browne, and that is probably the reason why it has been difficult to assess his contribution to politics, the law, and to academic life. One of the achievements of this book is that it skilfully deploys those public records to allow Browne's actions to speak for themselves. Readers can make up their own minds about Browne's decisions on critical issues, most notably the union, but they can do so by reading his own explanations, and the book provides a nuanced, contextualized account of some key periods of Irish history. It also contains a detailed analysis of Browne's contribution to international admiralty law by one of the leading international experts on that subject. So there is much here that will be of interest to legal scholars as well as political historians.

We hope that this study will appeal to an American (and international) audience as much as to an Irish one, and Professor Sweeney has deliberately included as much general information as possible to assist readers unfamiliar with the political and social landscape of late-eighteenth-century Ireland (and indeed the American context from which he came). For years Arthur Browne was dismissed as one of the 'slaves who sold their land for gold/As Judas sold his God'. What emerges from this book is a much more sophisticated portrait of a gentleman lawyer, scholar and politician who wrestled with some of the biggest issues of the day during one of the most turbulent periods of Irish history. Not all political careers end in failure, although perhaps there is a warning here about the fate of the intellectual scholar who embarks on that career.

Patrick Geoghegan is a professor of history at Trinity College Dublin and is a vice president of the Irish Legal History Society.

---

20 Ibid., 1133.

Acknowledgments

THE PERSONNEL OF THE Fordham University Law Library, especially Kate McLeod (now librarian of Elon University Law School), Alison Shea and Juan Fernandez, made this work possible. Many thanks are due to interlibrary loan personnel of Columbia University, St John's University, Houghton Library of Harvard University, Princeton University, Yale University, Trinity College Dublin and the Representative Church Body Library, Braenor Park, Churchtown, Dublin. I have also benefited from the encouragement of my brilliant colleagues at the Fordham University School of Law, and distinguished colleagues in the faculty of arts and sciences: John P. McCarthy, professor emeritus of history and director of the Irish studies programme and the late John F. Roche, professor emeritus of American history. The manuscript was prepared by Ms Judy Haskell, Mr Daniel Fairfax, Mr Alfred Bobek, Ms Xiamara Perez, Ms Jamie Baldwin and Ms Lourdes Ramirez. Mr Sean Murray, Fordham Law School JD '17 prepared the bibliography. I extend my profound thanks to the publications committee of the Irish Legal History Society, and to the Society's senior vice president, Dr Patrick M. Geoghegan of Trinity College Dublin, for the close and careful shepherding of this book since its first submission in November 2009. I am also most grateful for the meticulous work of Sam Tranum, my editor at Four Courts Press. I remain responsible for any errors.

Introduction

I

THIS BOOK TELLS THE STORY of a great lawyer, who lived in a period of wars, revolutions and political turmoil. Arthur Browne was a careful scholar and teacher of law, as well as an independent politician who did not hesitate to speak in defence of a free press and the rights of citizens threatened by repressive government.

Born in Newport, Rhode Island, Browne was educated at Trinity College Dublin and prepared for the Bar at Lincoln's Inn, London. He served seventeen years in the independent Irish Parliament of Henry Grattan, yet voted for its downfall when it failed to protect the liberties of the innocent, and condoned murderous military abuses.

His textbooks on civil-law subjects – admiralty, ecclesiastical, international, matrimonial and testamentary law – were used in America, Ireland and Great Britain long after their publication. Unfortunately, no collection of his papers exists. Thus, his story must be derived from his published writings and the history of his times.

His contemporaries certainly recognized his fight for civil liberties, as the author of one of his obituaries wrote:

> [Browne] used the most vigorous intellectual efforts to protect the liberty of the subject against the encroachments of power and oppression. His countrymen will not readily forget the zeal with which he protected the freedom of the press, that grand bulwark of our liberties 'and' on Catholic emancipation and the suspension of the habeas corpus, he exerted himself to the astonishment of everyone who heard him.[1]

Forty-seven years ago, Professor Paul O'Higgins wrote:

> Arthur Browne was one of the most distinguished academic lawyers to teach in Trinity College Dublin, perhaps the ablest. His writings are still worth reading; and not merely for their historic interest. His life reveals a lawyer of wide culture and compassion who tried in the turmoil and cruelty of eighteenth century Ireland to reconcile opposition to popular violence and

1   *The Hibernian*, October 1805, p. 599.

an attachment to the established state and church with opposition to arbitrary state power. His views on legal education and on many aspects of the law were enlightened for the time. Browne deserves a place in the history of Irish law; and not merely as the last Irish prime serjeant.[2]

A very distinguished American judge, Harold R. Medina, called Browne, 'a commentator whose influence on the development of American admiralty law cannot be overstated'.[3] The modern historians of Trinity College have described Browne as a congenial colleague:

> He set a new precedent by taking seriously the duties of the chair [of civil law] … In Parliament he was respected for his independence, and he courted ministerial displeasure on more than one occasion by standing up for civil liberties but his loyalty was never in doubt … [He] was a man of very wide culture; philosophy was his hobby and his writings, as well as the auction catalogue of his library, show that he read widely and fluently in Greek, Latin, French, Italian and Spanish … [His *Miscellaneous sketches*] leave with the reader the impression – confirmed by the opinions of his contemporaries – of an agreeable companion and good conversationalist, and of a man who combined, as happens all too rarely, charm with integrity … Browne died before he was fifty at the height of his powers and reputation.[4]

Professor Daniel Coquillette has written of Arthur Browne, comparing him to Jeremy Bentham and Joseph Story, '[they] were all dedicated to the rationalization of commercial law, to legitimation by utility of legal doctrine, and to the expression of the legal principles in a comprehensive and clear manner whether by statute or treatise'.[5]

This book will tell the story of Arthur Browne, beginning with his family's mission to America and his youth in the great seaport town of Newport as the approaching American Revolution darkened the prospects of the young orphan. Then the story will move across the ocean to Ireland and his scholarly achievements at Trinity College. It will track his preparation for the teaching and practice of law in London as the American door closed firmly behind him. His success as a teacher brought him into Parliament as representative of his university. He served for seventeen years in Parliament as an advocate for civil liberties and critic of governmental efforts to subvert the 1782 'constitution'. Then, at the close of the eighteenth century, constitutional liberties were imperiled in the 1798

2   P. O'Higgins, 'Arthur Browne (1756–1805): an Irish civilian', 20 *Northern Ireland Legal Quarterly*, 255–73, 270 (1969).
3   Maryland Tuna Corp. v. M/S Benares, 429 F. 2d 307, 321 (2nd Cir. 1970).
4   R.B. McDowell and D.A. Webb, *Trinity College Dublin, 1592–1952: an academic history*, p. 81 (1982).
5   D.R. Coquillette, 'Legal ideology and incorporation IV: the nature of civilian influence on modern Anglo-American commercial law', 67 *Boston University Law Review*, 877, 969 (1987).

Revolution and the repression that sought to undo the reconciliation of minority and majority populations in repeal of the penal laws. The ferocious Protestant vengeance on the innocent after the 1798 Rising pushed him into the ranks of unionists who destroyed home rule for the next one hundred twenty years. This is a story involving the emergence of the rights of the citizen as the age of democracy and industry began.

II

This study differs from many similar biographies in that there is no collection of the subject's papers; very few personal or family letters have turned up to fill in his life. Some professional letters have appeared from Trinity College Dublin archives and from archives in the United Kingdom, but they do not tell much of the story. His published writings and parliamentary speeches, together with references in secondary sources, are the available materials. Needless to say, published works do not reveal character in the same way as personal letters never intended for publication. In the end, Browne's biography must be a history of his times.

There are materials about Browne's family life in America, but the search for information about his family life in Ireland has been frustrating and largely unproductive. No will or administration of his estate has been found, although there is reference to a will in the declaration filed by his widow with her life-insurance claim. Eustace's *Abstracts of wills in the registry of deeds* had no information. Nothing has been found in McAnlis' *Consolidated index to the records of the genealogical office*. Nothing significant was found in the Representative Church Body Library of the Church of Ireland at Braemor Park, Churchtown, although he frequently acted in support of the church, nor in R. Hayes' *Manuscript sources for Irish civilization* (Boston, 1965), nor in the archives of the Royal Irish Academy or the King's Inns. Browne's home at the time of his death was on Clare Street, Dublin, east of Trinity College and west of Merrion Square, but the *Treble almanack* and the *Dublin directory* had no information.

Arthur Browne was buried in the churchyard of St Ann's church, Dawson Street, Dublin in June 1805, and there ought to have been family information there, but the original records no longer exist. The established church kept official records of marriages, births (baptisms) and deaths (funerals), but in the disestablishment of the Church of Ireland in 1869, Parliament required its parishes to send their original records to the Public Record Office in the Four Courts complex in Dublin (38 & 39 Vict. c. 59). During the Civil War, on 28–30 June 1922, the Irish Republican Army, embedded in the Four Courts, was attacked by the Free State Army, and in the fires and explosions, most of the paper records were destroyed. Excerpts of some of the St Ann's records had been previously made and were preserved in the manuscript room of the National Museum of Ireland, Kildare Street; I have examined them and found no reference to Arthur Browne and his family. The fire of 1922 probably accounts for the absence of records of the probate of his estate.[6] Because my search for Browne family records proved to be unsuccessful during several visits to Dublin, I engaged the services of the genealogical research firm Eneclann, at Trinity College, but their experienced and careful search did not discover the family records I sought.

Of course, there could be another reason beside the fire of 1922 for the absence of written records. Arthur Browne was a fellow of Trinity College Dublin from 1778 until his death in 1805. He married twice, although fellows were expected to remain unmarried. Despite the celibacy requirement, many fellows married, but by custom these marriages were not publicized and there were no references to wives and children of fellows at Trinity.

III

History was my favourite subject at Boston Latin School, and I was especially interested in the colonial and revolutionary eras, remnants of which surround everyone in Boston. At Harvard College, I was able to pursue eighteenth- and nineteenth-century historical studies with some marvelous teachers.[7]

During my years in Newport, Rhode Island, as a naval officer, I was introduced to the study of eighteenth-century Newport by a great friend, the Revd Canon Lockett F. Ballard, twenty-fifth rector of Trinity Church.[8] On the east wall at the north side of the church is a memorial to the fifth rector of the church, Marmaduke Browne, which notes that it was a gift in 1795 of 'Arthur Browne, esq. now senior fellow of Trinity College Dublin, in Ireland, and representative in Parliament for the same'. Thereafter I came across references to the admiralty law text of Arthur Browne in early decisions of the United States Supreme Court and I realized the connection. I published a study of the admiralty law of Arthur Browne in 1995 in the *Journal of Maritime Law and Commerce*.[9]

In May 1989, as a new member of the Irish Legal History Society, I met Professor Nial Osborough, then of Trinity College Dublin, who gave me a tour of

6   H. Wood, 'The public records of Ireland before and after 1922', 13 *Trans. Royal Hist. Soc.*, 4th series, 17, 34–6 (1930).

7   In American history: Samuel Eliot Morison, Frederick Merk, Arthur Meyer Schlesinger and Arthur Meyer Schlesinger Jnr. In English history: Elliott Perkins and David Owen. In French history: Crane Brinton and Donald McKay. Unhappily, I did not study Irish history with John V. Kelleher, a deficiency I now try to remedy.

8   Revd Canon Lockett Ford Ballard (1912–79): AB, Hamilton (1934); BD, General Theological Seminary (1940); ordained priest (1941). He served as a first lieutenant in the field artillery (26th Division) 1942–5, and received the Bronze Star and a Purple Heart. On release from the army he became rector of St Phillip's church, Garrison, NY (1945–54), and then rector of Trinity Church, Newport (1954–72), where his vision of its beautiful waterfront was realized in Queen Anne Square in 1976.

9   26 *J. Mar. L. & Comm.*, 59–132 (1995).

the college and suggested I read Prof. O'Higgins' article on Browne in the *Northern Ireland Legal Quarterly*. I also encountered Browne in Peter Stein's article, 'The attraction of the civil law in post-revolutionary America'.[10] My pursuit of Arthur Browne's career in Ireland was aided by research undertaken during five summers in Belfast and Dublin teaching in Fordham's programme of international law studies at Queen's University Belfast and University College Dublin. My work was also assisted by faculty fellowships granted by Fordham University.

IV

The significance of Arthur Browne, beyond his admiralty text, is his position as one of a trio of lawyers who were practitioners, scholars and teachers of the law, as well as practical politicians, whose wisdom was aided by practical experience to analyze and explain the system of laws that influence international trade. The other two were William Scott in England and Joseph Story in America. It is at least arguable that these three shared a common understanding of the general maritime law as a unifying force among trading nations.

Sir William Scott (1745–1836) was the person to whom the second or admiralty volume of Arthur Browne's treatise was dedicated.[11] Scott was eleven years older than Browne, and there were substantial differences in their backgrounds: Scott was a 'high Tory', violently opposed to political change, and especially opposed to any form of Catholic emancipation, while Arthur Browne was an independent Whig, suspicious of government and supportive of Catholic emancipation. Further, Scott inherited a substantial fortune from his father, while Arthur Browne made his own living by teaching and practising the law. Both men, however, benefited from lucrative appointments from the established churches and their courts. After nineteen years of admiralty practice, Scott was appointed judge of the high court of admiralty in 1798, a position he was to hold until his retirement twenty-nine years later.

Undoubtedly, William Scott had more practical experience than Browne, especially in view of his services as advocate for the navy from 1782 to 1795, and as king's advocate from 1788. Browne, on the other hand, was able to devote more time to teaching and research, leading to his synthesis of the subject in his text. Yet during Scott's long time on the bench (including seventeen years of the Napoleonic Wars), he became the authority on prize law, and wrote enough admiralty judgments to fill almost eleven volumes of reported decisions, thereby assuring himself an enduring place in both England and America on the subjects

10 52 *Virginia Law Review*, 403–34 (1966).

11 H. Bourguignon, *Sir William Scott, Lord Stowell: judge of the high court of the admiralty, 1789–1828* (1987). Scott was AB, Corpus Christi, Oxford, 1764; AM, 1767; BCL, 1772; DCL, 1779; Middle Temple, 1781; MP for Oxford, 1801–21; House of Lords 1821 as Lord Stowell.

of customary international law, prize law and admiralty jurisprudence. Scott's views on neutral shipping were never accepted in America.

There are also parallels in the career of Joseph Story (1779–1845) in the United States.[12] He was born in the commercial fishing village of Marblehead, Massachusetts, where his father, Elisha, a former Son of Liberty, practised medicine. Story studied at the Marblehead Academy before his entry into Harvard College. Upon graduation in 1798, second in his class, he was apprenticed to a famous Marblehead lawyer, Samuel Sewall.[13] After three years he was admitted to the Massachusetts Bar and began to practise law in the towns of Essex County. During a business trip to Washington in 1807, he met James Madison, then secretary of state, soon to be president of the United States. Madison was a classmate at Princeton in 1771 of Joseph Story's father, Elisha Story. Joseph had been elected to a seat in the state legislature as a Democratic-Republican, a follower of Jefferson and Madison. After three years, he was elected to Congress for a single term (1808–9); he was defeated in his bid for re-election because of the unpopularity of President Jefferson's embargo on foreign trade during the Napoleonic Wars. Story returned to the state legislature, where he became speaker of the House. In his active practice of law, he successfully argued the case of *Fletcher v. Peck* before the US Supreme Court.[14]

In 1810, William Cushing, of Massachusetts, one of Washington's original Supreme Court appointees, died, and President Madison had the opportunity to appoint a member of his political party to the Supreme Court, but his first three nominees refused the appointment and the fourth was rejected by the Senate. In that situation, Madison turned to young Story – at 32, the youngest man yet appointed – who was confirmed by the Senate on 18 November 1811, and began his service under Chief Justice John Marshall just as the United States entered the War of 1812 against Great Britain. That war produced a large number of cases, both on circuit and in the Supreme Court, dealing with international law, prize law and admiralty, for which Arthur Browne's treatise was invaluable.[15] Unfortunately, Story never wrote a treatise on these subjects, despite twelve volumes on other legal topics. In his thirty-four years on the court, he wrote 269 majority opinions, 3 concurrences with the majority and 14 dissents.

12 R.K. Newmeyer, *Supreme court Justice Joseph Story: statesman of the old republic* (1985). See also G.T. Dunne, *Justice Joseph Story and the rise of the Supreme Court* (1970) and J. McCallan, *Joseph Story and the American constitution: a study in political and legal thought* (1971).

13 Unlike in England and Ireland, legal education in America was entirely by apprenticeship (observing trials and copying pleadings) before the revolution, although a very few men, like South Carolina's John Rutledge, travelled to London for training at the inns of court. Apprentice training of at least three years was required for admission to practice.

14 10 US (6 Cranch) 87 (1810). The case held a Georgia statute unconstitutional, the first exercise of that power.

15 Story cited Browne authoritatively in his famous decision applying admiralty law to marine-insurance contracts, De Lovio v. Boit, 7 F. Cas. 418 (No. 3,776) (C.C. Mass. 1815) at 419, 420, 431, 435, 436, 438, 439, 440, 441 and 444.

In 1829 Story was appointed to the new Dane Professorship of Law at Harvard Law School,[16] while continuing his service on the Supreme Court. (The court held one term a year beginning the first Monday in October, terminating often before Christmas.) Newly developed steamboats and railroads (after 1835) made this dual service possible. Like Arthur Browne, he was a much beloved teacher. His Harvard lectures soon became a flood of treatises.[17]

V. BIBLIOGRAPHIC NOTES

Many of the Irish people mentioned herein were students, graduates or faculty of Trinity College Dublin. The initial information on them comes from G.D. Burtchaell and T.U. Sadleir, *Alumni Dublinenses* (1924), covering the years 1637 to 1846. In the eighteenth century, their status on entry was crucial: most students were pensioners who paid normal fees for board and lodging. Very wealthy students were fellow commoners, who paid double fees and might dine with faculty. Sizars were recipients of charitable grants in exchange for service in the college.

Unattributed biographical information was compiled from many sources: the *Dictionary of national biography* published by Oxford University Press (2004); the *Irish biographical dictionary* published by Cambridge University Press (2005); *Merriam-Webster's biographical dictionary* (1980); and the latest *Encyclopedia Brittanica*. Where modern biographies are available, they were used and cited.

VI. BIBLIOGRAPHY OF ARTHUR BROWNE

Professional subjects

1. Browne, Arthur, *A brief review of the question: whether the Articles of Limerick have been violated? By Arthur Browne, esq. representative in Parliament for University of Dublin* (Dublin, 1788).
2. Candidus, *A full display of some late publications on the subject of tithes and the sufferings of the established clergy in the south of Ireland, attributed to those dues. With strictures necessary for the further elucidation of that subject by Candidus* (Dublin, 1788)

16 In 1817, Harvard opened a law school to train lawyers through lectures and texts. The course lasted eighteen months without examinations or an academic degree. The case method of instruction and three-year course of study for a degree were introduced after 1870 by Dean C.C. Langdell.

17 In twelve volumes: *Bailments* (1832); *United States Constitution* (3 vols, 1833); *Conflict of laws* (1834); *Equity jurisprudence* (1836); *Equity pleading* (1838); *Law of agency* (1839); *Law of partnerships* (1841); *Bills of exchange* (1843); and *Promissory notes* (1845). In the last year of his life, he wrote the statute expanding admiralty jurisdiction to the Great Lakes to alter one of his earlier decisions, The Thomas Jefferson, 23 US (10 Wheat.) 428 (1825). Story had limited admiralty jurisdiction on rivers to those within the ebb and flow of the tide, overruled in The Genesse Chief, 53 US (12 How.) 443 (1851). He also prepared the Supreme Court admiralty rules of 1844, which lasted until 1966.

3. Browne, Arthur, *A compendious view of the civil law, being the substance of a course of lectures, read in the University of Dublin. By Arthur Browne, esq. S.F.T.C.D. professor of civil law in that university, and representative in Parliament for the same. To which will be added, a sketch of the practice of the ecclesiastical courts, with some cases determined therein in Ireland, and some useful directions for the clergy,* 2 vols (Dublin, 1797, 1799).

4. Browne, Arthur, *Remarks on the terms of the union. By Arthur Browne, esq., M.P. for the University of Dublin* (Dublin, 1800).

5. Browne, Arthur, *A compendious view of the civil law and of the law of the admiralty, being the substance of a course of lectures read in the University of Dublin. By Arthur Browne, LL.D., S.F.T.C.D., professor of civil law in that university, and representative in three parliaments for the same. The second edition. With great additions* (London, 1802).

6. Browne, Arthur, *A compendious view of the ecclesiastical law of Ireland, being the substance of a course of lectures read in the University of Dublin. By Arthur Browne, esq., S.F.T.C.D. professor of civil law in that university, and representative in three parliaments for the same. To which is added, a sketch of the practice of the ecclesiastical courts, with some cases determined therein, in Ireland. Second edition, with great additions* (Dublin, 1803).

Occasional subjects

1. Browne, Arthur, *Thoughts on the present state of the College of Dublin addressed to the gentlemen of the university* (1782).

2. Browne, Arthur, *Miscellaneous sketches: or, hints for essays. By Arthur Browne, esq., fellow of Trinity College Dublin* (London, 1798).

3. Browne, Arthur, *Some few brief principles of tacticks, extracted from Guibert. By Arthur Browne, esq. For the use of the College Corps* (Dublin, 1797).

4. O'Dil, Hussein, *Beauty and the heart, an allegory; translated from the Persian language. By Arthur Browne, esq., senior fellow of Trinity College Dublin* (Dublin, 1801).

5. Browne, Arthur (trans.), *Translations from various languages, mostly illustrative of the old Spanish poetry and romance. By Arthur Browne, esq. senior fellow of Trinity College Dublin* (Dublin, 1802).

6. Browne, Arthur, 'Brief strictures on certain observations of Lord Mondobbo respecting the Greek tenses', *Transactions of the Royal Irish Academy,* 3 (1790), 11–43.

7. Browne, Arthur, 'The comparative authenticity of Tacitus and Suetonius, illustrated by the question, "Whether Nero was the author of the memorable conflagration at Rome?"', *Transactions of the Royal Irish Academy,* 5, 3–16.

8. Browne, Arthur, 'Some observations upon the Greek accents', *Transactions of the Royal Irish Academy,* 7 (1800), 359–80.

9. Browne, Arthur, 'Some accounts of the Vicars Cairn, in the County of Armagh; communicated to the committee of antiquities in two letters, one from Dr Browne, senior fellow of Trinity College Dublin; the other from the Revd John Young, curate of Mullabrack', *Transactions of the Royal Irish Academy,* 8 (1802), 3–9.

10. Browne, Arthur, 'An account of some ancient trumpets, dug up in a bog near Armagh. By Arthur Browne, esq.; senior fellow of Trinity College Dublin', *Transactions of the Royal Irish Academy,* 8 (1802), 11–12.

CHAPTER ONE

The Browne family in Ireland and America (1699–1756)

I

WHEN YOUNG ARTHUR BROWNE, an orphan from America, disembarked in Dublin after his ocean voyage in March 1772, he was continuing a family connection with Ireland that had lasted more than one hundred years, through four generations. He brought a vision of democratic opportunity from the New World, which he later described in glowing terms:

> The state of property in New England tended to happiness, the land was divided in moderate portions, every man held his little lot in fee or perpetuity; there was no landlord, no tenantry, every man owned his own field, every man sat under the shade of his own tree; he paid neither tithe nor rent ... Beggars literally there were none ... neither poverty nor riches [were known] ... nobility [i.e. aristocracy] was unknown ... a real equality reigned ... The innocence of the people made them capable of liberty ... This obedience to the laws was fostered by religion which flourished with universal vigor ...[1]

And yet he never returned to that paradise, but lived for the next thirty-three years in Dublin, a crowded and dirty city where enlightened elegance and wealth contrasted with crippling poverty and ignorance.

The Browne family of Ireland were not old English or native Irish but new British (i.e. Scots or English) planters who arrived in Ireland in the wake of Cromwell's conquest in the mid-seventeenth century. The family progenitor may have been an army chaplain from Scotland. Religion was the family business: Arthur Browne's great grandfather, grandfather, father and son were graduates of Trinity College Dublin and priests of the Church of Ireland, and two of these were missionaries of the Church of England in America.[2]

Arthur Browne's great grandfather was the Revd John Browne (1624?–1700), who held several ecclesiastical positions: as perpetual curate of Tullyallen near Mellifont in County Louth and as archdeacon of Elphin in County Roscommon,

---

1 Arthur Browne, *Miscellaneous sketches*, pp 194, 201–2 (1798).
2 Revd Arthur Browne (1699–1773) and his son Revd Marmaduke Browne (1731–71). G. Lewis, 'Clergymen licensed to the American colonies by the bishop of London, 1745–1781', 13 *Hist. Mag. Protestant Episcopal Church*, 129 (1944).

a see founded by St Patrick, where St Mary's Cathedral had been destroyed in 1641 and reconstructed in 1661.

Tullyallen, in the Boyne Valley, is at the heart of Irish Christianity. Nearby is the Hill of Slane, where St Patrick, around the year 433 AD, challenged the Druids by lighting the Easter fire at a time forbidden by the high king, Laoghaire. Tullyallen is also near the site of the battle of the Boyne where the Protestant army of King William of Orange defeated the Catholic army of King James II on 12 July 1690. That fact would have been foremost in the minds of eighteenth-century Irish, especially Protestants.[3]

Arthur Browne's grandfather, also named Arthur Browne, was born at Mellifont in 1699, the third son of Revd John Browne and Margery Donellan Browne. He was schooled at Drogheda, the nearest large town (the scene of a frightful massacre by Cromwell after a siege in 1649). He entered Trinity College as a sizar in June 1718, and received a BA in 1726 and an MA in 1729. He married Mary Cox, daughter of Revd Thomas Cox, vicar of St Peter's, Drogheda, and later dean of Ferns in County Wexford. Browne served as private secretary to Jonathan Swift, dean of St Patrick's Cathedral, Dublin, in 1726–9, before his ordination. He and his wife took the Browne family to America in 1729 as missionaries of the Society for the Propagation of the Gospel (SPG).

The father of the subject of this book was Marmaduke Browne, born in Providence, Rhode Ireland, in 1731, where his father was rector of King's Chapel. The family moved to Portsmouth, New Hampshire in 1736. Marmaduke entered Trinity College Dublin as a pensioner on 1 May 1750. He received a BA in 1754. He married Anne Franklin of Bristol, England before returning to America as an SPG missionary in 1755. After the death of his wife, and while serving as rector of Trinity Church in Newport, Rhode Island, he returned to Ireland in 1770 and received an MA from Trinity College Dublin. He died in March 1771, shortly after his return to America, leaving an orphan son, Arthur Browne.

II. MISSIONARIES OF THE SPG IN AMERICA

> Westward the course of empire takes its way.
> The four first acts already past,
> A fifth shall close the drama with the day
> Time's noblest offspring is the last.[4]

Missionary zeal for the conversion of the Indians of America came very slowly to the established churches of England and Ireland in the seventeenth century, unlike

---

3 See P. Beresford Ellis, *The Boyne water* (1976). For background, see D. Ferriter, *The transformation of Ireland*, pp 612–62 (2004) and M. Tanner, *Ireland's holy wars: the struggle for a nation's soul, 1500–2000*, pp 6–10, 422–8 (2001).

4 George Berkeley, *On the prospect of planting arts and learning in America* (1726, revised in 1752 shortly before his death).

the French and Spanish conquerors. English colonial outposts in America – for example, Virginia in 1607 – were not notable for proselytizing among the Indians.[5] The Pilgrims and Puritans of Massachusetts were escaping religious conformity in the mother country and did not devote much of their energy to converting their Indian neighbors.[6]

Religious wars and persecution had been the characteristic feature of seventeenth-century English and Irish life. Thus, it was not until the end of that century that Dr Thomas Bray organized two groups to raise funds from government and private sources for the purposes of preserving Christianity among the settlers in the colonial outposts and preaching the Christian gospel to Native Americans. The first was the Society for Promoting Christian Knowledge (SPCK), founded in London in 1698 to provide books for the colonies, especially Bibles and the Book of Common Prayer.[7] The second was the society for the Propagation of the Gospel in Foreign Parts (SPG), to which a royal charter was granted in 1701.[8] While the SPG was clearly a legitimate response to the missionary command to go and preach to all nations, Prof. Carl Bridenbaugh has taken a less benign view, calling it, 'British imperialism in ecclesiastical guise'.[9]

From its beginning until 1785 when its work in the newly independent United States ceased, the SPG established 202 missions, from Maine (then part of Massachusetts) to Georgia, and sent 422 ordained priests to the colonies.[10] No bishop was ever sent, and the absence of a bishop to supervise the churches, confirm the faithful and ordain new clergy was a serious obstacle to the growth of the Church of England in America. (Calvinist Presbyterians and Congregationalists, as well as Baptists and later Methodists and Lutherans, did not require bishops; French and Spanish Roman Catholic missions were very soon governed by bishops.) The efforts of the SPG clergy to persuade the British government to send a bishop to America led to a fierce pamphlet war in the mid-eighteenth century when the Calvinist clergy rolled out all the polemics of the English Civil War to prevent 'prelates' from descending on a free people.[11]

---

5 Virginia: S.E. Morison, *The European discovery of America: the northern voyages*, pp 617–79 (1971); J. Axtell and W. Sturtevant, *The European and the Indians: essays on the ethnohistory of North America*, pp 295–315 (1981).

6 Massachusetts: S.E. Morison, *A history of the American people*, pp 61–74 (1965); G.D. Langdon Jnr, *Pilgrim colony: a history of New Plymouth, 1620–1691* (1966); N. Philbrick, *Mayflower* (2006); J.M. Bumsted, *The Pilgrims' progress: the ecclesiastical history of the old colony, 1620–1775* (1989); W. Bradford, *Of Plymouth Plantation* ed. S.E. Morison (1970).

7 See C.W.K. Lowther, *A history of the SPCK* (1959).

8 See C. Pascoe, *Two hundred years of the SPG* (1901); E. Midwinter, 'The SPG and the church in the American colonies', 4 *Hist. Mag. Protestant Episcopal Church*, 70 (1935).

9 C. Bridenbaugh, *Mitre and sceptre: transatlantic faiths, ideas, personalities and politics, 1689–1775*, p. 51 (1962).

10 See O.W. Elsbree, *The rise of the missionary spirit in America, 1790–1815*, pp 49–51, 63 (1928, reprint 1980).

11 Bridenbaugh, *Mitre and sceptre*, pp 207–29 (1962).

An Irishman, George Berkeley,[12] was most influential in the recognition of a spiritual dimension to the approved colonization schemes by the Virginia and Maryland planters, where commerce had been the guiding principle. (The earlier Pilgrims and Puritans in Massachusetts had fled the efforts of the established church to force conformity in ritual, theology and morals.)

Berkeley was senior fellow of Trinity College while Arthur Browne, grandfather of our subject, was a student there. Berkeley's powerful friends obtained for him the position of dean of St Columb's Cathedral in Derry (then called Londonderry) in 1724, the second wealthiest deanery in Ireland (at £1,100 per year). That position required only occasional appearances, and even for these, his place could be taken by a deputy. Thus, Berkeley was free to pursue channels of power and influence in Dublin and London. In the year he became dean of Derry, Berkeley published *A proposal for the better supplying of churches in our foreign plantations and for converting the savage Americans to Christianity*.

In 1724, power in London was in the hands of Sir Robert Walpole,[13] head of the government and effectively prime minister. Walpole served the German-speaking Hanoverian, George I, until the king's death in 1727 and continued to serve the similarly German George II until 1742, when Walpole lost effective control of Parliament. Walpole had been the bridge between the Tory Queen Anne and the Whig Hanoverians. Both George I and George II had abandoned English and Irish affairs to Walpole, who sought to keep his kings out of European wars. He did not discourage the private interests that were developing the American colonies and favoured a policy of free trade with the colonies.

George Berkeley's answer to the religious problems of the colonies went beyond the efforts of the SPCK and the SPG in his plan for the creation of a college to educate young colonial men, near their homes in the colonies, for the ministry of the established church. Neither Harvard nor Yale suited his purposes as they were both controlled by dissenters. Without much information about the geography of the New World, its patterns of trade or its dissenting populations, Berkeley proposed to locate his college of St Paul in Bermuda, equidistant from all colonial outposts. Berkeley successfully began to enlist private funds for the project, but substantial government support was needed and he sought and achieved a royal charter, with the promise of a grant of £20,000 from the government. Having raised £5,000 privately and relying on his comfortable position in Ireland, accompanied by his new wife, Anna, George Berkeley left England and crossed the Atlantic to Newport, Rhode Island, where they arrived on 23 January 1729,

---

12 See J.D. Wild, *George Berkeley: a study of his life and philosophy*, pp 280–307 (1936); see also A. Luce, *Life of George Berkeley, bishop of Cloyne* (1949) and D. Berman, *George Berkeley: idealism and the man* (1994).

13 Robert Walpole (1676–1745) entered Parliament as a Whig in 1701, but served under Queen Anne's Tories as secretary of war, treasurer of the navy and paymaster of the army. He was ennobled as earl of Orford. His strong support of the Hanoverian succession in 1714 saved him from charges of corruption. See J. Black (ed.), *Britain in the age of Walpole* (1984).

accompanied by fifty-eight boxes of books.[14] Berkeley's purpose in Newport was to buy and develop a farm to provide supplies for the Bermuda college, while awaiting the government grant.

III. GRANDFATHER, REVD ARTHUR BROWNE (1699–1773)

Almost eight months after Berkeley's arrival, Revd Arthur Browne, newly ordained and accompanied by his wife and baby son, arrived in Newport, Rhode Island on 2 September 1729. After receiving his AM degree earlier in that year, Browne had travelled to London, to the headquarters of the SPG, where he was accepted as a missionary by the society after delivering a sermon and being examined by a committee of priests acting for Edmund Gibson, bishop of London whose jurisdiction had included all the American colonies since 1634. Browne was ordained to the priesthood by Bishop Gibson, and then the family began their voyage to America, all within a few weeks in 1729.[15]

It is possible that Berkeley's enthusiasm for the colonies may have influenced Revd Arthur Browne's choice of missionary life in the SPG, but it is uncertain whether Browne was to have been part of Berkeley's new college. In any event, the government grant was never paid and the Bermuda college never opened. George Berkeley stayed in Newport for less than three years, developing Whitehall, his 92-acre farm in Middletown, and preaching occasionally at Trinity Church, Newport, and other missions such as Wickford and Providence. Finally, he gave up hope of government assistance, and on 21 September 1731 sailed from Boston to London, where his patrons had arranged a prestigious new job for him. He was appointed bishop of the ancient diocese of Cloyne in County Cork in 1734, where he served until his death in 1753 at age 68.

Trinity Church, Newport,[16] founded in 1698, was served by SPG missionaries. Its rector from 1704 to 1750 was James Honyman, a former navy chaplain. Berkeley often preached and performed weddings and baptisms there. He later provided the funds for an organ for the church. It is possible that Revd Arthur Browne also preached there in the weeks before he and his wife sailed the 35 miles up Narragansett Bay to Providence, where the new King's Chapel, founded in 1722, awaited. Browne began his duties in Providence in 1730.

14 Wild, *George Berkeley*, pp 308–29 (1936); A. Brayton, *George Berkeley in Newport* (1954) and E. Gaustad, *George Berkeley in America*, pp 105–33 (1979).

15 E. Pennington, *The Reverend Arthur Browne of Rhode Island and New Hampshire* (1938) and M. Rogers, *Glimpses of an old social capital (Portsmouth, New Hampshire), as illustrated by the life of Revd Arthur Browne and his circle* (1923). G. Ripley and C.A. Dana, *American cyclopaedia* (1873); E.A. and C. Duyckinck, *Cyclopaedia of American literature*, p. 91 (1877). A portrait of Revd Arthur Browne by J.S. Copley (1757) was in the General Theological Library in Boston, it is now in Historic Deerfield, MA.

16 J.B. Hattendorf, *Semper eadem: a history of Trinity Church in Newport, 1698–2000* (2001); G. Mason, *Annals of Trinity Church, Newport, R.I., 1698–1821* (1890). Revd Canon Lockett F. Ballard, *Trinity Church in old Newport on Rhode Island* (1979), MS on file with Trinity Church.

Six years later, he and family moved to Portsmouth, New Hampshire, where another SPG outpost, Queen's Chapel, founded in 1732, required his services, at an increase in salary. Revd Arthur Browne served that church and the colonial government for thirty-seven years, until his death in 1773.

New Hampshire had been lightly settled by Puritans as part of the Massachusetts Bay Colony until 1679 when a separate colonial administration had been established by royal charter with Portsmouth as its capital. It was a thriving port, from which the timber resources for the royal navy were exported, a source of great wealth for the colony. That prosperous trade brought English merchants and traders, whose success was reflected in the substantial Georgian mansions and the classic Queen's Chapel (now St John's church).[17]

In addition to his parochial responsibilities and missionary travels to new towns seeking to establish new churches, Revd Arthur Browne became chaplain to the governor and council of New Hampshire.[18] His family grew in size and his importance increased in the society of merchants, mariners and administrators. After twenty years at Portsmouth, a book of his sermons was published and a formal portrait was made. He returned to England and Ireland once, in 1750, to enter his son Marmaduke in Trinity College Dublin and to accompany his daughter, Lucy, to England, where her new husband had been transferred by the military to South Wales.

During this time, he vigorously opposed the Great Awakening preached by Revd George Whitefield and others to the un-churched frontier settlers in ecstatic revivals.[19] After a 1738 tour of the Georgia missions of John and Charles Wesley, whom he had met while a student at Oxford, Whitefield had been ordained a priest in the Church of England in 1739. He was a gifted pulpit orator, passionate but occasionally hysterical or histrionic in open-air extemporaneous preaching. Whitefield subsequently made seven preaching missions to America; during the last trip (1769) he died at Newburyport, Massachusetts. Whitefield had abandoned the doctrines and discipline of the Church of England for those of Calvinism and the Wesleyan Methodists. His preaching was a vital part of the Great Awakening (1748–56) that spread through the wilderness areas, affecting Calvinists, Baptists, Methodists and Presbyterians. The principal American revivalist was the Puritan Revd Jonathan Edwards (1703–58), but Revd Arthur Browne feared the effect a rogue Anglican priest might have on the missionary efforts of the SPG. He wrote in 1742 to the SPG about 'STRANGE COMMOTIONS OF A RELIGIOUS NATURE ... sown by Mr Whitefield ...' where 'impressions, impulses, experiences are

---

17 Rogers, *Glimpses of an old social capital* (1923); E.F. and E. Morison, *New Hampshire: a bicentennial history* (1976) and D.E. Van Deventer, *The emergence of provincial New Hampshire, 1623–1741*, pp 93–106, 182–97 (1976).
18 Revd Arthur Browne appears in Nathaniel Hawthorne's *Tales of a wayside inn* (1863) in the story of Governor Benning Wentworth's marriage at age 60 to his 20-year-old housekeeper.
19 See F. Lambert, *Pedlar in divinity: George Whitefield and the transatlantic revivals, 1737–1770* (1993).

altogether in vogue, preached by the most presumptuous and unintelligible ... who boldly anathematize all that dissent from him'. Revd Browne's 1744 letter to the SPG complained of 'the new-fangled, lately revived, much boasted chimerical notions ... Whitefield's legacy ... [but are] much abated'.

The missionaries of the SPG enjoyed an occasional festive day, as when they assembled on 20 September 1738 in Puritan Boston to hear a sermon from Revd Arthur Browne entitled 'The excellency of the Christian religion' at Christ Church (the Old North). The ten or so missionaries were entertained after the sermon by the Old North vestry at the Exchange Tavern, where they consumed thirty-one bottles of Madeira, 14 chickens, ducks, pigeons, beef, bacon, apple pies, custards, fruit tarts, punch, cider and beer.[20]

Revd Arthur Browne also engaged in a pamphlet war on the question of a bishop for the American colonies, using his vigorous pen to combat the Calvinists' disapproval. He responded that the Calvinist critic of an American bishop, 'had licked up the spittle of his Oliverian [Cromwellian] predecessors and coughed it out again, with some addition of his own filth and phlegm'.[21] No bishop was ever sent by the SPG or the crown; after independence, an American loyalist, Samuel Seabury, was elected and consecrated bishop from Connecticut in 1784 at Aberdeen, Scotland, and in 1787, an American loyalist refugee, Charles Inglis, was consecrated bishop for the colony of Nova Scotia. (The first Roman Catholic bishop in the United States was John Carroll of Maryland, consecrated in 1790.)

In 1757, the wealthy congregation of Christ Church in Boston sought to call Revd Arthur Browne as rector, but the SPG refused to permit it, perhaps because the position was intended for an Englishman.

Revd Arthur Browne finally received the assistance he had long requested for his mission when his son Marmaduke was assigned as an itinerant preacher in 1755, but Marmaduke was called to Newport in 1760, and not replaced in New Hampshire until 1767.

After thirty years at Portsmouth, Revd Arthur Browne saw that the strong attachments of the people to the British crown were weakening, in view of the fierce resistance to British taxation to support the war against the French. Fear for the future of the British connection can be seen in a letter to the SPG from a convention of the society's fifteen missionary priests in New England, including Arthur Browne of Portsmouth and his son, Marmaduke Browne of Newport.

Boston, 22 Sept. 1768

[...] The general state of the churches in this part of America are indeed in as good a condition as can be reasonably expected under the present troublesome state of these colonies. All that we are able to do in these times

---

20 H.P. Thompson, *Into all lands: the history of the Society for the Propagation of the Gospel in Foreign Parts, 1701–1950*, p. 89 (1951).
21 Revd Arthur Browne, *Remarks on Dr Mayhew's incidental reflections* (1763).

is only to cultivate among the people committed to our care a spirit of peace and patience under the various insults to which they are exposed for refusing to join in the popular clamors which now prevail. We are neither allowed to speak nor scarcely to be silent unless we join with those who we believe to be labouring the destruction of our constitution, civil & religious. The civil government is too weak to afford us protection; & ecclesiastical superior we have none on this side the Atlantic, from whom we may receive timely advice or direction under our present trials. We can only look up to God and cast ourselves upon the divine providence for protection ...[22]

Shortly after the death of his wife Mary on 5 April 1773, Revd Arthur Browne visited his daughter in Cambridge, Massachusetts, where he died on 10 June 1773, before the American Revolution drove many Church of England clergy out of the country.[23]

The sermon at Browne's funeral was preached by Revd Edward Bass, an SPG missionary at Newburyport, and future bishop of Massachusetts. Bass said:

This man of God came into our country a young man. Soon after entering into holy orders, and for more than forty years with very little interruption, he laboured in the work of the ministry which he executed with great reputation, having been all along esteemed an excellent preacher and orator and a faithful parish minister.[24]

Revd Arthur Browne was buried in the churchyard of his parish at Portsmouth.

IV. FATHER, REVD MARMADUKE BROWNE (1731–71)

Revd Marmaduke Browne, the father of our subject, was born in Providence, Rhode Island, grew up in Portsmouth, New Hampshire and was educated at Trinity College Dublin (AB 1754). His name, Marmaduke, was that of an earlier seventeenth-century cleric; he was called Dukey by his mother. During his student days in Dublin, Trinity Church, Newport, sought him as 'catechist' to teach in its parish school. That position was not sufficiently remunerative, nor was the position in Providence. He declined and sought appointment as an SPG missionary. He

22 D. Addison, *The life and times of Edward Bass, first bishop of Massachusetts*, pp 101–2 (1897).
23 See generally, B. Steiner, *Samuel Seabury: a study in the High Church tradition*, pp 157–88 (1971). See also D.L. Holmes, 'The Episcopal church and the American Revolution', 47 *Hist. Mag. Protestant Episcopal Church* (1978) and N.L. Rhoden, *Revolutionary Anglicanism: the colonial church of England clergy during the American Revolution*, pp 75–83, 148–52 (1992). In 1793, Arthur Browne sent a large and elegant Bible to his grandfather's church in Portsmouth as a token of affection and respect for his grandfather's congregation.
24 Addison, *The life and times of Edward Bass*, p. 122 (1897). A later rector, Charles Burroughs, eulogized Revd Arthur Browne in 1857 as 'faithful, revered and beloved'. Pennington, *The Reverend Arthur Browne* (1938).

travelled to London, where he was approved by the society and examined for the priesthood. Marmaduke Browne was ordained by Thomas Sherlock, bishop of London, on 29 January 1755. Following in the footsteps of his parents, Marmaduke Browne married his English wife, Anne Franklin of Bristol and they crossed the Atlantic in a stormy fifty-eight-day voyage to Portsmouth, where he began his work as a travelling missionary in the new towns being settled in the valleys of the New Hampshire hills at New Holderness, Claremont and Haverhill. He also served other SPG missions in Massachusetts and Rhode Island.[25]

During four years of missionary status, Marmaduke Browne travelled the 135-mile journey from Portsmouth to Newport eight times, where he preached in Trinity Church. In the meanwhile Trinity Church, Newport, had been the beneficiary of the will of the late Nathaniel Kay, a wealthy merchant and customs collector whose estate provided a salary and a house for an assistant to the rector who would also be responsible for the school. That amount was sufficiently attractive so that Browne accepted the second call to Newport. In the Kay house in Newport, probably in 1756, Arthur Browne, the subject of this study, was born.[26] In 1760, when the rector, Revd Thomas Pollen, moved to Jamaica to serve in Kingston, Revd Marmaduke Browne became the fifth rector, at a salary of £100 per annum; he held that title until his death in March 1771.

Marmaduke Browne was a dynamic and learned preacher who attracted such a large congregation that the church building had to be enlarged in 1762 from five bays to seven bays to accommodate forty-six new box pews at a cost of £600.[27] An assistant, Revd George Bisset of Aberdeen, Scotland was sent by the SPG in 1767. In his first report to the SPG, Marmaduke described the town and his congregation:

> There are in the town of Newport between seven and eight thousand inhabitants whites & blacks; of these about nine hundred souls, are of the Church of England, one hundred & twenty of which are actual communicants. The rest are divided into the following sects; viz, Congregationalists or Independents, three sorts of Baptists, one of them observing the Seventh Day as their sabbath, Quakers, Moravians or Hemputers, & a number of Jews who have lately erected a synagogue … professed deists or unbelievers are not common …[28]

25 Lewis, 'Clergymen licensed to the American colonies' (1944).
26 There is no formal record of Arthur Browne's birthdate or place. He stated that he was born in the Kay house in Newport. The year of his birth can be inferred from conjectures as to his age being 17 when he arrived in Dublin, where he said in Parliament that he had never seen a Roman Catholic until he was 17 years old. See O'Higgins, 'Arthur Browne (1756–1805): an Irish civilian', quoting 12 *Parliamentary Register*, 189. In his *Miscellaneous sketches*, he speaks of his residence in New England, 'to the age nearly of seventeen'. A. Browne, *Miscellaneous sketches*, p. 193 (1798). See also Rogers, *Glimpses of an old social capital*, p. 60 (1923).
27 Mason, *Annals of Trinity Church, Newport* (1890).
28 Ballard, *Trinity Church in old Newport*, p. 328 (1979); letter of 29 Aug. 1763 to the SPG.

In that non-ecumenical age, Marmaduke Browne had good relations with the majority of Newport's people, who were Quakers and Baptists, for whom the ritual, discipline and organization of the Church of England was anathema. He reported to the SPG that, there was 'a better harmony of understanding subsisting between the church & dissenters', and that 'the Quakers ... express their regard for the church from the experience they have had of its mildness & lenity of its administration'. Newport people, including his congregation, were 'fond of the church, *they like religion, but they like it cheap*'.[29] The popularity of Marmaduke Browne persisted despite the aristocratic tendencies and Tory politics of his congregation.

Marmaduke Browne's reputation for learning and gentle character was recognized by wealthy merchants who were not 'churchmen', and in 1764 he was selected to be one of the twelve founding fellows of Rhode Island College (the others were Baptists), the seventh college to be established in the American colonies.[30] The college's name was changed to Brown University in 1804 to honour the many gifts of Nicholas Brown and his family.

Much of Marmaduke's correspondence with the SPG concerned its orders to its missionaries to establish schools to educate the children of black slaves. Many leaders of the SPG were opposed to slavery, but the best they could do in the face of the political power of slave traders was to teach the gospel to the children of slaves. Many of Browne's wealthy congregation and vestry were opposed, because of their participation in the slave trade. They undermined the society's plans by limiting the number of students and hiring a barely qualified schoolmistress. Although frustrated by this opposition, Marmaduke reported that 'eighteen ... said their catechism in church last Lent without missing a word, & several of them have made some proficiency in reading & the girls in sewing'.[31] It took four years of efforts to bring the school for slave children up to expected standards. Marmaduke, however, saw his duty, 'to bring the neglected blacks to the knowledge of our holy religion & in some measure to recompense them for the servitude which uncivilized paganism, & I fear not the most justifiable traffick on the part of Christians has involved them'.[32]

In 1767 Anne Franklin Browne died, leaving a legacy for her son in England. Securing that legacy, advancing his professional standing with an MA degree from Trinity College and enrolling his son, Arthur, at Trinity were Marmaduke's goals. He also sought to report personally in London on the status of the missions, and to secure additional parts for the organ given to Trinity Church, Newport, by George Berkeley. These were the reasons he used to justify his voyage to England

29 Mason, *Annals of Trinity Church*, p. 113 (1890), underlined in the original.
30 J.B. Hattendorf, *Semper eadem: a history of Trinity Church in Newport 1698–2000*, p. 110 (2001). See also John F. Roche, *The colonial colleges in the war for American independence*, pp 9–10, 34–6, 62, 167 (1986).
31 Ballard, *Trinity Church in old Newport*, p. 336 (1979).
32 Ibid.

and Ireland. Content with the services provided by Marmaduke's assistant, Revd George Bisset, the Trinity congregation consented to a paid leave, and the voyage, already approved by the SPG, began in June 1769. Marmaduke was accompanied by his son Arthur. We do not know the details of this expedition other than he successfully visited Dublin, London and Antwerp, but in autumn 1770, Marmaduke and Arthur Browne began the homeward voyage that was to take eleven stormy weeks of fighting contrary winds. We do not know the circumstances of Marmaduke's fatal illness, other than that a fever and the lengthy voyage weakened him, so that he died at the age of 40 in Newport on 16 March 1771, and was buried in Trinity Church on 19 March 1771, on the north side of the altar.[33] Ministers of the first and second Congregational churches (Samuel Hopkins and Ezra Stiles) were among the pall-bearers.

Almost a quarter century after the death of his father, Arthur Browne, by then a successful lawyer, politician and teacher in Dublin, commissioned a marble memorial of his parents to be sent from Dublin to the independent United States and installed on the north or gospel side of the altar in Trinity Church, Newport. It was the work of John Smyth, son of Edward Smyth, the master carver of the sculptures in Dublin on the Four Courts (1785) and the Custom House (1791).[34] After a relief portrait of Marmaduke Browne, and a family coat of arms, the memorial reads:

> To the memory of the Reverend Marmaduke Browne, formerly rector of this parish, a man eminent for talents, learning and religion, who departed this life on the 19th of March [sic] 1771 and of Anne, his wife, a lady of uncommon piety and suavity of manners, who died the 6th of January 1767.
>
> This monument was erected by their son Arthur Browne, esq., now senior fellow of Trinity College Dublin, in Ireland, and representative in Parliament for the same, in token of his gratitude and affection to the best and tenderest of parents, and of his respect and love for a congregation among whom and for a place where he spent his earliest and his happiest days.

> *Heu! Quanto minus est,*
> *Cum alliis versari*
> *Quam tui meminisse*
> MDCCXCV[35]

---

33 Mason, *Annals of Trinity Church*, p. 133 (1890).

34 John Smyth (1775–1834), sculptor of monuments in Dublin's St Patrick's Cathedral. Son of Edward Smyth (1749–1812), whose buildings were badly damaged in the Civil War of 1922–3, but have been faithfully restored.

35 'How much less is it to/converse with others [i.e. the living]/Than to remember you.' Browne used the same Latin expression in *Miscellaneous sketches*, in 'The tale of Amyntor and Zelida', p. 8 of additional notes to vol. 1.

CHAPTER TWO

A Newport youth (1756–72)

I

AS A 40-YEAR-OLD LAWYER, travelling to the west of Ireland on circuit in 1797, Arthur Browne recorded his memories of Newport, Rhode Island, the distant paradise where he had spent his first seventeen years. He wrote:

> there was a mid-season consisting of about six weeks or two months in spring and as many in autumn, which exceeded in delight all the creations of poetic fantasy ... Even in summer the heat was perpetually moderated by occasional thunder showers of short duration which refreshed the earth and left behind them a chearful [sic] verdure and a brilliant sky while now and then a refreshing breeze deliciously qualified the heat, and in winter the brightness of the sun and purity of the air enlivens the spirits, invited to exercise, and cheered the very soul.[1]

He also noted the countryside of farms and woods:

> The face of the country was beautiful beyond description. The vistas through the woods, the breaks of light through the trees, with an orient sun and the brightening sky formed a paradise.[2]

Arthur Browne was fortunate to have been born in a wealthy and cosmopolitan community that sharply contrasted with the dreary Puritan settlements of the New England countryside. The town of Newport on Acquidneck Island owed its existence to commerce and not to religion, unlike the towns of the Providence Plantations founded in 1636 by Roger Williams, who had been exiled from Massachusetts for heresy.[3] Newport's initial settlers were another group of dissidents from Puritan Boston, which founded the town in 1639, led by William Coddington.

---

1 A. Browne, *Miscellaneous sketches*, p. 197 (1798).
2 Ibid., p.195.
3 See generally, S. Brockumer, *The irrepressible democrat: Roger Williams* (1940); E.S. Morgan, *Roger Williams: the church and the state* (1961) and J.M. Barry, *Roger Williams and the creation of the American soul: church, state and the birth of liberty*, pp 264–341, 353–63 (2011).

Under a new royal charter of 8 July 1663 from Charles II, there was to be 'full liberty in religious concernments'.[4] A heavy influx of Baptists and Quakers as well as some Church of England merchants soon arrived in the Puritan town, to be followed later by Jews and Roman Catholics, two groups usually excluded from colonial immigration. A Boston Puritan described Rhode Island as 'the asylum for all that are disturbed for heresy, a hive of hornets and the sink into which all the rest of the colonies empty their heretics'.[5]

Neither Acquidneck Island nor Newport had Native Americans in Arthur Browne's time, the result of King Philip's War (1675–6). The sachem, Philip, son of Massasoit, who had befriended the starving Pilgrims at Plymouth in 1621, had led an army of many different tribes, including Rhode Island's Narragansetts, Pokanokets, Pocassets and Sakonnets, against an English army made up of the troops of Plymouth, Massachusetts Bay and Connecticut, and their Indian allies (but not Rhode Island's Quakers). While the English colonists suffered grievous losses, the Indian population was virtually exterminated by battle, famine, disease and exportation to slavery in the West Indies.[6]

Newport was a town of merchants in the classic eighteenth-century sense: men who were at the same time part-owners of ships, part-owners of cargoes, mariners, wholesalers or retailers – as circumstances required. Lives devoted to business operations did not mean that they shared common political and social views. There were, however, a few non-denominational groups through which citizens could meet together, such as the Masons, the volunteer artillery and firefighters, the Redwood Library and, after 1765, the Sons of Liberty. Newport was always a town of great diversity of opinions, beginning with religion, and it is arguable that toleration of religious diversity among Protestants produced the spirit of independence and political liberty that led to separation from the English mother country.

The town and its population expanded rapidly in the seventeenth and eighteenth centuries and grew rich from trade because of its many distilleries and its access to rich fishing grounds off Block Island, which provided the essentials of the triangle slave trade.[7] Newport rum was carried to the southern colonies and then to the slave coasts of West Africa, where it was exchanged in the local slave markets for black Africans who were carried to the plantation islands of the West Indies where the slaves were sold in exchange for the raw molasses (from sugar cane) that would be distilled into rum in New England. Further trade

4 See also W.G. McLoughlin, *Rhode Island: a history* (1978). See also C. Bridenbaugh, *Fat mutton and liberty of conscience: society in Rhode Island, 1636–1690*, pp 5–8, 10–26, 32–42 (1974).

5 S. James, *The colonial metamorphoses in Rhode Island*, pp 38–42, 241–55 (2000). C. Bridenbaugh, *Cities in the wilderness: the first century of urban life in America, 1625–1742*, pp 98, 104, 176–9 (1993).

6 N. Philbrick, *Mayflower*, pp 311–48 (2006).

7 H. Thomas, *The slave trade*, pp 153–7, 431–45 (1997); R.S. Dana, *Sugar and slaves: the rise of the planter class in the British West Indies, 1624–1713* (1972); and R. Pares, *Yankees and creoles: the trade between North America and the West Indies before the American Revolution* (1956).

opportunities arose with the sale of salted fish to the West Indians and lumber, fish and rum to Europe, in exchange for manufactured goods.

Slave plantations had been established in the British sugar isles (Jamaica, St Kitts, Antigua, Dominica, St Lucia, Barbados, the Grenadines and Trinidad), and these were the prime markets for slave labour. British trade laws did not discourage the trade in slaves, and it is likely that slaves were also provided illegally to Spanish, French, Danish and Dutch islands. There is little doubt that Newport's eighteenth-century prosperity was built on the slave trade. In fact, slaves were not only bought and sold in Newport, but the sale itself produced taxable revenues for governmental operations.[8] Many wealthy Newport merchants had household slaves.

The merchants of the town accepted and profited from slavery unashamedly, but it was not accepted in the surrounding towns and farmlands, and the slave trade was finally prohibited in the state after 1787.[9] The minister of the First Congregational Church in Newport, Samuel Hopkins, was an early and ardent opponent of slavery,[10] while the Church of England remained silent; in fact, owners and masters of slave-trade vessels were often members of the Trinity Church vestry.

Trade in slaves required many voyages to Africa, the West Indies and North American ports but few to the British Isles, because Boston dominated the transatlantic trade.[11] In fact by the 1760s, Newport was second only to Boston as a port in the North American colonies. The shipping industry provided the most employment, through shipbuilding, rope-walks, sail lofts, riggers, coopers, ships' carpenters and makers of navigational instruments. Trades that provided the cargoes, such as distilling, fisheries, meat packing and grain milling, furnished further skilled employment opportunities.[12] Luxury trades could also be found, with portrait painters, furniture makers, cabinetmakers, upholsterers, carvers, candlemakers, clockmakers and silversmiths.[13] Dealers in imported china, silks and

---

8   R. Stensrud, *Newport: a lively experiment, 1639–1969*, pp 96–108, 118–23, 147–80, 219, 253–5 (2006); C.P.B. Jeffreys, *Newport, 1639–1976*, pp 13–15 (1992); James, *The colonial metamorphoses in Rhode Island*, pp 159–60 (2000); Bridenbaugh, *Cities in the wilderness*, p. 410 (1993); and C. Bridenbaugh, *Cities in revolt: urban life in America, 1743–1776*, pp 72–4, 88, 253, 354–6 (1955).

9   J. Coughtry, *The notorious triangle: Rhode Island and the African slave trade, 1700–1807* (1981). E. Crane, *A dependent people: Newport, Rhode Island in the revolutionary era*, pp 24–31 (1985). Members of the Society of Friends were forbidden to own slaves after 1761. James, *The colonial metamorphoses in Rhode Island*, p. 230 (2000).

10 Samuel Hopkins (1721–1803), AB Yale (1741), a disciple of Jonathan Edwards, was called to Newport in 1770. In 1776, he published *Dialogue concerning the slavery of the Africans*, and he later published *System of doctrines contained in divine revelation, explained and defended (1793)*.

11 R.G. Albion, W.A. Baker and B. Labaree, *New England and the sea*, pp 32–9 (1972). A comprehensive survey of maritime trades in Narragansett Bay can be found in A.B. Hawes, *Off-soundings: aspects of the maritime history of Rhode Island*, pp 108–78, 267–73 (1999).

12 Jeffreys, *Newport, 1639–1976*, pp 15–18 (1992). See also C. Bridenbaugh, *The colonial craftsmen* (1950).

13 John Goddard (1724–1785) was the most famous of the Newport cabinetmakers and designers of furniture. See Jeffreys, *Newport, 1639–1976*, pp 19–25 (1992). See also M. Moses, *Master craftsmen*

brocades could also be found. Their wares were exported to New York, Maryland and the Carolinas, as well as being sold in the Newport market.

There were several printers in Newport, one of whom was James Franklin (1697–1735), elder brother and first employer of Benjamin.[14] There was also a weekly newspaper, the *Newport Mercury*, which began to be published in 1758. Lastly, in a town of itinerants such as sailors and tradesmen, there were twenty licensed taverns and many boarding houses.[15]

The Newport of Arthur Browne's youth was a cosmopolitan, lively seaport and a political centre, capital of the colony, seat of several provincial courts and a royal court of vice admiralty. The census taken in 1774 recorded 9,208 inhabitants in what has been described as, 'the most modern ... the most entrepreneurial of the thirteen colonies'.[16]

As the legal centre of Rhode Island in Arthur Browne's time, many lawyers and court officers were present in and about the Old Colony House, where the courts were held. It was the site of the superior court of judicature, the highest appellate court, composed of five justices, created in 1746 out of the original general court of trials (1647), to review the courts of general sessions for crimes and the courts of common pleas for civil disputes, established in each of the five counties of the colony. (A peculiar feature of Rhode Island practice was the power of the General Assembly to accept petitions from litigants for relief from court decisions.)[17]

The colony had created its own court of admiralty in 1653, which was principally concerned with prize law and letters of marque in the many wars of the period. This colonial court was suppressed in 1704 and replaced by a royal court of vice admiralty, authorized by Parliament in 1696 to enforce the Navigation Acts.[18] That court was part of the Boston court of vice admiralty created for a district that comprised Massachusetts, New Hampshire and Rhode Island.[19] The admiralty court had been selected to enforce the navigation laws and the customs regulations because of the absence of juries, regarded in London as possibly corrupt and at least unreliable.[20]

    of Newport: the Townsends and Goddards (1984). John Smibert, Robert Feke, Joseph Blackburn and Gilbert Stuart were portrait painters in Newport.

14 Jeffreys, *Newport, 1639–1976*, pp 15–17 (1992).

15 See E.B. Lyman, *A reminiscence of Newport before and during the Revolutionary War* (1906). Among the few surviving tavern buildings are the White Horse Tavern (1673) and the Pitt's Head Tavern (1757). Bridenbaugh, *Cities in the wilderness*, pp 112, 269–72, 433 (1993).

16 *Census of inhabitants of the colony of Rhode Island*, p. 239 (J. Bartlett ed. 1859). G. Wood, *The radicalism of the American Revolution*, p. 140 (1992).

17 P.T. Conley, *Liberty and justice: a history of law and lawyers in Rhode Island, 1636–1998*, pp 15–22 (1998).

18 Ibid., 80–7. See also, F. Wiener, 'Notes on the Rhode Island admiralty, 1727–1790', 46 *Harv. L. Rev.*, 44 (1932). The 1696 Navigation Acts are in 7 and 8 Will. 3 c. 22.

19 Snell, *Courts of admiralty and the common law*, pp 136–180 (2007). See also H. Crump, *Colonial admiralty jurisdiction in the seventeenth century* (1931) and L. Wroth, 'The Massachusetts vice admiralty court and the federal admiralty jurisdiction', 6 *Am. J. Leg. Hist.*, 251 (1962).

20 C. Ubbelohde, *The vice-admiralty courts and the American Revolution*, pp 46–53 (1960).

Parliament had given these colonial admiralty courts jurisdiction over, 'all marine and other cases ... occurring on the high seas, in port or on navigable rivers'. This was a jurisdiction wider than in England.[21]

Reports of cases are scant before 1720 but it seems that they dealt with collisions, salvages, possession of vessels, seamen's wages and injuries, maritime contracts, materialmen's liens and bottomry bonds.[22] Prize law also might be heard, but piracy was often heard by special commissions that included the admiralty judges.[23] Rhode Island gained great notoriety when one of these commissions tried the cases of Charles Harris (of London) and his crew of the pirate sloop *Ranger*, which had been taken captive by HMS *Greyhound*. Twenty-eight men were arraigned and pleaded not guilty, alleging that they had been forced to serve on the pirate vessel after the loss of their ships. Twenty-six were convicted and hanged at Gravelly Point in Newport harbour at noon on 19 July 1723; the bodies were buried on the shore at Bull's Point 'between the flux and reflux of the sea'.[24] Of the twenty-six hanged men, 16 were in their twenties; 13 were from England and 6 from New England.[25]

Two career paths: church and law, were daily in evidence to the young American growing up in comfortable circumstances in a town with intimate connections to the best offerings of the eighteenth-century world.

Just a short distance from the centre of the harbour is Trinity Church, built in 1725–6 for a parish founded in 1698. It is of clapboard construction, 96 feet in length by 46 feet in width, with a steeple of 150 feet, topped by a golden mitre, towering over the town, all painted a brilliant white; arguably, it is the most elegant Georgian church in the American colonies.[26] Arthur Browne's grandfather and father had served in it for more than 40 years. As with most of the colonial buildings made of wood, preservation is a constant problem. In Arthur Browne's youth, the Trinity steeple was the most prominent feature of Newport harbour, but

21 See also J. Sweeney, 'The Silver Oar and other maces of the admiralty: admiralty jurisdiction in America and the British empire', 38 *J. Mar. L. & Comm.*, 159 (2007).

22 M.P. Harrington, 'The legacy of the colonial vice admiralty courts', 26 *J. Mar. L. & Comm.*, 581 (1985) and 27 *J. Mar. L. & Comm.*, 323 (1986). Snell, *Courts of admiralty and the common law*, pp 202–11 (2007) and D.S. Towle, *Records of the vice admiralty court of Rhode Island, 1716–1752* (1936).

23 D. Owen and M. Tolley, *Courts of admiralty in America: the Maryland experience, 1634–1776*, pp 73–4 (1995).

24 Conley, *Liberty and justice*, pp 88–103 (1998); W. Updike, *Memories of the Rhode Island Bar*, pp 293–4 (1842).

25 Conley, *Liberty and justice*, pp 94–5 (1998).

26 J.B. Hattendorf, *Semper eadem: a history of Trinity Church in Newport, 1698–2000*, (2001); L.F. Ballard, 'Trinity Church in Old Newport on Rhode Island', unpublished MS at Trinity Church (1979); Mason, *Annals of Trinity Church* (1890); M.H. Elliott, *This was my Newport* (1944). A.F. Downing and V.J. Scully Jnr, *The architectural heritage of Newport, Rhode Island, 1640–1915* (1952); D. Guinness and J.T. Sadler Jnr, *Newport preserved: architecture of the eighteenth century* (1982); N. Isham, *Trinity Church in Newport, Rhode Island: a history of the fabric* (1936); C. Bridenbaugh, *Cities in the wilderness*, pp 263, 310–11 (1993).

it was also seen as a challenge to the Baptist and Quaker majority of townsfolk, because it was a symbol of the authority of the British system. The royal coat of arms was displayed in the Trinity sanctuary. Unlike Puritan meeting houses, Trinity Church has always had an altar at the east end, to the rear of the three-level wineglass-shaped pulpit. Almost unique in New England, the church had an organ, the gift of George Berkeley in 1733.

The passage of 250 years has not greatly changed many of the familiar sights of Arthur Browne's youth. It is estimated that 350 buildings of that era are still standing, especially the simply designed Quaker merchants' and tradesmen's homes of Easton's Point.[27] There are also a number of elegant homes of the colony's ruling class – the members of the Trinity congregation. Many of the wealthy merchants' homes and places of business were at the waterfront along Thames Street, but these have not survived.

Newport was blessed with a deep, ice-free harbour, screened from the ferocious weather of the North Atlantic, and capable of accommodating a large fleet of warships. Newport's prosperity depended on the movement of cargoes on the Long Wharf. High wharfage fees ensured that many ships preferred to anchor in the large, safe harbour, awaiting the opportunity to quickly load and unload cargoes at the Long Wharf. Many merchants had their own wharfs and warehouses along Thames Street. The wharfs and public buildings of that day are still there, relatively untouched by the passage of time. The Colony House, built of brick in 1739 to the designs of Trinity's architect, Richard Munday, was the capitol building of the royal colony. At the opposite (western) end of a large public space, the parade (now called Washington Square), stands the Brick Market, designed by Peter Harrison, built in 1761 and intended for multiple uses – in the New England tradition – as a marketplace on the street level, town and mercantile offices, a lecture hall and a warehouse.

The largest church was the Great Meeting House of the Society of Friends (Quakers). Originally a barn-like structure erected in 1699, it was enlarged at least five times. There were ten other churches of various denominations, now gone except for the Seventh Day Baptist church of 1729, incorporated in the building of the Newport Historical Society. America's oldest synagogue building, the Touro Synagogue of 1759, designed by Peter Harrison, architect of the Brick Market, applied eighteenth-century ecclesiastical styles to the needs of a Sephardic congregation, resident in Newport from about 1658. Another work of Peter Harrison is the Redwood Library and Atheneum of 1748, a membership library built with the classic proportions of a Roman temple but made of wood that seems to be stone. Diagonally across from the Redwood Library stands the Viking Tower, thought to have been built in the eleventh century by followers of Leif Ericson, a legend long since questioned.

27 In Easton's Point, 60 colonial houses remain. A similar neighborhood, Prospect Hill, has a large number of colonial houses, but they are greatly deteriorated by commercial uses. L.F. Gracey, *The Point* (1985).

There was no public school, although there were several private institutions, including a Latin school founded before Trinity Church established its parish school in 1741. The Trinity school curriculum was the eighteenth-century minimum: arithmetic, writing, English, Latin and scripture. The masters did not spare the rod. Arthur Browne's studies at that school would surely have been supplemented by his father and grandfather, but he said very little about his schooling before his acceptance to Harvard in 1771 and his entry into Trinity College Dublin in 1772.

Although Newport had no collegiate institution, intellectual life was not neglected; there was the Society for the Promotion of Knowledge and Virtue by Free Conversation founded in 1730 by Peter Bours and Revd James Honyman, and influenced by George Berkeley, which convened every Monday night to converse and debate some useful question.[28] Another institution was a chapter of the American Philosophical Society, which had been founded by Benjamin Franklin in Philadelphia in 1743.

Browne's *Miscellaneous sketches* describes his love of his American home, and in it he briefly details the joys of a Newport summer: 'parties in the woods and dinners under their charming shade with dances afterward ... and the country resounding with songs and serenades'. And 'the choruses of the birds, the hunt for hares and foxes'.[29] He does not mention clambakes by the sea or sailing in Narragansett Bay. Nor do we hear about the perils of a New England winter: the vicious winds, the penetrating rains, the mantels of ice and snow, occasionally producing snowbound days; he merely notes that some strangers object to the 'excessive cold of the winter ... unnatural in that latitude' but owing to the 'continental wind blowing over an immense tract of frozen lakes'.[30] While he rejoices in the delight of autumn, he does not attempt to describe the colours of that season – the bright red, yellow and orange mixed with gold, green, brown and purple – that make New England famous.

He could never forget the Americans' 'ease and freedom of manners, unrestrained by European form',[31] and contrasted the manners of old Europe, 'the insolent air of London and ferocious look of Dublin', with the 'mildness and simplicity' characteristic of American manners.[32] Unfortunately, he noted, the British military mistook American character as unwarlike, an error 'fatally acknowledged by General Burgoyne' at Saratoga in 1777 'at the hands of American farmers and yeomen'.[33]

These are his memories of the country where, 'I spent my earliest and my happiest days.'[34] He had grown up during the peak years of Newport's prosperity, but the wealth and civilization of eighteenth-century Newport disappeared during the Revolutionary War as merchants and skilled artisans abandoned the town during three years of British military occupation and devastation. Fifty years later,

28 C. Bridenbaugh, *Cities in the wilderness*, p. 459 (1993).
29 A. Browne, *Miscellaneous sketches*, p. 209 (1798).
30 Ibid., p. 197.   31 Ibid., p. 210.   32 Ibid., p. 205.   33 Ibid.   34 Ibid., p. 210.

a new class of wealthy Americans discovered the pleasures of Newport summers and the town was reborn as a summer resort for the wealthiest people of New York and the South.

II

Arthur Browne's preparation for college had been in the Trinity parish school, established in 1741 under the Kay Foundation. He later wrote of his preparatory education:

> Of their [Americans'] schools self love inclines the author of this sketch to give a favourable account, having never received any school education elsewhere, yet their teachers were often from Europe, and it was his own fate to be instructed by a German and a Scotchman.[35]

The schoolmaster from 1763 to 1767 was a German émigré, Johan Ernst Knotchell, originally hired as the church organist. Revd George Bisset of Aberdeen, Scotland had been sent in 1767 by the SPG to be the schoolmaster and assistant to the rector, but the full responsibility for the very large and wealthy congregation had fallen on his shoulders during Marmaduke Browne's European absence and last illness, so it is uncertain how much time he could have devoted to the school.

The parish school offered instruction in Latin, but Arthur Browne must have received additional instruction from his father during the long ocean voyages, and from his grandfather, in view of his admission to Harvard College in 1771 for the class of 1775, since the Harvard of 1771 required written and oral examination in Latin and Greek.

During his schooldays Arthur Browne (b. 1756) had two schoolmates of roughly the same age, whom he would later encounter as a young man in London. They were Benjamin Waterhouse (b. 1754) and Gilbert Stuart (b. 1755). During their schooldays in Newport, in addition to the daily lessons, these students lived close to a waterfront filled with seafaring adventures and the trade of Europe, Asia and Africa. (None of them gives any picture of the slave trade.) In that sense, Newport itself was an international school about Europe and distant places, and Waterhouse later recounted his memory of the yearnings of the three classmates to visit Europe.

Waterhouse, who became a famous physician and professor of medicine, attended the Trinity parish school, although his parents were Quakers. His father, Timothy, was a furniture maker and also a politician and member of the governor's council. Benjamin decided early on a medical career, and, after apprenticeship to a local doctor, John Halliburton, left Newport in 1775 for London to study with a wealthy uncle, Dr John Fothergill,[36] who had a very large London practice.

35 A. Browne, *Miscellaneous sketches*, pp 202–3 (1798).
36 P. Cash, *Dr Benjamin Waterhouse: a life in medicine and public service (1754–1846)* (2006).

Waterhouse spent an academic year at the medical school of the University of Edinburgh, and then spent sixteen months in London until November 1778.

Gilbert Stuart, who became the most famous American portrait painter of the early republic, attended the Trinity school for nine years after his father, also named Gilbert, had moved his family and his snuff-making business across Narragansett Bay, from North Kingstown to Newport. His teenage years were filled with adventures. He travelled – as a 16-year-old apprentice of Cosmo Alexander, an itinerant artist from Scotland – to Philadelphia, Delaware and Virginia. At 17, he accompanied Alexander to Scotland, but the sudden death of his master forced him to return home as an apprentice seaman to Newport, where he remained for two years before returning to Europe in 1775 to study painting and practise his craft.[37]

In 1777 and 1778, Waterhouse, Stuart and Browne were together in London. We know very little about the adventures of these young men in the greatest city of Europe. We do know that Waterhouse's Quaker relatives in London knew the American Quaker artist Benjamin West of the Royal Academy, who took Stuart as a pupil, and later as his assistant. Working with Benjamin West, a painter of royal and aristocratic subjects, brought Stuart into contact with Sir Joshua Reynolds, president of the Royal Academy, to whom Arthur Browne was indebted for an introduction to the dinners of Doctor Johnson's Literary Club.[38]

Gilbert Stuart fled his London creditors and arrived in Dublin in September 1787, where he remained for more than five years, again pursued by creditors, until April 1793, when he returned to America for good. Stuart's problem was too many clients and his inability to finish portraits on time.

After London, Benjamin Waterhouse travelled to the medical school of the University of Leyden, where he was a roommate of young John Quincy Adams. He received the academic degree of doctor of medicine in 1780, and sailed for America in 1782 in a naval vessel bound first for the Canary Islands and Cuba, but on the way his ship was captured by the British. On his eventual arrival in Boston, Waterhouse was appointed to the new faculty of medicine at Harvard, where he served for thirty-four years.

Of the three Newport schoolmates, Waterhouse lived the longest – to the age of 92. Both Stuart and Waterhouse had long and profitable careers in America but Browne never returned to the place of 'my earliest and my happiest days'.

III

In June 1769 Marmaduke Browne sailed to Europe with his son, Arthur, for the threefold purposes of settling his late wife's estate in favour of his son, who would be entered at Trinity College Dublin, obtaining additional stops and other parts for

37 C.M. Mount, *Gilbert Stuart: a biography* (1964) and D. Evans, *The genius of Gilbert Stuart* (1999).
38 See chapter 4, n. 10–11. Benjamin West (1738–1820), portraitist in Philadelphia and New York; to

the Trinity Church organ, and pursuing professional advancement by obtaining the AM degree from Trinity College. Their return began in August 1770. Marmaduke was 'indisposed, 'tho tolerably cheerful'[39] after an absence of fourteen months. There is no documentary evidence that Arthur Browne at age 14 accompanied his father on the European voyage, but it is a reasonable inference, since there was no one to care for him in Newport, and Marmaduke had accompanied his father, Revd Arthur Browne, to England and Ireland in 1750. Marmaduke's 1770 return voyage to America began at Antwerp, Belgium, in the winter of 1770–1.

The cause of Marmaduke Browne's sudden death in March 1771 at age 40 was unknown, although the stresses of an eleven-week voyage were mentioned, as well as possible fevers. The writer of the above letter continued that Marmaduke was 'seized with fatal symptoms of the convulsive kind, only four days before his death'.[40]

The future of an orphan in eighteenth-century America was certainly perilous in the absence of social welfare, insurance and pensions, so the immediate concern of Arthur Browne and his grandparents, who lived 140 miles away in Portsmouth, was to find a way to finance his education in the family profession of service to the established church.

College students of the eighteenth century usually began their studies in their mid-teens, so it was clearly time for Arthur Browne to begin serious academic work in a collegiate atmosphere. The sudden death of his father seemed to foreclose the possibility of study in Dublin, so he was forced to consider an American alternative, Harvard College.

Arthur Browne visited Cambridge, Massachusetts, seat of Harvard College, where his aunt Mary was the wife of Revd Winwood Sarjent, an SPG missionary since 1767 and rector of Christ Church, only a few steps away from the Harvard College yard. He wrote of the town:

> What could be prettier for instance than the village of Cambridge near Boston? Its colleges, its scattered mansions, most of them splendid, the seats of rich West-Indians, whose health had induced a change of clime, surrounding a smooth and verdant lawn, and rising up peeping though thick clumps of wood perhaps exceeded in beauty the prettiest village in England.[41]

Of Harvard College itself, he wrote:

> The principal [college in New England] was that of Cambridge, consisting of about 180 students, who were lodged in four handsome and extensive

Italy 1760, then to London 1762; historical painter to king 1772; president of Royal Academy 1792–1820.
39 Letter to the SPG from missionary priest J. Graves, quoted in Ballard, 'Trinity Church in Old Newport on Rhode Island', p. 357 (1979).
40 Ibid.   41 Browne, *Miscellaneous sketches*, p. 196 (1798).

brick edifices. The sciences were taught much in the same order as with us [Trinity College Dublin] beginning with logic, ending with ethics, though the books perused were different. One of the professors of this college, Dr Winthrop, was well known in Europe as an astronomer.[42]

The Harvard College of 1771 consisted of about 200 students; the class in which Arthur Browne was entered matriculated with 56 and graduated 63 men in 1775, the largest group since the foundation in 1636.[43] Most of them came from New England. The faculty consisted of the president (an ordained minister of the Congregational church), three professors and at least four tutors. Daily attendance at chapel services was required. A fire in 1764 had destroyed the library of 5,000 volumes, but within two years it had been replaced and even enlarged. Heavy drinking, the hazing of freshmen and all the tricks and entertainments of naïve adolescents were practised there, as was undoubtedly also true at the nine American Colleges in 1776, as well as Oxford, Cambridge and Trinity. A loyalist lady complained about the Harvard students, that, 'the independency and liberty with which the youths are brought up and indulged, makes too many of 'em proficient in vice'.[44]

Arthur Browne was entered in Harvard College after the death of his father as the best alternative to the European education planned for him, although Harvard would not have been a congenial place to the Brownes, since they would have disapproved of the Puritan theology of the college administration. The political views of the students and faculty undoubtedly terrified Arthur Browne's guardians. Professor Samuel Eliot Morison has noted that only 196 of 1,224 Harvard graduates living in 1776 (a mere 16 per cent) could be termed loyal to the British crown.[45]

Furthermore, insubordinate attitudes were loose in the college since the Butter Rebellion of spring 1766, when the students conspired to refuse to eat in the college commons because it was serving rancid Irish butter, of which the college had a surplus.[46] Two years later, a 'liberty tree' appeared in the college yard, and students voted to abstain from drinking tea because it was subject to British taxation.[47] Lastly, there was a major distraction in the presence of the disorderly Massachusetts legislature, the Great and General Court, which sat in Harvard's buildings from March 1770 to March 1773, having been moved from Boston by Governor Hutchinson to escape the effects of Boston mobs controlled by opponents of the crown, such as Samuel Adams.[48]

42 Ibid.   43 S.E. Morison, *Three centuries of Harvard*, p. 102 (1936).
44 Ibid., p. 135. Of the 63 graduates in 1775, there were 6 lawyers, 14 clergymen, 15 medical doctors and 5 schoolmasters.
45 Ibid., p. 147.   46 Ibid., p. 118.   47 Ibid., p. 133.
48 Ibid., pp 136–7. See J.C. Miller, *Sam Adams: pioneer in propaganda* (1936), S. Beach, *Samuel Adams: the fateful years, 1764–1776* (1965) and M. Puls, *Samuel Adams: father of the American Revolution*, pp 97–114, 127–51 (2006).

It is not possible now to determine whether Arthur Browne attended lectures at Harvard between his admission in summer 1771 and his voyage to Ireland in March 1772. He does not mention classes or lectures in his descriptions of the college.

In addition to upsetting Arthur Browne's plans to study in Dublin, the death of Marmaduke Browne also produced an unexpected financial crisis in the affairs of Trinity Church, Newport. The vestry wrote to the SPG on 17 April 1771 reporting the death of the society's missionary, which 'had deprived the parish of this great and inestimable blessing', requesting the continuation of the mission status, necessarily including the salary of a new rector, asking for financial assistance to reduce the debt incurred for rebuilding the church steeple, and asking that the society agree to Revd George Bisset as the new rector at the same salary level.[49] The SPG acted three months later to approve the choice of Mr Bisset but to deny any further financial assistance to the parish because of the 'flourishing state and opulent circumstances of their parish'.[50] Trinity would have to rely on local resources.

Before this devastating rejection was received by the Trinity vestry, Arthur Browne wrote to John Bours, the senior warden of the parish, from his grandfather's house, two months after his father's death:

Portsmouth, May 16, 1771

Dear Mr Bours:

It seems to me most proper to write to you concerning the following affair, both as church warden, and as being one of my best friends. My grandfather declines drawing upon the society, and thinks it would be best for the gentlemen who are church wardens, not to draw, but to write to the society, informing them of my father's death, of his leaving me wholly unprovided for, by which means there was a great chance of my losing a liberal education at home, whither my father designed to send me. He says I may be pretty sure, if those gentlemen would be so kind as to write of the society's doing something handsome for me, especially if they would represent me in as favourable a light as they think proper, as a lad of some merit, who, if properly encouraged, might turn out something.

These are his words, not mine; for not all the vanity natural to man should induce me to write thus of myself, were it not his direction. I know your friendship will excuse the trouble, which, notwithstanding after having troubled you so often, I am to give you, and I hope poor Peter was recovered before you got home. My love to Mrs Bours.

I received Mr Sam Bours' kind letter, and found that I must chuse a guardian as he says. I hope poor Mrs Bours has had no more ill turns. My

---

49 Ballard, 'Trinity Church in Old Newport on Rhode Island', pp 356–8 (1979); quoting vestry letter of 18 Apr. 1771.

50 Ibid., p. 359.

compliments to all friends. My grandfather and all the family join with me in love to you and Mrs Bours, and believe me always, your affectionate, humble servant, etc.

Arthur Browne[51]

The recipient, John Bours, a lawyer and senior warden, would later be the man to hold the parish together as lay reader after the rector (Mr Bisset) fled with the British army in 1779. In 1771, he wrote to the SPG for the vestry, seeking support for the education of the 16-year-old orphan, Arthur Browne. The vestry's letter was a most enthusiastic endorsement:

Newport, May 29, 1771

Revd. Sir:

The subscribers, wardens of Trinity Church in Newport, beg leave to address the honorable society on behalf of Mr Arthur Browne, a minor of sixteen years of age, son of our late worthy minister the Revd Marmaduke Browne, of whose death we informed them in a letter of April 1st, in conjunction with the vestry of said church.

The Revd. Mr Browne was blessed with only this child, in whom, very early in life he had discovered marks of early genius and was thence prompted to use his endeavors to give him an education suitable to his capacity; to this end it was, that he undertook his late voyage to Europe; principally to recover a small estate in Ireland, to which the lad was heir in right of his deceased mother. He succeeded so far as to recover about forty pounds sterling, per annum, this sum, with what he thought he could by great economy spare out of his annual income from the honble society, he had resolved [to] appropriate towards giving him an education at the University of Dublin; and had settled a plan to send him the ensuing summer to the care of Dr Foresaith. One of the fellows of the university. But how unfortunate for the youth is the death of his father; with him his expectations are cut off and he will be disappointed of a liberal education unless he can obtain some assistance from his friends; his father having left him nothing but a small library not worth above fifty pound sterling at the extent & a little household furniture. As we are sensible the honble society had a regard for the father we flatter ourselves that they will not take it amiss, or think it impertinent in us to recommend to their notice his son as a lad of singular modesty, and of a capacity rarely to be met with in one of his years; have no sinister views in saying this much of him: justice and his merit demands it of us. We would beg leave of the venerable Society to give us some directions about drawing upon them for what salary was due his father at the time of his death. Any small assistance he may receive from them towards forwarding him to his laudable undertaking, will be acknowledged with the most grateful sentiments, by him, as well as by

John Bours

Isaac Lawton[52]

Seven weeks later, the SPG acted generously to provide Arthur with half of his father's yearly salary, voted on 19 July 1771. The favourable light requested by Trinity Church also produced £25 passage money to Ireland from the SPG. (Transatlantic passage varied from £6 to £10 in mid-century.) It is not known when he received this news, but now assured of an annual income of £40 from his mother's estate and the promised assistance of Dr John Forsayeth, senior fellow of TCD, and armed with the base of an eighteenth-century education, Arthur Browne was able to make the voyage to Ireland (probably from Boston) in late winter 1772. He enrolled at Trinity College Dublin on 24 March 1772.

The Newport and the America that Arthur Browne left in 1772 was three years away from the open rebellion that began at Lexington and Concord, Massachusetts on 19 April 1775. It is, however, necessary to review the build-up of disaffection and hatred that led to war, witnessed in Newport by Arthur Browne and his family.

In 1768, Arthur Browne's father and grandfather had joined in a letter to their missionary superiors in London summing up the 'troublesome state of these colonies', and the insults to which their congregations were exposed for failing to 'join the clamours'.[53] They did not need to describe the mob actions already officially reported. It would have been impossible to ignore the noise and tumult that endangered Arthur Browne's family's livelihood and even survival. He undoubtedly suppressed thoughts and nightmares of civic strife and violence in favour of the idylls of a happy youth. Thirty years later, however, the turmoil in Dublin before the 1798 Revolution must have been a vivid reminder of adolescent experiences.

The privileged life of Arthur Browne in Newport was confined to his father's church, its rectory and its parish school; but this commercial town was a centre of angry political discourse, which became violent protests concerning British tax and trade policies. The disaffection of the people with the mother country might not have been initially apparent because his father's congregation of some 200 families consisted in large part of wealthy merchants, seafarers and government officials, assumed to be Tories or loyalists,[54] but the clamour and shouts soon surrounded them and drowned their loyalist sympathies.

---

52 Ibid., p. 147.
53 D. Addison, *The life and times of Edward Bass, first bishop of Massachusetts*, pp 101–2 (1897).
54 E. Stiles, *Extracts from the itineraries, 1755–94* (1962).

IV

The Seven Years War with France had brought prosperity to Newport, from smuggling and privateering, but the peace treaty of 1763 left George Grenville and the British government burdened with a heavy war debt that it was determined should be shared with the American colonies.[55] Widespread rumours that the colonials had traded profitably with the enemy French colonies during the war meant that there was little sympathy for the colonials in Parliament. Rigid enforcement of existing trade and navigation laws, especially the 1733 import duties on molasses (used for distillation into rum), sugar, coffee, wines and manufactured goods, presented an immediate solution to the financial problem, as it was known that enforcement of these duties had been notoriously lax. One obvious choice was to use the surplus warships of the peacetime British navy to assist in the inspection of colonial shipping. Thus, some forty-four naval vessels were dispatched to operate in American waters.[56] A naval vessel was stationed in Newport harbour continuously from 1763 until the final withdrawal of British forces in 1779. Another possible revenue enhancement, not realized until 1768, was the use of the British standing army to conduct searches and seizures of smuggled goods.

Before the Stamp Act, but in the face of strict enforcement, Revd Ezra Stiles of the Second Congregational Church in Newport expressed the view of many merchants and mariners in a 1764 letter to the Connecticut colony's agent in London:

> Indeed a parliamentary taxation of America effectually strikes at the root of American liberty and rights and effectually reduces us to slavery. We are already equal to England in numbers, and it will be hard to subject one half the king's subjects to the taxation of the other half. Britain has expended several millions in our defense which we shall soon pay in sale of lands, in commerce & c. And why should she claim perpetual subjugation in return for defense? Why should we be treated as a conquered country?[57]

The actions of the warships and their crews involved rigorous inspections and occasional impressment of seamen and were perceived by Newport merchants as

---

55 See P. Lawson, *George Grenville: a political life*, pp 181–204, 224–6 (1984) and J.L. Bullion, *A great and necessary measure: George Grenville and the genesis of the Stamp Act, 1763–1765* (1982).

56 N.R. Stout, *The royal navy in America, 1760–1775: a study of the enforcement of British colonial policy in the era of the American Revolution* (1973); A.B. Hawes, *Off-soundings: aspects of the maritime history of Rhode Island*, p. 167 (1999). Royal navy vessels stationed in Narragansett Bay and Newport for the ten years before the revolution were HMS *Squirrel*, *St John*, *Maidstone*, *Liberty*, *Cygnet*, *Gaspee*, *Rose* and *Swan*.

57 Morgan, *The Stamp Act crisis: prologue to revolution*, p. 224 (1953); Hawes, *Off-soundings*, p. 9 (1999). See also E. Crane, *A dependent people: Newport, Rhode Island in the revolutionary era*, pp 112–13 (1985) and F.B. Wiener, 'The Rhode Island merchants and the Sugar Act', 3 *N.E.Q.*, 464 (1938).

the source of actual losses where their profitable operations had been tax-free for many years. These perceptions produced the first hostile actions against British imperial authority even before Parliament imposed the Stamp Act in 1765.

The financial crisis in Britain, precipitated by the French war, came in a period of political instability during which weak governments made poor choices that shattered the unity of the empire. The great war leader, William Pitt, retired for reasons of health just as the new king, George III, began to free himself from the Whig potentates that had run the country for forty-five years. The king's friends were not yet a political party to replace the Tories of Queen Anne's time. Pitt's Whig successors were power-hungry politicians and canny traders but without leadership skills. Their short-lived administrations could not deal consistently or fairly with America (or Ireland).

It was the Whigs who created the sources of disaffection in America: the Sugar Act (1763), the Stamp Act (1765), the Declaratory Act (1766), the Townshend Duties (1767) and the Army of Occupation (1768). By the time Lord North began his twelve-year Tory administration (1770–82) the damage had been done and revolution was inevitable. The military policy and even the strategy of the American War of Independence was the responsibility of Lord George Germain, secretary of state for North America, who succeeded in 1775 the earls of Hillsborough (1768) and Dartmouth (1772). Disaffection leading to rebellion is more appropriately the responsibility of Hillsborough, first holder of the office of secretary of state for the colonies. He was an absentee Irish landowner deeply involved in British Whig politics before he turned his ignorance of America and political inexperience to preserving the empire. With the British army in occupation, his peremptory orders to royal governors to use the power of legislative dissolution to prevent colonials from debating taxation assumed this would end discussion rather than perpetuate it.

In Newport, mobs of sailors and dock workers fought with customs officials in the summer of 1764, recapturing molasses seized for non-payment of duty. Under mob influence, town cannons were fired (ineffectively) at HMS *St John*. The effort of the navy to board a suspected smuggler in Newport in December 1764 led to warlike resistance and exchange of serious wounds. In April 1765, the sloop *Polly* was seized by Customs Collector John Robinson, but a mob removed the cargo, stripped off the rigging and ran the vessel aground, damages for which the vessel owner asserted the personal liability of the collector, in lengthy and humiliating proceedings. Impressments of seamen for naval service led to a riot on 4 June 1765, when a longboat of HMS *Maidstone* was seized by a mob, estimated to be 'above 500 sailors, boys and negroes'. The officer was verbally abused and released but the longboat was paraded through the town before being set ablaze. No perpetrators were ever identified for prosecution.[58]

58 D.S. Lovejoy, *Rhode Island politics and the American Revolution, 1760–1776*, pp 38–9 (1958); E.S. and H.M. Morgan, *The Stamp Act crisis: prologue to revolution*, pp 23–47 (1953).

The ready availability of mobs of distressed workers raised the question of whether wealthy merchants were leading or encouraging the mobs. In the subsequent Stamp Act riots there is no doubt that young gentlemen were part of the mobs that were later described as 'Sons of Liberty'.[59] Because of the economic issues involved in taxation and impressments, it is undoubtedly true that the mobs involved all classes of society.

On 22 March 1765, the royal assent was given to a new scheme of colonial taxation for which George Grenville was responsible.[60] After 1 November 1765 a paper stamp had to be affixed to all legal and commercial documents, including bills of sale, leases, deeds and ships' papers, and to most types of printed paper, specifically to newspapers, pamphlets (usually called 'broadsides') and almanacs.[61] Anticipating trouble from colonials, Grenville proposed that Americans, instead of émigré Britons, be appointed to administer the scheme and sell the stamps. Enforcement through civil and criminal penalties was entrusted to the courts of vice admiralty for trial by royal judges alone rather than by 'unreliable' colonial juries.[62]

Word of the new tax flew across the Atlantic, and committees of merchants immediately reacted. On 29 May 1765 the House of Burgesses in Virginia declared its opposition in the Virginia Resolves.[63] The Massachusetts Great and General Court (the lower house), published circular letters on 8 June 1765 to all colonies, suggesting a congress of the colonies to take united action against the new tax.

Mob action against the Stamp Act began in Boston as soon as the list of stamp-tax distributors was published in early August 1765. Andrew Oliver had sought the stamp-distribution appointment through the influence of his brother-in-law, Chief Justice Thomas Hutchinson. On Wednesday, 14 August 1765, his effigy was hanged from a 'liberty tree' in Boston, and then carried in an evening procession to his house, where the head was struck off. His house was ransacked by the mob; he resigned the next day.[64]

The pressure and noise increased over the next twelve days and a violent eruption after the Puritan sabbath occurred in Boston on the evening of Monday, 26 August 1765, when a mob gathered on King Street (now State Street). The mob first attacked the home of William Story, registrar of the court of vice admiralty, ransacking it and setting fire to its contents, and then attacked the house of Benjamin Hallowell, controller of the customs, pillaged it and set it afire. The mobs increased in size and noise and then marched to the much grander mansion of the

59 W.M. Fowler, *William Ellery: a Rhode Island politico and lord of admiralty*, pp 9–11 (1973).

60 E. Channing, *A history of the United States, 1761–1789*, pp 35–40 (1912).

61 5 Geo. 3 c. 12. See generally, Morgan, *The Stamp Act crisis* (1953), Bullion, *A great and necessary measure* (1982), Lawson, *George Grenville*, pp 224–6 (1984) and P. Thomas, *British politics and the Stamp Act crisis* (1975).

62 5 Geo. 3 c. 12. See Ubbelohde, *The vice-admiralty courts and the American Revolution* (1960).

63 Stamp Act Resolves of the House of Burgesses, 28 May 1765. Hutchinson, *History of the colony and province of Massachusetts Bay*, vol. 3, p. 333 (1936).

64 Channing, *A history of the United States*, pp 58–9 (1912).

chief justice (and lieutenant governor), Thomas Hutchinson, in the north end of the town.[65] Axes were used to shatter the front door, after which the mob broke into the library, where books, paintings, official papers and colonial archives were seized and tossed onto a bonfire made up of the furniture, draperies and household belongings of the chief justice, who was despised by the mob as an enforcer of royal authority, although he had opposed the Stamp Act. Efforts to tear down or burn the three-storey brick structure were abandoned at dawn – possibly because the mob had consumed the contents of the ample wine cellar. Hutchinson and his family had fled at the approach of the mob to the house of friends and then to a warship in the harbour before abandoning the city for his summer estate on Milton Hill, about 8 miles south of Boston. There had been no serious injuries in the melee, but one of the finest houses in the colonies had been turned into a desolate ruin. A reward of £300 was offered for the apprehension of the leaders of the mob, and several men were initially arrested, but they were subsequently released, after their jailer was threatened with mob violence. No one was ever prosecuted for this outrage. By legend, the leaders of the 1765 mob were also the 'Indians' who destroyed the tea eight years later in the Boston Tea Party.

It is possible that news of the resignation of Boston stamp master Andrew Oliver after the 14 August hanging of his effigy persuaded leaders of the Newport Sons of Liberty to apply the same remedy to local Tories: Augustus Johnston, attorney general of the colony; Martin Howard Jnr, Tory lawyer, Trinity parishioner and pamphleteer; and Dr Thomas Moffat, a Scottish follower of George Berkeley. Their outspoken views were known to favour cancellation of the 1663 Rhode Island Charter and substitution of direct royal government. On 26 August 1765 a scaffold was erected on the parade, with effigies of the three Tory leaders. After dark a mob, furnished with drink (probably rum) by Newport merchants, assembled on the parade. The effigy of Howard was carried from the parade in front of the Colony House the few steps to his house, the Wanton-Lyman-Hazard House on Broadway. Forewarned, Howard fled before his effigy was hanged and burned by the unruly crowd, whose frustration at the absence of Howard was quickly transferred to his home, which was opened and the contents destroyed.[66] The mob then moved to the opposite side of the Colony House to the house of Dr Moffat, who had also abandoned it to the mob, which hanged and burned his effigy before ransacking the contents. Both Howard and Moffat rowed out to the safety of HMS *Cygnet* at anchor in the harbour. They never returned to Newport. The home of customs collector John Robinson adjacent to the Customs Wharf was ransacked the next day.[67]

65 Hutchinson's own account of the riot is in his *History of the colony and province of Massachusetts Bay*, vol. 3, pp 85–93 (1936). See also Channing, *A history of the United States*, pp 59–60 (1912).

66 Fowler, *William Ellery*, pp 9–11 (1973); Hawes, *Off-soundings*, pp 158–60 (1999); D.S. Lovejoy, *Rhode Island politics and the American Revolution, 1760–1776*, pp 103–15 (1958); Crane, *A dependent people*, pp 112–16 (1985); and S.V. James, *Colonial Rhode Island: a history*, pp 325–32 (1975).

67 Lovejoy, *Rhode Island*, pp 105–18 (1958). Howard was rewarded by the ministry with appointment as chief justice of North Carolina.

The Newport stamp master, Augustus Johnston, a well-known political figure then serving as attorney general of the colony, was not immediately threatened on 26 August, but two days later the mob reassembled to deal with the hated stamps, not yet arrived. Johnston forestalled destruction of his property and danger to his person by notifying the mob leaders of his intention to resign the stamp office, which he did, conditionally, on 29 August.[68]

Howard and Moffat sailed to England, where they later testified about their treatment at the hands of the Sons of Liberty.[69] Johnston remained in Newport but when the non-importation strategy of the Stamp Act Congress was forced on the Newport merchants, he resigned the office of the stamp master unconditionally on 24 December 1765. No stamps were ever used in Rhode Island. Agents of Howard and Moffat sought compensation from the colony, which was apparently awarded in 1773.[70]

The town centre around the Colony House and Trinity Church was quite congested with homes and shops. The Trinity rectory, which was at the corner of what are now High and Touro streets, and the parish school, which was at the corner of what are now School and Mary streets, were two short blocks from the church. Close to the rectory was the Colony House, at the head of the parade and a few steps north of the home of Martin Howard Jnr (the Wanton-Lyman-Hazard House on Broadway), while the home of Augustus Johnston was a few steps south of Division and Mary Streets. Thus, the rectory was in the middle of the Stamp Act riots of August 1765.

The Rhode Island legislature convened in September 1765, and decided to send two official delegates to the congress being organized by Massachusetts to consider united action to deal with the stamps. Rhode Island's elected governor, Stephen Hopkins, certainly echoed the Massachusetts Resolves in his 1765 pamphlet, 'The rights of the colonies examined', to the effect that neither the people nor the Parliament of Britain had the power to tax the colonies. Thus, the view of Rhode Island's Assembly was that the Stamp Act was a nullity and officials were expected to conduct business without the stamps.[71]

Official delegations arrived in New York City from Massachusetts, South Carolina, Rhode Island, Connecticut, Pennsylvania and Maryland for the Congress. Unofficial representatives from Delaware, New Jersey and New York also attended. Of the twenty-eight attendees – mostly merchants or lawyers – a number became famous in the continental congress and the revolutionary army: James Otis of Massachusetts; Eliphalet Dyer and William Johnson of Connecticut; Robert Livingston of New York; John Dickinson and John Morton of Pennsylvania; Caesar Rodney of Delaware; and Christopher Gadsden, Thomas Lynch and John Rutledge of South Carolina.

68 Ibid., pp 100–12.
69 James, *Colonial Rhode Island*, p. 330 (1975), and Lovejoy, *Rhode Island*, pp 110–12 (1958).
70 Lovejoy, *Rhode Island*, pp 110–12 (1958).
71 Ibid., pp 113–15, and James, *Colonial Rhode Island*, pp 330–2 (1975).

The Stamp Act Congress, meeting without royal authority, assembled on 7 October 1765, before the effective date of the stamp tax (1 November 1765). Votes were taken by colony and not individually. The product of their deliberations, which continued until 23 October, were fourteen resolutions opposing taxation without actual representation in the enacting legislature, an agreement not to import British manufactured goods and a condemnation of trial in the courts of vice admiralty, which deprived citizens of the right to trial by jury.[72]

Mob gatherings and threats of violence by tar and feathers had persuaded official stamp distributors in every colony to resign their appointments before the effective day of the tax. By 1 November 1765 there were no stamp distributors and no customers to buy them. Business in which stamps were required for ordinary operations suspended such activities, as did most courts where stamped documents were required. After several weeks of inactivity, however, businesses and courts resumed their normal un-stamped proceedings.

The 30-year-old John Adams, practicing law in Boston, summed up this remarkable year in his diary:

> The year 1765 has been the most remarkable year of my life. That enormous engine fabricated by the British Parliament for battering down all the rights and liberties of America, I mean the Stamp Act, has raised and spread through the whole continent a spirit that will be recorded to our honor with all future generations. In every colony from Georgia to New Hampshire inclusively, the stamps distributers and inspectors have been compelled by the unconquerable rage of the people to resign their offices ... This year brings ruin or salvation to the British colonies. The eyes of all America are fixed on the British Parliament. In short, Britain and America are staring at each other – and they will probably stare more and more for some time.[73]

By the new year, 1766, the effect of non-importation was clear to British exporters, whose distress was felt by members of Parliament. The House of Commons took testimony (as committee of the whole) from Benjamin Franklin, agent for Pennsylvania, and other colonial agents, and debated military enforcement or total repeal. Repeal of the provocative legislation was the ultimate choice, and the king gave the royal assent to repeal on 18 March 1766, just four days shy of the Stamp Act's first anniversary,[74] but the repeal was accompanied by an assertion of Parliament's authority to legislate for the American colonies in all

---

72　C.A. Weslager, *The Stamp Act Congress* (1976); Channing, *A history of the United States*, pp 56–8 (1912); and S.E. Morison, *Sources and documents illustrating the American Revolution, 1764–1788*, pp 31–7 (2nd ed. 1929). The legal issues between the colonials and the mother country are reviewed in J.P. Reid, 'In accordance with usage: the authority of custom, the Stamp Act debate and the coming of the American Revolution', 45 *Fordham L. Rev.*, 335–68 (1976).

73　L. Kinvin Wroth & Hiller B. Zobel (eds), *Legal papers of John Adams* (Cambridge, MA, 1965), i, p. 282.

74　6 Geo. 3. c.12. See Channing, *A history of the United States*, pp 68–79 (1912).

cases. This declaration led to further colonial protests on import duties in 1768 and would eventually be the precipitating factor in the 'tea parties' of 1773.

V

The next phase of the struggle involved the Townshend Duties of 29 June 1767, when Parliament imposed duties on the import into the American colonies from England of glass, lead, paint, paper and tea. The duties were accompanied by the creation of a superior court of vice admiralty in Halifax, Nova Scotia, a navy town without Sons of Liberty, for trial of offences,[75] and the law revised the writs of assistance authorizing customs searches without probable cause on suspicion of possession of goods on which duties had not been paid.[76] The effective date of the new legislation was 20 November 1767. In the Stamp Act crisis of 1765, a distinction had been made in England and America between the internal (local) stamp as a tax and external (foreign) customs duties or tariff. By 1768 Americans saw no distinction, but Britain justified the new scheme as imperial rather than local.

Agents of the colonies quickly informed their principals, who determined to repeat the non-importation tactic of 1765. (Non-importation did not yet involve non-exportation; the total embargo on trade with Great Britain did not come until 1774, when war became inevitable.) Lord Hillsborough's order to the Massachusetts legislature to rescind its circular letter of 1765 to other colonies was met on 30 June 1768 with defiance, in a vote of 92 to 17 not to rescind. Paul Revere memorialized the vote with an engraved silver 'liberty bowl'.

Merchants of Boston, Providence, Newport, New York and Philadelphia reluctantly agreed to impose non-importation of British goods on 1 January 1768. Non-importation remained in force for twenty-eight months, but this time American merchants as well as British exporters began to suffer the effects of the cessation of business activity. By the end of October 1769 some Newport merchants who were not involved in the profitable slave trade sought exemptions from non-importation of some products and a resumption of traditional relations with British trading partners. The Newport merchants' actions were resented in neighboring colonies as seeking unfair advantage over righteous sufferers. Threats were made that Boston, Providence, New York and Philadelphia would refuse to deal with Newport, an early form of boycott. The threats restored the united front so that British export trade to the American colonies had ceased by January 1770.[77]

At this point, British politics intervened. An attempt to respond to the demands of British traders and the newly vocal friends of the American colonies provided

75 8 Geo. 3 c. 23. See Ubbelohde, *The vice-admiralty courts and the American Revolution* (1960).
76 7 Geo. 3 c. 41.
77 A.M. Schlesinger, *Colonial merchants and the American Revolution, 1762–1776*, pp 152–543 (1918); Lovejoy, *Rhode Island*, pp 143–7 (1958), and James, *Colonial Rhode Island*, pp 334–7 (1975).

King George with the opportunity to be rid of the hated Whigs. The king replaced the unpopular duke of Grafton with Lord North, who became the prime minister who lost the American colonies. Lord North served the king from January 1770 to March 1782. His government achieved repeal of the Townshend Duties – all but the tax on tea – in April 1770.[78] This action brought a quick end to the unified non-importation action of the colonies, but only briefly. North's pledge of no new taxes was scorned in America.

Customs enforcement by the royal navy and installation of British military forces in Boston and New York created new crises, which would lead to war. Another product of the Townshend Duties legislation was the creation of the board of commissioners of customs for the colonies, to be located at Boston.[79] The commissioners were assisted by a 50-gun frigate, HMS *Romney*. Customs officials seized the sloop *Liberty*, which belonged to John Hancock, for non-payment of duty on a cargo of Madeira wine on 14 June 1768, and then moved the sloop to an anchorage next to the warship to guarantee its safety from the type of mob action that had occurred in Newport, when seized cargoes were released by the mob. This time the mob proceeded to the private homes of the customs officials to demonstrate with threats of tar and feathers; customs officers on the dock were also assaulted. The customs officials and their families fled from the town to the protection of Castle William, the fortress that guarded Boston's inner harbour.[80] With the mob in control of the streets and the General Court defiant, Governor Francis Bernard dissolved the legislature on 30 June. In response, an unauthorized 'convention' of representatives from ninety-six towns met for five days in Boston to plan further opposition, but cooler heads prevailed and the result was a petition to the king for redress of grievances.

VI

The flight of the customs officials occurred just before the deployment of British army units to Boston. The gradual transfer of the peacetime British army from England and Ireland to occupation duty in America began in autumn of 1768 and the numbers continued to increase annually before the major invasion of 1776. The effect of removing British military power from Ireland to America was the origin of the Irish Volunteers and even Grattan's independent Parliament in 1782.[81]

Two regiments (about 1,200 men) of British troops landed in Boston in October 1768 in the face of intense resentment of the 'lobster backs', so called because of

78 10 Geo. 3 c. 17. The expected return was £10,000 per annum from America.
79 O.M. Dickenson, 'Commissioners of Customs and the Boston Massacre', 27 *N.E.Q.*, 307 (1954). See also J. Tyler, *Smugglers and patriots: Boston merchants and the advent of the American Revolution* (1986).
80 B. Carp, *Rebels rising: cities and the American Revolution*, pp 45–55 (2007).
81 See chapter 5, n. 5–10. A comparison of the similarities in the colonial experiences of Massachusetts and Ireland is found in J.P. Reid, *In a defiant stance*, pp 114–15, 135–49, 152–9 (1977).

the red uniforms or the flogging of bare backs for disciplinary reasons. Similar forces landed simultaneously in New York City.[82] Newport did not then receive British troops, although there was always a warship on duty in Narragansett Bay to suppress smuggling.

In Newport, abuse of customs officers became common, especially after the local collector, John Robinson, was replaced by an Englishman, Charles Dudley – he was assaulted on the wharf.[83] In July 1769 a royal customs ship, the *Liberty*, attempting to enforce the customs and navigation laws, was abandoned by her besieged crew, then set adrift, beached, pillaged and burnt by the mob of Sons of Liberty, who had already decorated a 'liberty tree' (like the ones at Harvard and Boston) on the principal thoroughfare, Thames Street.[84] Sons of Liberty at Providence applied tar and feathers to a customs official who had not resigned his office.[85]

The first bloodshed from the 'army of occupation' occurred in New York City, in a battle between soldiers and civilians on 19 January 1770, although only one life was lost in the encounter.[86] The New York incident is known as the battle of Golden Hill. (It took place near the modern intersection of John and William streets.) On 16 January 1770, British soldiers cut down the 'liberty pole' celebrating repeal of the Stamp Act and deposited the pieces in front of Montayne's Tavern, a meeting place of the Sons of Liberty. Three days later, Sons of Liberty, now armed with cudgels and swords, were looking for trouble and soon found it when they came upon members of a British regiment from Ireland. In the fight, blows and cuts were exchanged, and one civilian was fatally wounded by a soldier's bayonet. British officers broke up the fight and ordered the soldiers to their barracks; thirty or forty people may have been involved.

Greater loss of life – five civilians– occurred in Boston on 5 March 1770, in the 'Boston Massacre'.[87] There had been continued verbal tauntings between soldiers and Sons of Liberty, but the situation became more serious when economic conflict emerged. British soldiers sought to supplement their meagre pay with work as longshoremen, labourers or artisans in their hours off-duty, depriving civilian workers of job opportunities. This conflict was undoubtedly the source of the Boston trouble. Belligerent townsmen, including boys and longshoremen, verbally and profanely insulted and threw snowballs at the sentry on duty in front of the custom house, near the Town House (now the Old State House) about 9 p.m. on Monday, 5 March 1770. The sentry called out the full guard and a squad lined

82 Channing, *A history of the United States*, pp 96–8, 211–16 (1912); O.M Dickerson, *Boston under military rule, 1768–1769* (1936, reprint 1971).
83 Lovejoy, *Rhode Island*, pp 154–5 (1958). Dudley eventually fled to the station warship, HMS *Rose*.
84 Ibid., pp 157–8. Customs ship *Liberty* in Newport must not be confused with Hancock's sloop *Liberty* in Boston.
85 James, *Colonial Rhode Island*, pp 345–7 (1975).
86 E.G. Burrows and M. Wallace, *Gotham: a history of New York City to 1898*, pp 210–12 (1999).
87 H. Zobel, *The Boston Massacre*, pp 205–307 (1970).

up facing the mob, which had grown to eighty people. A soldier hit by a stick or iced snowball yelled 'Fire!' and five soldiers fired into the crowd, killing three people instantly. Two others later died of wounds and six more were wounded. The victims were buried after a public funeral followed by 15,000 mourners. There are still many unknown facts concerning the incident: did the mob contain Sons of Liberty? Was the mob assembled by the Sons? And what part did provocation by Samuel Adams play? Captain Preston denied giving any order to fire and was acquitted by a Boston jury.

With Paul Revere's engraving of the British shots and Samuel Adams' committees of correspondence[88] spreading exaggerated tales of the 'Boston Massacre', dangers of serious confrontation increased. Violent encounters between soldiers and townspeople ceased, temporarily in 1771 and 1772, because the soldiers were moved out of city streets. In Boston, Lieutenant Governor Hutchinson ordered the troops to Castle William and other harbour islands,[89] and in New York the commander also restricted the soldiers to the harbour fortifications.[90]

Legends persist at Boston Latin School of bloodless confrontations of the schoolboys with the Lobsterbacks, leading Governor General Gage in January 1775 to remark, that it was 'impossible to beat the notion of liberty out of the people; as it was rooted in 'em from their childhood'. The headmaster, John Lovell, however, was a loyalist who gave the order *'Deponite libros'* ('Put down your books') after the April 1775 battles of Lexington and Concord, closing the school.[91] He joined the evacuation of the British army in March 1776 and died in Halifax in 1778. (The school reopened on 5 June 1776 under Samuel Hunt, an even more vigorous flogger than his predecessor, who remained until 1805.)

Patriots confined their protests to a refusal to drink the tea subject to the tax of 3 pence per pound under the East India Company tea monopoly. However, it was acceptable, even virtuous, to drink smuggled tea.

Revolutionary incidents must have been prominent in his mind as Arthur Browne boarded the ship that took him from his home to a new life. American and British historians have argued that the source of disaffection that led to independence was the Stamp Act of 1765. Reviewing the history of the period thirty years later, Arthur Browne considered that the peace treaty of 1763 with France, limiting American access to French and Spanish colonies, and the British currency Act of 1764, forbidding the issue of paper money in the American colonies, were the greater sources of disaffection. He wrote:

88 R.P. Brown, *Revolutionary politics in Massachusetts: the Boston Committee of Correspondence and the towns, 1770–1774* (1970).
89 Zobel, *The Boston Massacre*, p. 209 (1970).
90 Burrows and Wallace, *Gotham: a history of New York City*, p. 212 (1999).
91 P. Holmes, *A tercentenary history of the Boston Public Latin School, 1635–1935*, pp 16–18 (1935).

The discontents of America are usually dated from the Stamp Act in 1765, but they really originated in 1763 immediately after the peace from the interdiction of their trade with the Spanish Main. It was the only trade which brought specie into the country, and hence no money was seen except paper, having half johannes, dollars, pistereens; a guinea or English crown seldom seen. The depression of the value of paper money was greater in Rhode Island than anywhere else ... The insulting mode of treating America in the beginning, encreased the flame ... 'Yankee [Doodle]' was a tune frequently played in reproach, and America afterwards wisely adopted this tune of reproach as its favourite national music.[92]

92 Browne, *Miscellaneous sketches*, p. 205 (1798).

CHAPTER THREE

Dublin and Trinity College (1772–6)

1. 'OFF TO DUBLIN IN THE GREEN'

THE IRELAND TO WHICH ARTHUR BROWNE travelled at age 17 differed from his American home in many ways, not least the weather, but most obviously in the political organization of England's oldest colony. The green isle did not suffer the extremes of New England weather, where the seasons of the year are clearly distinguished: periods of intense heat in summer and extreme cold and heavy snow in winter, as opposed to the persistent dampness of Ireland from frequent rainfall. Ireland's northern situation also created longer summer days and longer winter nights than those experienced in New England.

Overall, because of the action of glaciers in the ice age that ended about ten thousand years earlier, the landscapes of the two areas were similar, featuring mountains in the west, descending to gentle hills and plains. Browne's destination, Dublin, was situated between the Wicklow Mountains and the sea, and spread along the banks of the River Liffey. The most significant difference from New England is the presence of the great bogs covering most of Ireland's central plain and serving as a fuel source when dried. Woodland areas were scarce in Ireland, because of intense clearance for agriculture since the Stone Age, while the rocky infertile soil of New England discouraged clearing woodlands, which still cover most of the region.[1]

New England's history is essentially that of the European settlers, beginning only in 1620, while the historical record of Ireland extends at least three thousand years, from the 'invasions' of the Celts, Vikings, Normans and British planters, to the suppression of the majority native Irish by a minority of British people (English, Scots and Welsh) differing in language and religion, who came to be called 'the Ascendancy'.

In his biography of John Foster, the last speaker of the Irish House of Commons, A.P.W. Malcomson has clearly summarized the Ascendancy:

> The Anglo-Irish were the descendants of people of English origin who had settled in Ireland during the fifteenth, sixteenth, seventeenth and eighteenth centuries, usually after receiving grants for military and other services to the

---

1 A full description of the state of agriculture and animal husbandry in the Ireland of this time is provided by the English agricultural expert Arthur Young (1741–1820), in his two-volume work, *A tour in Ireland, 1776–1779* (1780, reprint 1970).

45

British crown. In religion, they were not only Protestant, but Anglican, in distinction to the Protestant dissenting families of Scottish origins who were planted in Ulster in the early seventeenth century, or who planted themselves in the late seventeenth century. The Anglo-Irish were a social elite rather than a strictly ethnic group [and] for most of the eighteenth century [they] held a virtual monopoly, legal or practical, of political power: a legal monopoly in that Catholics were excluded by law from Parliament, the parliamentary franchise and corporations; a practical monopoly in that Protestant dissenters, though never excluded by law from Parliament or the parliamentary franchise, numbered only a handful of members in any House of Commons.[2]

In other words, Irish government was sectarian in favour of a minority of the population. That Protestant minority did not include Presbyterians, usually called 'dissenters' as the word Protestant was then confined to the established church (Church of Ireland). Eighteenth-century writers understood the nature of the Irish government, especially the proselytizers of the United Irishmen in the 1790s, who clearly described the basic problem of Ireland in contrast to England:

Where the great body of the people have no interest whatever in the soil: there are not many so far from absolute poverty as to have anything absolutely worth defending. The religion professed by government and established by law is not that of the majority of the people. Much landed property is held by the tenure of forfeiture and confiscations. The chief magistrate is not a native: the ministers who compose his council are not natives. They have an interest to take care of separate from and possibly incompatible with that of the country which they govern and which they may prefer. They can, of course, have no common cause with the people and have not a shadow of security in their affections.[3]

The plight of the majority of the people was expressed graphically by the Belfast lawyer and poet Samuel Ferguson (1810–86) in 1834, in a possible translation of a 1580 Irish poem:

We starve by the board,
And we thirst amid wassail –
For the guest is the lord,
And the host is the vassal!
Through the woods let us roam,

---

2   A.P.W. Malcomson, *John Foster: the politics of the Anglo-Irish Ascendancy*, p. 14 (1978), as quoted in part by O. Knox, *Rebels and informers*, p. 304 (1997). See generally, S. Connolly, *Religion, law and power: the making of Protestant Ireland, 1660–1760*, pp 262–79 (1992).
3   The *Dublin Press*, 28 Sept. 1797, the radical newspaper edited by Arthur O'Connor, suppressed in 1798, cited by K. Whelan in *1798: a bicentenary perspective*, p. 383 (2003).

> Through the wastes wild and barren;
> We are strangers at home,
> We are exiles in Erin!

The major differences between Newport and Dublin were economic and social, the official humiliation and impoverishment of the majority Roman Catholic population by the Protestant minority for economic and religious reasons in the confiscations and penal laws contrasted with Rhode Island, where there was no land-owning nobility or established church, and opportunity to advance in society was available to all.

The amount of land owned or controlled by the peerage – whether Catholic or Protestant and whether resident or non-resident – had increased dramatically in the seventeenth century, thereby transforming political power in Ireland from a 'family' basis to a land-ownership basis.[4] The effect was to decrease the percentage of land owned by those who actually laboured in the fields. Arguably, in the eighteenth century less than 15 per cent of the land belonged to the Catholic majority, although opinions differ sharply.[5]

Loss of land held by Catholics was initially the result of two major confiscations that followed English military victories. First, in 1652–4, there was the confiscation of the lands of Catholic gentry involved in the Confederation of Kilkenny, suppressed by Oliver Cromwell in 1649–50. Second, in 1691, there were the forfeitures of lands of Catholic people involved in support of King James II during his Irish invasion of 1689–91.[6]

The Irish penal laws dealt with essentials: land ownership, public offices and learned professions, education and public worship. There were also petty prohibitions, such as the regulation that a Catholic could not own a horse of value greater than £5 (7 Will. 3 c.5), the price of a horse for the cavalry.

Much of this legislation was routinely ignored, although occasional Protestant zealots (the 'priest catchers') sought to have Catholic clergy imprisoned. However, as a spur to conversion, the penal laws were a failure, and it is doubtful that conversion of the majority was intended. After thirty-five years of these laws, the bishops of the Church of Ireland were ordered to report on the state of the Roman Catholic church in the dioceses of the established church; in 1731, they reported 1,440 Catholic priests, 890 Mass houses and 60 religious houses (convents or monasteries).[7] It is unlikely that these figures were overstated.

---

4   J. Ohlmeyer, *Making Ireland English: the Irish aristocracy in the seventeenth century*, pp 84–95, 475–82 (2012).
5   Ibid., pp 87, 90–8, 113–17, 301–35, 478.
6   See generally, K. Bottigheimer, *English money and Irish land: the adventurers in the Cromwellian settlement of Ireland* (1971) and J.G. Simms, *The Williamite confiscation in Ireland, 1690–1703* (1956).
7   R.B. McDowell, *Ireland in the age of imperialism and revolution*, pp 174–5 (1979). See also W.P. Burke, *The Irish priests in penal times (1660–1760)* (1914).

The penal laws did not attempt to exterminate the majority. Rather, their purpose was to make the majority powerless and prone to abandon their Catholic faith and accept Protestant rule. In any event, eighteenth-century Ireland was not a modern totalitarian state with hordes of bureaucrats to keep constant watch over the citizens, as in the days of the French Revolution or communist supremacy in the Soviet Union and Eastern Europe. Enforcement of the penal laws depended on the zeal or lack of zeal of the minority, during the Age of Enlightenment, when the rigours of creed were being relaxed by an indifferent and licentious society devoted to hunting, horse races and pleasure. By the 1780s, Catholicism was professed and practised openly but discreetly under the supervision of twenty-four bishops (not all resident). Harassment of the clergy became sporadic but was always a possibility.

The penal laws have been summarized by Professor Connolly:

> Far from being a systematic 'code' reflecting a consensus among the Protestant elite as to how its security could best be preserved; penal legislation against Catholics was in fact a rag-bag of measures, exacted piecemeal over almost half a century. These were drawn up in response to a variety of immediate pressures and grievances and to the accompaniment of continual disagreement over both the principle and the detail of measures taken.[8]

Although the penal laws (or 'laws against popery') are fully laden with religious bigotry and impoverishment of the majority population, there was another side to them: to discourage actual treason. The Stuarts were allied with the Catholic king of France, Louis XIV, the traditional enemy. For more than 500 years, England was perpetually at war with France, especially during the Hundred Years War (1336–1453), which held memories of English victories at Crécy (1346) and Agincourt (1415) and defeat at the hands of Joan of Arc at Orleans (1429). In fact, war with France was endemic in the eighteenth century and British politicians as well as Irish Protestants regarded Tories and Catholics as potential traitors.

Irish Protestant attitudes to the Catholic population reflected a paranoid fear of assassination, on the one hand, and a more logical fear of loss of lands that had been confiscated from ancestral Catholic owners by victorious Protestants in the seventeenth century, on the other. Fear of retaliation and retribution by a newly empowered Catholic majority was not unreasonable. But English governments were not interested in zealous enforcement of the penal laws, because of their frequent international alliances with European Catholic monarchs, and the assistance of Catholic citizens as allies became necessary for survival when the traditional French enemy became anti-Catholic and revolutionary.

8   S.J. Connolly, *Religion, law and power: the making of Protestant Ireland, 1660–1760*, p. 262 (1992). See also M. Wall, *The penal laws, 1691–1760* (1967) and J.A. Froude, *The English in Ireland in the eighteenth century*, vol. 2, p. 217 and vol. 3, p. 312 (1881).

Since eighteenth-century gentlemen – and politicians – did not engage in trade, there were few restrictions on commercial activities by Catholics in the penal laws, so Catholic enterprise was directed to commerce, which allowed them to influence the merchant class in the next century and undo the power of the Ascendancy. Another area untouched by the penal laws was the sea – fisheries and maritime commerce (and smuggling) – probably because these were regarded as insignificant when compared to agriculture and grazing.

II. TRINITY COLLEGE DUBLIN

Both the Harvard College Arthur Browne left behind and the Trinity College Dublin to which he journeyed were important centres of learning, strongly connected to political power, wealth and influence in church and state. Because of his family background, including service to the established church, and his prospective education at Trinity College, Arthur Browne was a member of the Ascendancy on arrival in Dublin. Whether he ever overcame this inheritance is the story of his next thirty-three years.

Having arrived in Dublin, thanks to the SPG, and assured of an annual benefice of £40 from his mother's estate – enough for a student in college, although not enough for a family man – he must have been concerned about his finances in his first years. The cost to parents of TCD students was from £40 to £50 per year. He does not speak of family connections in Ireland that might have been of assistance to him. Arthur Browne had been entrusted by his father to the care of Revd Dr John Forsayeth, senior fellow of TCD and an old friend of his father. In the sale of Forsayeth's library after his death in 1785, it appears that most of the volumes dealt with theology and church history, so it is likely that he may have guided Arthur's studies in the direction of the church career that Arthur later rejected. Arthur Browne entered Trinity College Dublin as a pensioner on 24 March 1772.

Arthur Browne's college was already 180 years old when he matriculated in 1772, one of about 140 young men, mostly 16 to 18 years of age, overwhelmingly the sons of professionals (clergy, doctors and lawyers) or gentlemen, mostly from Leinster and Munster. They usually had some connection to the established church.[9] The academic regime was firmly in the hands of the clergy of the established church, and there was always movement between college offices and the bench of bishops or holders of wealthy 'livings' (as parishes were then called). The course of study for the first degree in arts (BA) was four years. Entrance examinations, chiefly on the *Aeneid* and the *Iliad*, were held four times a year. The total population of undergraduate and graduate students was about 600 at that

9 R.B. McDowell and D.A. Webb, *Trinity College Dublin, 1592–1952*, pp 499–501 (1982). In America, the sources of the student body and the fees were similar for the nine degree-granting colleges, but in England, students at Oxford and Cambridge were drawn from the aristocracy and the fees were much higher. See J.F. Roche, *The colonial colleges in the war for American independence* (1986).

time, divided into three classes: the (fee-paying) pensioners, who were the majority; the very wealthy fellow commoners, who were privileged to eat and associate with the fellows while paying double fees; and the sizars, who were charity students, waiting tables or performing other services at the college – there were usually about a dozen.

The senior academic of Trinity College Dublin was the provost. (During Arthur Browne's years the provosts were not the usual clergymen, but wealthy lawyers with substantial political connections: Francis Andrews, 1758–74, and John Hely-Hutchinson, 1774–94.) Instruction of the students was provided by twenty-two fellows; of these, seven were senior fellows, who, together with the provost, constituted the all-powerful board. There were ten formal professorships, usually held by fellows. Appointment as a junior fellow resulted from public examination.[10] Students selected the fellows as their tutors and paid fees for the privilege of supervised instruction.

The students were feared for their boisterous, even riotous conduct in the city, especially during elections and popular celebrations such as Guy Fawke's Day (5 November). Student expeditions into the city required a written pass from the tutors, which was usually initially denied, but then granted under clever excuses. Student rowdiness took on a political tone during the regency crisis (1789), the Fitzwilliam crisis (1795) and the events leading up to the 1798 Revolution, although students were forbidden to attend political demonstrations after 1795.[11]

The gates were guarded and locked at night, but adventurous students discovered ways to go 'town haunting' to visit taverns and gambling establishments such as the cockfights and bull-baiting in the Liberties district. Organized sports in college were not well-developed then, although there was a bowling green and Provost Hely-Hutchinson encouraged dancing, fencing and riding (hence his nickname, 'The Prancer').

The students dined together at midday, initially at 2:40 p.m. until 1791, and then at 3 p.m., the usual dinner hour in aristocratic circles.[12] Like their elders, the students had a passion for duelling and wagering on anything, especially horse races and other games.

Students were required to wear academic gowns, and were compelled to attend a daily service in the college chapel, offered at 6 a.m., 10 a.m. or 4 p.m., as well as a Sunday service, when there were choral services and sermons. The requirement varied for non-residents and seniors, although the majority of students were required to attend at least seven times per week. Penalties for lateness or non-attendance were enforced. Needless to say, the fellows of the college were expected to attend the chapel services, and the ordained fellows were expected to preach.

10 McDowell and Webb, *Trinity College Dublin*, pp 41–80, 97–110 (1982).
11 For student life and regulations, see H.A. Hinkson, *Student life in Trinity College Dublin* (1892). See also C. Maxwell, *A history of Trinity College Dublin, 1591–1892* (1946); J.W. Stubbs, *The history of the University of Dublin from its foundation to the end of the eighteenth century* (1889); W.B. Taylor, *History of the University of Dublin* (1846), and W.M. Dixon, *Trinity College Dublin* (1902).

Students at Trinity, like those in America, were interested in joining groups of fellow students for entertainment, conversation and even knowledge. By the time Arthur Browne was a student, the college historical society, known as 'the Hist', had been founded (or refounded)[13] on 20 March 1770 by thirteen students, mostly scholars, so that the members could acquire historical knowledge, compose research papers and practise oratory. Provost Andrews and the board encouraged this development, and granted the Hist the use of the fellows' common room (over the dining hall) for its weekly Saturday-evening meetings. Although the fee on admission to membership was quite steep for students (£1 1s.), membership (by election) increased to fifty by the second year.[14]

Documentary evidence of Arthur Browne's membership is lacking; full membership lists of the early years disappeared during the moves of the Hist. However, it is very likely that he was a member, in view of his life history as a joiner of similar organizations: the lawyers' corps of Volunteers, the Monks of the Screw, the Reform Club, the Whig Club, the Society for Discountenancing Vice and Promotion of Virtue, the Trinity Defence Corps and the Royal Irish Academy.

Spirited debate soon became a feature of the Hist's meetings. In May 1771, the society debated, 'That America would not flourish more as a monarchy than as a republic'. Twenty years before the vote in Parliament, on 6 January 1779, the society debated, 'Whether an union with Great Britain would be of advantage to Ireland?'[15] After parliamentary independence in 1783, membership, including graduates, increased dramatically, beyond the capacity of the common room. The French Revolution (1789) and the rise of the United Irishmen (1791–4) introduced dangerous subjects that frightened Provost Hely-Hutchinson and some members of the board. In consequence, the society was forced to move out of college buildings to a rented hall on William Street in April 1794.[16] Many famous parliamentary orators received their early training in the Hist before joining the Monks of the Screw or the Whig Club.

The physical appearance of Trinity College has scarcely changed since 1772. The library (begun in 1712), with its famous Long Room (240 feet long and 40 feet high), then stuffed with 50,000 books, one of the most handsome library buildings in Europe, made the south end of a square, with the Rubrics, a much older student residences, on the east. A second square, the Front Court, with offices and residences, begun in the 1750s, looked outward to the busy streets surrounding the old Irish Parliament buildings (begun in 1728). The inward view from the Front

---

12 Stubbs, *The history of the University of Dublin*, p. 334 (1889). Student life at TCD in the eighteenth century is featured in the novel, *Charles O'Malley: the Irish dragoon* (1841) by Charles J. Lever (1806–72); see pp 129–72 (1891 edition).

13 Antecedents were Edmund Burke's club for discussion and debate (1747–48) and a brief historical club in 1753. J.V. Luce, *Trinity College Dublin: the first 400 years*, p. 69 (1992).

14 D. Budd and R. Hinds, *The Hist and Edmund Burke's Club*, pp 1–41, 127–8 (1997).

15 Ibid., pp 145–7.

16 T. Swift, *Animadversions on the fellows of Trinity College*, pp 128–37 (1794).

Court faced the dining hall (1759) on the north side, and the old chapel, which was demolished and replaced by the present chapel (1798). On the south side was the theatre or examination hall (1777) and the provost's house (1758), the scene of substantial social functions at which the college entertained the important members of the Ascendancy and foreign visitors.

When Trinity College was created in 1592 on the grounds of the dissolved monastery of All Hallows, the south side of the Liffey River (where Viking Dublin began) contained the port and the administrative centre of English rule, the castle (begun in 1204), but the wealthy and powerful lived on the north side of the Liffey. By 1750, the areas south and east of the college had been developed into substantial Georgian residences around St Stephen's Green, Leinster House (1745) and Merrion Square (after 1762); Trinity thus became surrounded by the elegance and wealth of the Enlightenment. It was and is a twenty-eight acre oasis of green lawns and granite fortresses in the heart of a busy city.

The Trinity curriculum in classics covered the principal Latin authors then available (Virgil, Horace, Juvenal, Livy, Suetonius, Caesar, Plutarch, Cicero, Tacitus, Terrence and Pliny) and the Greeks (Homer, Sophocles, Euripides, Demosthenes, Theocritus and Xenophon). The curriculum in science included logic, philosophy, astronomy, physics, mathematics, metaphysics and ethics; many of the scientific texts were by Continental scholars, but John Locke's philosophy was required reading.[17]

Arthur Browne may have been describing his undergraduate days when he wrote, 'the Irish are rather formidable at the bottle; however, much less so than formerly, and after all the names they have acquired, the Scotch drink twice as much without being noted for it at all'.[18] Nevertheless, his college years enlarged his views of the eighteenth-century world, and he acquired skills and discipline that would serve him in any public capacity. He summarized the benefits of his college education as:

> habits of study – regular division of time – habits of discipline and obedience – of early rising – of early retirement in evening – diligence – labour virtuous emulation ...[19] ... the skill to read with utility and effect ... reading is an art, and an art taught ... by scholastic system; when [one] is obliged to weigh every period – to consider its purport – its tendency – its real meaning – with previous consciousness of obligation to render an analysis of it, [one] will confess the utility of habits thus acquired ...[20]

The lifelong habits of study were certainly obvious in the very substantial library he acquired over the next thirty years.

---

17 McDowell and Webb, *Trinity College Dublin*, pp 45–9 (1982); Locke's *Treatise on government and essay on human understanding* (1690).
18 A. Browne, *Miscellaneous sketches*, p. 139 (1798).
19 Ibid., p. 9.   20 Ibid., pp 11–12.

III

Of course we cannot overlook the physical location of Trinity College in the heart of Dublin, the second city of the British empire, surpassed only by London. It was the national capital of the Kingdom of Ireland, seat of the nearly regal court of the viceroy or lord lieutenant, always one of the wealthiest and best connected of the English dukes. The national Parliament, government offices and the most important royal courts of justice were also located there. The professions of medicine, law, science and arts were well established. Dublin was also the centre of shipping and the pre-industrial-age manufacturers of woolens and silk, as well as a great variety of shops. In addition to TCD, there were libraries, bookshops, printers, art galleries and a full range of luxury trades. There was also a vigorous intellectual life in theatres, concert halls and salons, where the work of the great Irish writers of English, such as Dean Jonathan Swift, William Congreve, Lawrence Sterne, Oliver Goldsmith and Richard Brinsley Sheridan were known and appreciated. For various reasons, the Irish language was virtually unknown in the city, which was then heavily Protestant; Ascendancy people did not appreciate the subtleties and beauty of Irish which was considered to be the language of primitive agriculture, and was expected to disappear in the near future.[21]

Dublin (and Ireland) had not yet developed a middle class between the gentry and those who worked for a living, unlike Rhode Island and cities like Boston, New York and Philadelphia, where a powerful middle class was developing that not only voted but could be elected to public office.[22]

Unlike Arthur Browne's Newport home of about 9,000 people, Dublin had a population of 128,750 in 1772, but many were desperately poor people living in dilapidated, unsanitary conditions, the source of disease and crime. The situation became much worse in the next forty years as the population of Dublin increased to 175,319 in 1814.[23] Dublin was always crowded with people, including many visitors. It was a city full of taverns, inns and coffee houses, as well as temptations. It was also a city full of horses for transport of people and goods, but also for sport at race meetings in the county. The smells of the city must have been overpowering.

IV. THE AMERICAN DOOR CLOSES

On 9 June 1772, while Arthur Browne was beginning his studies at Trinity, an undisguised mob of sixty men from Providence, led by John Brown, attacked the

---

21 C. Maxwell, *Dublin under the Georges, 1714–1830* (1936); M. Craig, *Dublin 1660–1860: a social and architectural history* (1969); and T. Barnard, *Making the grand figure: lives and possessions in Ireland, 1641–1770* (2004).

22 S.M. Blumin, *The emergence of the middle class: social experience in the American city, 1760–1900* (1989).

23 Maxwell, *Dublin and the Georges* (1936).

revenue enforcer HMS *Gaspee*, a 50-foot schooner with eight guns and crew of thirty-eight that had run aground at Nanquit Point in Narragansett Bay while chasing smugglers. The commanding officer, Lt William Dudingston, was wounded in the fight; he and his crew were put ashore and the ship was set on fire by the mob. Despite a reward of £500 and a lengthy formal investigation, no one was ever accused of the crime.[24]

In 1773, events led irresistibly to war. The Massachusetts legislature demanded that the king dismiss Governor Hutchinson and Lt Governor Oliver (16 June 1773), a consequence of the publication of the governor's private letters to the assistant of the colonial secretary. Tea became an issue because the proceeds of the tax were to be used to pay salaries of judges. Protests about the tea tax and the East India Company monopoly led to mob action in Boston in the Boston Tea Party of 16 December 1773, when 342 chests of East India Company tea, worth about £10,000 and subject to a direct British tax (3 pence per pound), was poured into Boston harbour by fifty or more Sons of Liberty disguised as Indian warriors.[25] Again, no offenders were discovered. This resulted in the British government's decision to punish Boston by closing the port after 1 June 1774 until compensation had been paid for the destroyed tea. This punishment was part of a series of measures called Coercive Acts, but known to the Sons of Liberty as the Intolerable Acts,[26] which made an example of Massachusetts by abrogating its charter, enlarging the powers of its royal governor, terminating the power of town meetings, providing for trial in Great Britain for offences against the revenue or riots committed in the colonies and quartering British troops at the expense of the colony. Massachusetts absolutely refused to pay compensatation for the tea. Newport's answer was to send provisions over land to the relief of oppressed Bostonians. Many cities and towns in other colonies did the same.

Responding to the parliamentary punishment of Boston and Massachusetts, Samuel Adams, the genius of revolutionary communication, organized committees of correspondence to circulate Boston's claims of British tyranny; within a short time some eighty committees in Massachusetts alone were at work to inflame popular resentment from Maine to Georgia. The outcome was the call by Massachusetts, Rhode Island, Pennsylvania and New York for the first continental congress to assemble at Philadelphia on 5 September 1774.

The new governor, General Gage, arrived in Boston on 13 May 1774, and was soon confronted by the General Court's call for a continental congress on 17 June. Accordingly, the governor dissolved the legislature on 18 June. The Intolerable Acts had silenced town meetings, as Gage had silenced the legislature, but counties

---

24 R. Stensrud, *Newport: a lively experiment, 1639–1969*, pp 187–9 (2006); A.B. Hawes, *Off-soundings*, pp 92–5 (1999); C. Rappleye, *Sons of Providence: the Brown brothers, the slave trade and the American Revolution*, pp 102–26 (2006); and N. York, 'The uses of law and the *Gaspee* affair' in P.T. Conley, *Liberty and justice: a history of law and lawyers in Rhode Island, 1636–1999*, pp 132–53 (1998).

25 B.W. Labaree, *The Boston Tea Party*, pp 126–69 (1964).

26 Intolerable Acts, 14 Geo. 3 c. 19, 39, 45 and 54.

had been overlooked. Representatives of the towns in Suffolk County met in Milton to consider a plan of opposition.[27] Dr Joseph Warren, then of the committee of correspondence, later chair of the committee of public safety, presented a draft that became the Suffolk Resolves of 9 September 1774: local militias were to be armed and exercised regularly, taxes intended for the crown were to be paid to local governments until the Intolerable Acts were repealed, detention or imprisonment of patriots was to result in the seizure of loyalist hostages, a total abstention from consumption of British-origin merchandise was required and a provincial congress was to assemble without royal authority. Nevertheless, a renewed harmony with the mother country was anticipated once the unconstitutional Intolerable Acts had been repealed. Paul Revere carried the resolves to Philadelphia.

The illegal Massachusetts provincial congress assembled at Salem on 7 October 1774. Many of the twenty-six delegates had been members of the prorogued legislature. It appointed a committee of public safety to observe and react to developments, under the chairmanship of John Hancock. (When Hancock went to the Philadelphia congress, he was replaced by Dr Joseph Warren.)

Fifty delegates from twelve colonies assembled in Philadelphia to prepare lists of grievances and create the Continental Association, a pressure group, to carry out a complete embargo on all trade with Great Britain. Open warfare was only six months away. While war with the mother country was inconceivable to the Brownes and the other SPG missionaries, it was not inconceivable to many Americans to whom England was a foreign country across 3,000 miles of ocean, abandoned by their ancestors three or four generations earlier.

The separation from the mother country appeared more ominously in Billings' Revolutionary War hymn, 'Chester', published in 1770:

> Let tyrants shake their iron rod,
> And slavery clank her galling chains.
> We fear them not, we trust in God,
> New England's God forever reigns.
>
> The foe comes on with haughty stride
> Our troops advance with martial noise
> Their veterans flee before our youth.
> And generals yield to beardless boys.
>
> What grateful offerings shall we bring?
> What shall we render to the Lord?
> Loud hallelujahs let us sing
> And praise his name on every chord.

27 E. Channing, *A history of the United States: the American Revolution, 1761–1789*, pp 14–49 (1912).

War deprived Newport of its skilled and prosperous population and scarred the town but did not destroy it. Newport remained the capital city of the new state of Rhode Island, but it never regained its pre-war eminence.

The colonial America of Arthur Browne's youth disappeared in the American Revolution lasting from 1775 to the peace treaty of 1783. There is no evidence that he ever returned to America; he had already crossed the Atlantic three times. In 1798, he wrote:

> I trust I have said enough to prove there were charms in the country [America], and to show what it is that makes every former resident in America think of it with affection, with melancholy, and with regret; it does not follow that he should wish to return to it; the death of friends; the total change of inhabitants within a few years, the wonderful alteration made by an intervening revolution; his welfare in the country in which he is [Ireland]; the kindness of that country and his obligation to it and the new ties he has formed in it, may totally eradicate such a wish from his heart; but he will now and then cast back a look to it, as if a distant paradise, and vainly imagine amidst cares and anxieties where he is, that they do not dwell in every country and are not the inhabitants of every soil.[28]

Arthur Browne's mastery of the Trinity curriculum was demonstrated midway through his college years by his designation in 1774, after examinations, as a 'scholar', which entitled him to financial benefits: free board, reduced rent and a £20 subsidy.[29] He received a BA degree in the spring of 1776, and it must have been around this time that he made his decision not to pursue the family profession into the ranks of the clergy of the established church.

---

28 Browne, *Miscellaneous sketches*, pp 210–11 (1798).
29 McDowell and Webb, *Trinity College Dublin*, p. 121 (1982).

CHAPTER FOUR

London and preparation for the law, during the war in America (1776–83)

I

HAVING JOINED THE COMPANY of educated men in the spring of 1776, Arthur Browne surely realized that there was no future for him in an America at war, and thus the obvious path was to take the first step in an academic or ecclesiastical career by seeking a fellowship at Trinity College, obtainable through public examination. The status of junior fellow or senior fellow, however, required the holder to be in holy orders, either deacon or priest, after ordination by a bishop, but there is no evidence that Arthur Browne ever took holy orders. In fact, the statutory requirements were regularly evaded, including the further requirement that the fellows be unmarried.[1]

In the year after he graduated, Arthur Browne underwent the gruelling oral examinations in public in the elegant new theatre before the provost, board and fellows, with an audience of interested spectators.[2] Because of his success in these examinations, he became a fellow of Trinity College, a position he held for the rest of his life: junior fellow in 1777 and senior fellow in 1795.

We do not know all the influences that moved him from the paths of his ancestors or the influences that moved him to the law. In any event, at age 21, Arthur Browne, junior fellow of TCD, travelled to London in May 1777 to join one of the inns of court, to qualify as a barrister with the right to appear in court and prepare legal documents.[3] It is not apparent which members of the Dublin legal community suggested Lincoln's Inn for his preparation for the Bar, but George Ponsonby, an ally in Parliament later, was at Lincoln's Inn at the same time.[4] (Most Irish lawyers trained at the Middle Temple.) Lincoln's Inn had the reputation as a place for serious students who intended to practise law. In those days preparation consisted of mandatory attendance at a series of dinners where moot court arguments were held; readings and studies were suggested but certainly not mandatory.[5]

London was a unique place to study law:

1 R.B. McDowell and D.A. Webb, *Trinity College Dublin, 1592–1952*, pp 50, 97–107.
2 Ibid., p. 105.
3 R.B. McDowell, *Ireland in the age of imperialism and revolution, 1760–1801*, p. 143 (1979). See C. Kenny, *King's Inns and the kingdom of Ireland: the Irish inns of court, 1541–1800* (1992).
4 See chapter 5, n. 34–6.
5 D. Hogan, *The legal profession in Ireland, 1789–1922*, pp 16–18, 33–5 (1986). The requirement of

the biggest city in Europe, with about 740,000 inhabitants (one of every ten Englishmen) ... a place of pains and pleasures. The death rate was far higher than in the countryside and only constant immigration ... increased the city's numbers. Though better paved and lit than Paris, much of the city stank. Air pollution from domestic coal fires caused smog and black rain. The streets were packed with traffic ... Food was often tainted or stale; the drinking water also tasted foul and could, moreover, prove fatal ... Crime, though less prevalent than in other large European cities, was commonplace ... Continental visitors to London were struck by the universal pre-occupation with politics ...

In 1776 this thriving political culture centered upon two institutions, the coffee house and the press, and was absorbed by one issue, America ... there were over 550 coffee houses ... London had seventeen papers ... British opinion on America, both in London and in the provinces, was sharply divided.[6]

The political turmoil had already produced the 'Wilkes and liberty' riots of 1768 and would produce the Gordon 'no-popery' riots of June 1780. These deadly riots point to the fact that it was a violent age, in which life was cheap. Death sentences (by hanging) were customary for 200 felonies, and hangings at Tyburn were popular entertainments, but neither death nor transportation was able to control the personal violence or offences to property (burglary, robbery and all types of larceny). This should not imply that life was safer or worth more in Dublin; the difference was that Dublin was smaller.

Concerning his legal education at Lincoln's Inn, Arthur Browne wrote:

> In all my preceding studies ... I had found the aid of some tutor, lecturer or instructor to guide my steps and direct my course of reading; on going to the Temple, which I supposed was to look for such aids, finding no person professing or appointed to give them, and no mental food whatsoever afforded me by those learned seminaries, the Inns of Court, though they obliged me to receive that of a corporal kind, I sat down like most of my brethren to read at random ... I read and read on, reports ancient and modern, cases, opinions, treatises, commentaries, all without order or method, but was particularly delighted with some modern essays on the subtle branches of contingent remainders and springing uses, on which I became very learned – a learning which, by the by, I never since have happened to find of any use to me ...[7]

a London inn of court continued until 1885. Ibid., p. 34. See also D. Lemmings, *Professors of the law: barristers and English legal culture in the eighteenth century*, pp 107–48, 225–30, 309–19 (2000) and V.T.H. Delany, 'History of legal education in Ireland', 12 *J. Leg. Educ.*, 396–406 (1959–60).

6   J. Brewer, 'The look of London, 1776' in K. Pearson and P. Connor (eds), *1776: the British story of the American Revolution* (1976). See also D. Marshall, *Dr Johnson's London* (1968) and C. Hibbert, *King Mob: Lord George Gordon and the riots of 1780* (1958).

He registered dismay at the time wasted because his reading was not properly directed:

> from its great reputation [I] naturally took up Coke upon Littleton ... I next made recourse to that elegant Pracés [*sic*] of the law written by Mr Justice Blackstone to get a general view of the subject, and was soon informed to my great surprise that I had been learning with much labour not, what was law, but what was not, i.e. what was law 200 years ago ...[8]

He soon realized that social skills rather than doctrine or theory were the key to success at the Bar:

> keep open house ... that is the way to get business; as you eat your way to the Bar, you must drink it into practice! ... [but] at the end of twelve months, I found an empty purse, an aching head, and some small tendency to the gout.[9]

Nevertheless, the London season provided an opportunity to dine with Dr Johnson and other intellectual leaders.[10] This dinner in the presence of Dr Johnson was owing to the fact that he was:

> invited by the kindness of Sir Joshua Reynolds (the greatest possible favourer to a young Templar) to dine at the same table with a number of eminent men ... to have seen whom, is a grateful recollection at this day: Mr Garrick, Mr Dunning, Mr Burke, and Mr Gibbon were of the company. Yet there was no opportunity for the display of Dr Johnson's talents, the conversation being ... extremely trifling.[11]

This dinner may have followed a meeting of the Club, the type of social and convivial group that Browne would later frequent in Dublin in the Monks of the Screw and the Reform and Whig clubs. Of polite conversations in the inns of court, he wrote:

> I have often heard the Temple [the inns] spoken of as the nest of infidelity; one would expect to find there a set of sceptic philosophers gravely disputing about religion. During two years residence there, though I saw much carelessness about sacred things, I saw little infidelity and so far from it being a constant topic, I never heard the conversations on the subject of religion

7   A. Browne, *Miscellaneous sketches*, pp 372–3 (1798).   8   Ibid.
9   Ibid., p. 380. He described the winter in London, 'amidst all its grandeur, its dark and misty air and shifting clouds of obscuring smoke', p. 199.
10 See W.J. Bate, *Samuel Johnson*, pp 366–7, 504–9 (1977).
11 Browne, *Miscellaneous sketches*, pp 82–3 (1798). For Joshua Reynolds (1723–1792), later appointed painter to the king (1784). See R. Wendorff, *Sir Joshua Reynolds: the painter in society* (1996).

during my stay; the courts, or the theater, or dissipation were the topics, but I am glad to add that I never heard but one man there seriously avow disbelief or contempt for religion.[12]

Browne does not mention how he made the connection with Sir Joshua Reynolds, president of the Royal Academy and the most prominent portrait painter of the day, a man described by Browne as mild and amiable. His Newport schoolmates Gilbert Stuart and Benjamin Waterhouse were in London at the time of Arthur Browne's studies. Stuart was working as a portrait painter at this time and was a pupil and assistant of the American painter Benjamin West, who was a great friend of Sir Joshua Reynolds (and succeeded him as president of the Royal Academy); Waterhouse, a medical student, stayed in London observing patients at Guy's Hospital under the guidance of his uncle, Dr John Fothergill.

The mandatory dinners having been eaten, 'having given much time to study and much more time to the amusements of London, I was admitted to the Bar, and became a complete jurisconsult, wigged and gowned'.[13] Browne never directly discusses visiting continental Europe, but in *Miscellaneous sketches* he mentions seeing the battlefields of Ramillies and Fontenay in 1779, thus he must have been in Belgium, France and Germany after his London years.[14]

His contemporaries always credited him with the social graces, good fellowship and sense of humor needed for the battlefields of the English and Irish bars.

Browne's call to the Bar in London did not signify the end of preparation for the practice of law: apprenticeship (for solicitors) and pupillage (for barristers) would customarily follow.[15] A third type of preparation was the pursuit of a doctorate (LLD) for practice in courts based on Roman law rather than English common law.

Arthur Browne returned to Dublin in 1779 and began the academic studies of the Romans and the legal system derived from them that germinated his classic treatise, *A compendious view of the civil law and of the law of the admiralty*, first published twenty years later. In the summer of 1779, he received an AM degree from Trinity College.

Formal legal education at Trinity College Dublin was in approximately the same primitive state as it was in Oxford and Cambridge.[16] A professorship of law was established at TCD in the period 1651–60, but little is known of it other than the salary.[17] By the mid-eighteenth century, the law was represented by a professor of civil and canon law, but the functions were unclear.[18] In 1761 the government established a professorship of feudal and English law, undoubtedly in reaction to

12 Ibid., p. 252.   13 Ibid., pp 373–4.   14 Ibid., pp 332, 339.
15 B. Abel Smith and R. Stevens, *Lawyers and the courts: a sociological study of the English legal system, 1750–1965*, pp 15–17 (1967) and T. Ruggles, *The barrister or strictures on the education proper for the Bar (1792)*.
16 McDowell and Webb, *Trinity College Dublin*, p. 19 (1982).   17 Ibid., pp 19–20.
18 Ibid., p. 41. Arthur Browne held this chair from 1785 until his death.

the Vinerian Professorship in English Law established at Oxford for William Blackstone in 1758. Again, it is uncertain what duties were actually performed – the first holder of the Trinity chair, Francis Sullivan, having been described as 'invincib[ly] indolent', even though some of his lectures were published posthumously.[19] A later successor, Patrick Duigenan,[20] gave entertaining and anecdotal lectures that were popular to instruct the gentleman landowner, magistrate or parson in the necessary rudiments of the law.[21] The existence of these professorships, regarded as sinecures for senior fellows, did not create a law school to replace on-the-job training for the young professional.[22]

Nevertheless, Trinity College awarded two degrees in law – LLB and LLD – which were awarded after perfunctory oral proceedings in Latin, presided over by either or both of the professors of law. Acknowledging the inadequacies of the current education of lawyers, Browne had an opportunity to comment on the need of lawyers to have a wide understanding of the liberal arts and sciences: 'Law is a regular science. To understand its theory, a knowledge of other sciences is previously requisite ... liberal sentiments should be early inculcated.'[23]

In spring 1780, Arthur Browne received the LLB degree, although he was already able to represent clients at the Bar, and in spring 1784 he received the LLD degree, whereby he was entitled to practice in the prerogative courts, the court of admiralty and other courts based on Roman law.[24] No doctoral dissertation was required nor is it clear how the exercises for the doctorate differed from those for the baccalaureate. In any event, Arthur Browne would hereafter be Doctor Browne; his appointment as professor of law followed in 1785.

II

The physical separation of Arthur Browne from his American home also became a mental isolation, as an independent nation emerged in the War of Independence that took place over the next important years. This war also led to changes in Ireland.

The war began accidentally when General Thomas Gage,[25] royal governor of Massachusetts, decided to send a secret night raid to Concord (18 miles west of

19 Ibid., pp 65–6. Francis Stoughton Sullivan, *An historical treatise on the feudal law and the constitution and laws of England* (1772).

20 See chapter 11, n. 25, where Professor Duigenan served as deputy to the archbishop of Dublin at the visitation of April 1798 in Trinity College by Lord Chancellor FitzGibbon.

21 McDowell and Webb, *Trinity College Dublin*, p. 66 (1982).   22 Ibid., pp 330–1.

23 Ibid., p. 138. McDowell and Webb describe the exercises for the degree as, 'some slight knowledge of Latin and a minimum of inventiveness and presence of mind'. A. Browne, *Thoughts on the present state of the College of Dublin ... (1782)*, pp 47–8.

24 K.J. Costello, *The court of admiralty of Ireland, 1575–1893*, pp 62–3, 173–8, 183–5, 187–202, 205–27 (2011).

25 Thomas Gage (1721–87) was educated at Westminster School and then commissioned in an infantry regiment. He fought at Fontenoy in 1745 and Culloden in 1746. He spent twenty-one

Boston) to seize arms and ammunition that the illegal provincial congress had been acquiring for the past year.

The governor's secret mission was under the command of Lieutenant Colonel Francis Smith and consisted of the 10th Regiment of Foot, some additional guides and royal marines under Major John Pitcairn – a total of about 700 men. These were carried in longboats from the foot of Boston Common across the Charles River basin from about 10 p.m. on 18 April 1775 to begin the 18-mile march to Concord. Earlier that night, Dr Joseph Warren of the committee of public safety had sent at least two riders out of Boston to warn the countryside and specific militia units that the regulars were on the march.

With the sound of a church bell, about 77 members of the 144 member Lexington militia had gathered at Buckman's Tavern to await the orders of Captain John Parker, who directed them to line up at the west end of the green but not to fire unless fired upon; Parker soon ordered his men to stand down and go home with their weapons.

Major Pitcairn's force marched into the town with fifes and drums at about 5 a.m. but stopped on the green as the major gave an order to the militia: 'Disperse ye rebels! Throw down your arms!' A shot was fired from an unknown source, and the British troops responded with two volleys that killed eight and wounded ten of the fleeing militia, which did not return fire.

The British troops did not pursue, but marched 6 miles further, to the town of Concord, arriving about 8 a.m., to begin the search for military stores, most of which had already been removed by the forewarned Concord militia, which had already left. News of the army's march and the Lexington encounter spread quickly through the countryside, and militias of twenty-two surrounding towns began to gather outside Concord.

At the North Bridge over the narrow Concord River, some 400 militia waited, standing in the way of three companies of British troops (about 100 men). The militia intended to prevent the search of the farm of a militia colonel, James Barnett. The soldiers fired into the militia, which immediately returned fire. Two soldiers were killed; two militiamen were killed. This was the 'shot heard round the world' on 19 April 1775.

No significant arms having been found, the return to Boston was ordered. It began in good order for the first mile, until the troops reached Meriam's Corner, where waiting militia began to ambush the troops from behind stone walls and copses of trees (not yet in leaf). Colonial sharpshooters easily picked off the young officers and even Lt Colonel Smith, who was wounded in the thigh.

years of his military career in America, beginning in the French and Indian War, including the conquest of Canada, where he became brigadier general in 1759, then major general in 1761. In 1763, he was appointed lieutenant general and commander-in-chief of British forces in North America at New York. In 1774, he was appointed royal governor of Massachusetts to succeed Thomas Hutchinson. He was recalled during the siege of Boston, returned to England on 10 Oct. 1775 and became general in 1782. See J.R. Alden, *General Gage in America* (1948).

Guerilla-style attacks from the rear and sides continued during the eleven weary miles to Charlestown, where, at sundown, longboats ferried the troops across the Charles River to the safety of Boston. Official reports of British army losses were 73 killed, 174 wounded and 26 missing. Colonial losses may have been 49 killed, 46 wounded and 5 missing.[26]

Official news from General Gage to the ministry did not arrive in London until 10 June, but the colonials had used a faster ship; Whig friends of the colonial cause were informed of the battle by 27 May, and the newspapers carried the American version two weeks before Lord North's government was in a position to blame General Gage.

Within four days, news of the fighting in Massachusetts spread to New York City, where the Patriot Party broke into the royal arsenal to seize 500 muskets, pillaged two ships holding army food supplies and forced the royal customs to close.[27] By May 1775, the royal custom house in Newport had also closed, and the few remaining royal officers fled after the last royal governor of Rhode Island, Joseph Wanton, a vestryman of Trinity, Newport, was removed by the legislature.[28]

The roadside skirmishes of April became traditional war on Saturday, 17 June 1775, a blazing hot and humid day, when British General William Howe made a disastrous attempt to end the rebellion by a frontal assault with a 2,500-man force on a redoubt at Bunker Hill, overlooking Boston harbour at Charlestown, expecting the 'peasants' to run away. Only about 300 men from the besieging force of about 12,000 colonial militia were entrenched there. Three assault waves of British troops, courageously led by General Howe, eventually forced the colonials, who had run out of ammunition, to retreat, but their volleys on the British advance had disabled almost 50 per cent of the attacking force – 26 killed, 828 wounded, and many scattered.

III

After the beginning of the war, governmental functions were gradually, almost haphazardly, assumed by committees of public safety of newly reorganized legislatures, while the authority of the British crown withered and died.[29] One year

26 Controversy still surrounds most of the details and precise numbers for many incidents of 18–19 Apr. 1775, although there is agreement about the proportions. The casualty figures are found in D.H. Fischer, *Paul Revere's ride*, pp 320–2 (1994). General discussions of the opening battles are found in E. Channing, 3 *History of the United States*, pp 157–62 (1912), A.B. Tourtellot, *William Diamond's drum: the beginning of the war of the American Revolution*, pp 91–204 (1959), Lt Gen. J.R. Galvin, *The Minute Men: a compact history of the defenders of the American colonies, 1645–1775*, pp 118–223 (1967), T. Fleming, *The first stroke: Lexington, Concord and the beginning of the American Revolution* (1977) and C. Bradford, *The battle road: expedition to Lexington and Concord* (1988).

27 E.G. Burrows and M. Wallace, *Gotham: a history of New York City to 1898*, pp 22–5 (1999). See also B. Schecter, *The battle for New York: the city at the heart of the American Revolution* (2002).

28 L.F. Ballard, *Trinity Church in old Newport*, p. 364 (1979).

29 See J.P. Reid, *In a defiant stance: the conditions of law in Massachusetts Bay – the Irish comparison*

after removing the governor, the General Assembly of Rhode Island seized the royal charter, and on 4 May 1776 repudiated all allegiance to King George III. The second continental congress called on the American colonies to form state governments on 10 May 1776, a prelude to the Declaration of Independence less than two months later on 4 July 1776. The declaration by Congress similarly rejected allegiance to the king, because king and Parliament had violated the fundamental contract with America.

The time of trial and persecution of the SPG missionaries and their mostly loyalist congregations began in earnest after independence, the problem being that the priests had taken an oath of allegiance to the king when they were ordained. Furthermore, the Book of Common Prayer required the congregation to say the mandatory prayers for the king and the royal family.

On 24 July 1776, by an Act of the Rhode Island legislature, prayers for the king were forbidden, and their recitation was made a high misdemeanor. The response of Trinity, Newport's rector, George Bisset, Arthur Browne's teacher, was to close the church for public worship so that the required prayers would no longer be said. The school was also closed. Parochial services that did not contain the forbidden prayers – such as baptisms, weddings and funerals – continued to be held.[30]

George Washington had secretly installed heavy artillery on Dorchester Heights above Boston harbour on the night of 4–5 March 1776, within range of the British fleet. Fleet batteries were unable to elevate sufficiently to hit the colonial fortification. Thus, General Howe gave the order to evacuate the city. By 17 March 1776, the evacuation on 120 vessels was completed.[31] Almost a thousand loyalists joined the evacuation, including two of Boston's three SPG missionaries and the Cambridge missionary, Revd Mr Sarjent, uncle by marriage of Arthur Browne. Each regiment was permitted to take six camp followers. Their initial destination was Halifax, Nova Scotia; the civilians could journey on to England or remain in British Canada,[32] while the British army and navy

and the coming of the American Revolution, pp 118–34 (1977). See also G. Wood, *The creation of the American republic 1776–1787*, pp 127–61 (1967). A British view of the war is found in P. Mackesy, *The war for America, 1775–1783* (1964). The situation was not unlike that in Ireland during the Anglo-Irish War (1919–22) when Dáil Éireann became the effective legislature instead of the Westminster Parliament, and the republican 'courts' gradually took over private disputes from the royal courts in the territory of the Irish Free State. R. Foster, *Modern Ireland, 1600–1972*, pp 495–501 (1988).

30 Ballard, *Trinity Church in old Newport*, p. 365 (1979).

31 D. McCullough, *1776*, pp 70–108 (2006). The artillery came from the British fort at Ticonderoga on Lake Champlain, after Ethan Allan's surprise attack there on 10 May 1775. Brig. Gen. Henry Knox (1750–1806), a Boston bookseller, had led forty-two sleds full of cannon and ammunition over snow-covered countryside for 300 miles from Ticonderoga. See N. Callahan, *Henry Knox: George Washington's general* (1958). Installation of the cannon was the work of Brig. Gen. John Sullivan (1740–95), a lawyer from Durham, NH, who served on Washington's staff in the siege of Boston. In his honour, Washington assigned 'St Patrick' as the password for 17 Mar. 1776, the day the British fleet sailed out of Boston.

32 See R. Calhoun, *The loyalists in revolutionary America, 1760–1781* (1965). Sarjent died in London

awaited reinforcements, which actually removed many British troops from Ireland.[33]

British forces, regrouped and reinforced at Halifax, then descended on New York with a mighty armada of 500 ships and 32,000 men.[34] As a result of disastrous defeats at the battle of Long Island (Brooklyn Heights) on 27 August 1776 and White Plains on 28 October 1776, Washington and the remnant of the colonial army fled across the Hudson River in November to New Jersey and Pennsylvania for five more years of war.

Ignoring Boston, held by colonial militia, the British selected Newport as its major naval base between Halifax and New York, and on 8 December 1776, a fleet of 17 warships and 70 transports with 4,000 British and Hessian soldiers occupied Newport and Narragansett Bay;[35] Trinity Newport's rector immediately reopened the church for the military and his congregation. The occupation of Newport by the British army and navy destroyed the pre-war elegance and prosperity, dependent on the slave trade, privateering and smuggling. It has been estimated that at least half of the population fled inland, and, except for those who serviced the army or the fleet, the pre-war trades ceased and the skilled workers removed to Providence, which rapidly overcame Newport in wealth and population.

A daring exploit of colonial militia after six months of occupation greatly embarrassed the British. Brigadier General Richard Prescott had moved his headquarters from the town to a farm about 5 miles outside for the summer. On 9 July 1777 colonial Colonel William Barton landed a force in darkness, overcame the sentries and captured the general, holding him in Providence for a year until an exchange could be arranged. Prescott reassumed his command in July 1778 with cruel vengeance on the townspeople, until the evacuation of forces was completed on 25 October 1779.

Washington and his army survived the campaigns of 1776 through 1779 by avoiding European-style battles and striking British weak points by stealth, but this strategy led to despair and defeatism – until a dramatic victory in upstate New York in October 1777 by General Horatio Gates, which caused the surrender of a British army of almost 6,000 men at Saratoga. About to travel to France, Benjamin Franklin, the new 'minister', brought news of the Saratoga surrender with him. The French court seized the opportunity to revenge the loss of Canada by a formal

shortly after his arrival. Subsequently, refugee loyalists could seek compensation for their financial losses from a royal commission in London. Loyalist claim records are preserved in the National Archives, Kew, and are analyzed in W. Brown, *The king's friends: the composition and motives of the American loyalist claimants* (1961).

33 See chapter 5, n. 6–13, for the Volunteers movement in Ireland.

34 McCullough, *1776*, pp 134–54 (2006). The size of the British forces (including 8,000 Hessian mercenaries) is well known, but the size of Washington's army varied almost daily, from a maximum 20,000 to 2,500 because of desertions after defeats and because of the varied lengths of militia enlistments, differing from state to state and within states.

35 Ballard, *Trinity Church in old Newport*, p. 366 (1979). The details of the occupation of Newport are described in R. Stensrud, *Newport: a lively experiment, 1639–1969*, pp 195–214 (2006).

recognition and alliance with the United States, signed on 8 February 1778.[36] Thereafter, French assistance was no longer clandestine,[37] and the French army, navy and treasury supported the American War of Independence.

In 1779, British strategy changed to accommodate a world war with France, concentrating new forces in the Carolinas while retaining New York. The British army evacuated Newport on 25 October 1779. Forty-six loyalists, including Trinity's rector, went with the British fleet. After the British evacuation, a mob invaded Trinity Church and tore down and destroyed the royal arms in the chancel.[38] The building was delivered to the Baptist congregation, which had been burned out by British forces.

The French fleet of 9 warships and 35 transports arrived at Newport on 11 July 1780 with an army of 5,500 troops under Comte General de Rochambeau.[39] This French army would play a major role in ending the war.

IV

The American war ended as accidentally as it had begun, and it was clearly the responsibility of Lord Charles Cornwallis,[40] who lost America for the British empire. The same Cornwallis saved Ireland for the same king and empire in 1798.

In the aftermath of the Irish Revolution of 1798, Arthur Browne praised Cornwallis for his rescue of the Irish nation from godless French republicanism and fanatical Protestant vengeance on the majority Catholic population, so it is appropriate to review the career of this imperial pro-consul and his experiences in America.

36 Benjamin Franklin (1706–90) had held a royal appointment as deputy postmaster general for the colonies (1753–74). He had served in London for more than fourteen years, was held in great esteem by French *philosophes* as an enlightened natural philosopher and had been a member of the second continental congress from the beginning. He was the obvious choice to lead a commission of official representatives. See Treaty of Alliance, 8 Stat 6 (1778); this treaty endured until the Quasi-War with France, when it was terminated by Congress, 1 Stat 578 (7 July 1798). See S.F. Bemis, *The diplomacy of the American Revolution*, pp 17–65 (1935).
37 France had secretly provided surplus military supplies to Congress, expecting payment in tobacco and rice, through a sham company, Rodrigue Hortalez et Cie., operated by Pierre Auguste Caron de Beaumarchais (1732–99), a watchmaker, entrepreneur, secret agent and playwright.
38 N. Isham, *Trinity Church in Newport, Rhode Island: a history of the fabric*, pp 69–71 (1936). Efforts of later rectors to restore the royal arms have been strenuously resisted; a copy is displayed in the parish house.
39 Jean Baptiste Donatien de Vimeur de Rochambeau (1725–1802). In the Seven Years War he was promoted to brigadier general (1756) and wounded in battle in Germany. After Yorktown he was made governor of Picardy, but was imprisoned for two years under the Terror. See A. Whitridge, *Rochambeau* (1965).
40 Charles Cornwallis (1738–1805), born in London, attended Eton and began studies at Clare College, Cambridge, before going on the Grand Tour of Europe (1757–59). He entered Parliament in 1760 as a Whig member for Eye in Suffolk. On the death of his father in 1762, he moved to the

Cornwallis had volunteered to accompany the 1776 invasion, but returned to Britain because his wife, Jemima, was seriously ill. After she died in February 1779, Cornwallis again volunteered for American duty and was sent to assist the new southern strategy of Sir Henry Clinton and the North administration.

Cornwallis' campaign to subdue South Carolina began very well, with a victory over General Horatio Gates and a largely militia army at Camden on 16 August 1780, with more than 900 American casualties and 1,000 prisoners (not including Gates, who fled). Despite the mild winters of South Carolina, the army tradition of going to winter quarters brought an end to the campaign in October 1780.

The war resumed in 1781 with a major battle at Guilford Court House on 15 March. Described as a Cornwallis victory, it was certainly pyrrhic, with 500 British casualties. Cornwallis then marched 200 miles into Tidewater Virginia, surprising Governor Thomas Jefferson and the Virginia legislature, who narrowly escaped capture on 4 June. Thereafter, Cornwallis, resupplied from New York, was able to operate freely during the torrid summer.

Cornwallis sought a convenient encampment where he might be reinforced and resupplied from New York, while Clinton demanded a deepwater port for future naval operations by an expected fleet from England that never arrived, therefore Yorktown – on a vulnerable peninsula near Chesapeake Bay – was chosen, and it became Cornwallis' headquarters on 1 August. Cornwallis expected the arrival of Admiral Thomas Graves and a fleet of warships from New York. Instead, French Admiral de Grasse appeared with a fleet of 25 warships and 3,000 marines from the Caribbean, establishing a complete naval blockade of the mouth of the York River by 1 September.

Five days later the 19 ships of Admiral Graves' fleet began to arrive at the mouth of Chesapeake Bay. Three days of battering, ramming and maneuvering followed, favouring the French. On 9 September, a French fleet under Admiral Barras arrived from Newport. On 10 September, Graves withdrew his ships from the scene of destruction and returned to New York. The battle of Chesapeake Bay led to a resumed blockade, which put Cornwallis' camp in peril. Retreat by land was still possible because Cornwallis' forces outnumbered the colonials in the vicinity, but Cornwallis, like Clinton, expected a new fleet and a new army from England and determined to stay at Yorktown. That fleet and army had gone to Gibraltar.

Washington's army was camped along the Hudson River north of British-held New York City, awaiting the moment when Clinton would have withdrawn troops and ships for service in the Caribbean or Carolinas. On 5 July 1781, Comte de Rochambeau arrived with 5,000 men at Washington's headquarters; joint operations against New York were being planned when news arrived on 14 August that the French fleet under de Grasse would be in the Chesapeake Bay for a limited

House of Lords, maintaining his Rockingham Whig connections in that body, voting against taxation of America and opposing the use of military force, but in 1776 he volunteered for service in America. See F. and M. Wickwire, *Cornwallis: the American adventure* (1970).

time in late summer and early autumn – hurricane season in the Caribbean – but would have to return to protect the French islands from British attacks expected in late autumn. The opportunity to trap Cornwallis was irresistible.

The French army had already marched more than 200 miles from Newport, and Clinton was aware of that augmentation to Washington's forces. The trick was to move the combined French-American army surreptitiously 500 miles to the Chesapeake without alerting Clinton to its absence. By small units over three different southerly routes the movement began on 15 August, but it was not until mid-September that all the components had arrived at Yorktown. Washington and Rochambeau now had about 16,000 men for the siege of Yorktown and its 7,000 to 9,000 British and Hessians.[41]

French engineers laid out traditional siege lines, and Washington set up French and American heavy guns. A fierce bombardment of Yorktown began on 28 September, and the siege lines crept closer. Hunger and the spread of diseases had their effect, and the council of Cornwallis' officers agreed that further resistance was futile. On 17 October, Cornwallis wrote to Washington proposing a ceasefire and a meeting of staff officers to discuss surrender.

The formal surrender ceremony began at 2 p.m. on 19 October 1781.[42] It was a bright fall afternoon. Cornwallis was not there; he claimed to be ill.

In his first report to General Clinton, his superior, on 20 October 1783, Cornwallis sought to locate the blame upwards, noting that his surrender occurred 'with mortification', but that he would never have been induced to accept Yorktown if he had not been 'assured by your Excellency's letters' of 'every possible means to relieve us'. Regardless of the breach of military etiquette, a large British army had become prisoners of war.

Military custom of the time treated the surrendered officers and enlisted men differently. By Article V of the capitulation agreement, 'The soldiers [were] to be kept in Virginia, Maryland or Pennsylvania and as much by regiments as possible and supplied with the same rations of provisions as are allowed to soldiers in the service of America.'[43] By Article VI, officers could choose to go on parole to New York, there to await embarkation to Europe (on British ships).[44] 'Parole' meant a solemn oath not to participate in any further hostilities against the victorious army until the end of the war. Officers who did not choose parole would have to await an exchange of prisoners of war.

---

41 See generally, T.J. Fleming, *Beat the last drum: the siege of Yorktown 1781* (1963) and B. Tuchman, *The first salute*, pp 245–90 (1988). The recent literature is extensive: R. Ketchum, *Victory at Yorktown: the campaign that won the revolution* (2004); J.A Greane, *The guns of independence: the siege of Yorktown* (2005); J. Grainger, *The battle of Yorktown 1781: a reassessment* (2005); J.E. Ferling, *Almost a miracle: the American victory in the War of Independence* (2007). An earlier study was H.P. Johnston, *The Yorktown campaign and surrender of Cornwallis* (1881).

42 Controversy surrounds most of the details of the formalities. See Wickwire, *Cornwallis*, pp 385–8 (1970); R. Chernow, *Washington: a life*, pp 406–14 (2010); and J.T. Flexner, 2 *George Washington in the American Revolution*, pp 459–64 (1968).

43 Fleming, *Beat the last drum*, pp 345–9 (1963).   44 Ibid.

Having chosen parole, on 4 November, Cornwallis prepared the necessary reports, suffered a humiliating interview with Clinton and then departed as quickly as possible. As it was nearing European waters, a French privateer intercepted and captured the *Greyhound* (and her passengers), intending to take it to a French port for condemnation as prize. But a vicious midwinter storm battered and exhausted the crew into seeking the nearest port of refuge, Torbay in Devon. From Torbay, Cornwallis proceeded by land to London, arriving on 22 January 1782, and the French crew was allowed to take their prize to France.

Despite the surrender, Cornwallis was well received by the king, Commons and Lords. He did not suffer popular indignation even though he had abandoned his army in American prison camps. He was, however, greatly disappointed about the future of the war, and that he could not be a part of it.[45] It was too late anyway; there would be no more war in America. Whig opposition to continued war was about to overcome the king, Lord North and the Tories.

What was the effect of America on Cornwallis? He had arrived in 1776 with the education and experience of a professional European warrior – something Americans knew they had no chance of becoming. He left six years later a prisoner of war on a parole, chastised by his superior, having experienced defeat and personal tragedy in the death of his wife. This could have been the source of the compassion and clemency he showed in Ireland.

Official reports of the surrender of Cornwallis and his army did not reach London until 25 November 1781. The king was immediately informed, but the next day, in the speech from the throne for the opening of Parliament, he did not mention Yorktown or Cornwallis. Instead, he called for the vigorous prosecution of the war in America. The prime minister, Lord North, knew it was all over, yet the king required North to persevere, hinting that unless Parliament pursued the war he would go to Hanover and abdicate the British throne.

The March motions declared that there must be an end to the war in America. By 15 March, the government lost its already slim majority by 9 votes and North pleaded with the king to accept his resignation.[46] The king accepted Lord North's resignation coldly on 20 March, and Lord Rockingham became prime minister on 27 March.[47] As ungraciously as possible, the king merely promised not to veto peace with America.

---

45 F. and M. Wickwire, *Cornwallis: the imperial years*, pp 3–9 (1980) and S. Weintraub, *Iron tears: America's battle for freedom, Britains's quagmire, 1775–1783*, pp 304–7 (2005).

46 J. Norris, *Shelburne and reform*, pp 148–50 (1963); there is an extensive analysis of each member's vote at pp 295–367.

47 Charles Watson-Wentworth, 2nd marquis of Rockingham (1736–82). He served as prime minister to George III in 1765 for a year and in 1782 for three months – both times involved conciliation with America. Edmund Burke (1729–97) became his private secretary and lifelong advisor during sixteen years of opposition. Rockingham died, apparently from influenza, after three months in office. See generally, R.J.S. Hoffman, *The marquis: a study of Lord Rockingham, 1730–1782*, pp 372–85 (1973). See also F. O'Gorman, *The rise of party in England: the Rockingham Whigs, 1760–1782* (1975).

V

Rockingham was the most experienced politician of his day and assembled a cabinet of the most important members of the Lords, plus Charles James Fox to lead the Commons and handle foreign affairs. Extensive reforms were planned, beginning with the settlement with the Irish Parliament and a new relation with America, but Rockingham died after fourteen weeks in office.

For years, legislation by the Irish Parliament required submission of the 'heads of bills' to pre-approval by the British privy council, pursuant to Poynings' Law of 1494 and the British Declaratory Act of 1720; the result was the inability of the Irish Parliament to legislate for itself, a situation clearly resembling what Britain had attempted in America with the Declaratory Act of 1766, now repudiated by the force of arms.

The final push to be rid of these British shackles began in February 1782 at the Dungannon convention of the Volunteers, which resolved that only the king, Lords and Commons of Ireland could make law to bind the kingdom of Ireland. On arrival in April, the new Whig viceroy, the duke of Portland, was empowered to resolve Irish disaffection while preserving the imperial connection.

On the opening of Parliament, on 16 April, Henry Grattan's motions, which had the effect of asserting the independence of the Irish Parliament – called the constitution of 1782 – were approved without opposition. The actual bill to deal with Poynings' Law was urged by the new attorney general, Barry Yelverton, with its key language that Irish bills would not suffer 'addition, diminution or alteration', as an amendment to the existing law. Henry Flood's proposal to substitute total repeal for amendment did not survive, but would come back later to divide the Whigs in their hour of victory.

Yelverton's bill passed in June 1782 and similar legislation was enacted by the British Parliament in January 1783.[48] Ireland's Parliament was no longer tied to the British privy council – a short-lived independence that expired at the end of 1800 with the union of Parliaments (see chapter 13).

Shelburne[49] succeeded Rockingham as prime minister, which was quite acceptable to the king. Fox resigned from the cabinet, to the delight of the king. Otherwise, the new cabinet was similar to that of Rockingham, with the 23-year-old William Pitt as chancellor of the exchequer. With Fox (and Burke) outside and

48 J. Kelly, *Poynings' Law and the making of law in Ireland, 1660–1800*, pp 315–54 (2007); E. Curtis, *A history of Ireland*, pp 310–16 (16th ed. 1950) and N. York, *Neither kingdom nor nation: the Irish quest for constitutional rights, 1698–1800*, pp 124–36 (1994). The Irish debates are in 1 Parl. Reg., pp 382–97 (1782); see also 21 and 22 Geo. 3 c. 47.

49 The earl of Shelburne (1737–1805) was born William Fitzmaurice in Dublin, son of John Fitzmaurice the earl of Kerry. His early years were spent at Lansdowne near Kenmare in County Kerry. He later went up to Christ Church, Oxford, where he studied under Blackstone. He joined the army and became aide-de-camp to the king. This early attachment meant that the king trusted him despite his political opposition. He became knight of the garter (KG) in 1782. In 1760, he entered the British House of Commons for Wycombe, and in 1761, the Irish House of Commons

Portland sent to Ireland as viceroy, Shelburne was weak and Fox conspired with the Tories until Shelburne lost the support of the Commons over commercial trade with America and resigned his office in accordance with what he believed to be the constitution; his great achievement, a generous peace with independent America, could not be undone, although commercial relations remained hostile until the renegotiation in Jay's Treaty in 1794.

The king's fury at the combination in the next government of North, his most loyal supporter, with Fox, his personal enemy, was a bitter pill coated with Portland as nominal prime minister.[50] The king considered any government that involved Fox a violation of his royal prerogative to choose his servants and therefore unconstitutional. He sought any opportunity to be rid of the Fox–North coalition. Eight months were required for the proper opportunity: Fox's India bill, creating a board of parliamentary commissioners to control the East India Company, thereby delivering the riches and patronage of the East to Fox and the Whigs. The India bill passed the Commons comfortably on 8 December 1783, but using every scrap of influence, including suggestions that supporters of the India bill would be his 'personal enemies', the king persuaded the Lords to reject it by a vote of 95 to 76 on 17 December. With this excuse, the king dismissed the Fox–North coalition and installed the very young William Pitt as prime minister without a parliamentary majority on 19 December 1783. All members of the cabinet, except Pitt, were in the Lords. The king's own unconstitutional action went unchallenged, and Parliament continued for three months until it was dissolved on 24 March 1784. In the elections of April 1784, Pitt gained 104 seats and Fox lost 108 seats, thanks in part to the financial support of the East India Company. With the king's backing and a parliamentary majority, Pitt was in charge of British affairs for the next 17 years, the life of the Irish Parliament.[51]

It is still uncertain why the king chose this young man to carry out a risky scheme that might have forced him to abdicate. Pitt was a brilliant orator, well schooled by his father in public affairs and political intrigue. Pitt had a taste of office as chancellor of the exchequer (and spokesman in the Commons) for the brief Shelburne administration, but most important, in appearance, style and manners he was the opposite of the king's enemy, Charles James Fox, and had no connections to the prince of Wales.

Preliminary peace negotiations with America had begun 13 April 1782 when Richard Oswald[52] met Benjamin Franklin in Paris. Parliament approved

for County Kerry. However, his father died in 1761 and he transferred to the British House of Lords as earl of Shelburne. See J. Norris, *Shelburne and reform*, pp 170–85, 240–70 (1963).

50 William Henry Cavendish-Bentinck, 3rd duke of Portland (1738–1809), was elected a Whig member of Parliament from Wembley in 1761, but his father died in 1762 and he transferred to the House of Lords as duke of Portland. Like Rockingham, he served twice as prime minister (1783 and 1807–9). He was sent to Dublin as viceroy by Rockingham in April 1782.

51 See J. Ehrman, *The younger Pitt: years of acclaim*, pp 118–53 (1969). See also D. Jarrett, *Pitt the younger*, pp 64–84 (1974) and J. Derry, *Charles James Fox*, pp 189–213 (1972).

52 Richard Oswald (1737–84), born in Scotland, went to Virginia for six years before thirty years of

negotiations with America 17 June. Oswald persevered for a time despite criticism in Parliament, but his health suffered and he eventually withdrew. In the end, the treaty was signed for Great Britain by David Hartley.[53]

The issues between Great Britain and America were heavily influenced by the October 1781 surrender at Yorktown, and the two armies imprisoned in America. Issues between Great Britain and France were influenced by Admiral Rodney's destruction of the French fleet – and capture of Comte de Grasse – at the battle of Saintes (near Martinique) on 12 April 1782.

With Franklin already in Paris, Congress established a commission of five representatives and prepared instructions, one of which required the commission to inform the French foreign minister, Comte de Vergennes,[54] and seek his concurrence.

Official negotiations began with the arrival on 23 June 1782 of John Jay,[55] and were virtually concluded by the time Adams arrived on 26 October 1782, because Jay had summarized the discussions in a draft treaty of 5 October that became the model for the final treaty.[56] The multilateral agreements concluded on 3 September 1783.[57] Ratification by Congress followed on 14 January 1784, and the ratifications were exchanged in Paris on 12 May 1784. The British army, preceded by 7,000 loyalists, evacuated its last stronghold, New York City, on 25 November 1783. After almost twenty years of disaffection, hatred and war, peace had returned.

trading in London. Shelburne frequently consulted Oswald about America and Oswald's previous business arrangements with Dr Franklin made him an obvious choice for the peace negotiations. He was an extremely successful dealmaker.

53 David Hartley (1730–1813), born in Bath, AB Corpus Christi, Oxford 1750. He entered Parliament in 1774 from Kingston on Hull, serving until 1784, with Wilberforce. He was an inventor and scientist, thus an early friend and correspondent of Franklin. He opposed war in America and the slave trade.

54 Charles Gravier, Comte de Vergennes (1717–87). His independent career as a successful diplomat began in Germany (1750–5), and then took him to the Ottoman empire at Constantinople (1755–65). At the accession of Louis XVI in 1774, he became foreign minister, an office he held until his death. He regarded the 1763 Treaty of Paris as a humiliating defeat that had to be avenged, thus his involvement with Beaumarchais in secret assistance to, and the alliance with, America. See generally O.T. Murphy, *Charles Gravier, Comte de Vergennes: French diplomacy in the age of revolution, 1719–1787* (1982).

55 John Jay (1745–1829), AB King's College (Columbia University) 1764, attended the first and second continental congresses. He was president of Congress (1778–9) and then minister to Spain (1779–82) and France. Jay spent fifteen weeks in England after the treaty was signed, during which time he was awarded the DCL from Trinity College Dublin. Jay returned to become secretary of foreign affairs under the Articles of Confederation (1784–9), and the first chief justice of the United States Supreme Court.

56 See R.B. Morris, *The peacemakers: the great powers and American independence*, pp 147–72, 311–410, 418–37 (1965) and R.B. Morris, *The forging of the union*, pp 1–79 (1987). Professor Morris has also edited the correspondence of John Jay; see R.B. Morris, *John Jay: the winning of the peace – unpublished papers, 1780–1784*, pp 237–477 (1980). Article 8 of the 1778 Treaty of Alliance required mutual consents to any truce or peace with Great Britain.

57 8 Stat. 80 (1783).

It was on 14 October 1783 that Arthur Browne entered the Irish House of Commons as member for Trinity College Dublin. His American homeland was no longer the enemy. Reviewing the American Revolution in 1798 he wrote, 'America, before the revolution was by far the happiest [land]. She has gained by the change in power, in wealth, in consequence – whether she has advanced in felicity may perhaps be questioned.'

Life for him in America no longer seemed possible because of 'the death of friends; the total change of inhabitants' and the 'wonderful alteration made by an intervening revolution'. This surely meant the dispersal of his father's congregation, and the flight of loyalists as the SPG closed its operations in America. Arthur Browne was not ready for a new world of independent and victorious American republicans unlawfully holding British properties, but his Newport heritage enabled him to bring principles of civil liberties to the newly independent Parliament of Ireland.

CHAPTER FIVE

Parliament (1783–8)

I

ARTHUR BROWNE WAS 27 when he was elected by the fellows and scholars of Trinity College to represent the University of Dublin constituency in the House of Commons of the Irish Parliament, which met across the street from the front gate of the college. The electors were the 22 fellows and about 70 scholars. This was, in fact, an unusually large number; some 'pocket' boroughs had no residents, or a very few who were employees of the borough owner or patron. Elections were public meetings without secret, written ballots, and the returns from elections were not often made public.

Arthur Browne had already become a popular figure with the students as a lecturer, and it is possible that he was chosen by young men to annoy the provost and reactionary guardians of traditions,[1] but the record of the published views of the electors makes it plain that they were denying re-election to John FitzGibbon, an MP who was no longer attached to the principles of the Patriot Party. ('Patriot' was a term loosely applied to members in opposition to the continuation or expansion of English interests by Dublin Castle.)

In the election of 1778, John FitzGibbon had been returned as one of the two members of Parliament for Trinity College. FitzGibbon was initially popular with the Patriot Party, but his temporizing on popular issues caused concern among the Trinity electors for the approaching election. Walter Hussey Burgh had been elected in 1776, but had been appointed to a judgeship, chief baron of the exchequer, just before his sudden death in 1783. Thus, two members were to be elected in 1783.

A meeting of the Trinity electors on 3 April 1782 issued demands for the positions to be taken by its members in Parliament:

> When the murmurs of a people, struggling for their rights have been heard even in the quiet retreat of science, we should deem it a breach of duty to our

1 E.M. Johnston, 'Members of the Irish Parliament, 1784–7', 71 *Proceedings Royal Irish Academy* (1971). 'Browne, Arthur, brought in for the University of Dublin by the young men against the provost, was born in America, a fellow of the college' (p. 171), 'both members are in opposition' (p. 215). This election was a reaction to the interference of the provost (Hely-Hutchinson) in a previous election of May 1776 when the provost's son, Richard, an Oxford graduate, was elected with Hussey Burgh. Richard's election was voided because some electors were minors, and John FitzGibbon was elected in his place. An obituary in Walker's *Hibernian Magazine* (Oct. 1805)

countrymen and ourselves, did we neglect to second their virtuous exertions ... we have not been the last to feel, the repeated injuries this country has suffered ... We are therefore convinced, that an express declaration of rights is the only measure upon which this country can build its legislative independence ... We therefore expect you will exert your most strenuous efforts to obtain a declaration of the rights of Ireland, a repeal or satisfactory explanation of the law of Poyning's; an Act for making the tenure of the judges independent of the crown, and a repeal of the perpetual mutiny bill ... [2]

Apparently the electors were dissatisfied with FitzGibbon's recent performance in Parliament on the constitutional issues favoured by Grattan and the Patriot opposition, thus in the election of July 1783, FitzGibbon lost, and Arthur Browne and Lawrence Parsons were elected to Parliament. It must have been clear to the electors in 1783 that Arthur Browne favoured Whig principles, despite his family background in the established church, often considered an adjunct of the Tory party. It must also have been obvious that he was an American, despite ten years in Dublin, and the electors knew that Americans had just defeated the royal armies at Yorktown to establish their independence.

For ten years Arthur Browne had lived within a few yards of an operating legislature with a substantial visitor's gallery that could be filled when dramatic issues were being considered, and whose sessions were public entertainment, like hangings. Trinity students in academic gowns easily became addicted to duels of repartee by the members. Arthur Browne did not speak of attending the House of Commons before his official membership began in 1783, but he soon mastered the language and customs of parliamentary debate, possibly under the tutelage of George Ponsonby or other Monks of the Screw. He later was a vigorous defender of the right of students to attend meetings of the House.

II. HISTORICAL BACKGROUND

The Irish Parliament of which Arthur Browne became a member was later to be known as 'Grattan's Parliament' after having been freed from the legal controls of the London administration in the repeal of Poynings' Law after 16 April 1782.[3]

described Browne as 'the idol of the students ... they loved him with the affection of fond children', and 'no person in the university was more beloved than Dr Browne'.

2 D.A. Fleming and A.P.W. Malcomson, '*A volley of execrations': the letters and papers of John FitzGibbon, earl of Clare, 1772–1802*, pp 3–5 (2005). FitzGibbon's defeat had been predicted in the press because of his 'amiable cullibility' (to serve government). See A. Kavanaugh, *John FitzGibbon, earl of Clare: Protestant reaction and English authority in late eighteenth-century Ireland*, p. 60 (1997).

3 1 *Parliamentary Register*, p. 334, Poynings' Law (10 Hen. 7 c. 4) of 1494 required the heads of bills introduced in Ireland to be pre-approved by the privy council in London. The Poynings' Law

Threats of an American-style trade embargo and the presence of 40,000 Volunteers quickly persuaded the new British Whig government of Lord Rockingham (who succeeded Lord North after word of defeat in America), to acquiesce in the unopposed decision of the Irish Parliament to undo Poynings' Law. It was the only achievement of Rockingham's three months in power before his untimely death.

The Irish government and population were not ignorant of the events of the American war thanks to sympathetic Irish and English newspapers and pamphlets that were often read (or translated and read) in pubs or shebeens in the country.[4] Irish military units had been posted to Boston in 1768, but the transfer of 4,000 British troops of a total military force of 12,000 from Ireland to America in 1776 raised concerns about agrarian disorders and potential French invasions.[5] These fears were greatly exacerbated by the American Alliance with France in 1778 and the war with Spain in June 1779. Without government permission, encouragement or financial assistance, groups of men were assembled by landlords from their tenants, also by groups of neighbors electing their own officers, for the purpose of home defence and repelling invasion. These unofficial military units were called Volunteers, and it was estimated that by 1779 there were 25,000 men in self-organized military units ranging in size from 30 to 100.[6] These groups were overwhelmingly Protestants in the south and Protestants and dissenters in Ulster, because of the penal-law prohibitions against Catholics bearing arms. Nevertheless, there were a number of Volunteers units where the penal laws were ignored, and Catholics were enlisted.[7] (Catholics could also be enlisted in the regular British army or navy.)

During the war emergency of 1779, the Volunteers began to take public positions on Irish constitutional rights: in favour of the repeal of British prohibitions on Irish trade, and against new taxes. Lord North presented a new series of bills responsive to Irish demands to allow Ireland to trade with British colonies, and to export woolens, and glass to England. Enactment of these bills in December 1779 and early 1780 eased the crisis,[8] but encouraged the Volunteers and the Patriot Party to insist on the independence of the Irish Parliament, clearly

principle had been restated in the 1720 Westminster Declaratory Act, 6 Geo. 1 c. 5. The Declaratory Act resulted from a legal dispute over the finality of Irish appellate jurisdiction in the case of *Sherlock v. Annesley*, a dispute over lands in County Kildare. See M. Flaherty, 'The empire strikes back: *Annesley v. Sherlock* and the triumph of imperial parliamentary supremacy', 87 *Colum. L. Rev.*, 593 (1981). The statute was repealed by 21 and 22 Geo. 3 c. 47 in Ireland and 21 and 22 Geo. 3 c. 53 in Great Britain. See J. Kelly, *Poynings' Law and the making of law in Ireland, 1660–1800*, pp 275–309 (2007).

4   V. Morley, *Irish opinion and the American Revolution, 1760–1783*, pp 71–4, 97–129, 148–50 (2002).

5   Ibid., pp 246, 263; N. York, *Neither kingdom nor nation: the Irish quest for constitutional rights, 1698–1800*, pp 105–6 (1994). A French and Spanish fleet, with troops aboard, cruised in the English Channel in summer 1779.

6   Morley, *Irish opinion*, pp 246, 263. See generally, T. MacNevin, *History of the Volunteers of 1782* (1882).

7   N. York, *Neither kingdom nor nation*, pp 174–84 (1994).

8   J.C. Beckett, *The making of Modern Ireland, 1603–1923*, pp 215–20 (1983).

demanded by Henry Grattan on 19 April 1780 and finally achieved in Dublin in 1782. In the past, the British army would have suppressed such radical notions, but by 1782 the Volunteers greatly outnumbered the active military (possibly 40,000 Volunteers and less than 9,000 British army).[9] Whether the Volunteers would have used military force to achieve their demands is uncertain. But a form of legislative independence of the Protestant Irish Parliament was achieved in May 1782 without bloodshed.[10] This was not American-style independence, and the Catholic majority of the population was hardly affected by this change, since no Catholic could be a member of the 'independent' Irish Parliament.

There was a Dublin Volunteers lawyers' corps of 100 barristers and solicitors. We cannot be certain whether Arthur Browne was a member as no list of members appears to have survived. He may have been, though, given his subsequent election as commandant of the Trinity Defence Corps. Arthur Browne was never a United Irishman.[11] His military experience came unexpectedly in 1796 when a corps of students and fellows was organized to repel threatened French invasions even before the failed French landings at Bantry Bay in December 1796.[12] The proposed Trinity Defence Corps was controversial, but the students were armed and organized into four companies. Arthur Browne became commander of the corps, and began to study and teach military organization, strategy and tactics, although he always described himself as an amateur and not a soldier.[13]

---

9 Ibid., p. 263. The Volunteers' commander-in-chief was James Caulfeild (1728–99), the earl of Charlemont. The duke of Leinster and Frederick Augustus Hervey, the bishop of Derry, were also commanders. James Caulfeild was one of the great Whig aristocrats of the eighteenth century. He was an improving landlord on his vast estates, a town planner at his village of Moy in County Tyrone and a great builder at his country estate, Marino, north of Dublin. He emerged prominently in the Volunteers movement as commander-in-chief and a major influence on the Dungannon Resolutions, a prelude to the 1782 constitutional changes pushed by Grattan. He became a leader in the Whig Club. He was described by FitzGibbon as, 'wild and boisterous on the subject of Ireland' (1787 letter, Fleming and Malcomson, '*A volley of execrations*', p. 56 (2005)). He was a great supporter and influence on the Royal Irish Academy. He strongly opposed the union in 1799. See J. Kelly, 'A genuine patriot: Lord Charlemont's political career' in M. McCarthy (ed.), *Lord Charlemont and his circle*, pp 7–37 (2001), and M. Craig, *The Volunteer earl: being the life and times of James Caulfeild, first earl of Charlemont* (1948).

10 See generally: R. Foster, *Modern Ireland, 1600–1972*, pp 167–286 (1988); L. Cullen, *The emergence of modern Ireland, 1600–1900*, pp 193–256 (1981); P. Smyth, *The Volunteers and Parliament*, pp 113–36; A.P.W. Malcomson, 'The parliamentary traffic of this country' in T. Bartlett and D. Hayton (eds), *Penal era and golden age: essays in Irish history, 1690–1800*, pp 137–61 (1979); P. Rogers, *The Irish Volunteers and Catholic emancipation* (1934); G. O'Brien, *Anglo-Irish politics in the age of Grattan and Pitt*, pp 52–7, 68–72, 93–6, 147–54 (1987).

11 There were 56 barristers and solicitors in the list of 425 Dublin United Irishmen. See R.B. McDowell, 'The personnel of the Dublin Society of the United Irishmen, 1791–4', *Ir. Pol. Stud.*, 12–53 (1940–1).

12 J.A. Murphy (ed.), *The French are in the bay: the expedition to Bantry Bay, 1796* (1997).

13 For Browne's membership in the lawyers' corps of the Volunteers, see chapter 10, n. 31. A. Browne, *Miscellaneous sketches*, pp 321–54 (1798).

III. PARLIAMENT

A. House of Commons

Arthur Browne's studies for the law occurred during the period when the Volunteers were preparing the way for an independent Protestant Parliament in Ireland, no longer controlled by London. His service as a member of the Irish House of Commons spanned the short life of that independent Parliament before it was extinguished in 1801 by the union of Ireland with Great Britain, governed by a single Parliament at Westminster.

The Irish Parliament was hardly a governing body in the modern sense, since the executive and the ministers were not responsible to the Irish Parliament, but to the ministry in London, and the Irish executive, headed by the English viceroy, usually achieved its goals through 'influence': pensions, peerages and privileges paid out to compliant members. Parliament never pretended to represent the people; it represented wealth in land. There were some actual voters (the 'forty-shilling freeholders') in county elections and in cities, but many members were chosen by borough owners.

There were no formal political parties, but rather shifting alliances of groups subject to the influence of powerful land owners. There were also independent members uncommitted to any faction. Relentless pursuit of office and bargaining for perquisites in church and state were the hallmarks of the Irish Commons. Government majorities were not permanent, as members refused to 'stay bought'. Service in the Irish House of Commons was regarded as the first step in a political career that could be played for advancement to wealth and nobility.

It was in fact an unrepresentative, corrupt and largely ineffective body controlled by the Ascendancy of the established church. Catholics could not vote nor sit as members in 1783. Presbyterians were disabled from sitting as members until 1780, but had minimal influence thereafter.

The House of Commons had 300 members: each of the 32 counties sent two members; and each of 110 boroughs (towns, villages and manors) sent two members; and each of 7 cities sent two members. To these 298 members were added the two representatives of Trinity College, the only collegiate institution in Ireland at that time.[14] The legendary price sought by borough owners of a seat in the Commons in 1783 was £2,000, but the buyer expected to recoup the cost by negotiating his vote, as necessary.[15] Intentional or negligent absenteeism was always

---

14 J.L. McCracken, *The Irish Parliament in the eighteenth century* (1971); B. Farrell (ed.), *The Irish parliamentary tradition*, pp 139–59 (1973); A.P.W. Malcomson, 'The parliamentary traffic of this country' in T. Bartlett and D. Hayton (eds.), *Penal era and golden age*, pp 137–61 (1979); and J. Gilbert, 3 *A history of the city of Dublin*, pp 127–8 (1854). In 1798, 67 of the 300 were members of the Bar, see K. Ferguson, 'The Irish Bar in 1798', 52 *Dublin Historical Record*, 32 (1999).
15 J.A. Froude, 2 *The English in Ireland*, p. 365 (1881). Seats in the Westminster Parliament sold for £3,000 to £4,000.

a problem. There was a statutory limit of eight years to the length of a Parliament.[16] After 1785, Parliament met annually instead of the previous biennial practice.

Despite the differing political viewpoints of the members, there was one overriding consideration: fear of the majority Catholic population. This was not fantasy, because the agrarian violence of the White Boys in the 1760s and Defenders in the 1790s was attributed to landless peasants or workers who were usually Catholic. The intensity of this concern is difficult to understand in the twenty-first century, but it can become understandable through the eyes of a modern analyst. Professor S.J. Connolly writes that:

> Ireland in the century or so following the Restoration [1660] is best seen as first and foremost a part of the European *ancien régime*. It was a pre-industrialized society, ruled over by a mainly landed elite, in which vertical ties of patronage and clientship were more important than horizontal bonds of shared economic or social position, and in which even popular protest was conducted with the assumptions that underlay the existing social order. It was also, like the rest of Europe, a confessional state, in which religion remained a central aspect of personal and political motivation, and in which differences in religious allegiance were a cause of fundamental conflict …[17]

B. The House of Lords

The other house of the Irish Parliament, the Lords, had about eighty-five resident members, but absenteeism was even more a problem there than in the Commons.[18] Unlike in England, the Lords in Ireland were not the ancient nobility; Catholics could not sit and many members were recent creations for military or political services. The Lords usually supported Dublin Castle because almost one-third of them held high offices, for which they were lavishly compensated; but their insatiable demands for patronage and promotions made them unreliable. The four archbishops and 18 bishops of the Church of Ireland were members of the House of Lords, always present and extremely protective of church privileges, but not uniformly compliant with the wishes of government. Government control, however, was assured through proxy votes of reliable members. The speaker of the Lords was the lord chancellor – from 1789 until the dissolution of the Parliament in 1800, John FitzGibbon, the earl of Clare. The Lords were certain to reject reform legislation not desired by the administration; and its function as a court of final appeal was restored by the 1782 constitutional changes.

16 7 Geo. 3 c. 3. (1761), called the Octennial Act. The death of the sovereign or the sovereign's decision to dissolve Parliament also terminated the existence of a Parliament. (In England, parliaments had had seven-year tenures since the 1715 Septennial Act.)

17 S. J. Connolly, *Religion, law and power: the making of Protestant Ireland, 1660–1760*, p. 2 (1992)

18 See F.G. James, *Lords of the Ascendancy: the Irish House of Lords and its members, 1600–1800* (1995).

IV. THE VICEROY OR LORD LIEUTENANT

The viceroys were very wealthy English nobles – earls or dukes – who were appointed by the British prime minister; before 1767 they were often absentees except for biennial sessions of the Irish Parliament, and were very uncomfortable being absent from the centre of political power in London, despite an annual salary of £20,000.[19]

When the viceroy was absent or had resigned, executive functions were performed by the lords justices – usually the archbishop of Armagh, the lord chancellor and the speaker of the Commons – three nobles representing the Parliament, the law and the established church. Important political decisions were made in London, but communication was difficult and unreliable, especially in winter months, when fierce weather defeated attempts to cross the turbulent Irish Sea. Thus, political reliability was the most important qualification for the viceroy and the lords justices, invariably Englishmen or men of English ancestry.

V. THE MONKS OF THE SCREW

Ten years within the narrow community of Trinity College was not the ideal preparation for a political life, but Browne may have acquired a proper preparation through his membership in the Monks of the Screw, the popular name of the Knights of St Patrick, founded by the lawyer and MP Barry Yelverton in 1779. It was certainly a convivial group that enjoyed good food, witty conversation and great amounts of wine and spirits in gatherings at the former home of the late Lord Tracton on Kevin's Street, Dublin. They met weekly on Saturdays during the four annual terms of the courts.[20] Although the society kept no formal records, it is apparent that the members adhered to general principles that were called Whig or even patriotic. It is likely that this club more closely resembled the London Literary Club of David Garrick[21] than the notorious London Hellfire Club, known formally as the Brotherhood of St Francis of Wycombe.[22] Arthur Browne may have

---

19 See generally C. O'Mahony, *The viceroys of Ireland: an anecdotal review of 700 years*, pp 179–211 (1912).
20 Michaelmas (originally from 29 Sept., later 2–25 Nov.); Hilary (11–31 Jan.), Lent (15 Apr.–8 May) and Trinity (22 May–12 June).
21 David Garrick (1717–79), playwright, producer and actor, a former pupil of Dr Johnson, he acted and managed theaters in London and Dublin.
22 The Brotherhood of St Francis was founded in 1746 by Sir Francis Dashwood at a London tavern, the George and Vulture. The meetings were later transferred to the secluded privacy of his estate at West Wycombe, Medmenham Abbey, in 1752, to perform parodies of the Christian sacraments such as the 'Black Mass' to celebrate Satan and his works amid depraved rites, largely of a sexual nature. Members of the order were noted for debauchery, wealth and high office; they included Lord Sandwich, Lord Oxford, John Wilkes, the Whig politician, and William Hogarth, the satirical painter. (It is likely that Benjamin Franklin and the young prince of Wales, later George IV,

been familiar with a literary group similar to the London Literary Club from his youth in Newport, where there were several similar groups.[23]

The Dublin society of 'monks' was overwhelmingly the resort of lawyers and political men, a grouping that lasted for approximately six years, 1779–85; it was replaced about 1789 by the Whig Club of members of Parliament.[24] Heavy drinking was the custom of the age, even among wealthy professional classes, and unquestionably wine was the major feature of the weekly sessions. Pranks and jokes also must have been prominent. The famous barrister John Philpot Curran was prior and wrote the anthem of the monks, ennobling the joys of the vine. Thomas Davis sought to extol the reputation of the club of the 'wisest, best and most brilliant spirits of Ireland', writing in 1845:

> It was an union of strong souls brought together like electric clouds, by affinity and flashing as they joined. They met and shone and warmed. They had great passions and generous accomplishments, and they, like all that was good in Ireland, were heaving for want of freedom. They were men of wit and pleasure, living in a luxurious state of society, and probably did wild and excessive things. This was reconcilable (in such a state of society) with every virtue of head and heart.[25]

According to Davis,[26] there were 54 members elected and sworn: 36 were lawyers[27] and 24 were members of Parliament;[28] 4 were members of the clergy; 2

attended some of the fashionable proceedings.) The members swore oaths of secrecy, but the notoriety was so great that secrecy was unlikely in the gossip of the London salons. The club broke up in 1762, largely because of political differences. Dublin also had a secret Hell-Fire Club from 1734–49, attracting young officers and nobles to taverns on Dame Street and Corn Hill for debauchery, blasphemy and satanic rites. See G. Ashe, *The Hell-Fire Clubs: a history of anti-morality* (2000). Novelistic treatment was given by F. Van Wyck Mason in *Brimstone Club* (1971), P. Straub in *The Hellfire Club* (1995) and E. Lord in *The Hellfire Clubs* (2008).

23 The Knights of St Patrick (Monks of the Screw) must not be confused with the Order of St Patrick founded in 1783 by George III to be the Irish equivalent of the English Order of the Bath or Order of the Garter; the Order of St Patrick used St Patrick's Cathedral in Dublin for its ceremonies.

24 The Whig Club is discussed in chapter 9.

25 T. Davis, *The life of the Right Hon. J.P. Curran* (1846), p. 26.　　26 Ibid., pp 27–8.

27 Arthur Browne MP, Walter Hussey Burgh MP, Beresford Burton KC, William Caldbeck KC, Tankerville Chamberlayne MP, John Philpot Curran MP, Robert Day MP, Robert Dobbs, William Doyle, James Dunkin, Henry Duquery MP, Temple Emmet, Matthew Finnucane, Richard Fitton, John Forbes MP, Richard Frankland KC, Henry Grattan MP, Thomas Hacket, Francis Hardy MP, Richard Herbert MP, John Hunt, Dudley Hussey MP, Robert Johnson MP, Mocawen, Richard Martin MP, Peter Metge MP, Thomas Muloch, Charles O'Neil KC MP, Joseph Pollock, George Ponsonby MP, William Preston, Charles F. Sheridan MP, Michael Smith MP, William Stawell, Arthur Wolfe MP and Barry Yelverton.

28 Seven members of Parliament who were not lawyers were: Isaac Cory, General John Doyle, Sir Henry Harstonge, Viscount Kingsborough, Sir Edward Newenham, George Ogle and Lt Col. Ross.

were medical men;[29] and 8 were members of the high aristocracy.[30] The membership was more closely connected to the Patriot Party than to the English interest. It already included Volunteers, and would include members of the United Irishmen. Membership in this august group of convivial spirits may not have produced immediate financial benefits or professional advancement, but it surely assisted the unknown American on his path in Dublin society. Certainly a major asset of the club was the fact that when Arthur Browne became a member of Parliament (1783) many of the cabinet of the viceroy (the duke of Portland, a Rockingham Whig appointee) were members of the club: Denis Daly, master general of the muster; Charles F. Sheridan, secretary of war; Barry Yelverton, attorney general; George Ponsonby, counsel to the revenue commissioners; Walter Hussey Burgh, prime serjeant; and Peter Metge, admiralty judge.[31] The duke of Portland subsequently made extraordinary efforts to preserve Browne's appointment as estate agent for the established church.[32]

VI. THE REFORM CLUB

In between the Monks of the Screw (1779–85) and the Whig Club (1789–95) was the loosely structured Reform Club, whose membership included future members of the Whig Club as well as opponents of the Whigs desiring merely moderate reform. It came together at the end of 1784. Reform Club members from the House of Lords included Charlemont, Powerscourt, Bristol and Aldborough. In the Commons, members included Arthur Browne and Lawrence Parsons (the Trinity members). John O'Neill of Antrim, William Brownlow from Ulster, Henry Flood, John Forbes, Sir Edward Newenham and Richard Griffiths were also participants. It was not especially convivial nor did it have a lengthy agenda. Members sought repeal of the hearth tax, reduction of the pension list, restructure of the navigation laws, reform of the tithe and tax on absentee landlords – measures unacceptable to Dublin Castle.[33] It was easily dispatched with the organization of the Whig Club after the regency crisis.

Despite his enthusiastic support of Enlightenment Whig principles, Arthur Browne does not appear to have been involved in Masonic activities. He may have been driven away by republican, agnostic and even anti-Christian sentiments expressed by prominent Masons. Many members of Parliament were part of the secret fraternity in England and Ireland.

29 Edward Hudson MD, also a dentist, and Frederic Jebb MD.
30 George, marquis of Townshend (after serving as viceroy), the earl of Arran, the earl of Carhampton, the earl of Charlemont (general of Volunteers), Viscount Kingsborough and the earl of Mornington.
31 R.D. Kennedy, 'The Irish Whigs, 1782–1789' (MA, University of Kansas, 1961), p. 19.
32 See chapter 7, n. 45.
33 R.D. Kennedy, 'The Irish Whigs, 1789–1793' (PhD, University of Toronto, 1969), pp 25–32.

VII. THE PONSONBYS

A significant factor in Arthur Browne's political career was his attachment to the Ponsonby family, and his contemporary, George Ponsonby. The other member of Parliament from Trinity, Laurence Parsons, was also devoted to the Ponsonby connection. This identification with the Ponsonbys does not mean that Arthur Browne always proceeded in lockstep with them. Notably, he differed from them in 1784, on the issue of the reform of Parliament proposed by Henry Flood,[34] and at the end of the Irish Parliament in 1800, when George Ponsonby led the 1800 rejection of union with Great Britain, and Arthur Browne finally supported it.

George Ponsonby was a principal architect of opposition to Dublin Castle. He also maintained the English Whig connection through his marriage to Elizabeth Cavendish, daughter of the duke of Devonshire; Ponsonby was especially prominent during the brief tenure of Earl Fitzwilliam in 1795. He usually supported measures of Catholic relief, but he was deliberately absent from Parliament from 1797 to 1799, in frustration at the overwhelming government majorities in that revolutionary era. He returned, however, to lead the opposition to the union with Great Britain in 1799.

The Ponsonby faction could normally muster two dozen votes (more or less) from Leinster and Munster,[35] but the effectiveness of the faction came from its ability to build on that support to negotiate temporary coalitions with the other interests in Parliament. Unlike the government, which paid 'up front' for support with jobs, promotions and pensions, the Ponsonbys more subtly traded votes for members' favoured projects.[36]

VIII. WHIG PRINCIPLES

The philosophical differences between the members of Parliament were, broadly, the differences between the supporters of the establishment in church and state (i.e. Dublin Castle), and those whose basic loyalty to the crown favoured reform, but did not extend to projects that might adversely impact the existing social order. Central to the thinking of the latter group, called Whigs in England, America and Ireland,[37] was the idea that good government resulted from a contract between the

---

34 See J. Kelly, *Henry Flood: patriots and politics in eighteenth-century Ireland*, pp 324–67 (1998). The Floods and Ponsonbys were frequently affiliated in local affairs.

35 Kennedy, 'The Irish Whigs', p. 19 (1961).

36 Kennedy, 'The Irish Whigs', pp 36, 47 (1969). The other principle borough owners for the purposes of negotiation were: the earl of Leinster, and lords Clifden, Hillsborough, Loftus and Shannon; they not only negotiated with one another but with Dublin Castle, exchanging support for patronage and promotions.

37 See generally, J. Beckett, *Protestant dissent in Ireland, 1685–1780* (1946); F. James, *Ireland in the Empire, 1688–1770*, pp 80–7 (1973), and O'Brien, *The great melody: a thematic biography of Edmund Burke* (1992). S.J. Connolly, 'Precedent and principle: the patriots and their critics' in S.J. Connolly (ed.) *Political ideas in eighteenth-century Ireland*, pp 130–55 (2000).

ruler and the ruled and that the best safeguard of the liberties of the subject from arbitrary oppression is found in a mixed government of king, Lords and Commons. In Ireland and America they were often called 'patriots'. Unlike the American merchants, lawyers and clergy who were the American Whigs, English and Irish Whigs were wealthy men of the world, dabblers in literature and the arts, sceptics, profligate lovers of food, wine and gossip. These Whig groups saw the liberty of a free people endangered by the 'influence' exerted by the king on the Lords and Commons. They shared a vigorous distrust of the crown. Thus, the common belief in England, America and Ireland was that 'the power of the crown has increased, is increasing and ought to be diminished' in the famous phrase of John Dunning in the English Commons on 6 April 1780.[38] The fact that English and Irish Whigs had similar views with respect to the power of the crown did not mean that they shared the same view with respect to Irish or American independence, which the English Whigs strongly opposed.

Still, they agreed that military force should not be used to impose the will of the English king, Lords and Commons on otherwise loyal subjects. The king's policy towards the American colonies was clearly rejected by Whigs. A strange phenomenon can be observed, however, in the execution of the American war by the general officers of the army, scions of the Whig nobility. It can only be called lacklustre, despite the duty to king and country that brought them to America to suppress armed rebellion. Their performance in the field was riddled with missed opportunities. However, Whig objections to the use of military force changed with events in revolutionary France and Ireland, shattering the unity of Whig opposition in England, America and Ireland.[39]

IX. BROWNE IN THE COMMONS

Unlike some parliamentary bodies, the Irish Parliament permitted undisguised reports of its proceedings – not verbatim but in a paraphrase that must have used some of the exact words and phrases of the speakers. Thus, it is possible to reconstruct the first substantive speeches that Arthur Browne made in Parliament in the 1783–4 session. He spent seventeen years in Parliament, speaking on many different subjects; his speeches on government, religion and civil liberties will be reproduced in this book as recorded in the *Parliamentary Register*, although some changes in punctuation and paragraphing were made to increase comprehension. Some speakers were allowed to improve their speeches for publication, thus it is not always an accurate record. Rules of debate were enforced by the speaker, resulting in curious circumlocutions: members never referred to the viceroy or

38 Dunning, a Shelburne Whig, submitted the resolution, which was carried by a vote of 233 to 215. See C.C. O'Brien, *The great melody*, pp 212–13 (1992).
39 See J. Ehrman, 2 *The younger Pitt: the reluctant transition*, pp 46–260 (1983); K. Feiling, *The second Tory Party, 1714–1832* (1959) and O'Brien, *The great melody*, pp 484–96, 501–3 (1992).

other members by name, and there could be no direct repetition of matters from a previous debate. Bills received three readings before enactment, and could be referred to committees or even the house itself as committee of the whole.

Following his victory on Irish legislative independence, Henry Grattan did not continue to lead a united group in opposition to Dublin Castle[40] – the 1782 victors quarrelled, and a bitter personal feud between Grattan and Henry Flood consumed the talents of a wandering group that could not overcome the 180 votes (more or less) that the administration could muster.[41]

The achievement of Irish parliamentary independence occurred through the combination of circumstances outlined in chapter 4, from the defeat of Cornwallis to the resignation of North and the return of the Rockingham Whigs. The Irish legislation, drafted by Yelverton, effected a simple repeal of Poynings' Law (21 & 22 Geo. 3 C. 47), and Shelburne was responsible for the contemporaneous repeal for the 1720 Declaratory Act (21 & 22 Geo. 3 C. 53), removing the British privy council's control of Irish legislation, but preserving the new empire, united under one crown. Grattan regarded this as British acquiescence in the permanent independence of the Irish Parliament.

During this process, Flood, however, had sought more – a renunciation of the British right to legislate for Ireland. This was probably a move to oust Grattan and regain leadership of the Patriot group. Grattan had opposed the renunciation as an unnecessary insult to Britain, but the idea of renunciation had caught the attention of the Volunteers, and appeared to have popular support. However, after a lengthy debate from 15 to 19 July 1783, Grattan's proposal defeated Flood's.[42] All manner of personal and political insults laced with malice and venom were exchanged, leading to the inevitable challenge on the field of honour. Flood's challenge was accepted by Grattan, and the two (with seconds) met at Blackrock on 30 October 1783. Law officers intervened and no shots were fired, the contestants being bound over to keep the peace on securities of £20,000 each.[43] The fracture of the patriot opposition refreshed the government, and the situation at the opening of the new

---

40 R.B. McDowell, *Grattan: a life* (2001). The legislative history of the post-1782 Irish Parliament is recorded in J. Kelly, *Poynings' Law and the making of law in Ireland, 1660–1800*, pp 36–57 (2007). Henry Grattan (1746–1820), born and raised in Dublin, son of a lawyer and member of Parliament, entered TCD as fellow commoner 1763, AB 1767, called to Bar at Middle Temple 1772, entered the Irish Parliament from the borough of Lord Charlemont 1775. He rapidly became a master of debate and powerful orator who led the effort to repeal Poynings' Law in 1782, having been defeated on several occasions after 1780. Parliament voted a reward of £50,000 to Grattan and he became LLD of TCD. He represented Dublin 1790–7. He returned to Parliament from Wicklow, where he had an estate, Tinnehinch, to oppose the union in 1799. After the union, he served in Westminster from Malton, a pocket borough of Earl Fitzwilliam. He was buried in Westminster Abbey.

41 Kennedy, *The Irish Whigs* (1961).

42 Kelly, *Henry Flood*, pp 317–35 (1998); McDowell, *Grattan*, pp 61–70 (2001); O'Brien, *Anglo-Irish politics in the age of Grattan and Pitt*, pp 55–62 (1987).

43 Kelly, *Flood*, pp 349–54 (1998).

Parliament cooled because Flood was absent, seeking the seat in the British Parliament for Winchester.

Arthur Browne's parliamentary career began on 14 October 1783, but his first major speech was not until 10 November 1783, reviewing the American war that had produced a political upheaval in England, and the independence of the Irish Parliament. Browne's target on this occasion was the augmentation of the standing army of Great Britain stationed in Ireland by the addition of British army veterans of the American War of Independence who had been prisoners of war, surrendered by Burgoyne and Cornwallis in America. Browne's intervention dealt with the need to reduce government spending and his target was the extravagant appropriation for the army:

> Mr *Browne*, of Trinity College, said, he was no party-man, yet declared himself obliged a second time at this early period of the session, to oppose an administration, which was such a determined foe to economy. An administration which not only was about to reject the single plan of retrenchment, which could be effectual, but had lately denied the necessity of any retrenchment at all. – He proved that retrenchment was absolutely necessary, by stating the formidable amount of the national debt, and shewed that as our expenditure exceeded our income by £200,000 per annum, the debt must perpetually increase, as we must borrow that sum every year. The example of England shewed the horrid consequences of an increasing debt, and the present was the best time for us to stifle the monster in its very infancy. He asked, why ministers, instead of abusing our common sense, by asking men to wait for committees of accounts, and committees of supply, to prove what everybody knew, did not think of forming a sinking fund? They could not do this, until they brought our expences below our income, and if they could do so, so as to save even the small sum of £20,000 per annum, even that in less than fifty years would pay off the debt, if the interest saved by the sums paid off was perpetually applied to the discharge of the remaining part of the principal.
>
> He proceeded to shew that retrenchment could be had only in the army establishment: he declared himself an enemy to standing armies: but if they must be, wished at least for a reduction ...[44]

But the army budget proved impregnable, and there was no support for a sinking fund, despite the favourite Whig argument of the need for economy. Browne returned to attack the augmentation in the military budget in prepared remarks:

> Mr *Arthur Browne* – Sir, I do not rise to trouble you with long encomiums on economy, I see plainly that economy is banished from your doors, and it would be folly to expect, that the neglected stranger will ever return. We have

44 2 *Parliamentary Register*, pp 81–2 (10 Nov. 1783).

nothing left but to look on in silent dismay, till the storm which in profusion is gathering, shall burst upon our heads.

But, though destruction will inevitably spring from prodigality, it is still possible to divert its course. Let it at least approach us through some other medium than that of the army; a pestilential medium which has ever been fraught with plagues and mischief – I speak not of armies absolutely necessary to the good of the state; I speak of idle and superfluous armies; of unnecessary augmentation. – I know invectives against standing armies have been so often repeated, that they are become offensive to the fastidiousness of modern ears. But if the truth has not had its effect, it ought to be repeated, and now repeated when it is possible to carry it into practice, and not to terminate is mere declamation. It is not less true, because it has been often, nor would it have been often said if it had not been founded in reason and in nature, and at these solemn pauses, which the constitution has ordained in passing our laws. At these sacred stations which it will not suffer us to pass without looking around us, to see whether we approach the precipice, I hope it will be pardonable to stay a moment where we have stayed before, and see whether the danger is less than it formerly has been.

Let us not deceive ourselves: if a superfluous unemployed army was ever dangerous, it is dangerous still. You have the augmentation now as fairly before you, as you had it in the year 1769; if you again agree to it, the army will go on increasing. – it will always be an object with the crown to increase it and there is no probability that the influence of the crown will ever diminish. The appearance of the times is fallacious. While the American storm raged, and the winds were all abroad, we had a temporary calm from the exertions of power at home; but things will revert to their old channel – It is the nature of power ever to wish to extend itself, and if you do not take this opportunity of curbing it, if you are not jealous of its advances now, you may never be able to impede its progress again.

He then referred to the Volunteers, the world war with France and Spain and the 1782 constitution:

In the midst of a profound peace, you introduce into the country a greater number of troops than were found necessary for its defence in the heat of contest, and that contest against the world in arms. When the territories of Britain are reduced, and her diminished orb shines with but half its former splendor, you support a greater army than was wanted to supply the lustre of her most brilliant day. When your finances are exhausted, and you are oppressed with a cumbrous debt, you maintain a greater peace establishment than when your treasury overflowed. When the spirit of the people is high, and virtue is at hand to assist you in pruning the luxuriance of power, you refuse to lop off that detested augmentation which was generated in the corrupted stream of former times. – It requires neither age, nor wisdom, nor experience to see that this is extraordinary. The people (for liberty is of a jealous nature) will not rest without knowing the cause. They will murmur at being obliged to contribute, not to the necessities of the state, but perhaps to its ruin. They will recollect that in all countries the excessive growth of armies has terminated without exception in the downfall of liberty, and at length of government itself. They will not rest satisfied with the flimsy pretexts which have been offered, not be lulled with soft unmeaning notes of gratitude: What gratitude! ... it is not to the liberality of Britain, but to circumstances, to necessity, to your own virtue, to America, that you owe your advantages. To America your temple and statutes are due, and to that generous patriotism which so ably seconded her at home. Britain was cruel and unjust for a century, and I will never believe that she learned justice and generosity in a day. It has been said, we at least owe her gratitude for opening the trade to the West Indian colonies. I deny it – she tied our hands behind our back, and then boasted she had given us food. If Europe was colonizing we should not have been idle; we should have had our West Indian and American settlements, and as it was, our blood and our treasure contributed to the acquisition and protection of the British colonies; but England alone reaped those crops which were sewn in that blood, and now that they have almost perished, she boasts of having admitted us to some little participation of the blasted fruits.

Browne then continued his denunciation of the war in America, which was lost by this army now thirsting for revenge, not on the enemy, but on the Volunteers, who had been organized to defend the nation while the British army fought in America. Unquestionably, this challenge to the administration (and especially to the attorney general, FitzGibbon) would mark him as a potential enemy, despite three generations of service to the Ascendancy establishment.

Other gentlemen have talked of wars and rumours of war, of wars in the south, and wars in the north, and chilled us with the terrors of an invasion from the frozen zone. They have talked of the Turks and the Tartars. – [Mr Ogle rose to order.] – *Mr Browne* proceeded. – If I have alluded to what passed in a former debate, I must say in excuse, that the order to the contrary has not been strictly observed by the House since I came into it. But, supposing we are in danger of a war, it is not by our navy we are to protect ourselves; this is the first and favourite tenet of the present ministry of England. No force you could raise could cope with the armies of France. It might be formidable to liberty at home, but would be laughed at by the insolent foe ... It might be formidable to scattered individuals falling one by one without union, and without strength, it might be dangerous to a trading nation, where every man poring on the ground does not look up at the encreasing blaze of power, till he is scorched by its rays; but it would never be a match for our foreign enemies. No, if you would really wish to be secure at home, preserve the country in its present state, encourage every man to bear arms, place an unbounded confidence in your people, and they will place an unlimited confidence in you. Imitate the generous policy of our ancestors, who, (you will find it on your statute book) in times of turbulence, when the minds of men were not yet civilized, nor taught to love order and good government, not only encouraged, but obliged every man to bear arms and to learn the use of them. Then with mutual confidence and universal discipline, you would be invincible indeed.

His real target then emerged as the English interest in the Castle:

I have done with the reasons offered by government for this measure; I will now tell them the reasons which the public without doors assign for them. They say, that it is not through fear of a foreign enemy they wish to keep up so large an army, but through fear of their real friends at home. Not through fear of hostile invasion, but through fear of virtue, and liberty, and public spirit; through fear lest these repeated struggles of the people, should at length effectuate, in a constitutional way, a rational reform. Through fear, not of the armies of France, but, it is time to speak plainly, of the Volunteers of Ireland; of those Volunteers whom you so coldly thanked in the beginning for what *they had done*, that it was evident you wished they should do no more. – [Mr FitzGibbon rose to order.] – *Mr Browne* in continuation. – I have a particular objection to the nature of this army, which is coming into the country, it is an American army fraught with slaughter, hostile to every idea of liberty, or rather unable to distinguish liberty from licentiousness. – [Major Doyle rose to order.] – You will have your four thousand men too, whom you sent abroad for their education, and a pretty education they have had. They will return, not as from a foreign foe with glory and patriotic ardour sitting on their crests, but with disappointment, and revenge, and depredation painted on their faded banners.

Let the profusion take any other shape than this. Divide your revenue board again, you would but add six men to those who might possibly distinguish your own interest from those of their country. Augment your band of pensioners, the drones cannot sting us. The eve of our declining day may retain its lustre. We may set like the tropical sun at once in night, without that long and lingering twilight, in which we now seem doomed to wander. We might wear the fair face of liberty to the last, and appear majestic though in ruin.

Sir, I speak not of chimaeras, or phantoms of my own brain; it is not more certain that empire hastens to decay, than that its ruin will be accelerated by a great national debt, and an increasing army; the calamity may not come today or tomorrow, it may not come upon the present generation, but it will come upon posterity, and the remedy will be out of their power. If there is any man mean enough to be regardless of the future generation, he may perhaps pass quietly through his own times. But this was not the care our ancestors took of us; they raised bulwarks sufficient to defend us, though almost virtue's self was dead. Every man who has a spark of heavenly flame about him will follow their example. You will never have such another opportunity. The spirit of your people will never be more high; the crown will never be more dependent on Parliament; you will never have another American war, and if you are silent now, you may be silent forever.[45]

The opposition was divided, the administration easily overcame Browne's objections and the army establishment was enlarged.

It must have been a challenge for Browne to remain circumspect about the war in America while in London (1777–80) in the presence of rabid supporters of it – both Tory and Whig. By 1783 a peace treaty had been signed, and he could speak in Parliament publicly about the failed war, but hatreds like those of Samuel Johnson and the high Tories lingered. Browne's reflections on Johnson's hatreds were not published until 1798, long after Johnson's death in 1784. By reason of Johnson's blast, 'I love all mankind except an American', or his description of Americans as, 'a race of convicts, and ought to be thankful for anything we allow them short of hanging', the description from Boswell of Dr Johnson as, 'in religion a bigot, in politics a tyrant and in manners a barbarian' would not have been too harsh and virulent from one 'who loves that country, which happens to be the situation of the author [Browne] who there spent his earliest and his happiest days'.[46]

Efforts to reform Parliament by reducing the powers of the great borough patrons remained underground during the American war and its aftermath, but with the new independence of the Irish Parliament, they re-emerged in bright sunlight, although Prime Minister Pitt was not ready to confront the issue and his lords lieutenant had been ordered to suppress it.

Browne's next substantive intervention concerned the narrow procedural issue of requesting leave for the introduction of the reform bill of Henry Flood, vigorously opposed by the administration, already exhausted by threats of reform. Grattan's personal enmity of Flood brought him to the side of the administration, but Browne and most of the Monks supported Flood's reform bill.[47]

The circumstances were very dramatic. The national Volunteers convention assembled on 10 November 1783 in the Rotunda Assembly with Lord Charlemont as chairman. Flood had returned from England and presented a plan for reform of Parliament to the delegates. (It is unknown whether Browne and other MPs who were members of Volunteers units attended, but both Grattan and Flood were officers in the Volunteers.) After three weeks, the convention approved Flood's plan of reform, which he, in Volunteers uniform, conveyed in a march of Volunteers to the House of Commons on Saturday, 29 November. Grattan was very uneasy about this method of presentation from an armed body of men to the unarmed Parliament, and Yelverton was totally opposed to receipt of the bill. Debate on

45 2 *Parliamentary Debates*, pp 99–102 (10 Nov. 1783).
46 A. Browne, *Miscellaneous sketches*, pp 69–70, 77 (1798).
47 O'Brien, *Anglo-Irish politics in the age of Grattan and Pitt*, pp 92–4 (1987).

leave to introduce the bill continued through that afternoon and until 3 a.m. on Sunday, 30 November, when it was denied.

Mr *Browne* (of the College) declared, the question came upon him unexpectedly; however he could not bear to be silent upon so grand an occasion. He could not endure the thought, that while the great names who offered the bill, floated down the stream of time, his little bark should not be seen to pursue the triumph.

The question is magnificent and simple; it is whether you will receive a bill of the first magnitude, introduced by the first men in the House? A bill which professed to restore the constitution to its pristine vigour, and that beauty with which it appears in theory and in history, which proffers to add sinews to virtue, and perpetuity to liberty. It seems to be the messenger of glad tidings. It bears a promising countenance ... We ought to receive it, even if its garb was a little exceptionable; but it is not; it approaches you in the robes of decency, with the modesty and firmness of determined virtue. It does not enter these walls with force; but it is met with violence. I have seen no violence this night, but on the part of administration.

He then dipped into history (the Stuarts):

No man, he said, had pretended to say, that a reform was not necessary; one gentleman had indeed asserted, that no instance could be produced of a contest between Parliament and the crown, where Parliament had not been victorious. But where could an instance be produced of such a contest of late years? The prevailing influence of the crown was too great to allow of such a contest; and where there was no contest, there could be no victory. In the last century there was a contest; and why? Because influence did not exist; but the phrenzy of administration had conjured up terrific forms, which no man in his sober senses could see. They were not afraid of Volunteers when we seemed to be on the eve of a quarrel with England; or when those Volunteers were raising the gentlemen, who now supported government, into consequence.

Gentlemen had intimated that there was a French influence at the bottom of the measure; if they meant that the proposers were conscious of it, it was a charge of high treason, and ought to be made in a solemn manner; if they supposed them to be dupes, he had too good an opinion of the abilities of the proposers, to pay credit to such a ridiculous assertion.

It had been said, it appeared from late events, Parliament had not been corrupt, and therefore a reform was not to be sought, i.e., a reform was not to be sought when Parliament was virtuous, and it was possible to acquire it; but the pursuit ought to be deferred till Parliament was notoriously corrupt, and there was no chance of succeeding in the attempt.

Gentlemen have talked of spurning the bill. It was not parliamentary or decent language, especially when the bill was introduced by the first men in the House. He was sure those who spurned it, treated virtue with contumely. They said to corruption, live for ever: what they said to their country, that country must judge.[48]

Fifty of the 182 members present spoke on the bill, but oratory alone could not overcome the power of administration. The motion was lost on a vote of 77 to 157. It had become clear that the Irish Parliament could not reform itself.

CHAPTER SIX

Teaching and practising the law
(1784–1805)

I. TEACHING THE LAW

IN 1782, A PAMPHLET APPEARED BY an anonymous author entitled *Thoughts on the present state of the College of Dublin addressed to the gentlemen of the university*. One library copy attributed it to Arthur Browne, while another copy attributed it to Revd Dr John Forsayeth, who had been Arthur Browne's sponsor in 1772 and was the classmate of Browne's father. In 1782, Browne had been junior fellow for five years, responsible for observing, encouraging and advising students. The likelihood of Browne's authorship may be confirmed by a letter he wrote to fellow TCD alumnus Edmund Burke on 3 May 1782, coyly acknowledging the pamphlet, without a specific admission.[1]

The pamphlet exults in the superior preparation Irish students receive because of the method of instruction:

> The Irish [student] is obliged to prosecute his studies during four years and upwards. He is periodically and frequently examined with great strictness. His merits and progress in Science are made public by judgments openly delivered. Shame and honour combine to spur on youthful emulation. He has the previous advantages of public and private lectures, where the knowledge he has acquired in his chamber is scrutinized, the assistance he wants is afforded, the mistakes he falls into are discovered and corrected.
> (pp 33–4)

The pamphlet rejoiced in the recent recognition of the independence of the Irish Parliament and its liberating effect on the (Protestant) nation, but then asked why that rejuvenation had not been felt in Trinity College. His praise of new political freedom from the restraints of Poynings' Law reflected his consistently rosy view of the Irish Parliament until the aftermath of the 1798 Revolution caused him to support its suppression.

---

1   In the Sheffield Archive collection of Burke's papers, once possessed by Earl Fitzwilliam, see WWM/BKP 1/1630. I am indebted to Dr S.P. Donlan of NUI Limerick for reference to the correspondence of Arthur Browne with Edmund Burke.

The sun of freedom had shone suddenly in the midst of darkness. Ye were dazzled by his rays, and could not distinctly discern every part of the glorious prospect before you. Animated by that generous ardour, which characterizes the natives of this country, ye disregarded the weight of your own concerns, while the fate of the kingdom was in the balance. But now, that all those great questions which agitated the nation have been discussed, and the ferment they occasioned has terminated in a success, though not equal to our wishes, yet sufficient to shew the utility of exertion; it behoves you to reflect on the injuries which the university hath sustained in the general calamity, and to remind the nation, that the mischiefs which affect it, are of great and universal concern.

The author then deplored the loss of prestige of TCD because of the absence of research and publication by the faculty, whose despondency and silence was caused by poverty, the result of governmental 'neglect and indifference approaching nearly to contempt'.

The problems of Trinity's faculty began with the amount of time and effort needed to achieve success in the examination for fellowship – wherein two-thirds of the candidates were unsuccessful. Yet, the successful fellow must become a full-time tutor of undergraduates to survive sixteen to twenty years of tutorial drudgery before achieving the status of senior fellow, when the financial benefits come along with oppressive managerial responsibilities. Furthermore, these scholars could not compete for the highest office (provost) because it was reserved for political favourites (p. 18).

The despondency and indifference of students could be attributed to a lack of opportunities that had been caused by the wretched state of trade and manufacturing imposed by the colonial master (p. 24). Even potential clergy had reduced expectations because strangers came over to gobble up the livings (p. 23 and 26). Looking to the law, he found it to be overstocked by lawyers without clients (p. 25). Nevertheless, collegiate experience can be valuable, 'sifted by all these trials, it is impossible that even the dullest or most indolent man should leave the college without a considerable degree of real and useful information' (p. 34).

II. ADMIRALTY AND CIVIL LAW

Arthur Browne's teaching career at Trinity College lasted for twenty years (1785–1805), during which time he also maintained an active practice in his civil law specialties and served in Parliament for seventeen years. After about twelve years of teaching Trinity students, he published his lectures as texts that would long outlive him on both sides of the Atlantic.

Arthur Browne's treatise, *A compendious view of the civil law and of the law of the admiralty,*[2] is in two volumes: the first, dedicated to his colleagues at Trinity

2 Vol. 1 was published in Dublin in 1797; vol. 2 followed in 1799. A revised and enlarged edition of

College, deals with the civil law, that is, the Roman law of Justinian's Corpus Juris Civilis, and proceeds from there into canon law.[3] The Corpus Juris Civilis (AD534) was prepared by a committee of ten scholars under the minister of justice, Tribonian, at the order of Emperor Justinian I (AD483–565) in the years AD528–34 at Constantinople. It is made up of four books: the Institutes, a treatise on law for beginning law students put together from the works of three earlier scholars, Gaius, Ulpian and Paulus; the Digest or Pandects, an authoritative compilation of those elements of a thousand years of Roman jurisprudence from the kings, the republic and the caesars regarded as still operative in AD534; the Code (or Codex Iustinianeus), a collection of older imperial decrees having the force of law in AD534; and the Novellae or Novels, the new legislation (154 sections) of the Emperor Justinian. The Corpus was in Greek (the language of the eastern empire), but was translated into Latin for use in the west; fourteen additional statutes were added by Justinian's successors. Browne's second volume, dedicated to Sir William Scott,[4] deals with the law of nations and the law of admiralty, Browne's specialties in practice. Its purpose was to provide the analytical tools for practitioners and judges in this esoteric specialty.

both volumes appeared in London in 1802–3. This second edition was used in teaching admiralty at American law schools, and was often cited by the Supreme Court. An American edition (allegedly 'with great additions') was released in 1840 by Halsted & Voorhies, a company of law booksellers located at the corner of Nassau and Cedar streets in New York City. The American edition is essentially a copy of the 1802–3 London edition. If there were 'great additions' it was in the changes made by Arthur Browne for the London edition. No changes seem to have been made by the publisher in the 1840 New York edition, despite the differences in legal systems. All citations in this book are to the London edition of Browne's work. The copy of the second (London) edition of Arthur Browne's admiralty text now in the Library of Congress was once owned by Thomas Jefferson, who purchased it in 1805 from the Philadelphia bookseller Patrick Byrne. After the Library of Congress was burnt by British soldiers on 14 Aug. 1814, Jefferson sold a large portion of his personal library in May 1815 to the United States to restock it. Allibone's *Critical dictionary of English literature* (1872) quotes earlier reviewers: 'His work has been deservedly popular, both on account of the learning, solidity and accuracy of his research, and because it is the best book in the language showing the connexion between the common law and the civil law ... It is often cited and always with respect,' vol. 1, p. 261.

3 An English translation of the work by S.P. Scott (1932) runs to 2,342 pages. See generally H.J. Berman, 'The origins of Western legal science', 90 *Harv. L. Rev.*, 894 (1977), and M. Cappelletti, H. Merryman and J. Perillo, *The Italian legal system*, pp 14–22 (1967). For the influence of Arthur Browne upon the civil law in America, see Stein, 'The attraction of the civil law in post-revolutionary America', 52 *Va. L. Rev.*, 403, 407, 425 (1966). See also S.P. Donlan, 'The debt is forgotten: a compendious view of Arthur Browne, *c.*1756–1805', 13:3 *Electronic Journal of Comparative Law* (Sept. 2009).

4 William Scott did not become a peer until 1821. As a result, he was still Sir William Scott at the time Browne penned his dedication; a biographical note on Scott may be found in the introduction. In a note preceding the history of admiralty, Browne wrote, 'The author begs that he may not be accused of plagiarism, if on controversial questions he has adopted the very words of Lord Mansfield, and Sir William Scott, even at considerable length. Where can the reader tread so safely as in the footsteps of those most celebrated men, to vary from whose very modes of expression, when they can be had, would be miserable affection of novelty, with total disregard of unity?'

The inclusion of all these subjects in a single work reflects the existing court structure in England, where doctors' commons and its membership – judges, advocates (barristers) and proctors (solicitors) – had a monopoly on those parts of the law with Roman or civil-law roots and without any common law tradition.[5] Thus, the members of doctors' commons practised in the courts dealing with probate and the interpretation of wills, matrimonial disputes and divorce, property disputes and the discipline of the clergy of the established church, and the law of admiralty. There was no formal doctors' commons in Ireland, but there was a specialized Bar whose members practised in the equivalent courts based on Roman law, separate from the courts of common law.

Arthur Browne defined his methodology as 'the method and order adopted by Mr Justice Blackstone … as nearly as the spirit of the two laws would possibly allow'.[6] William Blackstone published his commentaries on the canon laws of England in four volumes from 1763 to 1769, and even twenty-eight years later, when Arthur Browne was writing, that seminal treatise was still reverberating around the English legal world, perhaps in the same way that six centuries earlier, the discovery of the complete but long-lost Corpus Juris Civilis had 'exploded' on the scholars of the Middle Ages, and, by its methodology, changed the law of Western Europe for all time.

The portion of Browne's text devoted to admiralty proceeded, after Blackstone's analysis, 'to mark the great sources of the law of the admiralty in civil law'.[7] Defending his combination of civil law with admiralty law in a single treatise, Browne wrote that 'all our principles' are derived from the laws of Rome, listing the nature and effects of contracts; of masters and mariners: general average and contribution; collision of ships; shipwrecks and hypothecations. He also noted that admiralty practice was unintelligible without knowledge of the civil law, since the court of admiralty 'always proceeds according to the rules of the civil law, except in cases omitted'.[8]

A. Historical basis and summary

The work begins with speculation on the origin of the office of the lord high admiral[9] and the court established under that office.[10] It examines the Roman

5   See G. Squibb, *Doctors' commons: a history of the College of Advocates and Doctors of Law* (1977), and F. Wiswall, *The development of admiralty jurisdiction since 1800: an English study with American comparisons* (1970).

6   1 Browne, n. 2, p. iii.   7   2 Browne, p. vi.   8   Ibid., p. 507.

9   Ibid., pp 23–6. The first lord high admiral, according to Browne, may have been appointed by King John (about 1200), although some of the authorities cited by Browne and later scholars date the first appointment from 1272, in the reign of Edward I. Holdsworth believes the first mention of an admiral was in 1295. See W. Holdsworth, 1 *A history of English law*, p. 544 (2nd ed. 1937).

10   2 Browne, p. 28. Deputies of the lord high admiral were judges of the court from its earliest days. The admiral was usually a powerful baron surrounded by clerical advisors and assistants. See also authorities cited in Sweeney, 'The Silver Oar and other maces of the admiralty: admiralty jurisdiction in America and the British empire', 38 *J. Mar. L. & Comm.*, 159 (2007).

law[11] and the Rhodian law[12] before reviewing briefly the other authorities known at that time in Western Europe, such as the laws of Oléron,[13] the Consolato del Mar of Barcelona,[14] the laws of Visby[15] and the Black Book of the Admiralty (the source book for England).[16]

Under the first title, 'Perquisites of the admiralty court', there is a discussion of governmental rights in shipwrecks. Then the general title 'Jurisdiction of the instance court' examines both contract jurisdictions, including charter parties, bills of lading and seamen, and tort jurisdiction, including property rights in ships. A second chapter on the instance court deals with traditional maritime institutions: owners, masters and mariners; cargo carriage; general average; and rights of security in ships.

11 2 Browne, pp 34–8. Roman law is described as 'sterile'. Ibid., p. 38. After referring to the Lex Aquilia and parts of the Pandects and Code, Browne summarizes its provisions: the ship and shipowner are liable for the master's contracts, ibid., p. 35; fault liability applies in collisions except in cases of 'accident', ibid., p. 36; and the shipowner is liable for any loss of cargo (merchandise) and passengers' effects unless occasioned by shipwreck or pirates or any other causes which the civil law includes under *vis major*, ibid., p. 37.

12 Ibid., pp 38–9. The Rhodian law is described as the earliest sea laws of which any traces now exist, ibid., p. 38. Scholars remain divided about the authenticity and content of Rhodian law. See W. Ashburner (ed.), *The Rhodian sea law* (1909); Benedict, 'The historical position of the Rhodian law', 18 *Yale L. J.*, 223 (1909); F. Sanborn, *Origins of the early English maritime and commercial law* (1930); Lobingier, 'The maritime law of Rome', 47 *Jurid. Rev.*, 1 (1935); and Gormley, 'The development of the Rhodian-Roman maritime law to 1681, with special emphasis on the problem of collision', 3 *Inter-Am. L. Rev.*, 317 (1961).

13 Browne at pp 39–40 (reproduced at 30 F. Cas. 1171). The laws of Oléron allegedly were promulgated during the time of Eleanor of Aquitaine (1122–1204), who served as duchess of the region that included the port of Oléron at the mouth of the Gironde or Garonne river. Eleanor was married in turn to King Louis VIII of France (1137–52) and King Henry II of England (1152–89), establishing the legend that the laws of Oléron, produced by the clerics who administered her court, were the foundation of maritime law in France and England. See generally Stinson, 'Admiralty and maritime jurisdiction of the courts of Great Britain, France and the United States', 16 *Nw. U. L. Rev.*, 1 (1921), and Runyan, 'Rolls of Oléron and the admiralty court in fourteenth-century England', 19 *Am. J. Legal Hist.*, 95 (1975).

14 2 Browne, p. 41. A translation of the Consolato del Mar of Barcelona (thirteenth century?) can be found in S. Jados, *Consulate of the sea and related documents* (1975). See also Smith, 'The *Llibre del consolat de mar*: a bibliography', 33 *L. Lib. J.*, 387 (1940). Its provisions for shipowners' liability for damage done to the cargo by rats is notable: 'Art. 68 If any merchandise or cargo is damaged by rats while aboard a vessel, and the patron has failed to provide a cat to protect it from rats, he shall pay the damage … if there were cats aboard the vessel while it was being loaded, but during the journey these cats died and the rats damaged the cargo before the vessel reached a port where the patron of the vessel could purchase additional cats; [but] if the patron of the vessel purchases and puts aboard cats at the first port of call where such cats can be purchased, he cannot be held responsible for the damages …'

15 2 Browne, pp 39–41. The code of Visby, part of the 500-year-old Hanseatic League of German merchants in northern European cities reaching from London to Novgorod, is reproduced at 30 F. Cas. 1189. (Visby is a walled city in the Swedish island of Gotland, south of Stockholm.)

16 2 Browne, p. 42. The Black Book of the Admiralty is not a text but rather a compilation of sources for use by admiralty judges and practitioners. Sir Travers Twiss published it in four volumes in 1871.

A lengthy analysis of the prize court and the law of prize follows. Prize law had again become very active with the outbreak of the war with revolutionary France in 1793 and would continue to be until the cessation of the Napoleonic Wars in 1815. It was important in the American Civil War (1861–5), but has been used infrequently since then.

Court practice occupies the remaining first third of the work, beginning with an historical essay on practice in the Roman courts followed by an examination of practice in the instance court, the prize court, the criminal jurisdiction and the operations of the colonial vice admiralty courts, which customarily had a wider jurisdiction than the admiralty court in England.[17]

Browne briefly discussed the admiralty court of the Kingdom of Scotland, which also had a wider jurisdiction than England's[18] over 'the seas, fresh water within flood and mark and in all harbours and creeks'. This court also had jurisdiction in 'mercantile causes, even where they are not strictly maritime'. However, the statutory union with England in 1707 seems to have ended that court, admiralty jurisdiction thereafter being under the court of session or the lord high admiral (or the commissioners) of Great Britain respecting prize.[19]

Ireland had no lord high admiral, but Browne noted the existence 'from time immemorial of an instance court of admiralty'.[20] The Irish admiralty court was put upon a new independent footing in 1783, and by Article 8 of the 1801 Act of Union with Great Britain, the instance court for causes civil and maritime only was to continue, with appeals to the Irish court of chancery.[21]

B. Perquisites of Admiralty

Chapter III, on the 'Perquisites of the admiralty', deals mostly with the rights of the government in wartime (prize droits). The American edition of 1840 made no substantive changes in this chapter even though the rights of the crown were inapplicable.

---

17 Ibid., pp 490–5. See C. Ubbelhode, *The vice admiralty courts and the American Revolution* (1960). See also Owen, 'Admiralty practices in the 19th century', 13 *J. Mar. L. & Comm.*, 147 (1982). Admirers of the Aubry/Maturin novels of Patrick O'Brian will appreciate the colloquy between Dr Stephen Maturin and the deputy judge advocate at Gibraltar: '… Stephen asked him how, in naval courts, a suit for tyranny and oppression might be instituted in cases of extreme disparity of rank … whether the matter would have to be referred to the high court of admiralty, the privy council or the regent himself. "Why, sir … if the persecution were tortious and if it happened at sea, or even on fresh water or reasonably damp land, the admiralty court would no doubt have cognizance." "Pray, sir … just how damp would the land have to be?" "Oh, pretty damp, pretty damp, I believe. The judge's patent gives him power to deal with matters in, upon, or by the sea, or public streams, or freshwater ports, rivers, nooks and places between the ebb and flow of the tide, and upon the shores and banks adjacent – all tolerably humid."' P. O'Brian, *The far side of the world*, p. 51 (1984).

18 2 Browne, p. 30.   19 Ibid.

20 Ibid. Before construction of the Four Courts, it sat in the Apse area of Christ Church Cathedral.

21 Ibid., p. 32. See K.J. Costello, *The court of admiralty of Ireland, 1575–1893*, pp 172–85 (2011).

The civil droits are flotsam,[22] jetsam[23] and lagan,[24] referring to the ship's cargo or passengers' goods; wrecks (i.e., the ship herself);[25] and derelicts[26] and deodands.[27]

The disputes between the lord high admiral and the crown in Browne's time ceased with the transfer of these prize funds to the exchequer and the royal navy (prize law now being codified by statutes under the jurisdiction of a naval tribunal).[28] In the United States, however, the situation is more complex.[29] Most of Browne's chapter III on the perquisites of admiralty is today of historical interest only, as the principal controversy is now forgotten. That involved a

22 Ibid., p. 50. When goods (cargo or passengers' effects) are thrown (or jettisoned) into the sea in order to lighten a ship imperiled by storm and they continue to float they are called flotsam.

23 Ibid. Similar to flotsam, but the goods sink and remain under water.

24 Ibid. 'Lagan' (or 'ligan') is the word used to describe goods which, under circumstances similar to flotsam and jetsam, are jettisoned voluntarily but are tied to a buoy so as to be recovered when the storm ceases.

25 2 Browne, p. 46, distinguishes the common-law definition ('such goods as, after a shipwreck, are cast upon the land by the sea, and left there within some county'), from the admiralty definition of 'wreck at sea' ('a ship totally disabled by the force of a tempest at sea, though she doth not founder, and though one or two of her crew may have been by accident left behind, so that she is not a derelict, and being a whole ship and not a fragment, is not usually called flotsam, it is commonly called a wreck'), p. 49. His summary of the distinction is, 'floating wreck while the tide is in, is in the admiralty; stranded wreck when the tide is out, is in the king'.

26 Ibid., p. 51. Meaning 'boats or vessels forsaken or found on the sea without any person in them'.

27 Ibid., p. 56. Meaning 'things instrumental to the death of a man on shipboard, or goods found on a dead body cast on shore'.

28 See the 1948 Prize Act, 12 and 13 Geo. 6 c. 9. See generally C. Colombos, *The international law of the sea*, pp 747–56 (6th ed. 1965).

29 There is a federal-state controversy in the United States. A federal government under the second continental congress (1775–81) existed before the independent states ceased to be royal colonies. Some coastal states asserted their title to rights in the sea in devolution from the crown of Great Britain before the federal constitution (1787) and establishment of the federal government in 1789. Although case law asserted federal rights, the United States did not assert inherent rights from the British crown until 1978, when the federal government's assertions were rejected by the court of appeals in Treasure Salvors, Inc. v. Unidentified Wrecked and Abandoned Sailing Vessel, 569 F. 2d 330 (5th Cir. 1978). See The Siren, 80 US (13 Wall.) 389 (1871), a claim of prize by the crew of a Union naval vessel against a Confederate blockade runner scuttled and fired by her crew on the day Charleston surrendered to Union forces. The district court rejected the claim for prize, a decision that was later affirmed by the Supreme Court. In the course of the opinion, Justice Swayne wrote: 'In our jurisprudence there are, strictly speaking, no droits of admiralty. The United States have succeeded to the right of the crown. No one can have any rights or interests in any prize except by their grant or permission. All captures made without their express authority enure ipso facto to their benefit (at 393).' Much later, Justice Sutherland found the source of the foreign-relations powers of the United States (and the president as the sole organ of foreign policy) outside the constitution, in the devolution of international sovereignty from George III to George Washington. See Curtiss-Wright Export Corp. v. United States, 299 US 304 (1936). Justice Sutherland's historical theory has not stood up to critical analysis. See Levitan, 'The foreign relations power: an analysis of Mr Justice Sutherland's theory', 55 *Yale L. J.*, p. 467 (1946); Lofgren, 'United States v. Curtiss-Wright Export Corporation: an historical assessment', 83 *Yale*

struggle between the rights of the lord high admiral and his court (rights originating in a grant from the king to the lord high admiral) versus the rights of the king '*jure coronae*', the inherent rights of kingship without the intervention of the admiralty court. Even in Browne's time there was no longer an individual with the title of lord high admiral, the office being administered by commissioners.[30]

In this controversy and in the subsequent questions about maritime-contract jurisdiction, Browne was required to trace the problem back to a 1389 statute limiting the jurisdiction of the admiralty court to things done upon the sea, as well as a subsequent statute restating that admiralty was not to deal with things within the body of the counties.[31] Browne therefore distinguished between wrecks of the sea coming to land and thereby becoming subject to the king's prerogative rights, and wrecks of the sea, still at sea, and thus within admiralty jurisdiction.[32]

Browne then proceeds to an analysis of contract and tort, the traditional English analysis of obligations arising from agreement or by operation of law.

L. *J.*, 1 (1973); and L. Henkin, *Foreign affairs and the constitution*, pp 19–26 (1972). Congress subsequently legislated on the subject, asserting federal supremacy, see Archaeological Resources Protection Act, 16 USC. § 470aa (1979), the Marine Sanctuaries Research and Protection Act, 16 USC. §1431–9 (1983), but the Abandoned Shipwreck Act, 43 USC. 2101–6 (1986) has returned abandoned shipwrecks to state jurisdiction. See Giesecke, 'The Abandoned Shipwreck Act: affirming the role of the state in historic preservation', 12 *Colum.-VLA J.L. & Arts*, 379 (1988) and Sweeney, 'An overview of commercial salvage principles in the context of marine archaeology', 30 *J. Mar. L. & Comm*, 185 (1999).

30 The commissioners for executing the office of lord high admiral were appointed in 1673 under Charles II when his Roman Catholic brother (later James II) was excluded from holding the admiral's office because of his failure to comply with the Test Act (to receive the Holy Eucharist according to the rites of the Church of England). Since the Hanoverian succession (1714), the office has been held by commissioners. See 2 Browne, pp 32–3. In 1964, when the admiralty became part of the department of defence, the title lord high admiral was offered to and assumed by Queen Elizabeth II.

31 2 Browne, pp 46–7, 79, 86, 91–3. The 1389 statute, 13 Rich. 2 c. 5, dealing with 'thing(s) done upon the sea', was followed two years later to specify 'all manner of contracts, pleas and quarrels and all other things rising within the bodies of the counties'. See 15 Rich. 2 c. 3. The political background remains uncertain. Richard II (1367–1400) succeeded his grandfather in 1377 as a boy of 10 (subject to control by regents until 1389). One of the weakest of England's kings, he was badly advised by unpopular favourites and clashed repeatedly with Parliament. Following the Black Death, the country suffered very hard times, leading to the Peasants' Revolt of 1381 under Wat Tyler, which was suppressed with great bloodshed. Henry of Lancaster (later Henry IV) captured King Richard II, who was subsequently deposed by Parliament in 1399 and murdered by his jailers at Pontefract Castle. See G. Trevelyan, *England in the age of Wycliffe* (1909).

32 2 Browne, pp 48–9. In 1873 the jurisdiction of the admiralty court in the United Kingdom was freed from this medieval restriction on its jurisdiction after a series of exceptions by nineteenth-century parliaments. See 3 and 4 Vict. c. 65 (1840); 9 and 10 Vict. c. 99 (1846); 13 and 14 Vict. c. 26 (1850); 17 and 18 Vict. c. 104 (1854); 24 Vict. c. 10 (1861); and 31 and 32 Vict. c. 17 (1868). All were enacted before the transfer of the admiralty court to the probate, admiralty and divorce division of the high court of justice by the Judicature Act, 1873. The connection to Roman law was broken in 1970 by the reassignment of the admiralty court to queen's bench. See further Wiswall, *The development of admiralty jurisdiction since 1800* (1970), and Fitzgerald, 'Admiralty and prize

C. Contracts at Sea

Browne began with sources: 'The instance court is governed by the civil law, the laws of Oléron, and the customs of the admiralty, modified by statute law.'[33] Closer to his own time were the controversies of the seventeenth century between the admiralty court and the common law courts (king's bench, common pleas and exchequer),[34] wherein by writ of prohibition Edward Coke,[35] chief justice of the court of common pleas, sought to limit admiralty jurisdiction to the high seas by the statutes of Richard II.[36] The reasons for this struggle remain unclear: possibly it was due to a high-minded effort to preserve Anglo-Saxon jury trial against Roman inquisitorial practices (the courts of doctors' commons found facts by judge alone). The other possibility is less high-minded: a quarrel over fees. The consequence was that Browne had to deal with the residue of two hundred years of skirmishing between common law and admiralty that had produced much confusion in English case law and that has been repeated in the United States from the nineteenth century up to the present.[37]

A statute of Henry VIII[38] enlarged admiralty jurisdiction to include cargo damage, charter parties, general average, marine insurance, seaworthiness and negligent navigation of vessels, and bills of exchange, as well as all contracts made abroad, thereby confirming a 'maritime' jurisdiction similar to Continental practice.[39] But Lord Chief Justice Coke's prohibitions overcame even this statute, and, despite the general language of the Tudor statute, its terms were interpreted

jurisdiction in the British Commonwealth of Nations', 60 *Jurid. Rev.*, 106 (1948). See also Jackson, 'Admiralty jurisdiction – the Supreme Court Act of 1981', *LMCLQ*, 236 (1982).

33 2 Browne, p. 29. Admiralty appeals were to 'the king in chancery, who appointed delegates by commission to hear and determine it'. Ibid., pp 29–30.

34 King's bench descended from the king's personal administration of justice in the *curia regis*, with extensive criminal and civil jurisdiction after 1066. Common pleas had extensive real-estate jurisdiction but became, after 1178, the court for the trial of civil actions between individual subjects. Exchequer was originally a court in the royal treasury and later, by fictitious pleading, a court for civil actions between individual subjects (after 1154). See T. Plucknett, *A concise history of the common law*, pp 139–56 (5th ed. 1956).

35 Edward Coke (1552–1634) served as solicitor general (1592), attorney general (1594), chief justice – common pleas (1606), and was imprisoned in 1622 for opposition to royal prerogative. He favoured the law courts against other courts of royal prerogative, such as admiralty and chancery. See generally Holdsworth, *A history of English law*, vol. 2, pp 553–6 (3rd ed., 1922), and Mathiason, 'Some problems of admiralty jurisdiction in the 17th century', 2 *Am. J. Legal Hist.*, 215 (1958).

36 Plucknett, *A concise history of the common law*, pp 662–4 (1956). See 2 Browne, p. 1.

37 New Jersey Steam Navigation Co. v. Merchant's Bank of Boston, The Lexington, 47 US (6 How.) 344 (1848). See Sweeney, '*The Lexington*' 38 *J. Mar. L. & Comm.*, 65 (2008). On circuit, Justice Story had failed to apply the statutes of Richard II in DeLovio v. Boit, 7 Fed. Cas. 418 (No. 3,776) (C.C.D. Mass. 1815).

38 2 Browne, p. 28. Henry VIII was the first English king to claim the title king of Ireland, from 1541.

39 See generally J. Wigmore, 3 *A panorama of the world's legal systems*, pp 881–929 (1928), and E. Gold, *Maritime transport*, pp 18–30 (1981).

as being subject to the statutes of Richard II.[40] Accordingly, Browne was required to define marine contracts as 'contracts made on the sea,[41] whose consideration is maritime, and not ratified by deed[42] nor under seal'.[43]

Browne then reviewed the fictitious pleadings used to bring cases into admiralty despite the location of the making of the contract being on land, as well as the fictions used to force disputes arising at sea into the common law courts.[44] Browne contradicted the doctrine of the law courts that a contract truly made at sea lost admiralty jurisdiction if the execution of the contract was to be on land, using the example of a master obtaining necessaries while at sea by promising to pay money on land.[45]

Without concern for inconsistency he took up the question of the practice of the admiralty court in cases of suppliers (materialmen) where the tackle, furniture and provisions were clearly for use at sea, though the contract was made on land. This and other special examples (bills of lading, charters, and marine insurance) led Browne to conclude that 'all contracts which relate purely to marine affairs'[46] should be cognizable in admiralty, especially because of the ease and speed of the *in rem* process of the admiralty court, whereby the vessel is arrested and can be held liable and even sold to compensate the claimant (whose claims may have been ignored by distant owners).

In America, Justice Story clearly followed Browne's conclusion 'that the subject matter and not locality should determine the jurisdiction as to contracts'.[47] American courts – including the Supreme Court[48] – have added exceptions to Story's conceptual doctrine of the contract jurisdiction, but the trend is now in Browne and Story's direction.

D. Carriage of cargo

In American theory and practice, damage to cargo may be either breach of contract or tort. Europeans consider it solely contract. Browne clearly distinguished charter parties (a contract for use of the whole ship) from bills of lading (given for a single article, or more, laden on board a ship that has sundry merchandises shipped for

---

40 2 Browne, p. 94.

41 Ibid., p. 72. See also ibid., pp 78–9, 88. Browne defined 'sea' as 'that part of the water which is below low-water mark when the tide is out, and up to high-water mark when the tide is in', ibid., p. 91.

42 Ibid., p. 72.   43 Ibid., p. 96.   44 Ibid., p. 73.   45 Ibid., p. 74.   46 Ibid., p. 88.

47 See DeLovio v. Boit, *supra* n. 37, at 7, F. Cas, at 442.

48 In Minturn v. Maynard, 58 US (17 How.) 477 (1854), the Supreme Court held that admiralty contract jurisdiction did not apply to general agency contracts of vessels management. This was overruled in Exxon Corp. v. Central Gulf Lines, 500 US 603 (1991). Justice Marshall concluded that, 'Rather than apply a rule excluding all or certain agency contracts from the realm of admiralty, lower courts should look to the subject matter of the agency contract and determine whether the services performed under the contract are maritime in nature,' ibid. at 612. An extreme extension of maritime contract doctrine occurred in the train wreck of Austrailian goods in Norfolk Southern R.R. v. Kirby, 543 US 14 (2004).

sundry accounts).[49] Browne later dealt very briefly with charter parties and bills of lading simultaneously, using very few cases; thus it may be concluded that disputes between the cargo-owning interests (shippers or consignees and their insurers) and the ship-owning interest (shipowners and their insurers) were infrequent at the time Browne wrote his text. Possibly this may be explained by a unity of interests between shipowners and cargo owners. During the age of sail the theory that every voyage was a common venture was a reality. Many ships were owned in part by merchants (often in shares as small as sixty-fourths), and cargoes were similarly joint investments of many merchants. Accordingly, cargo owners may also have been shipowners and shipowners may also have been cargo owners, so that each voyage became a joint venture of many investors.[50] Bulk cargoes were seldom in great demand except in wartime. Voyages were usually not to deliver a cargo to a specific consignees but were made 'on speculation', accompanied by a 'supercargo', who looked out for the goods and arranged for their sale at the various ports of call. This mingling of ship-owning and cargo-owning interests may account for the apparent absence of litigation over cargo damage.

1. Charter parties

Browne listed the minimum contents of a charter party as: 1) the name and burthen (deadweight tonnage) of the vessel; 2) the name of the master and freighters (charterers, if any); 3) the place and time of loading and unloading; 4) the lay days and demurrage; and, 5) the penalties for non-performance.[51]

Today each trade has its own form of charter with familiar 'boilerplate' clauses providing the certainties and tolerable ambiguities common to that trade.[52] This practice did not yet exist in Browne's day. Further study of the staples of eighteenth-century shipping – the slave trade and the triangle trade – would be necessary, however, to reach definite conclusions about charter-party forms and the method of 'fixing' charters.[53]

---

49 2 Browne, pp 81–2.

50 A. Chandler Jnr, *The visible hand: the managerial revolution in American business*, p. 15 (1979).

51 2 Browne, p. 189.

52 See generally M. Wilford, T. Coghlin and J. Kimball, *Time charters* (3rd ed. 1989); 'Admiralty Law Institute: symposium on charter parties', 49 *Tul. L. Rev.*, 743 (1975); and the collection of forms in 2B and 2C Benedict on admiralty (7th rev. ed. 1986). Concerning eighteenth-century trade, see generally P. Curtin, *The Atlantic slave trade: a census*, pp 127–62 (1969); W. Du Bois, *Suppression of the African slave trade to the United States, 1638–1870* (1896); and J. Pope-Hennessy, *Sins of the fathers: Atlantic slave traders, 1441–1807*, pp 226–45 (1968). Outside the slave trade, see Bruchey, 'Success and failure factors: American merchants in foreign trade in the 18th and early 19th century', 32 *Bus. Hist.*, 272 (1958); Bailyn, 'Communications and trade: the Atlantic in the 17th century', 13 *J. Econ. Hist.*, 378 (1953); Andrews, 'Anglo-American trade in the early 18th century', 45 *Geographical Rev.*, 99 (1955); and S. Morison, *The maritime history of Massachusetts, 1783–1860*, pp 16–40 (1921).

53 See the description of fixing charters in Great Circle Lines Ltd. v. Matheson & Co., 681 F.2d 121, (2nd Cir. 1982); cf. Star S.S.Co. v. Beogradska Plovidba (the *Junior K*) [1998] 2 Lloyds Rep. 583

Browne specified a rule that has been altered in both England and America when he stated, 'A complete embargo, occasioned by war or reprisals, dissolves the charter party,'[54] and again, 'In case of embargo, the charter party is dissolved without charges to either party.'[55] His statements would be correct as to the international law consequences that upon a declaration of war, a subject (or citizen) may not trade with the enemy (neither with the enemy state nor any enemy private citizen).[56] However, as the Suez Canal cases in both the United Kingdom and the United States make clear, the addition of 8,000–10,000 miles to a voyage because of the closing of a major international waterway as the result of war does not invalidate a charter or a contract of sale.[57]

2. Bills of lading

Browne also listed the minimum contents of a bill of lading: 1) the quality, quantity, and marks of the goods; 2) the names of the shipper and consignee; 3) the places of departure and unloading; 4) the names of the master and ship; and, 5) the value of the freight (i.e., cargo).[58]

Bills of lading are to be prepared in triplicate for the shipper, consignee and master of the ship. In further distinction from the charter party, Browne said that the charter party settled the terms of carriage while bills of lading determine the contents of the cargo.[59] It was not then the custom to have the bill of lading perform the threefold function of receipt, negotiable document and contract of carriage.[60] Financing trade by letters of credit and CIF contracts would not become common practice until the latter part of the nineteenth century.

Respecting the bill of lading as a negotiable instrument, Browne noted, 'The indorsement [*sic*] and delivery of a bill of lading is, prima facie, an immediate transfer of the legal interest in the cargo.'[61] Dealing with the question of the possibility of dispute over the property in the goods because of triplicate original bills, Browne laid down the rule, still followed, that 'the person who first gets legal

---

54 2 Browne, p. 189. A reprisal in customary international law was a use of force short of war to punish a violation of international law.

55 Ibid.

56 See Calmar Steamship Corp. v. Scott, 345 US 427, (1953), and the Claveresk, 264 F. 276 (2nd Cir. 1920).

57 Tsakiroglou & Co. v. Noblee Thorl G.M.b.H. [1962] A.C. 93. See also American Trading & Produce Co. v. Shell Int'l Marine Co., 453 F.2d 939 (2nd Cir. 1972).

58 2 Browne, p. 190.

59 Ibid.

60 See the Pomerene Act, 19 USC. §§ 80101–16. See also Yeramex Int'l v. S.S. Tendo, 595 F.2d 943, (4th Cir. 1979), and Westway Coffee Corp. v. M/V Netuno, 675 F. 2d 30, (2nd Cir. 1982); cf. Bally, Inc. v. The Zim America, 22 F. 3d 65 (2nd Cir. 1994).

61 Note also that by the Act of 26 Geo. 3 c. 86, §3, the shipper must state in the bill of lading 'the true nature, quality, and value of such gold' in order to impose liability on the master or owners of a ship for loss to any 'gold, silver, diamonds, watches, jewels, or precious stones by reason of any robbery etc.'. 2 Browne, pp 145–6.

possession of one of them (bills) by delivery from the owner or shipper has a right to the consignment'.[62]

Browne appears to be disrupting the normal boundaries of English law between contract and tort in his discussion of cargo damage liability. He wrote that 'if the cargo be damaged, the owner of the cargo has in his turn his remedy against the ship or its owner', and, 'If either party fails in his part of the contract, the other is free, though it may be imprudent too rigidly to insist on the strict letter of the agreement … [a]nd he has also his remedy in damages against the party who failed in fulfilling his contract.'[63]

Although Browne seems to be setting up the tort of breach of contract of carriage,[64] the rigid distinctions between contract and tort at the common law would not have been part of the frame of reference of a civilian, for whom tort and contract were both simply obligations (with contract obligations growing out of the parties' agreement and tort obligations arising by operation of law).[65]

It is not possible to know whether Browne would have admitted the defences which the Supreme Court found to be the general maritime law in *The Niagra v. Cordes*.[66] In another place, speaking of charters, he says, 'If none of the contracting parties are in fault, and failure is occasioned by an Act of government, neither party suffers. If by the act of Heaven, or of an enemy, the ancient and modern laws are said to differ, though I believe they do not.'[67] Thus, governmental action (quarantine, restraint of princes, or arrest pursuant to the process of courts) was mutually excludable – neither shipper nor carrier were responsible,[68] whereas the effect of *vis major* (act of God) and acts of public enemies could be assigned to either party.[69]

62 Ibid., p. 190. See generally Allied Chemical Int'l Corp. v. Cia de Navegacao Lloyd Brasileiro, 775 F.2d 476, (2nd Cir. 1985), and G. Gilmore and C. Black, *The law of admiralty*, §3–4 to 3–5, pp 96–100 (2nd ed. 1975).

63 2 Browne, p. 191.

64 See P. Keeton, *Prosser and Keeton on the law of torts*, § 92, pp 658–67 (5th ed. 1984).

65 See F. Lawson, *A common law lawyer looks at the civil law*, pp 138–63 (1953).

66 62 US (21 How.) 7 (1859) ('the act of God, or the public enemy, or by the act of the owner of the goods').

67 2 Browne, p. 195.   68 Ibid.

69 Ibid., pp 192, 195. By the Act of 26 Geo. 3 c. 86, § 2, 'No owner of any vessel shall be subject to answer for any loss or damage which may happen to goods shipped on board such ship, by reason of any fire happening on board the said ship,' 2 Browne, pp 145–7. Browne notes that, 'This Act, in reality, only enacts the provisions of the old maritime laws. See the 41st article of the laws of Wisbuy and the 13th of the second fragment of the Rhodian laws.' In the United States there is a statute exonerating the 'owner' from liability for 'fire' unless caused by 'design or neglect' of the owner. See 46 USC. 30501 (enacted in 1851 in response to the Supreme Court's decision in The Lexington, 47 US (6 How.) 343 (1848), discussed *supra* n. 37). No special fire defence appears in the 1893 Harter Act, but there is a fire defence in 1936 COGSA. See 46 USC. app § 1304(2)(b) (1988). The various courts of appeal differ as to whether the owner must first prove seaworthiness before raising a fire statute defence. Compare Sunkist Growers, Inc. v. Adelaide Shipping Lines, Ltd., 603 F.2d 1327, (9th Cir. 1979), cert. denied, 444 US 1012 (1980), with In re Ta Chi Nav. (Panama) Corp. (The Eurypylus), 677 F.2d 225, (2nd Cir. 1983).

3. Deviation and freight

Browne compares the results under the Hanseatic laws of Visby with cases of his time, respecting geographical deviation.[70] Thus, where a shipper has loaded his goods for a voyage to one destination, but the voyage is to a different and more distant destination, the shipper pays 'half the damage that might happen to such ship'.[71] When a ship destined for one port arrives at another, the master and his chief mariners must swear under oath that they arrived at a port different from the destination port because of constraint or necessity.[72]

Browne noted that normally freight is 'collect' and not 'pre-paid', that is, there is no freight due until the completion of the voyage. Accordingly, the carrier has no right to a pro rata share of the freight for the proportion completed before shipwreck. Browne said nothing about clauses in charters or bills of lading that provide for freight prepaid and freight deemed earned on loading.[73]

E. Maritime torts

1. Locality rule

Browne's simple proposition was that locality is the criterion of admiralty jurisdiction, so that admiralty has a remedy for injury done to person or property upon the seas.[74] This jurisdictional rule has undergone the greatest doctrinal change in American admiralty theory with the addition of the element of maritime traditional nexus beyond location on the navigable waters needed to establish a maritime tort.[75]

70 2 Browne, p. 192.   71 Ibid.
72 Ibid. Oath-swearing was a feature of the Consolato del Mar and the Roll of Oléron. See *supra* n. 13 and 14.
73 Ibid., pp 193–4. On the differences between freight collect and freight pre-paid in the context of United States limitation of liability proceedings, see Complaint of Caribbean Sea Transport, Ltd, 748 F.2d 622 (11th Cir. 1984).
74 2 Browne, pp 201–2. See also ibid., p. 110 ('civil or private injuries to the person, committed on the seas are remediable in this [admiralty] court; but there, and in all matters of tort, locality is the strict limit … In torts, locality ascertains the judicial power').
75 Early case law, such as The Genesee Chief, 53 US (12 How.) 443 (1851), The Plymouth, 70 US 20 (1866) Atlantic Transport Co. v. Imbrovek, 234 US 52 [1914]) as well as more recent decisions, such as Nacirema v. Johnson (396 US 212 [1969]) and Askew v. American Waterways Operators, Inc., (411 US 325 [1973]) did not mention a required element other than location, although it might be said that those cases dealt only with problems in locality and no other possible element had been raised by the parties. The modern case law requiring that traditional maritime activity be present to invoke federal admiralty jurisdiction may represent nothing more than a technique to clear the crowded dockets of the federal courts. The Supreme Court found this required element of traditional maritime nexus in Executive Jet Aviation, Inc. v. City of Cleveland (409 US 249 [1972]) at a time when proposals were being considered to lessen the federal caseload by excluding vessels under 300 gross tons from the federal courts. Actual navigation of a vessel was removed as a mandatory element in Sisson v. Ruby (497 US 358 [1990]) and the necessity for relocation to navigable waters reemphasized in Jerome B. Grubart, Inc. v. Great Lakes Dredge & Dock Co. (513 US 527 [1995]).

2. Collision

It is a mystery why there are so few reported collision cases in Browne's treatise, given the increased volume of shipping produced by persistent war with France and other Continental nations from 1760 through 1815. The First World War and the Second World War produced a large volume of ordinary shipping litigation – excluding prize – and one would expect the same in earlier wars, but there is no evidence of substantial collision litigation and no ready explanation for its absence. Browne analyzed the collision situation under three types: when two ships are too near each other in port; when one is at anchor and the other under sail; and where both are sailing and strike together.[76]

Legal consequences in Roman law depended on fault. If the injury occurs without fault and by accident, neither party recovers;[77] but 'if the party occasioning the accident was in fault, he was to make full restitution and reparation to the injured'.[78] Browne then turned to the laws of Visby. Under Visby, where a ship under sail damages another ship under sail, 'the damage is to be borne by the ship that did it, unless her mariners swear they could not help it, and then to be borne by each equally'. Secondly, 'if two ships strike against one another, and receive damage, the loss shall be borne equally between them, unless the men on board one of them did it on purpose; in which case that ship shall pay all the damage'.[79] Lastly, Browne mentioned a rule of several liability to cargo: where, by accident, one ship perishes, the cargo loss 'shall be valued and paid for pro rata by both owners, and the damage of the ship shall also be answered for by both, according to their value'.[80] This latter statement is ambiguous. Does it mean that the allocation of fault is to depend on the value of the ships in collision, and if so, as of what time is the value to be determined, before or after the collision?[81]

Browne called on Bynkershoek's treatise to aid in interpreting this statement:

> the mercantile world was not reconciled to the idea that where it happens by accident, the doer of it should be perfectly free from the obligation of making some payment or retribution, because if so, it would always be contrary; on the other hand, if the principles of the noxal actions of the Romans, and of the action de pauperie were here applied, viz. that the theory which was the

---

76 2 Browne, pp 204–5. Professor Bourguignon suggests that collisions in crowded rivers and harbours would have been decided in common law courts. H. Bourguignon, *Sir William Scott, Lord Stowell: judge of the high court of admiralty, 1798–1828*, p. 96 (1987).

77 2 Browne, pp 203–4.   78 Ibid., p. 204 (described as 'the decree of fate').   79 Ibid.

80 Ibid., citing articles 29, 51 and 71 of the Visby Code. Unlike English law (The Milan, 167 Eng. Rpts. 167 [Adm. 1861]), American law has consistently adhered to the joint and several liability of colliding vessels to notionally innocent cargo. See The Alabama and The Gamecock, 92 US (2 Otto) 695 (1875); The Atlas, 93 US (3 Otto) 302 (1876); The Chattahoochee, 173 US 540 (1899); and United States v. Atlantic Mutual Insurance Co. (The Esso Belgium), 343 US 236, (1952). Owen, 'The origin and development of marine collision law', 51 *Tul. L. Rev.*, 775 (1977).

81 2 Browne, p. 205. Turkish law under the Ottoman empire provided that in a both-to-blame collision, the larger vessel was to bear the greater proportion of fault.

immediate cause or instrument of damage, should be given up, or otherwise the whole damage paid, it would be too severe a rule to be applied, if the case really happened by accident and misfortune: they therefore chose a middle course. In case of accident, the loss was to be divided between both parties, in equal proportions; in case of wilful fault or negligence, the guilty person was to pay the whole.[82]

Browne then goes on to the question of the vicarious liability of owners for the torts of masters and mariners. Under Roman law, each owner is liable to contribute in proportion to its share of ownership unless the master was authorized to do the act that caused the damage, in which case the owner's liability would be '*in solidum*' or joint and several, noting Bynkershoek's observation that masters are not authorized or instructed to run down ships.[83] The result was the non-liability of shipowners for the negligence of servants but the personified liability of the vessel remedied this defect.

Bynkershoek's writings are approved as 'guides in our courts',[84] and a case is put of a collision occurring through failure to carry lights at night, a fault of the master but not of the owners since not authorized by them. Browne prefers to say that while it is a fault of the owners, the liability does not extend beyond the value of the ship.[85] This interpretation by Browne illustrates the Anglo–American concept of the *in rem* liability of the ship for her own torts.[86]

Browne's last analysis on the subject of collision is from the laws of Oléron:

> if a vessel moored and lying at anchor be struck by another vessel under sail, the damage shall be common, because old decayed vessels have sometimes been purposely put in the way of better; and if in harbour, where there is little water, the anchor of one lies dry, the other may remove it, and the party preventing him must answer the damage; and every ship not having a buoy to the anchor is liable for any damage happening thereby.[87]

The first part of the quotation would be an exception to the presumption of fault when a moving vessel strikes a properly anchored vessel.[88]

Liability in both–to–blame cases was subject for many years to the inequitable rule of equal division of damages from English law.[89] When the United Kingdom

---

82 Ibid.
83 Ibid., pp 205–6 (citing chapters 18–23 of C. Bynkershoek's *Quaestiones juris privati* (1737)).
84 Ibid., p. 206.   85 Ibid., p. 207.
86 Ibid., p. 206. See Harmer v. Bell (The Bold Buccleuch) 13 Eng. Rep. 884 (P.C. 1852) and The China, 74 US (7 Wall.) 53 (1868).
87 2 Browne, p. 207 (citing articles 14 and 15 of the laws of Oléron).
88 See The Louisiana, 70 US (3 Wall.) 164 (1866); The Clara, 102 US 200 (1880); and The Oregon, 158 US 186 (1895).
89 The Woodrop-Sims, 165 Eng. Rep. 1422 (Adm. 1815), a decision of Sir William Scott. The House of Lords applied the rule of equal division of damages in a Scottish case, Hay v. Le Neve, 2 Shaw's Rep. 395 (H.L. 1824).

ratified the 1910 Brussels Collision Convention, English law was freed from the equal division rule. Because the convention also abolishes the rule of joint and several liability of colliding vessels to innocent cargo, the United States has refused to ratify the 1910 convention and continues the rule of joint and several liability.[90]

3. Seamen's injuries

Browne's discussion of mariners deals principally with wages,[91] desertion,[92] the supreme rule of the master,[93] flogging,[94] barratry[95] and the obligation of mariners to save and preserve the cargo to the utmost of their power.[96] He noted that all the old maritime laws provide that if a seaman is 'wounded in the ship's service, he ought to be cured at the expense of the ship, but if he is wounded in riots and quarrels, he must pay his own charges'.[97] Further, if he becomes sick during the voyage and is left on shore, he is entitled to his whole wages, after deducting what has been laid out for him, quoting the laws of Oléron, described as 'particularly humane', whereby the master is to furnish the sick sailor 'with lodging and

90 International Convention for the Unification of Certain Rules of Law with Respect to Collisions between Vessels (Brussels, 23 Sept. 1910), reprinted in 6 *Benedict on Admiralty*, Doc. No. 3–2 (7th rev. ed. 1986). See N. Healy and J. Sweeney, *The law of marine collision*, pp 312–20 (1998).

91 2 Browne, pp 155, 157, 166, 177–82. Browne quoted Lord Mansfield to the effect that if a ship is taken by the enemy before the voyage has been completed, the seaman is entitled to nothing because 'freight is the mother of wages, and the safety of the ship is the mother of freight', ibid., p. 177.

92 Ibid., pp 156–7, 164. Although seamen are permitted to go ashore for a short and reasonable period of time if the ship is safely anchored, the Hanseatic laws dealt harshly with seamen who went ashore without permission: such men were to be kept in prison on bread and water for one year if the ship suffered for want of hands, ibid., p. 164.

93 '[T]he mariners are to pay due obedience to the master, who hath the supreme rule on ship-board, and whose power and authority are by the law much countenanced', 2 Browne, p. 160.

94 Ibid. Described as 'moderate and due correction', referring to one blow in the laws of Oléron and Consolato del Mar, but also noting that under the laws of Oléron the penalty for striking the master was the loss of a hand. Browne preferred the punishment of loss of wages to corporal violence, ibid., pp 160–70. Flogging was abolished in the military in peacetime in 1868 in the United Kingdom. Richard Henry Dana's experiences aboard the brig *Pilgrim*, recorded in his classic work *Two years before the mast* (1840), made him a strong opponent of flogging and an advocate for its abolition. In Congress, Senator John P. Hale (1806–75), R-NH, the first senator elected on an anti-slavery platform, was the strongest proponent of the abolition of flogging. Flogging aboard United States naval and merchant vessels finally was abolished by the Act of 23 Sept. 1850, 10 Stat. 515. Today, the penalty for mariners' offences aboard ship is called 'logging', whereby amounts are deducted from wages for offences against ship's discipline.

95 2 Browne, p. 172 (quoting Beawes, *Lex mercatoria*, as an epidemical disease of seamen). The English Marine Insurance Act of 1906, 6 Edw. 7 c. 41, to which the Lloyd's S.G. Policy is appended, notes in the rules for construction of the S.G. Policy: '11. The term "Barratry" includes every wrongful act willfully committed by the master or crew to the prejudice of the owner, or, as the case may be, the charterer.'

96 2 Browne, p. 175. See The Niagara v. Cordes, 62 US (7 How.) 7 (1858).

97 2 Browne, p. 184, presumably in tavern brawls.

candlelight, and also to spare him one of the ship's boys, or hire a woman to attend him, and likewise to afford him such diet as is usual in the ship for men in health'.[98]

Browne's provisions seem to be very close to maintenance and cure in the general maritime law and the International Labour Organization's 1936 treaty on seamen's injuries.[99] Today, most of the maritime world has adopted worker's compensation as the exclusive remedy for seamen.[100]

F. General average

Arthur Browne's text on the system of general average was prepared eighty years before the appearance of the York-Antwerp Rules.[101] Those rules were required because of the divergence between French and British practices in statements on general average by 'adjusters' in Britain and '*dispacheurs*' on the Continent. In three pages he offers a glimpse of the provisions antedating statutory and even judicially declared marine-insurance law that he considered to be descended from Roman law. In general average, losses incurred for the safety of ship, personnel and cargo are spread among the financial interests in the voyage or venture. Thus, a contribution 'proportionably' must be made towards losses for the safeguard of the ship or of the goods and lives on the ship in time of tempest.[102]

Loss 'voluntarily suffered' is described as the great principle of general average. Browne then explains that 'voluntary' does not necessarily mean 'consenting' nor is every loss included. Thus, if masts or yardarms are destroyed by the tempest

---

98   2 Browne, pp 182–3.

99   See Shipowner's Liability Convention of 1936, I.L.O. Conv. No. 55, Shipowner Liability in Cases of Sickness, Injury or Death of Seamen, 54 Stat. 11693, T.S. No. 951, 77 L.N.T.S. 407.

100 Worker's compensation is available in the United States for longshore and harbour workers (33 USC. 901 et. seq.) But not for seamen whose labour unions oppose such legislation. Traditional maritime remedies are maintenance and cure and unseaworthiness in admiralty and at law under the Jones Act (46 USC. 30104).

101 The York-Antwerp Rules were the first maritime product of the International Law Association (ILA). Promulgated in 1877, they represented a melding of French and British practices. The ILA was founded in 1873 in Brussels, in the aftermath of the Franco-Prussian War (1870–1) and the American Civil War (1861–5), to reform and codify customary international law. The York-Antwerp Rules have been frequently revised (in 1924, 1949, 1974, 1994 and 2004), and are incorporated by reference in charter parties, bills of lading and other maritime contracts worldwide. See generally Eagle Terminal Tankers, Inc. v. Insurance Co. of USSR, 637 F.2d 890, (2nd Cir. 1981). See also R. Lowndes and G. Rudolf, *The law of general average and the York-Antwerp Rules* (11th ed. 1990), and L. Buglass, *Marine insurance and general average in the United States* (3rd ed. 1991). In Ralli v. Troop, 157 US 386, 403 (1895), the Supreme Court defined the elements of general average as follows: 'a voluntary and successful sacrifice of part of the maritime adventure, made for the benefit of the whole adventure, and for no other purpose, and by order of the owners of all the interests included in the common adventure or the authorized representative of all of them'. Today, the 'authorized representative' is usually the master.

102 2 Browne, p. 198. 'There is a general average act when and only when, any extraordinary sacrifice or expenditure is intentionally and reasonably made or incurred for the common safety for the purpose of preserving from peril the property involved in a common maritime adventure.' Rule A, York-Antwerp Rules (2004).

there is no voluntary loss, but if the same masts and yardarms are cut away there would be a general average. Similarly, if a ship runs on shore and is broken up but the cargo saved, there is no voluntary loss unless the ship was purposely grounded to save the cargo.[103] When a general average act has been performed, 'All persons for whose benefit the act was done, the freighters [shippers], the master, the owners, the sailors, the passengers, must contribute.[104] Furthermore, 'All things in the ship, except the victualing and provisions of the ship and the bodies of the men (unless servants) must bear a proportionable share in the contribution.'[105] Lastly, '[T]he master ought not to deliver the goods until the contribution is settled, they being tacitly pledged, as they are for the freight.'[106]

G. Maritime liens

Browne's study of maritime liens had to account for the home-port doctrine,[107] by which repairs and supplies to a ship in her home port would not create a maritime lien because the furnishers of repairs and supplies were presumed to have relied on the personal credit of the shipowner rather than the ship.

In another context Browne stated, 'The cargo is tacitly bound for the freight, which is preferred to all other debts affecting the cargo, though prior in time,'[108] a liability of the cargo itself whether the goods are carried under charter or bill of lading.[109] In another place he indicated the possessory nature of this lien, 'The master might always retain the merchandise until paid his freight', but this statement does not resolve the question.

Browne distinguished bottomry from the maritime lien for necessities (or hypothecation). Bottomry being a recent development, he had no Roman history or practice to fall back on and therefore defined it as a contract made at the home port for money lent upon the vessel on the condition that if the ship were lost the lender would forfeit its money, but if the ship returned in safety the lender would

103 2 Browne, p. 199. Cf. Barnard v. Adams, 51 US (10 How.) 270, 303–4 (1850): 'if the common peril was of such a nature, that the "jactus", or things cast away to save the rest, would have perished anyhow, or perished "inevitably", even if it had not been selected to suffer in place of the whole, there can be no contribution … The necessity of the case must compel [the master] to choose between the loss of the whole and part …'
104 2 Browne, p. 201.
105 Ibid. Cf. rule XI of the York-Antwerp Rules (1994), concerning wages and maintenance of the crew during prolongation of the voyage, and at a port of refuge, until the ship either resumes the voyage or is condemned.
106 2 Browne, p. 201. Today, a bond will be required for general-average contribution before the cargo will be delivered to the consignee. See The Jason, 225 US 32 (1912), origin of the Jason Clause to undo the effect of statutory unseaworthiness.
107 2 Browne, p. 191. See The General Smith, 17 US (4 Wheat.) 438 (1819). Browne wrote: 'it seems now settled that the ship cannot be hypothecated at home before the voyage commences', 2 Browne p. 80. The accompanying footnotes cite Lord Mansfield that, at home, it is simply a mortgage.
108 2 Browne, p. 191.
109 Ibid. See, for charter parties, The Bird of Paradise, 72 US (5 Wall.) 545 (1866); for bills of lading, see Alcoa S.S. Co. v. United States, 338 US 421 (1949).

receive its principal plus a rate of interest that could exceed the legal rate.[110] The lien for necessities or hypothecation is described as follows: 'The master ... cannot hypothecate the ship except for its own necessities, and that abroad; and the vessel itself is thereby subject to seizure in the court of admiralty to satisfy the debt, but no one is personally liable'.[111] Browne favoured extending admiralty jurisdiction at least to the part of the bottomry contract dealing with the ship and tackle, while the personal liability of the borrower would be at law;[112] admiralty process was *in rem* and not *in personam*, at that time.[113]

H. Possessory proceedings

Excepting felonious or piratical takings, for which the criminal jurisdiction was applicable, and takings as prize, for which prize jurisdiction only was applicable, Browne favoured applying admiralty jurisdiction to 'illegal possession of the ship in any other way'.[114] Disputes concerning ownership and control (but not title) led to petitory or possessory suits in admiralty.[115] Because the admiralty court could not determine title, Browne said the court was confined to the possessory action, the issue of possession for which the common law courts had concurrent jurisdiction.[116] The common law courts had exclusive jurisdiction over title disputes.

On the vexatious question of an illegal taking of a ship followed by a sale in open market, Browne disputed the view that admiralty lost jurisdiction because the sale was on land. He said that since admiralty had cognizance of the principal issue (the illegal taking), it should also have jurisdiction of the incidental issue, at least where the whole made one continued act (the sale after the taking being a continuation of the violence).[117] Respecting practice, the action *in rem* would be available for possessory actions.[118]

I. Limitation of liability

Noting the severity of the maritime liability of shipowners for damage or injury in case of accident, fire or theft, a major modification was introduced in English law by a statute of 1786 that limited the liability of owners of ships to 'the value of the ship, with all her appurtenances, and the full amount of the freight due or to grow due'.[119] The precondition is the absence of knowledge of the owners and the fact

110 2 Browne, p. 196.   111 Ibid.   112 Ibid.
113 Ibid., pp 98–101. In the United States, the Supreme Court has confused the clear distinction between *in rem* and *in personam* in transfers between district courts, Continental Grain v. Federal Barge Lines, 364 US 19 (1960).
114 2 Browne, p. 189.
115 Ibid., p. 113. Cf. The Tilton, 23 F.Cas. 1277 (No. 14, 054) (C.C.D Mass 1830) per Story on Circuit.
116 Ibid.   117 Ibid. Damages at law by replevin; restitution in admiralty.
118 Ibid., pp 118, 396–7, 430–2. In the United States, Rule D of the Supplementary Rules (F.R.C.P.) provides arrest of the vessel in possessory, petitory and partition actions.
119 26 Geo. 3 c. 86, see 2 Browne, p. 145.

that the master or mariners shall not be privy to loss or damage by reason of any fire or by reason of any robbery or embezzlement, secreting or making away with any gold, silver, diamonds, jewels, precious stones or other goods or merchandise. Browne noted the origin of this statute in an earlier Act dealing only with embezzlement by the master and mariners;[120] furthermore, he speculated that these English statutes merely enacted the provisions of the Rhodian law[121] and the laws of Visby.[122] Respecting distribution of the proceeds from the limitation fund made up of ship, appurtenances and freight, Browne wrote that the shippers 'shall receive their satisfaction thereout in average, in proportion to their losses', but equitable principles and the aid of the equity courts were to be enlisted for the resolution of disputes as to the value of the ship and the claims of the shippers.[123]

J. Salvage and rescue

In Arthur Browne's day, salvage cases were rare, probably because vessels driven onto the strand or impaled on rocks did not survive as commercial vehicles, having been stripped of cargo and recycled by looters or mooncussers. There was no professional salvor to save and restore commercial vessels. Even if the wreck remained a visible ship there were sure to be claims of the crown or the lord high admiral. Nevertheless, where the owner has not abandoned the vessel, a volunteer who succeeds in restoring the maritime property to the owner, has a lien that requires the owner to pay a reward to the rescuer.[124] More prominent in a century of naval warfare was the rescue of a captured vessel from the enemy, whether naval or privateer, possibly leading to a salvage award.[125]

A concern in salvage cases was the moiety rule – to the effect that in ordinary circumstances the salvage award will not exceed half (*moitié*) of the value of the rescued property[126] – a sensible solution at a time when valuations of ship and cargo were likely to be fanciful or at least unscientific.

---

120 7 Geo. 2 c. 15, see 2 Browne, p. 145.

121 Oléron, *supra* n. 13, Section 13 of the second fragment.   122 Visby, *supra* n. 15, art. 41.

123 2 Browne, p. 146. Cf. The Mauch Chunk, 154 F. 182 (2nd Cir. 1907); see generally, Sweeney, 'Limitation of shipowner liability: its American roots and some problems of collision', 32 *J. Mar. L. & Comm.*, 241 (2001).

124 2 Browne, pp 47–53. Conflicting principles of French and English salvage law were compromised in the first international maritime convention of the Comité Maritime International in 1910 (Convention for the Unification of Certain Rules of Law Relating to Assistance and Salvage at Sea, T.S. No. 576). A new salvage treaty taking account of environmental disasters was prepared in 1989, in force 1995. See generally G. Brice, *The maritime law of salvage* (2nd ed. 1993).

125 2 Browne, pp 266–270. The legal consequences of recapture are spelled out in terms of a wartime (1793) statute, 33 Geo. 3 c. 66. However, the international applications of the law of recapture (*ius postliminis*) were analyzed, going back to the Romans.

126 The moiety rule rejected as mandatorily applicable in Columbus-America Discovery Group v. Atlantic Mutual Ins. Co. (The Central America II) 56 F.3d 556 (4th Cir.) cert. denied 516 US 938 (1995). The Supreme Court applied the moiety rule in its famous analysis of salvage awards, The Blackwall, 77 US 1(1870).

III. ECCLESIASTICAL LAW

Browne's study of ecclesiastical[127] law is dedicated to William Newcome, archbishop of Armagh and is designed to assist canon lawyers and judges, like himself, but also non-lawyer clergy. It is of course, in English, unlike many of the sources, which are in Latin. It begins with the note that the Reformation Parliaments intended to revise the ancient canon law of the pre-Reformation church,[128] but that after 250 years no revision had been attempted, and accordingly, all the old canon law was still in force unless repugnant to the law of the land and the king's prerogative;[129] where appropriate, comparison to common law was attempted. As was his custom, there are references to historical disputes and decided cases.

The first three chapters concern persons in holy orders (bishops, priests and deacons) and are of historical interest only, concerning their privileges and immunities as well as their rights to possess church properties. The text also deals with the origin and development of tithe[130] and the rights of patrons to appoint clergy and the resolution of disputes thereon.[131] In discussing the duties of the clergy, the text provides a brief history of the forms of Christian worship. The text notes that clergymen are to be sober in eating and drinking, not wear long hair and abstain from games of dice, cards and taverns. Weddings are to be performed by them in church between 8 a.m. and noon (for fear of abducted brides and secret marriages) and not during Lent, fast days or the great festivals of Christmas, Easter and Pentecost.[132]

Chapter 4, on church property, including the subject of tithes, is also now of only historical interest, although the frequency and the number of disputes about church property is remarkable.

Chapter 5 examines the then existing ecclesiastical court structure in Ireland (the prerogative court and diocesan courts) and England, as well as the practices of the medieval papacy. While the 1869 disestablishment of the Church of Ireland altered the public-law aspects of this jurisdiction, it may yet be relevant to the court of arches of the established church in England.

Chapter 6, on ecclesiastical jurisdiction, is most valuable for modern readers, as it contains the law of matrimonial disputes and divorce, as well as the law of wills and the probate of estates.[133] The matrimonial actions are suits for specific performance of marriage, annulment, divorce and alimony.

---

127 A. Browne, *A compendious view of the ecclesiastical law of Ireland* (1797, 2nd ed. 1803); all citations *infra* are to the 2nd ed. Archbishop Newcome was appointed under Earl Fitzwilliam. Arthur Browne was agent for church properties during his tenure. Allibone's *Critical dictionary of English literature* (1879), vol. 1, p. 261, quotes earlier reviewers: 'His great powers of mind he improved by incessant study and by intercourse with the most distinguished scholars and the most able and virtuous statesmen of his day.'

128 2 Browne, p. x; 28 Hen. 8 c. 13 (in England, 25 Hen. 8 c. 9).

129 Ibid., pp 158–65, 241ff.   130 Ibid.

131 Ibid., pp 93–112. The term 'advowson' was used for the patron's right to appoint clergy.

132 Ibid., pp 75–91.   133 Ibid., pp 241–371.

A. Matrimonial disputes

Browne begins with the rule that *res judicata* will not prevent a new suit after an earlier dismissal where new proofs are offered because the subject matter is the health of the soul of the promovent (plaintiff).[134] Specific performance of contracts to marry had been changed by statute in England but not in Ireland and is compared to suits to enforce conjugal rights, to which adultery or cruelty or condonation is a defence. Annulment of compelled marriages (abductions) or marriages of minors without parental consent are distinguished from voidable marriages when consanguinity, affinity or impotency before marriage are concerned.[135]

Respecting divorce, the distinction is made between divorce *a vinculo matrimonio*, where there may be another marriage and divorce *a mensa et thoro*, which was really a legal separation, where remarriage was not possible, and the children were not considered illegitimate.[136] The causes are adultery and cruelty, but may require payment of alimony. (Browne was quite familiar with sham adulteries, as practiced in New York before the reform of the marriage laws.)[137]

B. Testamentary disputes

Concerning wills, Browne reviewed the claims of ecclesiastical jurisdiction since William the Conqueror (1066–87) and noted the supremacy of such courts in issues of probate and administration, but the concurrence with chancery in suits for legacies.[138] Formalities of the will are reviewed, especially testamentary disabilities for infancy and insanity, felony and excommunication (a frequent penalty in these courts).[139] The next subject is what may be devised by will (goods and chattels) and those lands devisable by will. (Most land estates passed by primogeniture to the heir.)[140]

The essence of the will is the appointment of an executor in writing, properly witnessed as to signature (by two witnesses).[141] Exceptions as to witnesses and writing (as in nuncupative or oral wills) are considered. A nuncupative will, during the last illness, must be reduced to writing within six days and requires three witnesses present in the testator's dwelling, if the value of the estate exceeds £30.[142] Disqualification of witnesses for conviction of felony, for infancy, for insanity and for 'affection and kindred' (i.e. a legatee) is also reviewed.[143] Women, poor men and foreigners may be witnesses but 'infidels'– unexplained – are excluded. (Note, *infra*, that these courts regularly excluded women from giving testimony.)[144]

Probate of the will by the executor(s) taking the required oaths is contrasted with the challenges to probate (caveats) for fraud and undue influence.[145]

---

134 Ibid., pp 257–8.   135 Ibid., pp 260–72.   136 Ibid., pp 276–9.
137 Ibid., pp 274–80. The question of divorce in the Republic of Ireland became a political as well as a religious question from 1983 to 1996. See R. Foster, *Luck and the Irish*, pp 42–53 (2006).
138 2 Browne, pp 281–3.   139 Ibid., pp 286–94.   140 Ibid., pp 294–7.
141 Ibid., pp 298–9.   142 Ibid., pp 299–303.   143 Ibid., pp 304–7.
144 Ibid., pp 306, 413–23.   145 Ibid., pp 306–15.

Revocation by oral declaration had been abolished by the statute of frauds requiring a new writing, unless the testator burns, tears or obliterates the former will.[146] Codicils to alter a will require three witnesses, by statute, where the will itself required only two. Presumptive revocation because of later marriage or birth of a child is noted.

The executor's duties: to probate the will, bury the deceased, collect debts, inventory the estate, pay debts, distribute legacies and tender accounts to the court are all analyzed, along with legal actions on behalf of the estate.[147] Lastly, the text deals with administration where there is no will probated, beginning with the preferences among the next of kin for appointment as administrator, comparing the duties to those of the executor, with the exception of the statutory provisions for distribution of the residuary estate.[148]

C. Procedure and evidence

Chapter 7, on the practice of ecclesiastical courts, involved a review of the medieval courts of canon law. The law of evidence is especially interesting; testimony of two witnesses, on oath, was required for many facts, but the person refusing to give testimony could no longer be tortured, merely subjected to excommunication. Jews, pagans, heretics and infidels could not testify against Christians; slaves and women could not be witnesses,[149] although Browne called the last 'barbarous and absurd'.[150] Domestic servants and family members were also excluded as witnesses.

Chapter 8 applied the principles of canon law of the preceding chapter to the eighteenth-century courts based on Roman canon law in England (the courts of doctors' commons), as well as the Dublin prerogative court and the consistorial courts in each of the dioceses of Ireland. Browne is concerned in this chapter with the failure of individuals to comply with the process of these courts and their orders – contumacy, for which the penalty was excommunication.[151] (The decree was to be read out by the clergy at the Sunday service of the parish to which the contumacious person belonged.)[152]

The pleadings – libel, exceptions to the libel and the replication (answer) – are compared to similar documents at common law.[153] The contestation (the cases in chief of libellant and respondent) and the methods of proofs to conclusion and sentence are examined,[154] followed by a review of the appeal process,[155] distinguishing 'grievances' about proofs and witnesses and 'sentences' or the merits of decision below.[156] Intricate rules dictate the use of new evidence, but the use of new evidence on appeal is possible.[157]

---

146 Ibid., pp 315–20.   147 Ibid., pp 323–45.   148 Ibid., pp 346–64.   149 Ibid., p. 388.
150 Ibid.   151 Ibid., pp 405–11.   152 Ibid., p. 407.   153 Ibid., pp 413–23.
154 Ibid., pp 424–48.   155 Ibid., pp 453–64.   156 Ibid., pp 453–4.
157 Ibid., pp 453–64. Browne explained the use of new evidence on appeal: 'The new allegation or proof therefore must be something which should not be suggested or occasioned by the evidence already published, though it should spring out of the pleadings below', p. 463.

The 1803 revision updates the 1797 work and contains an extensive appendix of statutes and excerpts or discussions of twenty-two Irish cases and short summaries of twenty-three new English cases.[158]

IV. THE LAW OF NATIONS (INTERNATIONAL LAW)

Arthur Browne's extensive treatise on admiralty law necessarily included the practical application of the customary law of Western European nations in his time, a period of persistent naval warfare, especially prize law[159] for naval vessels and privateers,[160] the rights of neutrals, letters of marque and reprisal[161] and the law of blockade. These subjects were known to him as 'the law of nations'; today they are part of international law.

The expression 'international', although created from Latin roots, is actually a nineteenth-century invention. In Roman law and medieval law, relations of peace and war were known as the law of nations. Jeremy Bentham,[162] famous as the philosopher of utilitarianism, was a lawyer who desired to codify the customary law of relations between nations, which he called international law. In nineteenth-century France, '*droit des nations*' became '*droit international*'. By 1873, David Dudley Field of New York and his European colleagues who desired to codify the

158　Ibid., appendix, pp 1–28.
159　Prize law refers to the wartime capture of enemy property at sea, as opposed to 'booty', the wartime capture of enemy property on land. The capture as well as the liability of the vessel and cargo must be approved by a prize court; in England, the admiralty court had a special jurisdiction as a prize court. See 2 Browne, pp 281–346.
160　A privateer was an armed merchant vessel not owned by a government but owned and operated by private persons for the purpose of capturing, seizing or destroying enemy ships and cargoes in wartime. The only thing distinguishing the privateer from the pirate was possession of a letter of marque and reprisal issued by the government of the flag state authorizing or licensing hostile actions against enemy property in wartime. The word is also used to describe the owner, master and even the crew of such a vessel. European nations abolished the practice by the Declaration of Paris of 1856 after the Crimean War. See 2 Browne, pp 338–41.
161　Letters of marque and reprisal authorize private owners of vessels to search out and capture enemy vessels seizing their cargoes and the vessel or destroying both, in wartime. '*Marcer*' was an old French Provençal word meaning to take reprisal action on an offending ship or town. In the United States constitution, Congress has the right to issue such letters: Art. I, Sec. 8. A key date in the struggle between the American colonials and the British empire was the decision of the continental congress to encourage states (former colonies) to grant letters of marque and reprisal (Second Cont. Cong. 25 Nov. 1775).
162　Jeremy Bentham (1748–1832), a graduate of Oxford (AM 1766), was called to the Bar in 1772 but became an essayist in favour of many reforms of existing society, criticizing Blackstone as anti-reform (1776). He also published on criminal law and punishments (1778), the economics of usury (1787), legislation and the justice system (1789), the poor law (1797) and judicial evidence. The principle of avoiding pain and seeking pleasure to produce the greatest happiness in the greatest number is in his *Introduction to the principles of morals and legislation* (1789). Towards the end of his life he took up the subject of codification of civil laws and the law of nations in *Constitutional code* (1827).

law of nations following the American Civil War and the Franco-Prussian war, formed the International Law Association. Today the concept 'international' is found in all modern languages.

Arthur Browne's chapter on the law of prize (2 Browne, pp 281–346) was the most valuable portion for his contemporaries. It is sad to read his conclusion that the chapter is now (1802) less useful since sudden and joyful tidings of peace have burst upon us. Unhappily, the Peace of Amiens lasted less than two years, but Browne recognized the reality: 'whatever may be our love or our hopes of peace, wars in the nature of things must recur' (p. 345). Browne then outlines procedural steps and requisite proofs for a successful prize in thirteen sections.

Browne's discussion of the right to search neutral ships extending beyond the ship's papers to the cargo itself – authorized by the court of reason (p. 321) – but denied in America, laid the ground for the second American war with Great Britain (1812–14) and the First World War (1914–18).

While treatises on the law of nations and specific aspects of the law of war on land and sea were well known to eighteenth-century lawyers, the idea of university courses in the subject did not emerge for another fifty years. Arthur Browne included a number of international law issues in his lectures (and text) on the civil law and the law of admiralty.[163] He also published in 1788 a polemical treatise on the highly controversial 'treaty' during the war between King William and the Irish Catholic forces of James II, after their surrender in the siege of Limerick in 1691. It is a 101-page pamphlet entitled *A brief review of the question whether the Articles of Limerick have been violated?* (1788).

A. The treatise

Eighteenth-century legal scholars did not want the law of nations to be mandated by an imperial crown (such as the Holy Roman empire) nor an imperial church (such as the Roman Catholic church). Seventeenth-century scholars had been satisfied to join together 'natural law' and 'the law of nations' into a single entity so that the provisions of the law of nations came from God through the universal truths of the law of nature, its authority having been found in scripture and the Latin classics. But the eighteenth-century mind understood the reality of the European status quo in religion after 150 years of religious warfare; so a law of nations had to be authenticated without a scriptural basis that would surely be viewed as heretical by some readers.

Browne's search began with his threshold questions:

1) How can there be a law between independent states?
2) What is the obligation to obey the law of nations?
3) Are there sanctions for violating the law of nations?[164]

---

163 2 Browne, *supra* n. 2.   164 Ibid., p. 2.

Since there was no international court to provide a resolution to disputes, he reflected his times in the statement, 'the law of nations is originally no more than the law of nature applied to nations'.[165] But, 'Why then is [the law of nations] distinguished from the law of nature?' Browne then admitted that 'numberless cases arise peculiar to nations, and not incident to individuals, and therefore making a separate science'.[166] A system is necessary 'to mitigate the horrors of war and preserve the blessing of peace',[167] Browne found. He distinguished the types of provisions in the law of nations under the following heads:

1) The natural law or necessary law, always obligatory upon a nation with respect to its own duty.
2) The positive law of nations: a) arising from custom and dependent on the consent of states; and b) arising from express or implied compacts (treaty law). The illustration is the just war, previously declared,[168] so the conquests are lawful, whereas undeclared warfare does not create lawful conquests.[169]

His search for authority in the law of nations reached back to the Roman empire, and included works from post-Reformation Europe and his contemporaries.

1. Roman sources

The principal classical author on international law from the period of the Roman empire was Ulpian, whose 'science' distinguished just laws from unjust laws, because he distinguished *ius naturale* from *ius gentium* so that state practices, such as slavery, that had hardened into customary law could at the same time be a violation of natural law. Efforts to distinguish the just war from the unjust were part of a futile exercise until the twentieth century, when the declaration of war before commencing hostilities became essential.[170]

2. Post-Reformation Europeans

Browne did not deal with important treatise writers of the Renaissance such as Victoria, Suarez, Bellini, Ayala or even Gentili, the Italian Protestant scholar who flourished in England. Possibly they were unavailable to him; it is doubtful that they were omitted simply because of their Roman Catholic background. Browne was unusually sensitive to doctrinal developments, regardless of denominational adherence, although in fact six scholars cited by him were all Protestant and two were children of the Enlightenment. Browne's sixteenth- and seventeenth-century

---

165 Ibid.   166 Ibid., p. 7.   167 Ibid., p. 13.   168 Ibid.
169 Ibid., p. 14. Declaration of war was required by the 1907 Second Hague Peace Conference. Convention III, 2 Malloy's Treaties, p. 2259.
170 J. Sweeney, 'The just war ethic in international law', 27 *Fordham Int'l. L. J.*, 1865 (2004).

authorities were: Grotius (1583–1645);[171] Hobbes (1588–1679); and Pufendorf (1632–94).

Grotius was a legal scholar and this was the despair of political philosophers, who did not appreciate his use of careful definitions as he analyzed the relations between nations without developing a theory of the state. He finally detached natural law from its entanglement with religious authority during a period in which force was the only arbiter in the dealings of states with one another.[172] The law of nature, like the principles of mathematics, lay behind the laws of various states, binding all peoples, and therefore lay behind the law of nations and its fundamental principle: *pacta sunt servanda* (treaties must be complied with).

3. Eighteenth-century contemporaries

Browne's authors from his own century were: Wolff, Barbeyrac and Vattel. These authors are often condemned as mere popularizers, since they benefitted from enormous improvements in the preparation and distribution of printed materials, so their works were not confined to university libraries but could be found in the libraries of enlightened citizens, such as the 'founding fathers' of the American nation, as well as in government offices dealing with foreign affairs.

Emmerich de Vattel, who was Swiss, was the most well-known authority on international law at the end of the eighteenth century and well into the nineteenth. He was trained in philosophy at the University of Basel. Despite his Protestant heritage and training, he was hired by Augustus III, the Catholic elector of Saxony (also the king of Poland) in 1746. In 1758, the elector appointed him to be the privy councillor in charge of foreign affairs at the Saxon court in Dresden. His principal treatise, *Le droit des gens ou principes de la loi naturelle appliqués á la conduite et aux affairs des nations et des souverains*, appeared in 1758. While Vattel was not a trained lawyer but a diplomat, his quasi-philosophical work became the chief source of international law for the new United States.

Browne concluded this discussion of authorities with the observation that the law of nations is enforceable without a superior authority to compel obedience.

> But great is our error, if we suppose that the law of nations has no influence on the wicked; it checks where it does not guide. No prince, no potentate, dare refuse an apparent allegiance to its sway ... The disposition of nations tends to punish the violators of their common law; that disposition will often control the intrigues of courts, and the confederate artifice of mutually corrupting states.[173]

171 Alexander VI's bull 'Inter caetera', 4 May 1493, divided lands and seas along a line 100 leagues west of the Azores and Cape Verde islands between Spain (west of the line) and Portugal (east of the line).
172 H. Grotius, *Prolegomena* § 15; G. Sabine, *A history of political theory*, pp 420–1 (1950). Rights of prisoners of war and the freedom of the high seas from national appropriation are part of the legacy of Grotius.   173 Ibid., p. 18.

B. The pamphlet on the Articles of Limerick

Arthur Browne's polemical pamphlet *A brief review of the question whether the Articles of Limerick have been violated*, appeared in 1786 in the course of a debate on the penal laws. Browne does not describe this 'surrender' document as a treaty, although many contemporaries did, and the place of signing on the banks of the Shannon River in Limerick is called the 'treaty stone'. In the terms of modern international law it would not be considered a treaty, but Browne applied customary international law concepts to it.[174] Even in his own day the Limerick Treaty was very controversial, and it was his task to absolve the Irish Protestant Parliament from accusations of bad faith and treachery in its treatment of Roman Catholic citizens. Browne's task was made necessary by John Curry's book, *An historical and critical review of the civil wars of Ireland* (1786).[175]

The heart of the problem was the legislation of the Irish Parliament known as the penal laws (or popery laws) that began to be enacted in 1695, a few years after the surrender and exile of the Catholic military nobility that had abandoned millions of their innocent followers to go to France to serve alien masters.[176] As an agreement, the 'Treaty' of Limerick failed by its ambiguities, especially the key provision for Roman Catholics 'to enjoy such toleration as they had enjoyed during the reign of Charles II'. Opinions might well differ on the meaning.[177]

---

174 Modern treaty law is based upon the Vienna Convention on the Law of Treaties (prepared in 1968–9, entered into force in 1980). It is prospective only. Article 1 defines its subject matter as an agreement between two nations, in writing, to be governed by international law.

175 John Curry (1702?–80) was born in Dublin, son of a wealthy Catholic merchant who sent him to France for his education in medicine at Paris and Rheims from which he received his MD. He was licensed in Dublin and developed a large practice. He published medical works on fevers in 1743 and 1774. In 1747, he began to publish contradictions of anti-Catholic legends in Protestant propaganda concerning the 1641 rebellion and the Cromwell repression, pointing to land confiscation and Protestant vengeance as sources of rebellion. His 1747 and 1758 works were republished posthumously by Charles O'Conor as *An historical and critical review of the civil wars in Ireland* (1786), to which Browne responded in his Articles of Limerick pamphlet. Dr Curry's historical works, like those of his Protestant competitors, were light on documentary research other than reminiscence. More importantly, Dr Curry was involved in the original Catholic Committee in 1756 and its subsequent revivals in 1760 and 1777. Curry corresponded regularly with Edmund Burke from 1764 to his death. He was a close associate of Charles O'Connor (1710–91), the Gaelic scholar and Catholic enthusiast, and supported the new oath of allegiance to the British crown.

176 Following defeat at the battle of the Boyne (12 July 1690), James II fled to France; the armed remnant of his army under Patrick Sarsfield crossed Ireland to Limerick, where one year later William's general, Ginkel, defeated the Irish-French forces at the battle of Aughrim (12 July 1691), which was followed by their siege of the city of Limerick for nine weeks. Sarsfield and Ginkel reached agreement to surrender the city if the Irish-French forces were sent to France by William's fleet. Sarsfield and 11,000 Irish went to France, where they became the Brigade Irelandaise of the French Army in the wars of the eighteenth and early nineteenth centuries. See R.F. Foster, *Modern Ireland, 1600–1972*, pp 146–53 (1988).

177 The key provision is in the first article: 'The Roman Catholicks of this kingdom shall enjoy such privileges in the exercise of their religion as are consistent with the laws of Ireland, or as they did

The public record of King Charles II involved the king's promise of liberty of conscience (Declarations of Breda, April 1660) before his coronation and the Declaration of Independence (March 1672) to remove statutory restrictions from dissenters and Catholics. Charles married the Catholic princess of Portugal in 1662; they were childless. Parliament enacted (with the royal assent) the Test Act of 1673 requiring office holders to take the Eucharist annually according to the established church, and the Papist Disabling Act of 1678 specifically excluding Roman Catholics from sitting in Parliament – the parliamentary response to the fraudulent 'popish plot' of Titus Oates.[178] The king's private history, unknown at the time, involved secret treaties of 1670, 1676, 1678 and 1681 with Louis XIV of France promising to support France in its European wars and join the Roman Catholic church in exchange for an annual payment of £20,000; this was despite his 1668 alliance with Protestant Holland and Sweden to support their wars with France.[179] King Charles allegedly converted to the Roman Catholic church on his deathbed, on 6 February 1685. His brother and heir, James, had announced his own conversion in 1671 and married the Catholic Princess Mary of Modena on 21 November 1673. (The Test Act of 1673 was designed to force James from the office of lord high admiral.) Under Charles II, England had a state church of which the king was the 'supreme head'; but those outside the state church (dissenters and Roman Catholics) were not full citizens, while the king's allegiance to the state church was at least questionable.

In defence of Parliament's failure to observe the treaty, Browne offered a doctrine from international law: *clausula rebus sic stantibus* – the little clause implied in all treaties that all things must remain the same. Browne alleged, unconvincingly, that papists' disloyal actions changed the circumstances of the treaty. In effect, there was no mutuality.[180]

Browne also offered 'constitutional' arguments: that the army negotiators did not have parliamentary authority to commit the Irish Parliament, and so Parliament was not bound by the agreement; that the ambiguity of language made the treaty unenforceable; and that by the penal laws the Parliament had acted to

enjoy in the reign of King Charles the second; and their majesties as soon as their affairs will permit them to summons a Parliament in this kingdom, will endeavour to procure the said Roman Catholicks such further security in that particular as may preserve them from any disturbance upon the account of the said religion.'

178 Titus Oates (1649–1705), an adventurer and liar, was possessed by the idea that he had discovered a plot by Roman Catholics to assassinate King Charles II, kill parliamentarians, burn London and exterminate Protestants (1678), causing a hysterical panic that killed innocent people. He was subsequently convicted of perjury (1685), but pardoned by King William. See G.M. Trevelyan, *England under the Stuarts*, pp 317–31 (21st ed. 1946).

179 A. Fraser, *Royal Charles*, pp 268–78, 325–47, 385–408 (1979) and H. Pearson, *Merry monarch*, pp 185–91, 199–200, 209–18 (1960).

180 The agreement of 3 Oct. 1691 provided for ratification within eight months. The joint sovereigns William and Mary consented to the articles on 24 Feb. 1692 and the English Parliament confirmed the Articles of Limerick in 1695, but the Irish Parliament refused to confirm in 1695 and began the enactment of the penal laws.

protect the property rights of those who supported the constitution in church and state.

V. THE PRACTICE OF LAW

Arthur Browne argued cases as a barrister in the common law courts and as an advocate in the ecclesiastical courts and the admiralty for eighteen years, seven as king's counsel. In his last three years he was prime serjeant dealing with litigation for the crown. (In his reported cases in admiralty, he usually appeared for shipowners.)

No list of his cases has turned up, although he discussed a few of them in his treatise, *A compendious view of the civil law and of the law of admiralty*. Reports of cases do not list all the lawyers who may have participated in arguments. Thus, a brief description of the courts in which he practiced is the best approximation of the practice of law in his lifetime.

A. The common law courts

The Irish legal system in which Arthur Browne practised as a barrister and advocate from 1784 to 1805 was essentially the same as that of England; both systems began with a Norman conquest in 1066 in England and 1177 in Ireland. Except for disputes in local courts, nothing remained of the laws of the Celtic Britons or the Romans, the Vikings or the Anglo-Saxons in England. Similarly, in Ireland, the ancient laws of the Celtic tribes, called 'brehon law' from the title of the judge, 'brehon' (actually '*breitheamh*'), had ceased to be effective by 1605 in the face of English military rule in eastern Ireland.[181]

The first four Norman kings of England decided policy and resolved important disputes over land ownership and feudal obligations in the *curia regis*[182] – the king's council of great nobles, at which the king presided. By the time of Henry II, eighty-eight years after the conquest, this judicial function may have become burdensome, since it interrupted such royal diversions as war, the hunt, the hawk, the table and the bedchamber. Thus, trusted subordinates, the justiciars, could act in his place. The Norman origins were obvious from the use of Norman French language in pleadings and reports; this added an element of mystery to the law until it was finally abolished by statute (4 Geo. 2 c.26) in 1731 in England and Scotland, and then in Ireland, in 1737 (11 Geo. 2 c.6).

---

181 K. Simms, *The brehons of later medieval Ireland*, D. Hogan and W.N. Osborough, *Brehons, serjeants and attorneys*, pp 51–76 (1990). The passage of English law to Ireland is reflected in A.G. Donaldson, *Some comparative aspects of Irish law* (1957).

182 Materials for this brief summary came from T. Plucknett, *A concise history of the common law*, pp 106–57, 176–99, 353–78 (5th ed. 1956); H. Potter, *Historical introduction to English law and its institutions*, pp 104–68 (4th ed. 1958); W.S. Holdsworth, *A history of English law*, vol. 2, pp 3–5, 32–63, 194–241 (3rd ed. 1922) and B. Abel-Smith and R. Stevens *Lawyers and the courts*, pp 7–29 (1966).

The first part of the royal council to work without the presence of the king and the great lords (probably after 1150) was the treasury or exchequer – its name came from the square cloth divided like a chess board on which accounts were settled. Its function as the place to resolve civil disputes between subjects came from the fiction that one or both disputants would be less able to pay taxes and other feudal dues owed to the king because of the existence of the dispute. By 1172 the writ of *quominus* was used for these disputes, and a procedural law for the exchequer court had been analyzed in *Dialogus de scaccario*.

The court of common pleas appeared around 1178 to deal with land questions (the real actions tried by wager of battle) and other civil disputes such as covenant, debt and contract. This court and its 'law' was probably the subject of the first English law text, Glanvil's *Tractatus de legibus et consuetudinibus Angliae*.

The Norman kings were always on the move, travelling to each part of the kingdom with the entire retinue, thus, the exchequer (and the later king's bench) followed the king. It was the court of common pleas that was allowed to settle at Westminster during the frequent absences from England of Henry II, Richard and John before its home base was fixed in the Magna Carta (1215) at Westminster – the 'certain' location (17 John c. 17). The great royal hall at Westminster, begun in 1097, had been completed by the thirteenth century and the common pleas and exchequer found a home there until 1875.

The third court coming from the curia regis was the king's bench, not fully developed until the time of Edward I (1272). It owed its separate existence to the fact that the king was not always available to preside, for example when he was on a crusade, fighting a Continental war, or still a minor (Henry III). This court had criminal jurisdiction both as to trial and appeal (by the writ of certiorari). Its civil jurisdiction was based on the writ of trespass *vi et armis* (essentially intentional torts) and trespass on the case (essentially negligence). This court developed prerogative writs: *quo warranto*, *mandamus*, prohibition and *habeas corpus*. It also came to be a primitive form of appellate court by the writ of error to inferior tribunals.

These three courts were courts of common law – the unwritten law found by the judges. By the thirteenth century, disputed facts were found by a jury. In these common law courts decisions were based upon the precedents and analogies developed out of the forms of action, i.e. the various writs, so that substantive law and the writs were married. The absence of a specific writ to deal with a new problem helped to produce the fourth court, that of the lord chancellor.

B. Chancery

This court dealt with situations not governed by the common law writs or where application of the writs might be unjust. In medieval times a chancellor was a legal advisor to a high ecclesiastical or civil officer. The peremptory powers of a single individual as lord high chancellor of the entire realm must have been acquired gradually, so also the emergence of a court free from the presence of the king and great nobles. This new court, not yet called chancery, emerged in the middle of the fourteenth century, administering 'equity', i.e. the royal conscience, often by an order to a party not to do something – the injunction – a power not exercised by courts of common law. Chancery did not use the jury to find facts, and parties seeking relief were required to come into court with 'clean hands', i.e., without any suggestion of questionable conduct.

C. Statutes

Norman overlords brought their familiar institutions with them to Ireland,[183] for example, an Irish Parliament was assembled in 1297,[184] thirty-two years after Simon de Montfort assembled a Parliament or representative assembly in England. English statutes were applied in Ireland by a statute of 1495 (10 Hen. 7 c. 22). Controversy surrounds the exact dates when Irish courts on the English model were established in Dublin – near Dublin Castle and on the grounds of the present Christ Church Cathedral (begun in 1170).[185] Surely by 1541, when Henry VIII assumed the title king of Ireland proffered by the Irish Parliament, and the year the King's Inns received the Blackfriar's Abbey on the Liffey, common law courts were operating in those areas subject to English military rule.[186] It is uncertain the effect of statute law before the eighteenth century.

D. The Bar

The division of the practice of law into courtroom specialists (the king's serjeants and the members of the Bar) and the office lawyer who dealt with clients (the attorneys and solicitors) had become rigid by the end of the sixteenth century.[187] Thereafter, the serjeants and the barristers had the exclusive right to appear in the common law courts of common pleas, exchequer and king's bench. This custom was confirmed by the royal decree of Elizabeth I in 1574. In 1785, the three common law courts plus the lord chancellor's court were gathered into a single building in Dublin. (In London, the three common law courts sat at Westminster Hall, but the lord chancellor's court sat in the City of London in the vicinity of the inns of court and Chancery Lane.) In Dublin, barristers were once accustomed to await briefs from solicitors in the great hall of the Four Courts building, until the

---

183 E. Curtis, *A history of medieval Ireland from 1110 to 1513*, pp 112–32 (1927); J. Gilbert, 1 *A history of the city of Dublin*, pp 133–42 (1854, rep. 1972); W.N. Osborough, *Introduction to the 1995 reprint of the legislation of the pre-union Irish Parliament* (1995).

184 E. Curtis, *A history of Ireland* (6th ed., 1950), pp 189–94.

185 C. Kenny, *The four courts at Christ Church, 1608–1796* in W.N. Osborough (ed.), *Explorations in law and history*, pp 107–32 (1995).

186 See W.N. Osborough, 'Eighteenth-century Ireland's legislative deficit' in M. Brown and S. Donlan, *The laws and other legalities of Ireland, 1689–1850*, pp 75–96 (2011) and Curtis, *A history of Ireland*, pp 164–70.

187 W.N. Osborough, *The regulation of the admission of attorneys and solicitors in Ireland, 1600–1866*, and D. Hogan and W.N. Osborough, *Brehons, serjeants and attorney'*, pp 101–51, 112–31.

1830 construction of the law library of the Four Courts. Barristers' chambers were not located together at King's Inns, as they were in London's inns, but in their dwellings during the years of Arthur Browne's legal practice,[188] and this surely explains the 625 law books in his personal library.

An appreciation of the Bar in Browne's time can be gained from an article celebrating the 200th anniversary of its 9 December 1798 meeting, which denounced the union proposal. According to that study, there were 359 practicing barristers with Dublin addresses. Forty-two practicing barristers (out of 67 members of the Bar) were members of the House of Commons. Since Catholics had been admitted only after 24 June 1792 there were but a half dozen Catholic barristers in 1798 and several Presbyterians, and the remainder were associated with the established church. It was estimated that 180 were the sons of landed gentlemen, 78 were sons of clergy of the established church, 22 were sons of judges or barristers, 23 were sons of solicitors and 15 were sons of physicians.[189]

E. Courts of Roman law

Another part of the Norman system was the segregation of specialized courts that used the Roman legal system. In London, that produced doctors' commons where the ecclesiastical courts dealing with probate of estates, matrimonial disputes and the operations of the established church were joined with the high court of admiralty for the simple reason that these courts used classical Latin instead of Norman French, and relied on an authoritative Latin text, the Corpus Juris Civilis.[190] Dublin had no doctors' commons, but some members of the Bar specialized in the work of the courts based on Roman law and limited their practice accordingly. Arthur Browne was a barrister in the common law courts as well as an advocate in the ecclesiastical courts and in the admiralty court.

Prior to 1783, the admiralty court in Ireland was not really an Irish court, but a subordinate court of the high court of admiralty in London. In 1783, Grattan's Parliament, of which Browne was a member, enacted the Admiralty Court Act.[191] The effect of that statute was to put the Dublin admiralty court under Irish control: judges were appointed by the crown of Ireland (the viceroy) and were removable by the Irish Parliament. Furthermore, appeals were made before the court of delegates (chancery) rather than the London high court of admiralty.[192] The English lords commissioners of the admiralty could not exercise their

---

188 D. Hogan, *The legal profession in Ireland, 1789–1922*, pp 14–28 (1986).
189 K. Ferguson, 'The Irish Bar in 1798', 52 *Dublin Historical Record*, 32–60 (1999).
190 G.D. Squibb, *Doctors' commons: a history of the College of Advocates and Doctors of Law* (1977) and W. Senior, *Doctors' commons and the old court of admiralty* (1922). Doctors' commons in the cloister of St Paul's Cathedral, London was finally dissolved in 1858 after common-law lawyers were admitted to the practice of the courts of doctors' commons.
191 See 23 and 24 Geo. 3 c. 14. Costello, *The court of admiralty of Ireland*, pp 354–6 (2011); 2 Brown, n. 2, p. 13.
192 21 and 22 Geo. 3 c. 20; see also 23 and 24 Geo. 3 c. 14.

functions in Ireland, even though there was no lord high admiral of Ireland. In the 1801 Act of Union, the instance court of admiralty for civil and maritime disputes remained in Ireland, with appeals still determined in the Irish chancery court of delegates.[193]

The most lucrative part of the jurisdiction was prize law, but there was persistent conflict with the English admiralty court and the lords commissioners, and this jurisdiction was often forbidden by writs of prohibition.[194] Prize law disputes came from seizures during the American Revolution until 1783 and the war with France from 1793 until 1815. Other areas of civil admiralty practice were collisions, salvage, maritime liens for necessaries, possessory actions, suits on charter parties, suits on bills of lading, bottomry bonds and other securities (respondentia bonds), seamen's wages, unlawful impressment of seamen and droits of the crown. The last area of possible admiralty jurisdiction was the Criminal law for piratical offences.

When Arthur Browne began to practise there, the admiralty judge was Warden Flood,[195] cousin of the Whig politician Henry Flood. He had been appointed by the English Admiralty Court in 1776, but reappointed under the new Irish Admiralty Court Act in 1785. He served as admiralty judge until his death in 1797. He frequently used deputies, including Arthur Browne, to hear cases during his twenty-one years.

In 1797, Jonah Barrington was appointed Admiralty judge.[196] The appointment was purely political, as he had no educational background or practical experience in admiralty and seldom acted in a judicial capacity. His stormy career in this office lasted until he was removed by the Westminster Parliament in 1830. Barrington, no stranger to corruption in office, later accused Arthur Browne of having sold his vote on the union in 1800.[197] Arthur Browne also served as deputy to Judge Barrington. The judge's salary was about £500 per annum, no match for Barrington's lifestyle. Barrington spent years seeking an increase in salary; in 1806, George Ponsonby, as lord chancellor, raised it to £1,000 per annum.

---

193 40 Geo. 3 c. 38.

194 Costello, *The court of admiralty in Ireland*, pp 187–95 (2011).

195 Warden Flood (1735–97) was the son of a lord chief justice of king's bench. He entered TCD as a pensioner in 1753, AB 1757; Middle Temple, called to Irish Bar 1759, LLD 1776 (TCD) on appointment to the admiralty bench.

196 Jonah Barrington (1760–1834) from Knapton, County Laois, entered TCD as pensioner in 1773, AB 1778, called to the Bar in 1788, was elected to Parliament in 1790 and became king's counsel in 1793. He was elected from Tuam in 1790 and from Clogher in 1797. He was appointed admiralty judge in 1797. He received LLD from TCD, *honoris causa* in 1797. He seldom presided in court, assigning the cases to a deputy. He continued to practise as a barrister while serving as admiralty judge. He assigned his judicial salary to secure loans and misappropriated funds held by the court, the reason for his eventual removal by Parliament. Hearings before deputies often occurred while creditors and bailiffs were on his trail. He struggled unsuccessfully with the English admiralty court over prize jurisdiction. See Costello, *The court of admiralty in Ireland*, pp 156–72 (2011).

197 See chapter 14, n. 23.

Admiralty practice was bifurcated in the same way as the common law. Proctors, like solicitors, dealt with the clients while advocates, like barristers, advised on the law and argued the cases in court. In 1784, Arthur Browne was one of the fourteen advocates – there were also seventeen proctors. By the time of his death during the Napoleonic Wars there were twenty-two advocates but only twelve proctors.[198] Admission to practice in admiralty as advocate was granted by the judge to those who possessed the degree of LLD (doctor of laws); only advocates could sign pleadings and appear before the court.

When Arthur Browne became an admiralty advocate, the court was located on the grounds of Christ Church Cathedral, off Christ Church Lane, near Winetavern Street. The court was later relocated to an office in the Four Courts. Much admiralty business was also conducted in the 'offices' of the admiralty marshall (for execution of process) and admiralty registrar (for recording or copying documents). These were usually in the office holders' private residences, which were found in many parts of the city.[199]

Regardless of the number of admiralty cases actually tried by Browne, his background and learning in the operations of government was such that he was able to collate and synthesize a chaotic subject matter and present it in a system that endured from the days of unwritten custom to the age of statutes.

A final word about trials: live witness testimony presented a serious problem in the eighteenth century in cases in which many people spoke only Irish while the courts functioned only in English. Bilingual judges, barristers and jurors were not common, so oath-bound interpreters were required in most parts of the country.[200]

---

198 Costello, *The court of admiralty in Ireland*, pp 183–5 (2011).
199 Ibid., pp 178–82.
200 W.M. Wolfe, *An Irish-speaking island: state, religion, community and the linguistic landscape in Ireland, 1770–1870*, pp 149–67 (2014).

CHAPTER SEVEN

Family life and religion (1756–1805)

I. FAMILY LIFE

Arthur Browne's family life is veiled from our eyes by the passage of time. No records of his two marriages, other than his writing in *Miscellaneous sketches*, remain; in 1798, he dedicated the second volume of his *Sketches*, 'To the memory of Marianne', who was once 'tremblingly alive' to his pleasures and cares, even after the passage of nine years, implying that her death may have occurred in 1789.[1] The daughter from that marriage, Mary Tatham Browne, a 'resemblance in person, sweetness and understanding' of her mother, is the person to whom the first volume of *Sketches* is dedicated, although she was then too young to understand some of the contents.[2]

We can appreciate his grief at the loss of his Marianne in his prose writing, 'On the passion of grief',[3] and a poem 'written soon after a great domestic loss':

> The joys are o'er – the picture's gone
> Like shining transient clouds, 'tis fled
> By tears effac'd, in hope dissolv'd
> And all its magic colourings dead.
>
> Ah! False the colours fancy feigns,
> One radiant light alone was true,
> Sweet gleam of bliss! What now remains?
>
> To mourn and love the past and you.[4]

Browne, like many eighteenth-century intellectuals, felt compelled to express emotion in rhyming verse.

He opened his home life to view in his essay, 'On conjugal felicity':

---

1   A. Browne, *Miscellaneous sketches*, vol. 2, pp iii–iv (1798). An explanation for the absence of recorded information might have been to evade the requirement that fellows of TCD remain unmarried during their fellowship; Arthur Browne was a fellow of TCD from 1778 until his death in 1805.
2   Browne, *Miscellaneous sketches*, vol. 1, pp iii–iv.
3   Ibid., vol. 1, p. 125.   4   Ibid., vol. 2, pp 384–5.

The happy couple who really love and respect each other, think not of commanding or obeying. Such ideas never enter the heart of real friendship much less of real love. An eager desire to know and to anticipate each others' wishes is the character of genuine passion.

He praises:

> that affection which prompts to show mutual respect and attention, to elevate each other in the eyes of strangers, and to excite delightful surprise in the beloved breast, by doing that which intimate knowledge of character whispers will be agreeable ...[5]

His widow in 1805 was Bridget Browne. The obituaries mention that he left a widow and five children,[6] so there must have been four children from a second marriage. We know that one of these was a son, Arthur, who became a parish priest in the Church of Ireland,[7] and one was a daughter, Anne Maria.

II

In the eighteenth century, as in most of the Christian era, the practice of religion was not confined to the solitary retreat. Public men were expected to declare their religious faith and even proselytize. As the son, grandson and great-grandson of priests, attendance at public worship and family prayers and scripture readings must have been a large part of his life before his college days. Later he put religion into the heart of conjugal felicity:

> Without religious principle, permanent happiness evidently cannot be expected: the sacred vow of marriage will not be properly respected, the approach of sickness or loss of beauty will break the feeble bonds not formed by Christianity, the parental care will be slightly extended to a neglected offspring and the parental example will complete their ruining.[8]

To him:

5   Ibid., vol. 1, pp 171–81.
6   *Faulkner's Dublin Journal*, 11 June 1805. On 5 Mar. 1789 Arthur Browne obtained a policy on his life from the Society for Equitable Assurances of Lives to benefit Bridget Browne, amounting to £700.
7   His son, Arthur Marmaduke Franklin Browne (1804–69), entered TCD as a pensioner in 1822, AB 1830, ordained at Cloyne 1835, curate and vicar of Affane Church in the Lismore diocese of County Waterford, married in 1840; a daughter Sarah married an officer in the Indian Army. Arthur Browne's daughter, Mary Tatham Browne, died at Newtown, County Wexford in November 1844. A younger daughter, Anne Maria Browne, was married at Affane Church in 1844.
8   A. Browne, *Miscellaneous sketches*, p. 180 (1798).
9   Ibid., p. 76, from an essay on the character of Dr Samuel Johnson.

The spirit of Christianity is meek and lowly of heart … the spirit of fortitude neither despises nor trembles at death …[9]

Could we imagine a world in which religion universally prevailed, and Christianity was universally practiced; what health, what happiness, what peace would reign in such a scene! War must cease – disease would be almost unknown, for temperance and tranquility of mind would banish most of those maladies which afflict mankind. Extreme old age sinking in gradual decay without pain, without sorrow, would be the termination of the life of man …

When we turn back from such a vision to what the world really is, does it not seem almost the abode of daemons? It might be a paradise still. Nature and Providence inflict comparatively few evils; we ourselves are the cause of our own misery.[10]

He saw his Christianity as:

Balm of hurt minds – sole comfort of the oppressed, resource of misery, companion of solitude and source of cheerful confidence …[11]

His public position required him to endorse the Protestant form of Christianity:

I am a sincere Protestant, I know the errors of the church of Rome, but what import is it to me whether a man calls himself Protestant or papist if he violates every law of charity, humanity and Christianity? I detest him equally.[12]

He said that his Christianity was based on two facts: the divinity of Jesus Christ and the immortality of the soul. His first belief arose from the pure and perfect system of Christian morals; his second belief from man's unconquerable desire of immortality.[13]

Unlike American members of the established church, like Jefferson or Washington, or fashionable Londoners, Browne was never attracted to the deism widely accepted at the end of the eighteenth century. Edmund Burke's criticism of Tom Paine's *Age of reason* (1794) found an echo in Arthur Browne's 'Modern sophisms':

Mankind seem lately to have conceived, that the abilities of preceding ages exhausted truth and virtue with every thing real and genuine, and left for the

10 Ibid., pp 246–7.   11 Ibid., p. 245.   12 Ibid., notes to vol. 2, p. 5.
13 Ibid., pp 249–50: 'in every other instance where the deity has implanted a natural desire that cannot be eradicated, he has given a power of satisfying it. It would be inconsistent with his goodness to tantalize by irrefutable desires without possibility of their satisfaction, it would be to laugh at his creatures, and is incompatible with his wisdom; it must be so then with this desire, and as surely as I believe in the existence and attributes of God, so surely I think must I believe in the immortality of the soul.'

talents of posterity only the invention of fallacy, and improvement of sophism. Hence, whoever wishes to please modern taste, devises new courses of paradox, with entremets of deism or sauces of debauchery.[14]

He concluded his thoughts on religion with a prayer for himself and his adopted country, written in 1798 during a period of bloody revolution and repression:

> Father of all, for without thy assistance I can have no confidence in myself, grant that whatever be the lot of my distracted country, it may not be my miserable fate to make an affected boast of thy religion for interested purposes, nor on the other hand shamefully to deny thy name in the hour of danger or day of adversity.[15]

III. THE ESTABLISHED CHURCH

Arthur Browne's early parliamentary career concerned defence of the tithe to support the established church, and much of his entire career was involved in defence of its privileges, so it is important to consider the established church as a political institution early in his biography. This section will not attempt to explore the spirituality or pastoral effectiveness of Arthur Browne's church, but only its outward manifestations in the life of the society in which he lived.

Arthur Browne's earliest experiences of the Christian church were in his father's or grandfather's parishes, in colonies where there was no established church but both men were supported by an annual missionary salary from the SPG. There was no bishop in America to oversee the work of the clergy, and handle complaints of angry parishioners, so clergy were free to accept 'calls' from the vestries of larger or wealthier parishes without official interference. The physical upkeep of the colonial church buildings was dependent on the congregation through the sale or rental of pews. Without active persecution of 'popery' or 'dissent', the Newport clergy had to compete for believers at ten different houses of worship.

Ireland, however, had a monstrous and wealthy bureaucracy in church matters, supported in large measure through the tithe, paid by the agricultural majority of the people, who remained Roman Catholic, or Presbyterian rather than by actual adherents of the established church.[16]

---

14 Ibid., p. 58.   15 Ibid., p. 255.
16 On the wealth of the church, see S.J. Connolly, *Religion, law and power: the making of Protestant Ireland, 1660–1760*, pp 179–82 (1992). The tithe was essentially a tax to be paid from one-tenth of the produce of arable lands by the workers of the land (the tenants) and not by the owners (the landlords) for the support of the clergy of the established church of the parish where the land was located. It was collected by 'tithe proctors' and the right to collect tithes could be assigned or 'farmed out' to collection agencies. It often led to violence on both sides. (The practice ended in 1839 as a result of the Tithe War.)

The number of eighteenth-century adherents is difficult to estimate. The first reliable census of the entire island from 1834, before famine and massive emigration, showed a total population of 7,943,940 of which 6,427,712 (81 per cent) were Roman Catholic, 642,356 (8 per cent) were Presbyterian and 852,064 (11 per cent) were members of the Church of Ireland.[17] Most eighteenth-century estimates assume that 10 per cent of the population belonged to the Church of Ireland,[18] but it was the church of cities and towns and only lightly scattered in rural areas. It was strongest in Dublin, Cork City and Limerick in that century. In the eighteenth century, as in previous ages, people were born into the Christian community of their parents and continued that affiliation throughout their lives.

The unity of church and state is most clearly shown in the Irish Test Act of 1704,[19] following the precedent of the English Test Act of 1673.[20] In order to hold any public office (except insignificant or low-level public employment) the office holder had to have a certificate from a Church of Ireland clergyman that the office holder had received the sacrament of Holy Communion at a Sunday celebration at least once per year. (It should be noted that celebrations of the Eucharist were infrequent, outside of the cathedrals, in the eighteenth century.) The Test Act continued in force until its repeal in 1780,[21] despite many efforts to amend the statute permanently to exempt Presbyterians. As in England, there were evasions at the local level and 'occasional conformity' indemnifications. This transformation of the central act of Christian worship into a civil service examination was condemned by the 1787 framers of the United States Constitution as one of the few legislative acts forbidden to the United States Congress.[22]

17 *First report of the Commission of Public Education, Ireland*, pp 1–45 (1834). The name 'Church of Ireland' now describes the ecclesiastical branch of the Anglican communion in the Republic of Ireland and in Northern Ireland. Eighteenth-century sources generally refer to it as 'the established church', but the modern name was also used until the union in 1801, when it became the United Church of England and Ireland. The 1834 Irish population of 8 million should be compared with the 2005 population of 5,318,276 (4,015,696 in the Republic and 1,702,600 in Northern Ireland).
18 T.C. Barnard, 'Parishes, pews and parsons: lay people and the Church of Ireland, 1647–1786' in R. Gillespie and W.G. Neely (eds), *The laity and the Church of Ireland, 1000–2000*, pp 70–3 (2002).
19 3 Anne c. 2 (1704). See generally, J.G. Simms, 'The making of a penal law', 12 *Irish Historical Studies*, 105 (1960–1); Connolly, *Religion, law and power*, pp 166–71 (1992); see also M. Wall, *The penal laws, 1691–1760* (1967).
20 25 Car. 2 c. 2, applicable to all persons filling any office, civil or military. The target was 'popish recusants', specifically the king's brother, James, earl of York, and his Roman Catholic family and supporters. It did not apply in Scotland where the Church of Scotland was Presbyterian, but its application to Ireland immediately excluded thousands of Ulster Presbyterians. It was not repealed in England until the 1829 Catholic Relief Act. See G.M. Trevelyan, *England under the Stuarts*, pp 313, 429 (1904).
21 19 and 20 Geo. 3 c. 6. Part of a British government programme to pacify Ireland's Presbyterian minority and Roman Catholic majority; it was bitterly fought by the bishops of the Church of Ireland.
22 US Constitution, art. VI, para. 3, 'but no religious test shall ever be required as a qualification to any office or public trust under the United States'.

In Ireland, the established church considered itself to be both Catholic and Protestant. It was Catholic in the sense of inheritor of medieval traditions in ancient buildings. The Protestant nature of the Church of Ireland was not the result of the reformation of popular attitudes concerning the church, as occurred in sixteenth-century Germany, France and Switzerland, for the Reformation was rarely and never effectively preached to the Irish people in their own language. Instead, the Reformation of the established church occurred through the English sovereign's power to appoint bishops, deans and other high officials. This was combined with the appointing power of the wealthy landowners. They controlled the churches and abbeys on their lands. (The abbeys were legally dissolved in 1560.) The reformed religion did not move out of the English Pale or the cathedral cities into the rural districts until the proselytizing of the nineteenth century.

Arthur Browne was a member of the established church, i.e. the church established by law in Ireland as it was in England, but in Ireland, it could only pretend to be nationwide. It was then governed by four archbishops (Armagh, the primate; Dublin, Cashel and Tuam) and eighteen bishops, all of whom were members of the Irish House of Lords, where they were usually supporters of Dublin Castle and the English interest: they were also a powerful restraint on any official who might attempt to deprive them of any perquisite, privilege or prerogative.[23] Englishmen usually served as chaplains to the viceroy, while Irishmen were usually cathedral deans or TCD fellows: thirty-four were Irish, two were Scots.[24]

Because the income from sees varied greatly, there was much upward movement among the bishops, a process usually referred to as 'translation', from a small, poorly compensated diocese to a larger, wealthier diocese.[25] The appointment was for life, unless translated. As in most of Europe, whether Protestant or Roman Catholic, bishops had official functions in support of the state and many holders of the title were purely political creatures.[26] Their initial appointments and advancements were usually political acts of the government in power. A further problem for the Irish church, however, was the number of English clerics who were sent to wealthy Irish dioceses; it did not work in the reverse direction for Irishmen. No Irishman was appointed to an English diocese before William Connor Magee

23 'Nomination' of bishops to sees in England, Wales and Ireland was controlled by the prime minister of Great Britain always for political services rendered by the nominee or his family. Political reliability was essential. In the latter half of the eighteenth century, 175 men were appointed to the 22 Irish sees: 39 were of English origin.

24 D.H. Akenson, *The Church of Ireland: ecclesiastical reform and revolution, 1800–1885*, pp 6–10, 32–70 (1971).

25 As in the civil service, there was a ladder to be climbed by translations: there were 'starter' sees, lightly populated and lightly endowed, where the annual incomes were less than £2,400 (usually only £2,000), such as Killaloe and Kilfenora, Clonfert and Kilmacduagh, Cork and Ross, Cloyne, Down and Conor, Dromore, Kilmore and Killala and Achonry. At the apex were the archbishoprics: Armagh at £8,000, Dublin at £5,000, Cashel and Tuam at £4,000. See M. Legg, 'The parish clergy of the Church of Ireland in the eighteenth century', pp 128–41 in T.C. Barnard and W.G. Neely (eds), *The Clergy of the Church of Ireland, 1000–2000* (2006).

26 Akenson, *The Church of Ireland*, pp 16–17 (1971).

in 1868 to Peterborough. English holders of Irish sees for political reasons, however, could expect translation to wealthier Irish or English dioceses. Bishops were expected to make annual visitations of every parish in the diocese to confirm parishioners and oversee the physical and spiritual condition of the parish, but this chore was often avoided, especially in the country. Absenteeism from the diocese was always a problem, even for native Irish. (Bishops maintained Dublin residences for their attendance at the House of Lords.) The number and boundaries of dioceses had been fixed in the twelfth century and bore no relation to the actual needs of the people. The diocesan structure was not reorganized until 1833, a change challenged by the Oxford Movement in England. This was merely a prelude to the eventual disestablishment of the Church of Ireland by Gladstone in 1869.

At the local level, however, the medieval parish structure fell apart. There were theoretically 2,436 parishes, but only 1,001 were in condition for public worship because of the ravages of war, neglect and decay; and of these merely 335 provided housing for the clergy.[27] In the eighteenth century there were roughly 1,120 ordained priests to minister to a theoretical flock of 800,000 souls.[28] Outside of the cities and towns it was essential that the clergy serve several parishes – called pluralism. (Nevertheless, there were probably as many Roman Catholic priests caring for the spiritual needs of the majority, eight times the size of the Protestant population.)[29]

Unlike Roman Catholics and members of some dissenting groups, preparation for the priestly office was not possible for the poor in the established church. The qualifications for ordination were determined in each diocese by the diocesan bishop. The usual requirement was a university degree from Trinity College Dublin, Oxford or Cambridge. (There was no seminary for training clergy in the established church until 1833.) Ordination to the priesthood by the hands of a bishop followed service as a deacon, usually for a short period of time. For ordination as a deacon, the candidate had to be 23 years of age, and 24 was the minimum age for ordination as a priest. The candidate could be examined by the bishop or by a committee of priests acting for the bishop.

Assignment to parish service often involved seeking a patron who controlled appointment to a parish, called a 'living' or 'benefice'. This was usually the local

---

27 A. Ford, J. McGuire and K. Milne (eds), *As by law established: the Church of Ireland since the Reformation*, pp 136–65, 187–94 (1995). A. Ford, *The Protestant Reformation in Ireland, 1590–1641* (1985). A. Acheson, *A history of the Church of Ireland, 1691–2001* (2002). R.B. McDowell, *Ireland in the age of imperialism and revolution, 1760–1801*, pp 156–70, 202–5 (1979).

28 Akenson, *The Church of Ireland*, pp 56–7 (1971). See generally Connolly, *Religion, law and power* (1992). R.B. McDowell estimates that there were about 1,280 clergy of the Church of Ireland, 800 rectors or vicars and 475 curates during the time of his study (1760–1801). See McDowell, *Ireland in the age of imperialism and revolution*, p. 162 (1979). Arthur Browne reckoned about 1,200 ordained priests, A. Browne, *A compendious view of the ecclesiastical law of Ireland*, p. 74 (1803).

29 See generally S.J. Connolly, *Priests and people in pre-Famine Ireland, 1780–1845* (1992); Akenson, *The Church of Ireland*, p. 163 (1971). T. Barnard and W. Neely (eds), *The clergy of the Church of Ireland, 1000–2000*, pp 128–56 (2006); incomes at p. 143.

landlord, who regarded the appointment as a property right; the average annual income was £148 2s., ranging from £90 in Killaloe to £250 in Raphoe.[30] As with the bishops, there was a constant search for additional or wealthier livings. Parish service in rural Ireland was not as attractive to ambitious Englishmen as the bishoprics. Many rural rectors or vicars (parsons) regarded themselves as responsible for the spiritual welfare of all residents, regardless of faith.

The function of the clergy, at all levels, beyond the spiritual, was to support the state and the House of Hanover through the doctrine and practice of the Articles of Religion,[31] and the Book of Common Prayer,[32] both having been approved by Parliament and endorsed by the sovereign. A few of them supported the Volunteers, but only one openly supported the United Irishmen: Revd Henry Fulton of Nenagh, who was transported to Australia.

There was a Christian message hidden in all of this, but it must have been very difficult to discover in this rich and powerful church that only served a small minority of the population. While the scriptures and the Book of Common Prayer were eventually available in the Irish language, few of the clergy spoke Irish and there was never a serious effort to speak to the majority in their own language. (The services of the Roman Catholic church to the majority were conducted in Latin, although preaching might be in Irish when offered, which was not common.)[33]

---

30 Akenson, *The Church of Ireland*, pp 55–63 (1971). 'Livings' included all the benefits available to the holder of the appointment as rector or vicar of a parish, including a residence (the glebe or rectory), the glebe farm and the rents of parish lands; these could be assigned to others for collection. See Connolly, *Religion, law and power*, p. 61 (1992); McDowell, *Ireland in the age of imperialism and revolution* (1979); and R. Gillespie and W. Neely (eds), *The laity and the Church of Ireland, 1000–2000*, pp 152–95, 250–76 (2002).

31 The Articles of Religion were first determined and defined by the joint convocations of Canterbury and York under Elizabeth I (1571), consisting of 39 articles of belief and practice. Puritans would later describe them as the cat (whip) with 39 stripes. See M.S. Flaherty, 'The Irish Articles of Religion and the fall of the Stuart monarchies' in H. Harty and W.E. Nelson (eds), *Law as culture and culture as law: essays in honor of John Phillip Reid*, pp 81–118 (2000).

32 The Book of Common Prayer was first assembled by Archbishop Cranmer from various medieval Latin sources in 1549 under Edward VI. At the restoration of Charles II, Parliament enacted the edition used in England for more than 300 years; 13 and 14 Car. 2 c. 4 (1662). This book was adopted by the Church of Ireland convocation in 1662, but further additions were authorized in the eighteenth century.

33 For Irish language proposals, see McDowell, *Ireland in the age of imperialism and revolution*, pp 149–51 (1979) and Connolly, *Religion, law and power*, pp 122–3, 133–4, 298–305 (1992). The Irish language was used at TCD in the administrations of provosts William Bedell (1627–29), Robert Ussher (1629–34), Narcissus Marsh (1679–83) and Robert Huntington (1683–92) to encourage preaching the Reformation to non-English speakers, using translations of the New Testament (1603) and the Book of Common Prayer (1608) by TCD fellow William Daniel. Formal Irish language studies among the Ascendancy occurred after the failed bequest of the politician Henry Flood (1732–91) for a professorship in the Irish language and the addition of books and manuscripts in Irish for the Trinity Library. Nineteenth-century proselytizers resumed the use of Irish in the Irish Society (1810) and the Home Mission Society (1828). See also T.C. Barnard, 'Protestants and the Irish language, c.1675–1725', 44 *Journal of Ecclesiastical History*, 263 (1973)

Except in the wealthy cathedrals, little of medieval Christian ritual remained by the eighteenth century, and nineteenth-century evangelicals condemned any traces of popery. There was a rigid adherence to the prayer-book offices of matins (morning prayer) and evensong (evening prayer).[34] In many parishes the celebration of the Lord's Supper or Eucharist was infrequent – usually only at the major festivals of Christmas, Easter, Pentecost and possibly All Saints. Monthly celebrations occurred in the cathedrals and larger parishes but weekly celebrations were not common. It appeared that clergy and people feared an unworthy celebration, a phenomenon in America as well as in the established churches of England and Ireland.[35] (Except for the later Methodist movement, observance of the Lord's Supper was also infrequent in Baptist and Calvinist churches, but it was the essence of Roman Catholic worship in the weekly (or daily) Mass).

The Church of Ireland not only failed to serve the majority of the population, but it did not even serve its own adherents.[36] Absenteeism, pluralism and nepotism were frequent complaints of the faithful. In wealthy parishes the incumbent rector or vicar enjoyed the profits and handsome salary while the actual parochial tasks were performed by curates, usually young, inexperienced and underpaid. The church made no provisions for the retirement of elderly clergy, nor their infirmities, so the holder of a good 'living' clung to it until death. These financial factors undoubtedly accounted for the attractions of the clerical office to unsuitable younger sons who never experienced the call to a life of Christian service. Parishes were supposed to provide housing – the rectory or vicarage – and sometimes a farm or glebe that the incumbent could farm or lease to others. In most parts of rural Ireland, the rector or vicar lived as country gentlemen, sometimes becoming the squire of the vicinity and serving as justice of the peace. Opportunities for additional income also came from teaching at village schools, diocesan academies and even TCD. Fees were also generated by patriotic or funeral sermons and other parochial activities, although these were largely compensated 'in kind' in country parishes. Special fees were exacted for baptisms, weddings and funerals. However, plunder and greed were not the only legacy; many clergy beautified their churches and improved their land holdings to benefit their communities.

A nineteenth-century archbishop of Armagh and primate of all Ireland, William Alexander, gave a bleak description of his eighteenth-century predecessors: 'those were the days of a silken prelacy, a slumbering priesthood, a silent laity; of a

and N. Wolf, *Irish-speaking island: state, religion, community, and the linguistic landscape in Ireland, 1770–1870*, pp 111–48 (2014).

34 See Acheson, *A history of the Church of Ireland*, pp 95–6 (2002); Akenson, *The Church of Ireland* (1971).

35 Ibid. Infrequent celebration was the custom in Dublin except for St Patrick's Cathedral, where Dean Swift began weekly celebrations after 1713. J. Crawford, 'Retrenchment, renewal and disestablishment' in J. Crawford and R. Gillespie (eds), *St Patrick's Cathedral, Dublin*, pp 320–2 (2009). See Also B. Steiner, *Samuel Seabury, 1729–1769: a study in the High Church tradition*, pp 83–5 (1971).

36 See T. Barnard, *A new anatomy of Ireland: the Irish Protestants, 1649–1770*, pp 81–114 (2003).

theology precise in form, but pale, pulse-less and pedantic'.[37] Despite its inadequacies, the progeny of the established church were not a 'petty people', to borrow Yeats' phrase.[38] They were the literary giants of the eighteenth century,[39] the heart of the Celtic revival[40] and the heroes of Ireland's independence.[41]

IV. CHURCH BUSINESS

At an earlier time in the eighteenth century, there had been a 'church party', almost exclusively Tory politicians, but fifty years of Whig domination had diminished their effectiveness in the House of Commons. In the House of Lords, however, the twenty-two bishops routinely sat, while the great landowners were often absentees, so the problem for the church was to identify and reward members of the House of Commons who were available to protect church interests from hostile legislative proposals and unobtrusively guide measures desired by the church.

Due to the Church of Ireland's sixteenth-century origins in royal appointments to existing bishoprics, deaneries and abbeys, most of its church buildings were Romanesque and Gothic structures, some of historical significance. Thus, little new building was accomplished before the mid-eighteenth century,[42] but an expanding population and desire to build brought to prominence a somnolent government department, the board of first fruits, which in 1786 began to receive grants of £5,000 a year from Parliament for repairing old churches and building new ones and new glebe houses for clergy.

In the words of the archbishop of Dublin, Charles Agar, Arthur Browne was an 'able and zealous' friend of the Church of Ireland.[43] He was often charged with shepherding legislation desired by the church into Parliament, and he undoubtedly benefitted financially from the church, as agent and legal adviser, so it is not surprising that one of his early political battles concerned the question of tithes. Browne was often entrusted with sensitive legislation for the church, such as the funding of the board of first fruits to repair and build churches in the unchurched

37 Quoted in P. Comerford, 'An innovative people: the Church of Ireland laity, 1780–1839' in Gillespie and Neely (eds), *The laity and the Church of Ireland*, p. 173 (2002).
38 In a Senate debate on divorce, 11 June 1925, quoted in R.F. Foster, *W.B. Yeats: a life*, pp 297–8 (2003).
39 Jonathan Swift, George Berkeley, Edmund Burke, Oliver Goldsmith and Richard Brinsley Sheridan.
40 Douglas Hyde, Lady Gregory, John M. Synge, William Butler Yeats, Sean O'Casey and Samuel Beckett.
41 Henry Grattan, Henry Flood, Edward Fitzgerald, Wolfe Tone, Henry and John Sheares, Robert and Thomas Emmet, Arthur O'Connor, Bagenal Harvey, John Kelly, Thomas Russell, Thomas Davis, Smith O'Brien, Isaac Butt, Charles Stewart Parnell and Erskine Childers.
42 Obvious exceptions were St Columb's Cathedral in Derry (1628), St Carthage's Cathedral in Lismore (1633) and St Macartan's Cathedral in Clogher (1744); of parish churches, St Werburgh's, Dublin (1715) and St Thomas' Church, Wicklow (1700), are examples.
43 A.P.W. Malcomson, *Archbishop Charles Agar*, pp 571–2 (2002).

areas.[44] Furthermore, he performed legal tasks and acted as property agent for the church, appointed by Archbishop William Newcome in 1795; Browne's Whig connections, however, caused the loss of this job as property agent in 1800.

Arthur Browne's legal study of canon law as applied by the Church of Ireland, *A compendious view of the ecclesiastical law of Ireland* (1797),[45] made him very well qualified as an advocate as well as adviser to the bench of bishops. This scholarly work also made it obvious that he was well qualified to serve as vicar general, a judicial position he held for the ancient diocese of Kildare, which could be a step to a civil judgeship.

Despite its title, this 472-page work is the essential treatise on matrimonial disputes and the law of divorce (pp 257–80) and testamentary disputes and the law of wills (pp 281–364). It also deals with the law of defamation, in part, where the temporal context was accusations of adultery and illegal fornication. The bulk of the work concerns the clergy, their privileges and obligations and the practice in the ecclesiastical courts – the prerogative court, consistorial courts and the court of delegates for appeals. Disputes about tithes are also explained (pp 241–56).

V. THE TITHE CONTROVERSY

Arthur Browne's Whig principles clashed with his family background when it came to financial support of the clergy of the established church – especially in rural areas. Neither his father nor his grandfather had been dependent on tithe, which did not exist in Rhode Island. They had been paid annual salaries by the SPG. Irish rural clergy had no such salaried income source in the eighteenth century. While the established church possessed great wealth, it was reserved for the archbishops, bishops and cathedral deans, whose extravagant lifestyles were the perquisites of English and Irish politicians.

Support of the parish clergy of the established church came from the tithe. Historically a levy on agriculture of one-tenth of annual production to support the temple priests in the Old Testament, tithe had become the customary law of Western Europe. There was, however, no general agreement as to what was subject to tithe. Arthur Browne defined it as follows: 'Every thing is tithable which doth yield an annual increase by the act of God, and many things are tithable by custom which do not bear such annual increase.'[46] Controversies over turf, potatoes, flax, meadows, tin and lead mines and cows, sheep, goats and horses were frequent. An Irish statute of 1800 forbade the collection of tithe of agistment – the pasturage of cattle,[47] something that had not been attempted in Ireland since 1735.[48]

---

44 Ibid., p. 264.
45 The church law was briefly incorporated in his treatise *A compendious view of the civil law and of the law of the admiralty*, pp 451–508 (1802). It is a study of the practice in diocesan consistorial courts and the prerogative court.
46 Ibid., p. 163.   47 40 Geo. 3 c. 23 (1800).
48 McDowell, *Ireland in the age of imperialism and revolution*, pp 166–8 (1979); the lower house had

The likelihood that acreage could be used to produce tithable crops was a consideration in the sale or lease of farmland. A further consideration was the historical production of the particular fields over the years, as purchasers attempted to estimate whether tithe, and possible disputes about it in the future, could cloud the title in real-estate transactions, or subject the purchaser, his cattle and other properties to mob violence.

Controversies over the tithe were not heard in the common law courts by juries, but in the ecclesiastical courts by judges.[49] The person who farmed the land rather than the title holder was responsible for this tax, so the Catholic farmworker owed tithe to the established church on his potatoes and the Presbyterian farmworker also owed tithe on his flax, to the established church.[50]

Criminal activity, usually called 'agricultural unrest', developed widely after 1760 from the Whiteboys or Rightboys in rural areas of the south, and from the Oakboys or Peep O'Day Boys in the north, often due to rent increases by landlords or the aggressive exactions of the tithe farmers or tithe proctors, agents or the clergy.

The political strife and agrarian violence over tithe made life very difficult for country parsons isolated among a hostile majority; while the law may have been on their side, their sparse congregations were unable to protect them. Their peril was the source of Arthur Browne's opposition to tithe reform.

Conservative opinion blamed Catholic treason and French agitators for violence, ignoring the poverty and desperation of the countryside, while Whig opinion, often hostile to the church, saw tithe as the source of violence, ignoring the landlords' exactions in rent and evictions as a cause of the trouble. Grattan's repeated efforts to reform tithe were the result and a vigorous pamphlet war that had begun before Browne had entered the debate.

Needless to say, no one defended agrarian violence, but supporters of the existing tithe such as 'Theophilus' (Patrick Duigenan) and Richard Woodward, bishop of Cloyne, saw the effort to reform tithe as an attack on the established church, the constitution and the House of Hanover. Father Arthur O'Leary,[51] a frequent author of pamphlets, had pointed to poverty, aggravated by oppressive tithe collectors, as one reason for agrarian violence. This was misconstrued as Catholic support for violence, and the politics of tithe reform became religious conflict – always lurking in the background of the penal laws, which were being gradually repealed.

passed a resolution against tithe of agistment, but the Lords never acted, although legislation had been promised. Exemption of pasturage was a powerful incentive to abandon tillage of the soil in favour of grazing sheep and cattle.

49 Browne, *A compendious view of the civil law and of the law of the admiralty*, pp 241–56 (1802).

50 In the Parliament of James II in 1689, the tithe had been preserved, but Catholics were required to pay tithe to the parish priest, and Presbyterians to the minister. See Connolly, *Religion, law and power*, pp 151–8 (1992) and J.G. Simms, *Jacobite Ireland, 1685–91* (1969).

51 See J. Kelly, '"A wild Capuchin of Cork": Arthur O'Leary (1729–1802)' in G. Moran (ed.), *Radical Irish priests, 1660–1970*, pp 53–60 (1998).

Grattan's reform plan in 1788 included a revolutionary revision of tithe, beginning with removal of potatoes and flax entirely from tax on the land and exemption of 'barren' land from tithe or tax. Grattan's powerful arguments denounced tithe as uneconomic, unjust and oppressive in amount, giving examples of ruinous exactions forcing peasants into rebellion.[52] It was not just the clergy themselves but their agents, the tithe proctors, who surveyed the crops, or the tithe farmers, who guaranteed a flat amount to the clergymen (usually called parsons) in exchange for the right to pursue tithable crops with as much force as necessary. In Whig thinking the cause of agricultural unrest was the tithe, which should simply be abolished by Parliament.

Arthur Browne identified the real source of the problem as the seizure of Catholic lands by victorious Protestants in an earlier century, as he noted in Parliament in 1786:

> there was a faction in the country (and so there was and no man could deny it) hostile to the established church, hostile to the Protestant Ascendancy, hostile to the acts of settlement, and the tithes to their estates … the property of the country differed from that of any other country in the world. In other countries the landed title is purchase here it is forfeiture. The old proprietor feeds the eternal memory of his ancient claim. The property of this country resembles the thin soil of volcanic countries, lightly spread over subterraneous fires.[53]

And he clearly foresaw in his Candidus pamphlet (1788) the consequences to land titles of governmental change:

> Should a revolution happen in this nation there would be also considerable forfeitures of landed property besides that of absentees; as all the supporters of the present measures of government would most certainly be exiled and their estates, it is said, would be granted to such of the military as would abandon the cause of despotism and embrace that of liberty. This would make a transfer exceeding any that happened here since the Milesians, when the whole kingdom was transferred …
>
> The Roman Catholics (as Theophilus observes) remembering that their ancestors lost their estates by repeated acts of rebellion; which estates are mostly now in the hands of Protestants; and to the recovery of which they look forward with as anxious a longing as the Jews do after the land of Judea.[54]

---

52 R.B. McDowell, *Grattan: a life*, pp 93–100 (2001).

53 7 *Parliamentary Register*, p. 353 (20 Feb. 1787). Browne's opposition to legislation against the tithe was claimed to be a slur on Roman Catholics, to which he responded, 'he was sure great numbers of them were highly loyal, and most strongly attached to government: but that surely could not be alleged as a reason for raising them on the ruins of the established church, and with the risk of a subversion of all property', ibid., p. 354

54 Candidus, *A full display of some late publications on the subject of tithes and the sufferings of the*

Whig theory, however, had further determined that the avarice, pride and ambitions of the clergy in their unjust demands for tithe had produced the unrest and destruction unleashed by lawless men, and furthermore, that the miseries of the peasantry would be alleviated by statutory prohibitions of tithe. To that end, Henry Grattan, pilot of the 1782 constitutional changes, in a speech on 14 February 1788, proposed a commission of inquiry to consider the question of the tithe.[55] On the same day, Arthur Browne and his Trinity colleague Lawrence Parsons objected to such a commission as an attack on the constitution and the established church. It was surely an uncomfortable situation for Browne as he rose to refute his leader:[56]

> Mr Browne (of the College) said he rose with much hesitation to offer himself in opposition to a right honourable gentleman [Grattan], whose superior abilities, whose splendid talents, whose romantic success in all his measures, had thrown a lustre round his name, which it was difficult to meet with a steady eye. The right honourable gentleman, long and nobly employed in building up, had now exercised his talents in pulling down; he raised the civil constitution, he pulls down the ecclesiastical, with equal probity of intention (he was sure), but not with equal safety. The rapidity of destruction is always attended with more danger than the flow and regular steps of formation. The difficulty and danger of the enterprise naturally recommended it to the daring spirit of the author: but difficulty and danger merely would not recommend a system to this house. They would require some potent reason for this mighty change. Had the right honourable gentleman alleged any? Yes; some vague information, probably furnished by interested persons; was that a foundation for a committee in these disturbed times, when the country was teeming still with outrage and combination? When, if there were grievances, the House could not, consistently with their dignity,

---

established clergy in the south of Ireland attributed to those dues ... , pp 164–5 (1788). Prof. O'Higgins noted that on the copy in the library of the Royal Irish Academy was written, 'Dr Brown [*sic*]', an attribution accepted by Prof. McDowell; see P. O'Higgins, 'Arthur Browne (1756–1805): an Irish civilian', 20 *Northern Ireland Legal Quarterly*, 255, 272 (1969). Browne's choice of 'Candidus' (free of guile) as a pen name in 1788 raises the question of his relation to the thought of Voltaire (1694–1778), who had published *Candide* in 1759. Voltaire's satirical pen had caused his imprisonment in the Bastille in 1718 and 1726, but by 1754 he had moved across the Swiss border to Ferney outside Geneva. Apparently fifty editions of *Candide* were produced around the world from 1759 to 1789 (nine in English translation). Another Candidus pamphlet appeared in 1792: *Free thoughts on the measures of opposition, civil and religious, from the commencement of the last Parliament to the present period; with a modest plea for the rights and Ascendency of Episcopal Protestantism* by Candidus Redintegratus, assigned to Arthur Browne by Prof. Hill in *From patriots to unionists: Dublin civic politics and Irish Protestant patriotism*, p. 237 (1997). This is uncertain; while some views coincide with Browne's parliamentary orations, others are radically different: attacks on the Volunteers, Grattan, the regency and the Whig tradition make the attribution at least questionable.

55 8 *Parliamentary Register*, pp 255–7.
56 Ibid., pp 257–61. See also R.B. McDowell, *Irish public opinion, 1750–1800*, pp 124–5 (1944).

listen to the cry; when it was notorious that the only oppression relative to the clergy was, that under which the clergy themselves suffered.

The right honourable gentleman had come forward in the habit of a friend, but his design was evidently to shake foundations almost as ancient as the state, fortified by time and consecrated with hereditary veneration, which never fell but once, and in their fall precipitated the peerage – the monarchy and the constitution.

He [Grattan] had made himself the arbiter of all controversy between the clergy and the laity. Who had commissioned him? Not the people, their voice had not been heard, the cry indeed of violence and anarchy has been heard. Who did not remember when this cloud first arose in the south? A vapour engendered in the filth of a county election. The powers of the country, the nabobs of the peninsula had persuaded the people that tithe was the cause of their complicated misery, and that they should be freed from tithe.

Did he appear for the clergy? Had he consulted, as was natural, with the right reverend bench? No. Was he commissioned by the inferiors? No. They knew the inconveniencies of the present system – they knew the conveniences. The experience of ages had proved that the latter overbalanced.

At this point Browne's Trinity colleague joined the debate.

Mr Parsons. – Though there may have been exactions by some individuals of the clergy, I will never consent to have the established church of this kingdom dragged like a delinquent to your Bar, and arraigned, and evidences brought to asperse, perhaps to defame and to calumniate the ministers of the gospel – this would be an unseemly thing. I also object to a committee of enquiry, because for a subject so extensive as the conduct of all the vicars of the south, the whole length of the session would be unfair, and a general enquiry impracticable, I must oppose the mode in which this business is brought forward.

Attorney General FitzGibbon, the voice of the establishment, agreed with the most splendid display of oratory that no commission was warranted, since existing laws could deal with illegal demands by tithe proctors.

A few days later (16 February 1788) the issue of tithes shifted from defence to offence with a bill to relieve the clergy of unconscionable contracts by which the right to collect tithe had been suspended in exchange for promises of immediate payment without litigation, designated a compensation bill. (In these debates on tithe it should be noted that the severest criticism came from nominal members of the established church.)

Mr Browne (of the College) said the objection to a compensation bill must be either, that the clergy did not want it; or that they did not deserve it – As to the first, the violence and silent combination which still existed in the south (which had effectually deprived the clergy of Munster of their incomes last year, and reduced them to the greatest distress) were notorious to every one – As to the latter, viz. their deserts, much had been said on a former occasion, which he hoped it was allowable to answer now, as this was, in fact, a continuation of the former debate, as far as the conduct of the clergy was concerned.

Browne then moved from theory to observed facts from his legal practice.

He said the statement made of the rates demanded for tithes in Munster was, to his knowledge, as to a great part of the province, founded on misinformation. He spoke confidently, as being acquainted in one great diocese with much the greater part of the beneficed clergy, and knowing their situation and conduct; and in another large diocese he was one of those dreadful monsters that had been described, who eat up whole villages at a time – a vicar general – he had besides been employed as counsel in most of the compensation suits brought under this Act in the county Cork, and therefore must know the ratage of tithe tolerably well; and he did aver, that the highest rate ever demanded by a clergyman in that part of the world, for the tithe of the best crop, was much below the rates returned to the right honourable gentleman.

Browne then begn a spirited defence of the clergy who had been impoverished by the failure to pay tithe, especially in the rural south:

Much had been said of the state of the peasantry. He begged leave to say something of the state of the clergy. Robbed of agistment, by affidavit, the very way lately proposed to try their merits, and by which, conscious as he was about their innocence, he should not be at all surprised if the activity and perjury of their enemies had made them appear guilty, if a committee had taken place – robbed of agistment, deprived of their small dues, driven in most parts of Ireland to relinquish many species of tithe, to which by law they were entitled, they knew too well the temper of the times and the decay of religion to insist on their rights, as well as the difficulty of drawing. They were content, on an average, [with] a fourth-part of their legal claim. They had not increased their rates for thirty years. He spoke from knowledge, having in many cases seen the books of their predecessors; as to theirs, the rates were generally diminished. In this state of things, in a season of the greatest plenty, an outcry arose – the people refused to give more than half the payment accustomed for many years.– No famine, no additional demand, yet nothing was being given but White-boy prices. The distressed parson sometimes was driven to accept, then they would give him nothing at all. This showed their aim was not at reduction, but at abolition; the clergyman was not to employ a proctor, but to take the tithe according to the valuation of the landholder; if he did, the proctor was bribed or intimidated. He was then driven to farm his tithe at a very great loss to himself; this too was imputed to him a crime. It had been said, a parish which paid a tithe farmer £800 a year, did most gladly agree to pay the parson £600 per annum. It was therefore evident that nothing but the fraud of the parishioners, could have driven him to lease his tithe. If they sued in the spiritual court for subtraction, it was objected that the proctor was no accurate judge of value or quantity; though every man acquainted with tillage can easily estimate with his eyes, and walking over the ground, that the charges were always too low to make any mistake dangerous. If he sent a person to survey, he would be accused of avarice, and the gentlemen of the country would not endure the presumption, as they would call it.

He said the clergy had lately endured many sufferings, and in many instances they were reduced to a fourth of their old incomes, and sought to exchange at any loss, and found themselves and families in the greatest distress by debts they had incurred on the prospect of their usual incomes. Such men, he said, knew he compared the kindness professed to them by their opponents, to speech of the executioners to Don Carlos, prince of Spain, when they went to strangle him. 'We assure your Royal Highness it will be very much for your good.'

He then turned to other complaints concerning the legal disputes, defending the ecclesiastical courts and his clients, the rural clergy:

He said the ecclesiastical courts were said to be party courts; would the law courts be less so? Had the clergy much reason to expect justice from juries composed of the payers of tithe, if we may judge from the persecution raised against them of late? The costs in ecclesiastical courts were talked of; they never could exceed 1£ 6s. 8d. [and] often were less, according to the circumstances of the case. The clergy were accused of oppression: Was there any benefit of clergy which screened them from the weight of damages? Did not the total dereliction of legal remedy and to recourse to open violence prove their innocence more than a thousand facts? I wish to Heaven, said he, that gentlemen had seen as much as I have of the state of these fancied oppressors, labouring through life, with little to enjoy and nothing to spare, at length arrived at something like competency to support extensive families; if they had seen them as I have done, with ruined hopes and broken hearts, despondency sitting amidst the blasted comforts of declining life. Is all your pity confined to the peasant. Suspected pity! Whose handmaid is interest, and which extends not to your brothers – your friends – your immediate blood – they call not only on your pity, but on your faith. They embraced a profession on the public faith – plighted by you, plighted by the constitution – plighted by the monarch's oath. You enticed them to purchase education, and with it keener sensibility, nicer feeling of mental pain, aspiring thoughts, and elegant desires, which now but serve to sharpen the stings of disappointment. They call on you to fulfil the hopes with which you taught them to inspire their children, and to rescue them from violence, from pettifogging tricks, from calumny and malediction. These are their evils in old age, when the spring of action is gone down, and they expected ease and comfort to glad their declining day; like the wearied mariner coming into port, and finding the enemy's flag waving on the battlements.

His attack now narrowed to oppressive landlords and their agents.

He said the real cause of oppression was the land-jobber or middleman; he having racked the tenant to the utmost, knew not how to encrease his rent but by robbing the parson. He teaches the foolish peasant to curse the parson for the weight of his spade and the scantiness of his meat, though he has only to lift up his eyes to his tithe-free neighbour, and see him labouring under an equal want of comfort, an heavier load of rent. The rent of land tithe-free is always much higher than of other land; it follows plainly that not a holder in Ireland would be advantaged by the abolition of tithe to-morrow. The friends of humanity, these deliverers of the peasantry, would raise a structure of increased rent, whose basis would be curses and execration.

Undoubtedly, Browne and other eventual supporters of union with Great Britain would regret this reference to the king's coronation oath, as that was the legal reason for rejecting Catholic emancipation in 1800, which was an essential part of the argument in favour of the union and the end of the independent Irish Parliament, because the expectedly large Catholic vote of Ireland would be diluted by the even larger Protestant vote in England, Scotland and Wales.

Browne then returned to the constitutional argument in favour of tithe:

He lamented that the rights of the clergy had been treated with so much levity; they were not supported upon divine origin, they stood upon the laws, the constitution, the articles of union, the king's coronation oath; in times when religion was young and flourishing; they might have been donations; now, that support would not do in depraved times, and they were become property, was it safe to sport with property? Rights admit not of degrees, degrees of importance they may have, degrees of sanctity they cannot have; the rights of the clergy, said he, are sacred as those of the laity, both much founded in public opinion, much resting on popular reverence; if the common base melts away both structures will totter; sport with the rights of others, if the moment of your sport be not death to your own rights; is it policy to teach the mob all this subtle logic, to make your peasants logicians, and your ploughmen philosophers? See to what species of mental knight errantry this may not lead. – But it may be said, the clergy do not reside to do their duty. This is not true; non-residence in Munster is very rare; breach or neglect of duty may be punished by the law; but do you do your duty? Have you no duty to your country, to your friends, to yourselves? Do you do your duty? – The clergy have too much. Did you ever hear of agrarian laws? Do you think it is easy to persuade the famished beggar that it is right for one

1 'Reverend Arthur Browne' (1757) by John Singleton Copley, Historic Deerfield HD 55.084. Photo by Penny Leveritt.

2 Queen's Chapel, Portsmouth, New Hampshire. Photo by Joseph C. Sweeney.

3 Marmaduke Browne
monument by J. Smyth at Trinity
Church, Newport, Rhode Island.
Photo by Joseph C. Sweeney.

4 Trinity Church, Newport, Rhode Island, before the 1987 renovation. Photo by Joseph C. Sweeney.

5 Trinity Church, Newport, Rhode Island. Photo by Joseph C. Sweeney.

6 'John Bours' (*c*.1763) by John Singleton Copley. Funds from the bequest of Mrs. Hester Newton Wetherell, 1908.7. Image © Worcester Art Museum, Massachusetts.

7 'Self-portrait at 24'
(c.1778) by Gilbert Stuart.
Redwood Library and
Athenaeum, Newport,
Rhode Island.

8 'Dr Benjamin
Waterhouse' (c.1776) by
Gilbert Stuart. Redwood
Library and Athenaeum,
Newport, Rhode Island.

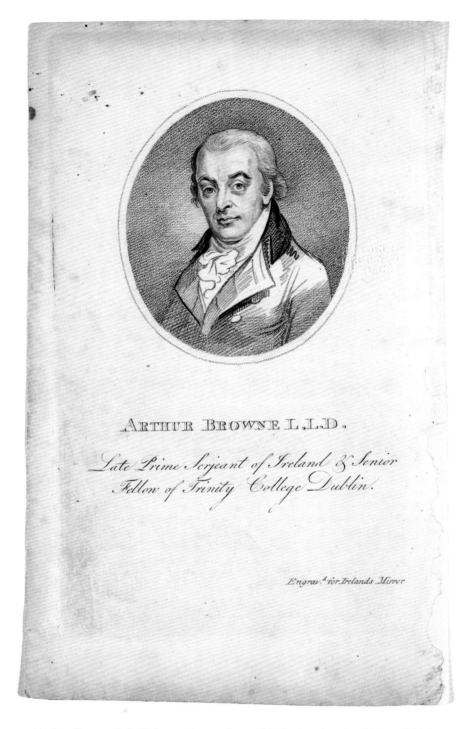

ARTHUR BROWNE L.L.D.

*Late Prime Serjeant of Ireland & Senior
Fellow of Trinity College Dublin.*

Engrav.ᵈ for Irelands Mirror

9 'Arthur Browne L.L.D. Late prime serjeant of Ireland and senior fellow of Trinity
College Dublin' (1805) by Gilbert Stuart. This image is reproduced courtesy of the
National Library of Ireland, EP BROW-AR (1B) 1.

10 'Trinity College, Dublin' (1799) by James Malton. West Front from College Green. This image is reproduced courtesy of the National Library of Ireland, PD 3181 TX 49.

11 Trinity College Dublin, West Front from Front Square. Photo by Joseph C. Sweeney.

12 Trinity College Dublin, examination theatre. Photo by Joseph C. Sweeney.

13 Trinity College Dublin, library.

14 Trinity College Dublin, dining hall. Photo by Joseph C. Sweeney.

15 'George Ponsonby'. Engraving by James Godby from painting by Alexander Pope. Historical & Special Collections, Harvard Law School Library, olvwork223587.

16 'Henry Grattan' (1792) by Charles Howard Hodges, published by George Cowen, after Gilbert Stuart mezzotint (NPG D15842), © National Portrait Gallery, London.

17 Lincoln's Inn, London. Photo by Joseph C. Sweeney.

18 'The Dublin Volunteers on College Green, 4th November 1779' (1779–80) by Francis Wheatley. Image © National Gallery of Ireland.

19 'Baron FitzGibbon' (1789) by Gilbert Stuart (American, 1755–1828). Oil on canvas; framed: 272.00 x 181.00 x 11.00 cm (107 1/16 x 71 1/4 x 4 5/16 inches); unframed: 245.00 x 154.00 cm (96 7/16 x 60 5/8 inches). The Cleveland Museum of Art, General Income Fund 1919.910.

20 'James Caulfeild, 1st Earl of Charlemont (1728-1799)' by William Hogarth; 1759 after; 1764 possibly; oil on canvas, 23 1/2 x 19 1/2 in.; 59.69 x 49.53 cm. Smith College Museum of Art, Northampton, Massachusetts. Gift of Mr. and Mrs. R. Keith Kane (Amanda Steward Bryan class of 1927).

21 'The Irish House of Commons, 1780' by Francis Wheatley, © Leeds Museums and
Galleries (Lotherton Hall) UK/Bridgeman Images.

22 'View of the law-courts, looking up the Liffey, Dublin' (1799) by James Malton. This image is reproduced courtesy of the National Library of Ireland, PD 3181 TX 87.

23 'Edmund Burke (1729–1797) in conversation with Charles James Fox (1749–1806)'
(*c*.1783–4) by Thomas Hickey. Image © National Gallery of Ireland.

24 'William Pitt the younger' (1805) by John Hoppner. Reproduced courtesy of Lincoln's Inn. Lincoln's Inn Archives. Ref. no. 51.

25 'William Wentworth, 2nd Earl
FitzWilliam (1748–1833), later
lord lieutenant of Ireland' by
Joseph Grozer, after Joshua
Reynolds. Photo © National
Gallery of Ireland.

26 'Charles Cornwallis,
1st Marquess Cornwallis' by
Thomas Gainsborough (1783)
© National Portrait Gallery,
London.

27 'Robert Stewart, Viscount Castlereagh 1769–1822' (1800) by Hugh Douglas Hamilton, © Parliamentary Art Collection, WOA 4053, www.parliament.uk/art.

man to have ten thousand a year, and another nothing? You open the way for every novelty which the fertile mind of man can breed.

He concluded this very lengthy oration with a warning for Grattan and his immediate circle:

> I am not fanciful in this, the thing has happened in the last age, in your own country. The right honourable gentleman is not the first Sampson who has pulled down the pillars of the temple and perished in the ruins; they altered the church, they then found it necessary to alter this house, to alter the monarchy and the constitution, and at last, which might come more home to the feelings of gentlemen, they found it was wicked for the Lord's people to pay rent – Take care, says an ancient author, how you pull down old fabricks, lest the dust put out your eyes, whose Lyncean opticks would be able to pervade the fog which might be raised around us; who would undertake to say to the mob, 'Thus far shall ye go, and no further?' Who thinks he can sooth Bedlam into peace, deserves a cell for his pains. Remember the Italian epitaph,
>
> *Stavo beno, stavo megliore, sto qui.*
> *I was well, I would be better, here I am.*
>
> After all I have to fear that any splendid novelty will spread ruin over this sacred ground; while the reign of reason and good sense continues; while religion lives, or even morality; while the memory of the revolution [1689] banner lives; the Protestant religion and the liberties of Ireland; so long will the church flourish in immortal youth; retaining the Athenian motto, 'dipping but not sinking', nicely interwoven in your constitution, closely connected with your monarchy you cannot sink it; if it merged in the rage of the people it would rise again in the dignity of this House; if it fell here it would shelter itself under the wings of the peerage; if they refused it perfection, it would hang to the title of the crown, stable as the throne itself.
>
> When I consider the magnitude of the subject and its native strength, I am almost ashamed to think I have presumed to come forward as its defender; and my only apology must be that bred in the seminary that feeds those holy fires, bound to protect its rights, I come forward to fight its battles almost from the foot of the altar.

Without the support of government and those Whigs supporting the established church, Grattan's plans for reform of the tithe failed utterly.

The tithe issue was never resolved by the Irish Parliament. After 35 years the Westminster Parliament of the United Kingdom abolished tithes, but only after a violent uprising during the Tithe War.[57] Abolition of tithe was another intermediate step to the disestablishment of the Church of Ireland by Gladstone in 1869.

57 R.F. Foster, *Modern Ireland, 1600–1972*, pp 309–10 (1988).

CHAPTER EIGHT

The regency crisis (1788–9)

THE PERIOD OCTOBER 1788 to March 1789 brought the most serious constitutional crisis of Grattan's Parliament and provided an opportunity for Arthur Browne to deliver some of his most significant speeches in the Irish Parliament. His attacks on the role of the Irish administration in delaying the offer of the regency to the prince of Wales were an important contribution, and were a major statement on his conception of the independence of Parliament.

The regency crisis was an issue which provided Prime Minister Pitt clear evidence that the Irish Parliament could be dangerous and must be suppressed. The cause was the mental incapacity of the sovereign. George III was 50 years old and had been king for twenty-eight years.[1] He had been happily married to the German Princess Sophie Charlotte of Mecklenburg-Strelitz for twenty-seven years. They were the parents of fifteen children: nine sons and six daughters. Unusually for that time period, only two of their children died in infancy. With those two exceptions, they were a healthy lot; nine of the fifteen lived to celebrate their sixty-fifth birthdays. Nevertheless, the king was clearly mad and had to be restrained and kept away from his family in late autumn 1788.

The physicians could not explain the source of the king's madness. Twentieth-century medical experts suspect a rare disease, porphyria, which produces symptoms similar to those of schizophrenia but can also be recognized from discoloured urine, abdominal pains and physical weakness, along with hallucinations, ravings and unintelligible speech.[2]

The constitutional crisis emerged from the conflict between the king and his eldest son and presumptive heir. The prince of Wales, then 26 years of age, was a firm opponent of the king's political friends; a further difficulty was the absence of legislation and historical precedents on sovereign incapacity.

I

Aside from political controversies over the American war, King George, called 'the farmer', was a popular monarch compared to other European sovereigns. He spoke

1   The king's personal life is portrayed in C. Hibbert, *George III: a personal history* (1998); also S. Ayling, *George the Third* (1972) and J.H. Plumb, *The first four Georges* (1956).
2   See M. Guttmacher, *America's last king: an interpretation of the madness of King George III* (1944); C.C. Trench, *The royal malady* (1964) and I. Macalpine and R. Hunter, *George III and the mad-business* (1969).

English, loved the established church and treated family, servants and visitors with respect and even courtesy.[3] His major fault was his hatred of Whig politicians, supporters of George II, his grandfather, who had mistreated and ridiculed his son, George III's father.

It was a tradition in European royalty that the sovereign and the adult heir to the throne became political enemies because of their friends. George III succeeded his grandfather at age 22, but his own father and grandfather had been estranged from their fathers. In the prince of Wales, the family estrangement was extreme. The prince's closest advisers and 'boon companions' were the king's enemies. The prince led a dissolute, even debauched, personal life and had contracted an illegal marriage with a Catholic widow, Maria Fitzherbert, in 1785, in violation of the Royal Marriage Act, which required the king's consent to his son's marriage.[4] Furthermore, king and prince were exact opposites in many ways: the king was pious, meticulous and abstemious in food and drink, kindly, shy and both generous and miserly, while the prince was licentious, careless, conspiratorial, extravagant – even spendthrift, gluttonous and inebriate. Most importantly, the king's friends were Tories and the prince's friends were Whigs, especially Charles James Fox and the opponents of royal prerogatives abused by George III.

Before the advent of the party system, responsible government meant that the prime minister and the members of the cabinet, although supported in Parliament, were personally responsible to the political wishes of the sovereign rather than a parliamentary majority, and the ceremony of the kissing the hands of the sovereign by the new prime minister was interpreted literally as an acceptance of the status of political servant of the crown. Thus, if King George III died or became permanently insane, Prince George would become king or regent with royal prerogatives; Pitt would be dismissed and the government would return to the Whigs, who had been out of power for a generation since the accession of George III (1760), except for an interlude in 1782–3 caused by American victory in war.

During the early autumn of 1788 the king suffered cramps, bilious attacks, rashes and discoloured urine and seemed very agitated and extremely eccentric. His physician, Sir George Baker, prescribed laudanum. An outburst of rage and physical violence by the king on the prince of Wales on 5 November resulted in the physician's decision that the king was under an 'entire alienation of mind'.[5] A number of distinguished London physicians were brought in to assist Dr Baker, but there was no improvement. By this time, however, London society and members of Parliament were aware of the king's madness and discussions about a regency and a new administration began among the prince's Whig friends, to the dismay of Prime Minister Pitt, who remained in power by delaying the transfer of royal authority until the king regained his sanity.

3 Hibbert, *George III*, pp 72–8, 193–8 (1998).
4 See A. Leslie, *Mrs Fitzherbert* (1960); J. Munson, *Maria Fitzherbert: the secret wife of George IV* (2003).
5 C. Hibbert, *George III*, pp 261–5 (1998).

Pitt and the cabinet agreed to move the king from Windsor Castle to the palace at Kew for restraint, and on 5 December 1788 the king's treatment was turned over to a family of physicians who maintained an asylum for restrained treatment of the insane at Gretford in Lincolnshire – Dr Francis Willis, his son Dr John Willis and his brother Dr Robert Willis.[6] Forceful restraint by the strong arms of Dr Willis' guards, and the frequent use of straitjackets, were part of the regimen. The king's madness continued unabated through December and January, but by 15 February 1789, for reasons unknown, there were noticeable changes in the king's behaviour and conversation. Steady improvement in the king's condition was clearly apparent in March, and on 23 April 1789, the king and the royal family attended a service of Thanksgiving for the king's recovery at St Paul's Cathedral, which was preceded and followed by a tumultuous procession through the streets of London.[7]

II

The legislation dealing with the madness of the king had proceeded on two different schedules in England and Ireland. Communications between London and Dublin often took a week or ten days due to the tempestuous winter weather conditions on the Irish Sea.

Official notice of the king's madness in England did not occur until 3 December 1788, when the privy council took sworn testimony from five of the king's physicians, from whose vague and highly qualified information about diagnosis and prognosis it could be discerned that the king was unable to perform his public duties. A week later, on 10 December, debate in the House of Commons began. In a reversal of customary positions, the Whigs argued for the royal prerogatives of the prince of Wales, while Pitt argued for parliamentary supremacy over the powers of a regent.[8] Uncertainty over the medical situation did not prevent the Whigs – Sheridan, Burke and Fox – from asserting the immediate right of the prince to succeed to all royal prerogatives, especially appointments, including the choice of prime minister and the cabinet. After unsuccessful negotiations with Prince George, Prime Minister Pitt introduced a bill naming the prince of Wales as regent on 5 February 1789, but severely limiting the royal prerogatives that might be exercised by the prince during the regency and committing the care and treatment of the king to Queen Charlotte. Discussions had not terminated before the Christmas recess; there were further adjournments because of the death of Speaker Charles Cornwall on 2 January 1789. Despite promises of future peerages,

6   The progress of the king's mental state and the restraints on his person are the subject of Alan Bennett's play, *The madness of George III* (1990), which was made into a film in 1994 as *The madness of King George*, featuring Nigel Hawthorne, Helen Mirren and Rupert Everett; it received the Academy Award for art direction.

7   Hibbert, *George III*, pp 300–3 (1998).

8   See J.W. Derry, *The regency crisis and the Whigs, 1788–89* (1963).

perquisites and offices, the Whigs were not able to overcome Pitt's healthy majority and the English restricted-regency bill passed the Commons on 12 February 1789, a time when the king was on the way to recovery.[9]

In Ireland, Parliament was not in session until 5 February 1789, being absent during most of the king's madness, but members, significantly the Patriot group with its English Whig connections, were aware of the king's fits of madness and Pitt's attempt to restrict the royal prerogatives of the regent, especially appointments and peerages. Thus, an unrestricted regency in Ireland became a weapon to attempt to force concessions from Pitt in England.

The Pitt administration was represented in Ireland by the marquis of Buckingham as lord lieutenant or viceroy. Buckingham had enjoyed a measure of popular support in his first administration as viceroy in 1783 when he favoured the Renunciation Act, strengthening the 1782 repeal of Poynings' Law, and again when he created the royal order of knighthood, the Order of St Patrick, of which he was grand master; but he was always an English politician who served the king's successful efforts to eliminate the Whigs from office, even while his brothers supported Fox in Parliament. On his unexpected return to Dublin on the death of the duke of Rutland, he did not entertain or flatter the powerful Irish nobility, and asserted a new regime of economy.

The viceroy's efforts to control the Irish Parliament by the influence of peerages, offices and cash (disguised as loans) did not conceal the fact that he despised the Irish, chiefly because he was in Dublin and not at the centre of power in London. These efforts at influence by corruption (i.e., 'jobbing') brought Arthur Browne to the floor of the House of Commons to denounce the viceroy's policies and actions at the beginning of the parliamentary session:

> Mr Browne (of the College) said that he came into the House extremely well disposed to lacerate the public character of the viceroy; but really it was now left in so miserable and mangled a condition, that it would be ungenerous, and unmanly, to attack the small fragment that remained. He could only now talk of what he intended to have done, which had been already anticipated by other assailants. He might have painted the acclamations with which the Administration began – the disgrace with which it terminated – the declarations against jobbing – the actual jobbing that succeeded – jobbing in the closet – coercion in the offices – A little gnawing, corroding, venomous scrutiny, which ate its way into the hearts of some poor men, who had not strength of body to bear violent accusation, or strength of mind enough to retort on greater offenders, which seemed to look out for crimes and forfeitures, as objects of prey, not of correction. He might have painted an economy, which instead of applying itself to great objects, such as the pension list, police establishment, or sinecure offices, fell upon a few

9 It was withdrawn from the Lords, and never enacted, although it appeared that the royal assent would be signified by the great seal.

miserable military taylors, and by depriving them of their little fire, in reality increased, instead of diminishing, the expence of clothing the army. He might have dwelt on a prorogation of Parliament, prejudicial to the public business and unnecessary, except for the purposes of a faction. But all these, and more, had been so amply discussed by others …[10]

As Buckingham privately knew of the king's madness, his first thought was to postpone the Irish Parliament, and then, knowing of Pitt's effort to restrict the regent's powers, his strategy changed to holding a normal session of Parliament to pass the money bills necessary to support the administration, as if there had been no change in the executive power by the substitution of a regent with limited powers.

The strategy of the Irish Patriot Party included use of the regency of the prince of Wales to correct defects in the 1782 settlement, most importantly to introduce 'responsible government', meaning that the lord lieutenant and his ministers would be responsible to the Irish Parliament rather than to the ministry in London. This distant goal could never be obtained from English politicians without a great crisis, like the American defeat in 1781.

In the regency crisis, the great landowners and nobles joined the Patriot Party, abandoning their customary attachment to the administration because of the possibility of greater rewards from a generous prince of Wales. The administration's strategy to restrict the prince's powers was announced in the Commons by John FitzGibbon, the attorney general (who Arthur Browne had defeated in the election of 1783). In the debate of 7 February 1789, FitzGibbon stated:

He asked, will any man, who is a lawyer, stake his professional character, by asserting that we are not sitting in a full Parliament; to support that assertion, he must prove that there is no species of government existing in this kingdom. He said if the consideration of his excellency the lord lieutenant's speech should be postponed to Thursday next, the money bills cannot be passed in the usual course; and if the right honourable gentleman will take upon him to risk the consequences that might result from such delay, and from the civil and military establishments falling to the ground, he should only say [alluding to Mr Grattan] on his head be it.[11]

After Grattan's response, Arthur Browne took up the challenge of the attorney general:

Mr Browne (of the College) said, notwithstanding the lofty words of the attorney general, he should not be afraid of losing his professional character, in case he should not be of the same opinion [on whether the House was only a convention] with Lord Loughborough, and many of the ablest and greatest

10 9 *Parliamentary Register*, pp 9–10 (6 Feb. 1789).   11 Ibid., p. 29 (7 Feb. 1789).

legal heads in England. However, at present; he should give no opinion upon it, but wait until the king's incapacity was ascertained, when the question would necessarily arise. In the mean time, he was against going into any business whatsoever, because it would be prejudging the question, and determining that we were a Parliament; and he could not help thinking, the wish to go into business immediately, a trick in government, which might affect hereafter the momentous questions expected as to the regency; for if any gentleman thought they had no power to debate a bill, to be ratified by some phantom of a commission appointing the regent, or to do any act, except address him to assume the administration of affairs, and of that opinion he was himself, they would be precluded by alluding to the present transactions; and being told that the House had already proceeded in a legislative capacity in going through the money bills, he was rather of opinion, they could do nothing whatever until a regent was appointed. It was the interest of Lord Buckingham to defer the business of appointing a controlling power over him. As long as the money bills went on in their usual course, there was nothing to urge him to expedition to that appointment; and he should expect every kind of trick and artifice, on the part of government, in order to obtain procrastination.

[Here he was interrupted by the chancellor of the exchequer.]

M. Browne observed, that the gentleman's haughty and overbearing manner had justly, upon many occasions, given offence to him, and many other gentlemen, and his observations should always be received by him with the utmost coolness and indifference.[12]

Henry Grattan took up the question of the king's madness on 11 February 1789 with a resolution to recognize the prince of Wales as regent of the kingdom of Ireland by an address to him from both houses of Parliament, in which the regent would have 'all royal powers, jurisdiction and prerogatives'. Grattan did this even though he knew that the regency in England was likely to be restricted.[13] Instead of a bill, requiring the royal assent, Parliament was asked to send an address to the prince of Wales to assume the regency of Ireland. The address was similar in language to the 1689 address of the English Parliament when William and Mary were invited to assume the throne. The address was approved without the necessity of a vote in the Commons and the Lords on 12 February 1789 and sent to the viceroy for official transmission to the prince of Wales.[14] Buckingham declared the procedure illegal and refused to transmit the address. Rejecting all the 'influence' that Dublin Castle had, the Irish Parliament repudiated the viceroy in a censure by 115 votes to 83.[15] A commission of members of Parliament was appointed to carry

12 Ibid., p. 29–30.   13 R.B. McDowell, *Grattan: a life*, pp 101–4 (2001).
14 9 *Parliamentary Register*, p. 75 (12 Feb. 1789); ibid., p. 116 (18 Feb. 1789).   15 Ibid., p. 155

the address to the prince by vote of 130 to 74.[16] It was in the context of this dramatic confrontation that Arthur Browne made one of his longest and most complicated orations on the legality of the independent Irish Parliament's action, on 20 February 1789:

> Mr Browne (of the College) requested the gentlemen who were and had been hostile to an address, to inform him how a bill was possible. A bill must derive its sanction and authority finally from the assent of the very regent whom they were about to appoint; it pre-supposed the very authority which it pretended to create; it contained the absurdity of a man's creating for himself that power, which from its nature could only be delegated. What was done at the revolution? The prince of Orange did not join in a bill making himself king; King William did not join in an act confirming himself on the throne. No: he was made king by a resolution of the two houses, and by that alone; had it been by address, containing the force of a resolution, it would have amounted to the same thing. The two houses alone were held competent to supply the defect of the executive power; they alone were competent then and now. Never was a doctrine more strongly insisted upon in theory, than this was of late in England by Mr Pitt's friends, though they deserted it in practice. It never had been denied by his opponents; they only differed whether the act of the House, should be election or adjudication.
>
> A bill of enaction then being absurd, he asked did gentlemen want a declaratory bill? Declaratory of what; that the regent of England was also regent of Ireland. If that were true, he said, a bill must be unnecessary, for we have a regent already. – a right honourable gentleman had said, it was true as to all imperial power, such as making war and peace; as to the use of the great seal, but not as to the use of the privy signet. Allowing this, the absurdity still remained; he was to be elected to the power annexed to the use of the privy signet, by an Act passed by himself; but the position he denied altogether; how was it proved? By the acts of annexation of the crowns, not by the letter of those acts; for they only say, the king of England shall be king of Ireland. Do gentlemen insist that king and executive power mean the same thing? If they do, a consequence will follow, which they may not like; it is this, the crown is hereditary; the crown and the exercise of the executive power mean the same thing, therefore, the exercise of the executive power is hereditary, and the prince has a right to the regency. But in truth the letter of those acts says no such thing; they say the king of England shall be king of Ireland; so he is at this moment. The law is obeyed, the throne is not vacant, but so strictly was that word king construed in former times, that it had been held not to extend to a queen regent.[17]

Browne then adverted to Ireland's independent choice of an English king:

---

16 Ibid., p. 153.   17 Ibid., p. 147 (20 Feb. 1789).

Proceed then to the spirit of those laws. They said we should follow England while she observed a certain rule, but they never said we should follow her through all the wanderings she might choose to take, while she was governed by the reigning family, or, if the line of succession should be altered, by king, Lords, and Commons, while she was governed by any other race so constitutionally elected. If the throne had become vacant by abdication, or extinction of the reigning family, and must necessarily be filled, we were bound to obey the person elected in England to fill it; but if without necessity, when the throne was full, England madly should choose to throw the exercise of the regal power into the hands of a stranger to the royal family, we were not bound to follow such absurdity. No: our loyalty, our honour, and every principle of the constitution would bind us not to follow it.

Where then was the bond of union between the two countries? In this – that neither nation could, without disobeying every principle of reason and the constitution, appoint any other person regent but the prince of Wales; if either nation varied from this rule, or imposed such conditions as made the prince refuse it, that nation was the cause of disunion, and ought not to accuse the other. The prince's claims were the true bond of union, and not the necessity of following any choice they might make, however absurd; those encouraged disunion who said any other person was as eligible.

Browne then had to confront the 1782 repeal of Poynings' Law, which required Irish legislation to be given the royal assent with the great seal of England:

A right honourable gentleman had said, we must elect the same regent with England, on account of the lord chief baron's act, and the necessity of the great seal of England to pass our laws. In the first place, this did not answer his original objections to the mode of a bill, as must be obvious to any man who would consider the argument; it only went to prove this, that we ought to wait till England had appointed, and then appoint, though it should be by address. He could only say, that in his opinion, if England put that great seal into hands totally improper, as, for instance, into those of a stranger to the royal family, who probably would take care that the prince never should come to the throne, Ireland ought not to appoint the same regent if she consulted loyalty, duty, or constitution, let the consequences be what they might. It was in fact a technical argument, an argument upon the letter of a law, (if, indeed, the letter supported it, which he did not admit) against the grand and first principles of loyal duty, wisdom and constitution. What would Ireland do in such a case? She would recur to first principles, and she would be driven to recur to them by her affection to the Hanover family, and by the madness of England. By first principles he did not mean war or commotion, but those powers which must necessarily devolve to both houses of Parliament in cases of extreme necessity.

It had been said, this magical great seal would make a bill practicable. How? He wished gentlemen to speak out. Did they mean by conjuring up such a phantom, as in England; by stealing the great seal, and supplying it as they might list – by an assumption of legislative power, by two houses of Parliament; if they did, let them avow the scheme, that it might meet with just reprobation.[18]

Browne proceeded next to notice the charges that had been made against the present proceedings in Ireland, as tending to disunite the two countries:

He said, if the prince of Wales was to be regent in both countries, of which no man doubted, the danger of disunion was visionary; but should England choose any other person, then how would the case stand? She had gone astray, without once consulting our wishes, or asking our opinions, and then accused us of disunion. Unity of sentiment, and unity of councils, must precede unity of action. If England had done wrong, rectitude could not be immolated to union; if she had done wrong through party, dignity should spurn at a unity in faction –

Ireland, in such a case, might speak thus – What did we do, when the wandering spirit of the monarchy had fled from its abode? The anxious eye of the nation, that pursued its errors with restless impatience, found repose by dwelling on the beloved image of the heir apparent. In that awful silence of the law of the land not commensurable to unbounded calamity, we recurred to the law of reason; to the law of analogy; to the law of public weal. With united voice they said – give to him that has the rights of permanent succession, give the temporary exercise of suspended power. Who is his rival in dignity? Who in interest to the public welfare? Who in affection to his afflicted father? We did not think it for peace to form divided empire – to erect altars to opposing deities – to force a minister upon the unwilling ruler of the land – imprison his wishes and enslave his mind – and seed a smothered war in the cabinet. We did not worship hostile principles, and warring spirits, and look for peace in systematic war. We did not think it for honour, to proclaim to Europe, in the successor to the throne, implied incapacity or suspected crime. We did not, while the reins of empire were passing through our hands, make the moment of conveyance, a moment of plunder. We did not in allocating the sovereignty, attempt to make ourselves sovereigns.

We said to the executive power, possess those aids without which you must perish; the power of reward so dear to sensibility; the power of calling to its councils whom it wills; the power of controlling aristocratical encroachment, by adding its friends to the number.

We beheld, in another country, a man of inordinate ambition, who after having crowded into his own family, and among his relations, the first places in the realm; the keys of the treasury and exchequer; the government of the navy; the king's seals; the lieutenancy of Ireland, contrived in the very

18 Ibid., p. 148.

moment of apparent downfall, to make his day of adversity a day of triumph. Who was able at that very time to say to the fountains of honour, you shall not flow; and to the coffers of patronage, you shall pour only from me; to offer proud indignity to princes, and to use the king's signet as his own; to say to the aristocracy thus far shalt thou go, and to direct the storming multitude at his will. We beheld him wishing also to hang this little satellite in a golden chain, to that proud planet over which he rules; to that system of ambition, of which he is the life and sun – and we resisted. We would not follow. We preferred truth, loyalty, and honour, to faction and absurdity.

What, said he, has England done in the present case? Departed from the plain principles of enlightened times, to musty precedents, drawn in blood, and indented with the sword. If we see in her conduct a commencement of awkward jealousy, and sullen suspicion; a middle act of speculative spiny controversy, with a long farewell to common sense; a conclusion in monstrous inventions, and wounded constitution; then are we rich in negative instruction; we know what we ought not to do; then will we not be entangled in the cobweb subtleties of party logic, though they came woven in the ancient curls of a lord president's wig, or floating on the solemn airs of youthful imposition. We will pay our duty to our rightful prince, and will not worship strange gods. We will appoint him, without limitation, or diminution from his power, because we know, to use a phrase of science, in politics the negative quantity never can perish. Diminution of one power, becomes addition to some other. The death of prerogative supplies food to some inferior ambition.[19]

Browne then dealt with the viceroy's claim of illegality and refusal to transmit the address of both houses of Ireland to the prince of Wales.

He said if his excellency had confined his answer to exculpation, no one could blame him for refusing to do that which was, in his opinion, contrary to his oath. But when he proceeded to reprobation, and to censure the conduct of the two houses, they were under the absolute necessity of defending themselves. The charge was made against them, and they must plead to it. It was evidently no less a charge than this that the two houses had requested the prince of Wales to do an illegal, nay a treasonable act. [Here a cry of hear, hear.] Gentlemen, then, said Mr Browne, agree with me, that we are charged with desiring him to do a treasonable act. If the act would be treasonable, so is the request. We are charged with treason. He said it was totally unprecedented, that one of the three estates should pass a censure on the other two. The three estates were mutually a check and controul each upon the other. They were to controul in turn, if necessary, but they were not to abuse. The king rejecting a bill, said mildly, '*Le Roi s'avisera*'; he never said I reject your bill because it is absurd, and illegal, and unconstitutional. It was

19 Ibid., pp 148–50.

not even one of the three states that had criminated the Parliament. It was not the king. It was a subject. He might say it was the Earl Nugent of Ireland, who had thus attempted to throw a stigma on the proceedings of the Parliament of Ireland. It was reserved for a deputy, and a subject, to use the language of malediction, and having been used, the dignity of the House required a vindication of its own honour.

He concluded by observing, that he had, as early as the third day of the session, given his opinion, that all intercourse, from the moment of the king's incapacity being declared, ought to be dropt with a government which would then cease to be under any controul, created by a volition which no longer existed, and unfriendly to the controuling power, which we wished to create over it; and which would try to prevent us from filling up the executive power, in order the longer to continue its own authority. If that opinion had been followed, we never should have met with the affront which we at present have experienced, and which might have been expected from a party always inclined to derogate from the dignity of Parliament.

He observed, with some humour, on the precedents which England had chosen to direct her conduct, particularly those from the time of Henry VI, when a duke of Gloucester was regent, opposed by a competitor for power, who contrived to keep back a great patronage from him, and by preventing his nominating the privy council, was able, says history, to set him at defiance, and who took advantage of embarrassed times, while his brother Bedford was flying from the victorious arms of Joan of Arc. He said he hoped there was no analogy between these times and those when the minister of the day was frightened at the fight of a maid, and when an ambitious cardinal of Winchester formed a determined confederacy against the regent of the land. One would not have thought these were exactly the times which modern Beauforts would have chosen for their example. He concluded by giving his hearty assent to the motion before the House.[20]

The delegation – made up of the dukes of Leinster and Charlemont, and members of Parliament Thomas Connolly, John O'Neill, William Ponsonby and James Stewart – proceeded to London, where they endured the celebrations for the king's recovery. It had been a fool's errand. Back in Dublin, the king's recovery was announced to Parliament on 2 March 1789, as members held whispered conversations about the expected vengeance of the viceroy, supported by Pitt and the king. That vengeance was quickly felt in the delegation, as the duke of Leinster and William Ponsonby were dismissed. Other parliamentary Whigs soon followed in exile, and John FitzGibbon became lord chancellor of Ireland, an office usually reserved for the English.

It is important to note the momentous events of 1789 elsewhere, while England and Ireland were engaged in the political struggles of the regency crisis. In the United States, the new Constitution was ratified by popularly elected conventions,

20 Ibid., p. 150.

and on 13 September 1788 the Congress under the Articles of Confederation adopted regulations to establish the new government at New York in 1789. Then followed the choice of electoral college members (7 January); a presidential election (4 February); the convening of the first Congress (4 March); and the first presidential inauguration (30 April). In France, the Estates-General met on 5 May 1789, and its Third Estate became the National Assembly on 17 June 1789. The people of Paris began a revolution at the Bastille on 14 July 1789. The fall of the Bastille electrified enlightened people to organize radical groups to challenge social and political establishments: the United Irishmen of 1791 and the London Corresponding Society of 1792. Both were suppressed in 1794. It took until 1793 for American radicals to organize Democratic-Republican societies. On the other side of the world, the first fleet had arrived at Botany Bay, and the settlement of Australia began at Port Jackson, later called Sydney, and destined to be a place of exile for Irish revolutionaries for thirty years.

CHAPTER NINE

The Whig Club, free speech and the Dublin police (1789–93)

I. THE DUBLIN WHIG CLUB

IN HIS 1798 *Miscellaneous sketches*, Browne spoke of the personal tragedy he had suffered in the death of his first wife, Marianne, nine years earlier, leaving him with a small daughter, Mary, to raise. This must have occurred in 1788, for on 5 March 1789 he arranged an insurance policy on his own life to benefit his second wife, Bridget. None of these private affairs are reflected in any other surviving speeches or documents.

With Pitt still firmly in power in London because of the recovery of the king's sanity, the position of Buckingham, the Irish viceroy, became impregnable, despite recent setbacks suffered by the administration in Parliament. Thus, many members prepared for viceregal vengeance in the form of loss of offices, privileges and promotions. The Patriot group was not the first target since they enjoyed few benefits, but those 'rats', the landed nobility who deserted the ranks of Castle supporters on the regency address, expected to suffer. Yet most of the 'rats' came from powerful families with long histories of support of Dublin Castle and the established church; viceregal vengeance might weaken the only effective support of the Protestant establishment, so there could not be a complete purge. The viceroy's goal of a restored majority for the administration could not be achieved as long as powerful members agreed to unite and stand with any member deprived of employment because of his vote to send the address to the prince of Wales. They did this in a round robin letter of 25 February 1789 to the viceroy.[1]

The day after the news of the king's recovery was informally announced (3 March) Grattan, unwisely, chose to test his strength with the almost customary resolution against the appointment of absentee officeholders in Ireland. While Grattan held on to 106 members in the division, the Administration came up with

---

1 R.D. Kennedy, 'The Irish Whigs, 1789 to 1793', pp 63–4 (PhD, University of Toronto, 1971), citing H. Grattan Jnr, 3 *Life and times of Henry Grattan*, p. 383 (1839–49). See also N.J. Curtin, '"A perfect liberty": the rise and fall of the Irish Whigs, 1789–97' in D.G. Boyce, R. Eccleshall and V. Geoghegan (eds), *Political discourse in seventeenth and eighteenth-century Ireland*, pp 270–89 (2001). Fifty-six important members from the Lords and Commons declared that their opposition to the administration would continue if members were penalized for their regency votes and that the offices of dismissed members would not be accepted by any of the signers. Forty-six signers joined the Whig Club.

115 votes to defeat the resolution, a clear sign that some of the great nobles had returned to the shelter of Dublin Castle.[2]

All the hopes of the English Whigs for office and the hopes of the Irish patriots and nobles for constitutional change had depended on the prince of Wales succeeding to the royal prerogatives. The king's recovery dashed these hopes, but the English Whigs were already a political party that was prepared to attempt to outmanoeuvre the king and Pitt.[3] In Ireland, the shock of the return of parliamentary power to the viceroy compelled the unusual necessity of closer cooperation. The Whig Club and later the Whig political party followed. That party would flourish briefly until weakened by the effects of revolution in France after 1791 and the disaffection of Burke's old Whigs in 1794.[4]

It was a consequence of the self-defensive discussions among the supporters of the address to the prince of Wales that Arthur Browne attempted to define the differences between factionalism and defence of the constitution:

> Mr Browne (of the College) said he rose to express his indignation at the charge of faction thrown out so frequently from the other side of the House, a charge so bold, he had almost said impudent, that it filled him with astonishment. Who were thus charged? The old country interest, the country members, that independent phalanx, who under all administrations had opposed the abuses and encroachments of government, with whom he had always the honour to act, and with whom he found himself acting still. And by whom were they thus charged? By the old veteran packhorses of government; those Issachars, who under every administration stooped down, like the strong ass, to take upon them every nasty burden that could be imposed; those dabchicks of government, who, as the poet describes, we have seen to creep, and wade, and swim, and fly, and hop through every mire of corruption that came in their way; those men whom we have seen turning with every shifting quicksand of vice, under that desert air where virtue could not breathe. He said, when the phrase, I am of no party, came from the honest enthusiasm of some gentlemen about him, he admired, and coincided in the declaration; but if it meant, as it too often did, that a man said he was of no party, because he did not know which party would come in, and wished to be well with all; or that a man had no political principle, and therefore was ready to prostitute himself to any measures, he detested and abjured the declaration. In one sense he would own himself of a party. He hoped he was of the party of honest men, of those men, who when the exercise of the executive power was to be supplied, did not assert the power of English

2   9 *Parliamentary Register*, pp 252–62.
3   See J.W. Derry, *The regency crisis and the Whigs, 1788–9* (1963); J.W. Derry, *Charles James Fox*, pp 214–92 (1972); L.G. Mitchell, *Charles James Fox and the disintegration of the Whig Party* (1970).
4   Kennedy, 'The Irish Whigs', pp 76–117 (1971); R.B. McDowell, *Ireland in the age of imperialism and revolution, 1760–1801*, pp 343–8 (1979); G. O'Brien, *Anglo-Irish politics in the age of Grattan and Pitt*, pp 124–34 (1987); N.L. York, *Neither kingdom nor nation: the Irish quest for constitutional rights, 1698–1800*, pp 199–202 (1994).

parliaments to make regents for Ireland, but had recourse to the plain principles of the constitution, and the natural and undoubted claims of the prince of Wales; who did not wander from the old track of the constitution without necessity, and who made necessity the limit of aberration. And he was not of that party, who attempted to undo the emancipation of this country, and to bring back the old detestable exploded ideas of the power of the Parliament of England over this country.

He abhorred the introduction of English party into their house as much as any man. But it was not to be of an English party to coincide in sentiment with a certain body of men there upon great imperial questions; not questions between the two countries, but questions common to both – the remedying defects in the executive power. – similarity of sentiment is not party. He must coincide with those men who had always opposed the improper influence, and supported the just prerogative of the crown; who had not rested in empty words, but carried these sentiments into effect – witness the contractors bill – the revenue officers bill – the household reform bill – the bill for limitation of pensioners: – whose determination did not melt in the heart of the closet, and who were willing, in support of these great principles, to rifle both power and popularity with a deluded people. Strange solecism in democracy! – obtain for the people what they have been for a century eagerly desiring, and you probably become unpopular. And he could not coincide in sentiment with that body of men who seemed to aim even at excluding the prince of Wales from the throne, who are inclined to assert the supremacy of the British Parliament over Ireland, by asserting their power to nominate a regent for us, let their choice be ever so ridiculous, wild or extravagant; who had been the authors of a declaratory bill, not of the meaning of the common and unwritten, but of the statute and written law, replete with all the Jesuitical doctrine of mental reservation, and of the assumption of legislative power, by the two houses of Parliament; replete with all the republican principles of the reign of Charles the first.[5] [...]

But above all, he urged the ridiculous situation in which we should be, if the lord lieutenant was suffered, by putting a rapid end to the session; to obtain an uncontrolled power, of opposing and contemning the resolutions of the two houses, and perhaps refusing to obey the regent appointed by the houses. A dangerous situation; for then the prudence and wisdom of Parliament not being collected, to take cool and necessary measures, the chief governor might be committed with the nation at large, who certainly would support the act of their representatives.

He concluded by observing, that to keep a check on the executive power might do good, and never could do harm. If it was an error it was an innocent error – it was an error on the right side; an error in defence of the constitution – in defence of the honour of the House – in support of the constitutional measures already taken, in opposition to artful and designing

5   9 *Parliamentary Register*, pp 192–3 (26 Feb. 1789).

men – an error proceeding from strong attachment and affection to the king's royal family. If that were error, he said, he would say, as Tully [Cicero] said of the doctrines of immortality, and as some modern has said of adoration of the fair – *Si hic fit error, libenter erro, nec hunc errorem, quo delector, mihi extorqueri volo.*[6]

The Dublin Whig Club initially replaced the dormant Monks of the Screw and Reform Club,[7] but soon expanded beyond the rarified atmosphere of enlightened aristocrats into the world of business and politics.

The remainder of the 1789 parliamentary session produced administration victories and partial victories against the patriot programme of the control of pensions, restructuring the Dublin police and disenfranchisement of revenue officers because of their alleged interference in electoral politics. As a Whig politician, Arthur Browne described the Whig ideal in a debate after the passage of legislation restricting pensions and places:

> He said he did not stand up to flatter the aristocracy, with which he had no connection, but he would say, that as he never desired to see the aristocracy supreme, so neither did he ever desire to see it linked to or enslaved to the crown. He was sure in a just counter-prise between those two powers, which might force each of them to appeal to the democratical part of that house, consisted the surest safeguard of the welfare and liberties of the people.[8]

Browne's devotion to the independence of the Irish Parliament is clear, but it is very hard to disentangle his connections with the British empire. He certainly agreed with Edmund Burke, who wrote, 'I cannot conceive how a man can be a genuine Englishman without being at the same time an Irishman. I think the same sentiments ought to be reciprocal on the part of Ireland.'[9]

Browne was well aware of British intolerance of Irish people – both Ascendancy and native – but he respected the British constitution, described by John Adams as 'a democracy disguised as a monarchy',[10] and reverenced the established church and the historical tradition of the British Parliament. He followed the victories and defeats of the British Whigs closely, and gave an apt description in his *Miscellaneous sketches*:[11]

> The English constitution does not object to virtue – it rejoices in it. But its wisdom is that it can abstract from virtue – it has provided for its absence, and depends more upon conflicts of parties and the balancing of powers to produce its salutary ends.

6   Ibid., p. 194. The quotation may be rendered, 'If this was a mistake, I freely made it and I do not wish to twist this mistake which I admit.'
7   See chapter 5.   8   9 *Parliamentary Register*, p. 287 (9 Mar. 1789).
9   As cited in D. Dickson, D. Keogh and K. Whelan, *The United Irishmen*, p. 103 (1993).
10 G. Wood, *The creation of the American republic, 1776–1787*, p. 48 (1969).
11 A. Browne, *Miscellaneous sketches*, p. 233 (1798).

By June 1789, friends of the 1782 constitution and the Whig regency supporters were dining together for political purposes, usually at Leinster House (town residence of the duke of Leinster and present seat of Dáil Éireann) or at Lord Charlemont's home (the Hugh Lane Gallery). These were political meetings without the frivolities of the Monks of the Screw, although the most prominent members had been Monks. The Whig Club was formally organized on 26 June 1789.

The club, of which Arthur Browne was an original member, was hardly a populist group. Its members were gentlemen, landowners or professionals, greatly influenced by Henry Grattan, organizer of parliamentary independence in 1782. They dined together for political discussions at least weekly. Originally they were fifty-five members of Parliament, of whom at least thirteen had been Monks of the Screw.[12] In addition to Grattan and John Philpot Curran, there were a number of members prominent in the history of the period, especially Robert Stewart (later Lord Castelreagh), Edward Fitzgerald (leader of the United Irishmen in 1798), Richard Brinsley Sheridan (playwright and theatrical manager), John Metge (admiralty judge), George and William Ponsonby, Edward Newenham, John Forbes, Thomas Connolly and Napper Tandy (Dublin businessman and political organizer). By 1791, there were probably 200 members of the Dublin Whig Club, including forty borough patrons, twelve landed peers and four bishops of the established church.[13] The Dublin Whig Club was concerned with issues of administrative reform through Parliament; other groups such as the Northern Whigs in Ulster and the Belfast Whig Club had broader democratic goals that would shortly be represented in the Society of United Irishmen, organized on 18 October 1791 in Belfast.[14]

The Whig Club dinners and discussions probably influenced parliamentary oratory, as the biting wit and sarcasm of Whig orators turned sessions of Parliament into political theatre.

In August 1789, the Whig Club prepared a political programme that would announce its constitutional principles following the end of the 1789 parliamentary session and before the departure of Viceroy Buckingham. The programme necessarily endorsed the connection with Great Britain through the royal house of Hanover while simultaneously declaring that only the Irish Parliament could legislate for Ireland. There followed a list of the legislation deemed essential: controlling the award of offices and pensions; reforming the Dublin police; disfranchising revenue officers; and making the Irish administration financially responsible to the Irish Parliament through an Irish treasury board.[15]

12 Kennedy, 'The Irish Whigs', pp 300–1 (1971), citing H. Grattan Jnr, 3 *Life and times of Henry Grattan*, pp 432–4, and H. Grattan, *Letter on the nature and tendency of the Whig Club and of the Irish Party* (1797).
13 Ibid., p. 83, citing *Dublin Evening Post* of 5 May 1791.
14 McDowell, *Ireland in the age of imperialism and revolution*, pp 343–7 (1979).
15 Ibid., p. 343.

Lord Chancellor FitzGibbon raged that the Whig Club was 'a horde of miscreant traitors professing peace but practicing corruption'.[16] There were many outward similarities between the Dublin and London Whig Clubs. The London Club dined together eight times per year; the admission fee and annual dues were £2 2s. 6d. The initial membership was limited to one hundred, but thereafter, every meeting enlarged the membership. Thus, in contrast to the exclusive Irish Whig Club, the London Whig Club was very large: 1,190 names were listed in 1799.[17] In January 1791, the privileges of honorary membership were extended to the new Irish club. The London Club had a list of ten toasts to be offered at every meeting, among which were: 'The sovereignty of the people', 'The rights of the people' and 'May the example of one revolution [1689] prevent the necessity of another.'[18]

The Dublin Whigs began an attack on the viceregal influence that corrupted Parliament through the use of sinecures and pensions, even as it appeared that the prince of Wales would not achieve the power to correct the deficiency of the 1782 settlement concerning responsible government. Browne had defended the future programme in February 1789:

> Mr Browne (of the College) said he had so often and strongly expressed his sentiments on the subject of pensions, that he should not at present argue upon a matter, which almost baffled all argument, by presenting intuitive conviction. He had often sanguinely supported it, in small minorities, from a firm persuasion, that its propriety and its evidence, would some time or other extort a majority. The auspicious time had at length arrived, when such a majority, from a concurrence of circumstances, might probably be obtained. He congratulated the country upon it; and he observed, that whoever deserted his post, at that critical moment, must be handed down to posterity, as betraying, and rendering fruitless, the only occasion that had ever offered for an effectual measure.[19]

In these remarks, he felt it necessary to deal with the objections of his Trinity College electors to cooperation with the aristocracy. He argued that the alternative was perpetual defeat for a necessary reform.

> It will be in vain to urge, that he did not like the men, who were ready to co-operate with him. The public will discern the conquest of private pique over public principle. It will be in vain to say he does not believe they acted from

16 Quotation from FitzGibbon speech in the Lords, C. Falkiner, *Studies in Irish history*, p. 124 (1902), as cited in T.D. Mahoney, *Burke and Ireland*, p. 286 (1960).
17 See J. Bellamy, *The Whig Club* (1799), which contains rules of the Whig Club (pp iii–xii) and a list of members, including deceased, suspended and excluded former members.
18 Ibid., pp xi–xii.
19 9 *Parliamentary Register*, pp 286–7. Persons receiving places or pensions after enactment of legislation could not sit or vote in Parliament. This legislation forced Browne to seek re-election in 1795 after he 'took silk', i.e. became king's counsel, thereby entitled to higher fees as lead counsel in litigation.

a regard for public good. Far be it from him to imagine that the respectable bodies of men, who had lately joined the independent interest, were not actuated by a regard to the prosperity of the country. If they were not, they were the greatest fools, for they were the greatest sharers in it. But, said he, let us suppose, for a moment, that they were only governed by interest, and their interest coincided with that of the nation; were independent men to reject the aid of every man, who was not actuated by pure patriotism? If they were, they might have the pleasure of declaiming in eternal minorities, but were never likely to carry any good measure for the country. [...]

The appeal has been made, by the aristocracy offering to join in grand measures beneficial to the kingdom; by the Castle offering any price for single votes, and offering, instead of argument, ridicule upon their opponents. It would have been more cunning in the Castle men to have brought forward the measure, and to have anticipated their opponents; but in the present state of things, he could have no doubt which appellants to join, or rather, which appellants he would suffer to join him. He said there was an artful language held by government, and addressed to the prejudices of independent men: do not be the dupes of aristocracy; they want to build their own schemes upon your shoulders. That is, do not accept the aid of aristocracy; drive them back to us, and then we can conquer your single power, without trouble, as we used to do. Was it to be the dupe of the aristocratical part of the country, to vote for measures which could not possibly serve the interests of that body of men; for measures which they had always voted? Or, should we not rather be the dupes of that government, which desired us to yield up our strength without offering any public measures in return?

If Lord Buckingham had stept forward, and said, join me, I will bring forward a pension bill, there might be some weight in the argument. He observed on the extraordinary means which government had used to captivate the independent part of that house. Though not a rich man, he was as independent as any man in that house; and he would mention the effect of their language upon him. Their attempts to win that part of the House were nothing but insult. In the beginning of the session they accused them of little less than treasonable practices – of dethroning the king. Very obliging indeed. They next called them a faction; – vastly kind. They then insinuated, that the way to reduce this faction – was by a price. They complimented them indeed with a high one, half a million, but still it was a price. And lastly, to-night government insinuated that they were not the king's friends, and that they were a parcel of fools, duped by an aristocracy. He said if any county members rode off, upon this pretext, of separating from what was stilled aristocracy, vulgar plain people without doors would say, that there were ways of corrupting members, not always ostensible, as by giving them the government interest in their counties. He said, far be it from him to charge with want of virtue any man who voted for a virtuous measure. There was no looking into the heart. But he had no scruple in saying, that great measures had usually at all times been carried by a jumble of motives, and a chaos of interests, superadded to the principle and virtue of a few; and if a good measure was carried for the country, he should care little by what concourse of circumstances, so the country was at length enabled to obtain it.[20]

Arthur Browne and his coalition persuaded the House of Commons to approve the bill to restrict pensions by 130 votes to 98, however the bill was defeated in the Lords, 49 to 40.[21]

Many Irish Whigs, such as George Ponsonby and Henry Grattan, were involved with the London Whigs, but the reverse was not common, with one great exception: Edmund Burke, who was known and respected in both countries.

Edmund Burke was the intellectual champion and eloquent voice of the parliamentary Whigs during the dark days of the administration of Lord North and the personal influence of the king (1770–82). Burke's leader, Rockingham, rewarded him with the lucrative office of paymaster of the forces during the brief time the Whigs were in office, but further advancement was foreclosed after the king installed the younger Pitt as prime minister for the seventeen years after 1783.

It was the savagery of the French Revolution after the Bastille (14 July 1789) that disrupted the Whig opposition, because Charles James Fox continued his enthusiastic support of the French at least until the war began in February 1793.[22] Burke published his strenuous opposition to the revolutionary chaos in France in his bitter *Reflections on the French Revolution* (1790). Disaffection between the old Whigs, who agreed with Burke, and the new Whigs, who followed Charles James Fox, became fatal for the Whig clubs and the Whig interests in both parliaments after January 1794, when the duke of Portland led the old Whigs to join forces and share patronage with the Pitt administration.

Arthur Browne had met Edmund Burke in London while preparing for the Bar (1777–9). Browne would have been drawn to Burke because of Burke's support of the Americans in the Stamp Act crisis in 1765, his opposition to parliamentary taxation in the speech on taxation (19 April 1774) and his speech on conciliation with America (22 March 1775).[23] After Burke's death (1797), Browne wrote a glowing tribute in his *Miscellaneous sketches*:

20 Ibid., pp 287–8 (9 Mar. 1789).
21 Kennedy, 'The Irish Whigs', pp 70–1 (1971). Defeat in the Lords was due to proxy votes.
22 See J.W. Derry, *Charles James Fox* (1972) and E. Eyck, *Pitt versus Fox: father and son, 1735–1806*, pp 323–76 (1946, English trans. 1950).
23 'In this character of the Americans a love of freedom is the predominating feature which marks and distinguishes the whole; and as an ardent is always a jealous affection, your colonies become suspicious, restive, and untractable whenever they see the least attempt to wrest from them by force, or shuffle from them by chicane, what they think the only advantage worth living for. This fierce spirit of liberty is stronger in the English colonies, probably, than in any other people of the earth ... They are therefore not only devoted to liberty, but to liberty according to English ideas and on English principles ... Three thousand miles of ocean lie between you and them. No contrivance can prevent the effect of this distance in weakening government ... An Englishman is

The torrent of anecdote and information which poured from the lips of that great man in private, as of eloquence in public, were the astonishment and delight of his friends. Lolling on a summer evening on his steps at Beaconsfield, or after a winter day in Parliament on his carpet in town … he spoke treatises fit to be published through the world.[24]

Arthur Browne visited Burke at Beaconsfield,[25] and kept up an occasional correspondence with him from 1780 to 1794.[26] Browne's criticism of chaotic conditions in France in his *Miscellaneous sketches*,[27] reflected his affirmation of Burke's condemnation in *Reflections*. Having concluded that the revolutionary chaos in France could not be justified, Browne wrote to Burke within the same month that *Reflections* was published:

I must be convinced that the oppression is intolerable, and that there is no other possible remedy. But, what tyranny if it existed, can justify its opponents in overturning all ancient institutions, in destroying all principles – in subverting all foundations of government.[28]

In the same letter, he had confessed his early enthusiasm for changes to the ancient regime:

When the French Revolution was in its infancy, I felt all the ardour of its success, which a generous love of liberty, found of the spirit of that country, America, in which my boyish days were spent, and nurtured and maintained by reason and reflection, could inspire.[29]

The London Whigs were rattled by Burke's *Reflections* and it is likely that most Whigs still supported the French Revolution before the ugly violence of 1792 when

the unfittest person on earth to argue another Englishman into slavery.' R.J.S. Hoffmen and S. Levack (eds), *Burke's politics: selected writings and speeches of Edmund Burke on reform, revolution and war*, pp 61–94 (1949).

24 Browne, *Miscellaneous sketches*, p. 222 (1798).

25 Burke bought the large country house called Gregories in 1768, in the town of Beaconsfield, Buckinghamshire, about 25 miles northwest of London, where he regularly entertained political allies and literary friends such as Garrick, Sheridan and Dr Johnson. Pitt's proposed peerage would have made Burke the earl of Beaconsfield, but Burke rejected it. Burke died there on 9 July 1797 and was buried at the parish church of St Mary.

26 I am indebted to Dr Sean P. Donlan of NUI Limerick for alerting me to the Browne-Burke correspondence in the Sheffield Archive. See S.P. Donlan, *Regular obedience to the laws: Arthur Browne's prelude to union*, pp 6–7 (2008). See also S.P. Donlan (ed.), *Edmund Burke's Irish identities* (2004).

27 Browne, *Miscellaneous sketches*, pp 48–52, 64, 228–9, 251, 255 (1798).

28 Letter of 30 Nov. 1790 found in WWM BKP/V2278, as cited in S.P. Donlan, *supra* n. 26, pp 6, 17. *The reflections* were published in London on 1 Nov. 1790. The most radical legislation of the Assemblé Nationale was the 14 July 1790 civil constitution of the clergy and abolition of hereditary nobility.   29 Ibid.

King Louis' Swiss guards were slaughtered (10 August) and prisoners were massacred (2–7 September). These events set the tone of revolutionary government before the execution of the king (21 January 1793) and Robespierre's reign of terror (June 1793 to 27 July 1794). The open breach among Whigs did not occur until the parliamentary debate that ended 6 May 1791; Burke replied to earlier provocations by Fox when Burke described the new (short-lived) French constitution as an abomination and horror that tore the bonds of society asunder.[30] Burke followed in August 1791 with *An appeal from the new to the old Whigs*, reviewing the differences, and the unity of the Whig party disappeared, replaced by open hostility. Burke and Fox were never reconciled.

Putting aside the French Revolution, Fox's thirty-three-year parliamentary career pushed the Whigs in the direction of popular sovereignty and civil liberties. Besides his support for the American cause from 1774 to 1783, Fox also advocated Roman Catholic emancipation in Ireland, abolition of slavery, reform of the East India Company's operations in India and reform of the Westminster Parliament (even though he had enjoyed a rotten borough). He saw through the Pitt scheme and opposed the union of Ireland with Great Britain in 1801. This record encouraged Arthur Browne to make a lengthy defence of Fox when Dr Duigenan proposed that Fox be censured by the Irish Parliament for a speech given in the Westminster Parliament, declaring:

> his veneration for Mr Fox and his indignation at those general charges which had been bellowed against every man who differed from the minister. He owned his veneration for Mr F. was extreme, and proportionate was the shock he felt at the calumnies poured forth to-night. He had often seen and heard Mr Fox in public, and had the honour of being slightly known to him in private. Whether he considered his talents, his integrity, his knowledge, that capacity of mind which seemed intuitively to see the consequences and conclusions, which, in the minds of others, required long and labourious deduction; that rapidity of vehement eloquence, only to be equalled by an almost miraculous rapidity of ideas – that foresight, had almost prophetic spirit which enabled him to forsee all the calamities into which we have fallen, and to point out; step by step, all those measures which would have prevented them; that suavity of manners, such a contrast to the ridiculous insolence and brutal haughtiness of little men in power, or that modesty of soul which made him apparently unconscious of his natural precedence to other men; in whatever light he viewed him, he had always appeared to him as a superior being.
> With respect to his integrity, no man can doubt that had he been made of common mould, of such materials as ministers are usually made of, he would have been in power these many years past, and many of those who now abuse him, crouching at his feet. With respect to his love for Ireland, he had

---

30 Hoffman and Levack (eds), *Burke's politics*, pp 390–400 (1949).

manifested it on every occasion; had he in 1782 and 1784 most ably contributed to its present constitution, and in the very speech now alluded to, and said to be his, declared the recognition of her independence a right, not a boon. He had endeavoured to avert the most dreadful calamities from our sister country – he was now striving to do so. [...]

The discontents of Ireland were an imperial concern, affecting the welfare, if not the existence of the whole empire. Were England in the same ruinous state, as her ruin would draw the ruin of Ireland along with it, he, as a member of the Irish Parliament, should think he had an equal right to move an address to the crown in a similar manner. Had Mr Fox, indeed, in the address, proposed any specific measure, or desired the House of Commons of England to dictate to the Parliament of Ireland particular acts, that might be interfering with our independence. He did no such thing; our independence was dear to him, and he had always proved it. He mentioned indeed his opinion, that certain measures would save this country; and had he not a right, as a member of Parliament, to mention his opinion? Where then was this mighty libel?

He believed he had found it out. Mr Fox had the presumption to say, that really the influence of the crown could produce effects in this house, and that those effects were not always agreeable to the people. Wonderful libel! Perfectly false to be sure! Had no man heard of such a charge before? had no body in that house ever hinted at such a thing? had any man a doubt of the fact? He was surprised how men could preserve their gravity, when they brought forward such accusations. After a variety of other arguments to prove the innocence of Mr Fox's address, and his remarkable love for this country so often manifested, Mr Browne proceeded to animadvert on the abuse and calumnies which had been thrown out that night, on the most respectable men. Mr Fox had been called the head of a rabble; – were the eighty gentlemen who supported him a rabble? Those who voted with him were accused of endeavoring to promote rebellion in England, and were disappointed of seeking to do it in Ireland. Was this meant to apply to the dukes of Norfolk and Bedford, the earl of Moira, the marquis of Lansdown, and the peers who were in the same opinion? He commented sharply on the impolicy, as well as the wickedness, of bringing charges of treason against every man who differs in opinion from the minister, or reprobates the conceptions of government; in higher life and strong minds, it might produce no sensation but contempt; in weaker ones, and among the vulgar, he knew nothing so likely to make a traitor, as the perpetually calling a man by that name.[31]

Although there was no censure of Fox, the speeches of Browne and George Ponsonby that day were the last signs of life of the Whig Club.[32] Only the threat of

31 17 *Parliamentary Register*, pp 513–15. Browne's speech of 3 May 1797 was delivered before Burke's death on 9 July 1797. The censure was rejected without a division.
32 Whigs 'seceded' from the parliaments of Dublin and London from May 1797. Irish Whigs

destruction of the Irish Parliament would bring back some of its members – especially Grattan, Curran and the Ponsonbys – for the unsuccessful struggle to prevent the union.

II. FREE SPEECH, FREEDOM OF THE PRESS

Arthur Browne's reputation as an advocate for civil liberties and free speech resulted from his fight against a notorious abuse of judicial office by the lord chief justice of Ireland. Those procedures that were used against the press were: first, contempt; then, attachment; and lastly, fiats.

Freedom of the press deals with two distinct problems: 1) censorship prior to publication; and 2) the civil and criminal consequences of publication. Censorship was the only problem recognized by Blackstone in *Commentaries on the laws of England* (1765–9), in which he wrote that 'The liberty of the press is indeed essential to the nature of a free state.'[33] Freedom from prior censorship did not foreclose consequential prosecutions for sedition, or civil damages for defamation. It was Browne's efforts to relieve John Magee, publisher of the *Dublin Evening Post*, of the consequences of publication that made him a champion of freedom of the press.

In Arthur Browne's time, journalism was not yet a profession, and the competition between newspapers in Dublin was not as robust and partisan as in London and America. Dublin newspapers relied on advertising, letters to the editor, gossip from the courts or politicians and material taken from English and foreign newspapers, copyright protection being non-existent. There were no reporters or columnists, just the proprietor, who served as editor or writer, and printers scratching out a precarious living from subscribers. Newspapers were not yet daily, appearing weekly or twice or thrice per week.[34]

It was the crisis of the 1780s – defeat in America, the Volunteers and Grattan's Parliament – that created lively partisanship and scandal for a readership that pondered and brooded over the four to six sheets in coffee houses and taverns. The first and longest surviving was *Faulkner's Dublin Journal*, founded in 1725, originally not involved in controversies, but gradually supportive of Dublin Castle.[35] Opposition to government was the reason for the existence of the *Freeman's Journal, Hibernian Journal, Morning Post, Volunteers' Journal* and *Dublin Evening Post*.[36] The *Volunteers' Journal*, subsidised by the wealthy father of its

---

returned to fight the union in 1799. For the end of the Whig Club, see G. O'Brien, *Anglo-Irish politics in the age of Grattan and Pitt*, pp 128–33, 173 (1987).

33 W. Blackstone, *Commentaries on the laws of England*, book IV, pp 151–3 (9th ed. 1793). See also L. Levy, *Emergence of a free press*, pp 173–281 (1985).

34 B. Inglis, *The freedom of the press in Ireland, 1784–1841*, pp 19–22 (1954); C. Maxwell, *Dublin under the Georges, 1714–1830*, pp 169–72 (1936).

35 Inglis, *The freedom of the press in Ireland*, pp 21, 44, 57–62 (1954).   36 Ibid., pp 239–42.

editor, Matthew Carey, was unrestrained in denouncing England and its trade policies. The voice of Dublin Castle was the *Hibernian Telegraph*, founded in 1795; government's initial reaction to criticism had been suppression – only in the emergency created by the United Irishmen had the Castle decided to subsidize its own newspaper.[37]

It was journalistic excess by the *Volunteers' Journal* that unleashed suppression in April 1784, when it described the House of Commons as a den of thieves and prostitutes, deserving American-style tar and feathers, and ridiculed the speaker of the House, John Foster, with a vicious cartoon. Foster was irate, and responded with a contempt proceeding before the House of Matthew Carey, the editor, who was imprisoned during the proceeding. Before this was concluded, Parliament was prorogued and Carey was released; Carey was not prepared for martyrdom, and he fled to America.[38]

Statutory press control was sarcastically labelled 'A bill to secure the liberty of the press' by Speaker Foster, its author and promoter. It provided that vendors of newspapers containing libels were subject to arrest.[39] Newspaper publishers were required to post a bond of £500 and file a statement of names and addresses of interested parties with the stamp tax commission. Acceptance of payment for printing a libel was made criminal, as well as extortion of money for non-publication.[40] Criticised by Grattan, Foster agreed to amendments to remove vendor criminality and the heavy bond. It was enacted and approved 1 June 1784.[41]

This legislation immediately caught the favourable attention of John FitzGibbon, then attorney general, as it 'secur[ed] the liberty of the press by preventing the abuses arising from the publication of traitorous, seditions false and slanderous libels by persons unknown'. His legal analysis followed in a letter of 18 November 1787 to his friend Lord Auckland (William Eden), then in Paris, for recommendation to the French government:

> The great difficulty which we found was to ascertain the printers, publishers and proprietors of our newspapers. Our Act, therefore, directs that no person whatever shall print or publish or cause to be printed or published any newspaper or anything in the nature of a newspaper, before he shall first have given in to the commissioners of the stamp duties or the distributors of stamps in the country, an affidavit containing his true name and place of abode, and stating whether he be printer, proprietor or publisher of the paper, and the name of every person sharing the profits of it; which affidavit remains at the stamp office to be made use of as occasion shall require in actions or prosecutions for any libel contained in the newspaper, and is by

37 Ibid., pp 33–8, 52–74.
38 Ibid., pp 22–7. E.L. Bradsher, *Matthew Carey: editor, author and publisher: a study in American literary development* (1912).
39 Inglis, *The freedom of the press in Ireland*, pp 34–45 (1954).
40 Ibid., pp 43–4.   41 Ibid., pp 44–5. See 23 and 24 Geo. 3 c.28.

the Act made conclusive evidence of the printing or publishing or property in the man who swears it; and by the Act, every proprietor as well as printer is bound to swear this affidavit.

A. Contempt

John Magee's *Dublin Evening Post*, with the largest press run in Dublin, began a campaign for parliamentary reform – especially the elimination of rotten boroughs controlled by the nobility and Dublin Castle – also demanding the removal of Attorney General FitzGibbon. An information was filed against Magee in November 1784, and prosecution was threatened, but the newspaper continued its attack.[42] After the 25 January 1785 issue, king's bench began an 'attachment' proceeding and Magee was arrested and confined to prison by John Scott, now Baron Earlsfort. For government, the attachment system for contempt of court avoided grand jury indictment (which might be denied in Dublin) and proceeded directly to sentence without the necessity of an adversary proceeding or jury verdict.

Contempt of court was charged whenever a defendant commented about the legal proceedings that had begun against him. Thus, Magee was not punished for the November 'libels', but for his criticism of the attachment procedure by which he was imprisoned. Earlsfort fined Magee £5, imposed one month of imprisonment and required him to post a bond 'to keep the peace'.[43]

B. Attachments

Arthur Browne began his assault on the non-jury contempt proceeding 'by attachment' a few days after Magee was imprisoned. He located free speech in the divinely ordained law of liberty:

> The power of attachment was certainly to be found in the British constitution, but confined to one instance, securing the administration of justice from disobedience, and contempt. It was founded in this case in obvious necessity; because without a power of punishing instantly the man who dared to affront them, neither their dignity, nor even existence, could be preserved. As far as their necessity extended, the power of attachment extended, and no further. The complaint of the people of Ireland, he might say of the people of England too, was, that this power had exceeded its bounds, and gone forth like a pestilential vapour to corrupt the constitution. Confined within its proper bounds it was salutary and useful. Though contrary to the great principles of the constitution, though very poison in itself, the wisdom which attempered the constitution knew how to mix the most subtle poison with the most wholesome materials, and from the composition to derive life and vigour; but when an unskillful hand dashes the

42 Inglis, *The freedom of the press in Ireland*, pp 47–57 (1954).   43 Ibid., p. 32.

cup, and destroys the temper, then it becomes poison again. When this power is applied to cases which have had no possible relation to the dignity of the courts of justice; to cases where the offender, if he was an offender, could not have had the courts in his contemplation in the most remote degree; to cases of politics; to cases where, if any contempt was offered, it was to the crown immediately, and not through the intervention of its courts of justice, who does not see the danger?

The trial by jury, ever estimable, was especially so when government was the real prosecutor. Who was to try whether there were tumult or sedition against the executive power? Surely not the executive power itself; judges appointed by the crown, and who represented the crown in its courts. No, a jury chosen from among the people; a temporary tribunal, which, after the trial, relapsed into the body of the people, and would take care not to set any precedent of oppression, to which the next moment themselves might become subject. The contrary doctrine confounded the judiciary and executive powers; these very things which Montesquieu, speaking of England, says, would destroy liberty. And that is substituted for the trial by jury! – why a trial which opposes three of the most known principles of the constitution? – that no man shall be obliged to criminate himself; that no man shall be condemned without a power of appeal; and, thirdly, that no one shall be judge in his own cause.

Yet this had been called a merciful mode of trial, though it gives to the courts, on account of its severity, to support their dignity; and though it contained something very like the old detested oath *ex oficio*. It was said to be merciful, because the innocent might swear himself innocent, and why should the guilty escape. The argument would prove that the trial by jury should be abolished; but how different was the clemency of the law – through a man confessed himself guilty, the judge would advise him to retract his confession, and plead not guilty, that he might have every chance of escaping, on cross-examination, for want of evidence, for want of prosecution, or on account of any trifling flaw in the record; and so far from being tried by offended judges, he might object to one of his judges, even if he disliked his countenance, in a capital case.

The late proceedings had introduced a dangerous doctrine of constructive contempt. It had been well said by a great nobleman of the last age, whose actions were the detestation, and whose defense of those actions the admiration of the world, that he liked not those new fangled and constructive treasons (the doctrine of which had been invented by his enemies); for if such subtleties prevailed, no man would know by what rule to govern his words or actions. So may we say, we like not these constructive contempts; for if these doctrines prevail, no man will be safe. Disquiet will be aggravated to sedition, and sedition into treason. Accusation will walk forth in triumph, and power, with voluntary credulity, shall swallow the idle tale. Every action may be construed a contempt: every man an officer of the courts. Why not, as well as in the present case? Which he defied any man to show cause within those definitions of contempts which he read from law books. He denied that Mr Reilly's being a sheriff made any difference; for, first, it was the quality of the offence, and not the quality of the man, which constituted the criminality. Every act that tends to bring the king's courts into odium or contempt, is the subject of attachment, let the man who commits it be who he may, whether magistrate or not; therefore it was in vain to say, that the precedent did not extend to every man. If Mr Reilly was attachable, any person who attempted to bring his county together would also be attachable.

Again, the sheriff acted *virtute officii*, or *colore officii*. Now gentlemen on the other side cannot say he acted *virtute officii*, because they denied his power to convene the county, for the purpose of appointing delegates, and he could not act by virtue of a power which he had not. There was a great difference between abusing and assuming a power – a man could not abuse a power which he had not. He then assumed a power, and there the gentlemen were in another difficulty, for if he assumed it, he was like any other man, for any man might have assumed the power, and then the precedent extends to all.

The gentlemen then are driven to say, he acted *colore officii*, and here he would appeal to country gentlemen, whether it were not sufficient to damn a measure, that it required such nice logic to defend it. When the trial by jury was open, and as no experiment was made, there was no ground to say, that a fair trial could not be had, why have recourse to a method which, if it could be defended at all, it must be with great difficulty? But to meet the argument – it depends upon this, that whatever wrong the sheriff does by *colour* of his office is a contempt of the courts. Now this is begging the question, for his office is multifarious – it sometimes regards Parliament, as in the case of elections; sometimes the crown immediately, as in the case of calling the county, to suppress rebellion or invasion; sometimes the crown immediately, through its courts of justice, as in the case of abusing legal processes. – Now, there may be contempt committed by the sheriff in all these different capacities, punishable by attachment however only in the last instance. The contrary doctrine confounds all sorts of contempts, and makes contempts against the crown immediately, and against the crown in its courts of justice, one and the same. Nothing can be more accurately distinguished than they are in books, and confounding them is most dangerous. Refusing to obey the king's writ, demanding a loan, and speaking seditious words in the House of Commons, have been in the time of the Stuarts construed contempts of the crown. What pity that they did not think of continuing them also as contempts of the court of king's bench, and punishing them by attachment. It would not be going much further, than the punishing a man who convenes a county to debate upon political matters by that mode.

Parliament, he said, could have taken care of its own privileges, and if Mr Reilly had been guilty of a contempt of them, would have ordered the attorney general to prosecute, but not, by attachment. Necessity had been pleaded. It was a dangerous plea, and proverbially called the plea of the tyrant. He concluded by saying that he was confirmed in his opinion of the danger of the measure, by the sentiments of some of the greatest men in England, particularly of one who had most uniformly opposed, and endeavoured to controul the encroachments of power [meaning Mr Fox]; he considered this as an impediment; one of those which, from the Middlesex down to the Westminster election, had been too perceptible to every observing man. This was the age of experiment. But he had seen the resolutions respecting Middlesex erased from the journals of England. The Westminster scrutiny would soon become the subject of universal abhorrence, as it now was with reflecting men; and if the measure should be by any resolution approved of, which heaven avert, he trusted he should live to see the day when that resolution also, with universal joy, should be obliterated from the record.[44]

In the last paragraph, Browne is referring to the case of John Wilkes in England.[45] In 1762 Wilkes founded a satirical newspaper, the *North Briton*, to ridicule the new king's administration and its Scottish prime minister, Lord Bute. No. 45 (23 April 1763), criticizing an advance copy of the speech from the throne, resulted in his arrest and confinement in the Tower of London, together with general search warrants applicable to anyone connected with that number: printers and bookstore personnel as well as anyone associated with John Wilkes – a total of forty-nine persons. Wilkes and his associates filed lawsuits for trespass *quare clausum fregit* and false imprisonment against individual officers and the secretary of state. The government eventually paid £100,000 to settle these suits. Freedom of the press was a reality in England, while the fight continued in Ireland. In 1768, Wilkes was elected to Parliament from Middlesex (metropolitan London).

The constitutional challenges to the attachment procedures may have been the reason another method of press-suppression was introduced by Lord Clonmel: the 'fiat'.

C. Fiats

The beginning of *Daly v. Magee* and an account of Arthur Browne's argument in the king's bench in 1790 can be found in William Fitpatrick's 1867 book *Ireland before the union* – a book with no pretence to impartial treatment of the circumstances of the union:[46]

Lord Chief Justice Clonmell is, we believe, chiefly remembered in Ireland for the obliging alacrity with which he extended the aegis of his judicial protection over the 'Sham Squire' and his colleagues, when the popular

44 10 *Parliamentary Register*, pp 375–8 (3 Mar. 1790).
45 See A. Cash, *John Wilkes: the scandalous father of civil liberty* (2006); C.P. Chenevix Trench, *Portrait of a patriot* (1962); G. Rude, *Wilkes and liberty: a social study of 1763 to 1774* (1962).
46 W.J. Fitzpatrick, *Ireland before the union with extracts from the unpublished diary of John Scott LLD* (1867).

journalist, Magee, laboured to reduce the overcharged importance of that person as an organ of the corrupt Irish government and puller of many complicated wires. Lord Clonmell signed a fiat or warrant to the officer of his court to issue a writ, marked in such sum as the fiat directed, on which writ the defendant, Magee, was arrested; and it ordered that he should either find bail to the amount of such sum, or remain in prison. The surety required by Lord Clonmell on the affidavits in question amounted to £7,800; and as few printers could produce such bail, the fiats became almost equivalent to perpetual imprisonment ...[47]

The fiat was an *ex parte* judicial order to confine the person of a named tortfeasor (or criminal) until security in the amount of the alleged damages had been posted with the court. Neither trial nor even determination of triable issues must be imminent.[48]

John Magee was a persistent and life-long thorn in the side of government,[49] but he could not be ignored because his newspaper had the largest circulation, the most advertising and the most intriguing scandal. He did not attempt to moderate his language nor were investigation or confirming witnesses sought or produced prior to publication. In the case of *Daly v. Magee* the publisher tangled with a government informer, Francis Higgins (the 'Sham Squire'), and his judicial protector, John Scott, the lord chief justice of king's bench. Fitzpatrick continued:

> One of the Sham Squire's colleagues, who succeeded in getting Magee imprisoned on a fiat, was Richard Daly ... George Ponsonby, afterwards lord chancellor of Ireland, showed the utter frivolousness of the grounds on which Daly sought and obtained a fiat for £4,000. Daly's affidavit recited a verse by Magee, describing young Roscius in great despondency, and he swore that he was the person indicated. How lines so innocuous could draw forth the heavy stroke of legal vengeance to which we have referred, seems strange.
>
> > This shall end my woes and me, he cried,
> > And drew the glittering weapon from his side;
> > But as too hard the yielding blade he pressed,
> > The tragic tin bent harmless on his breast.
>
> George Ponsonby was ably supported by Arthur Browne, who showed that the practice of granting fiats had been scarcely, if at all, heard of till the reign of Charles II, and was then introduced by the judges, as appears from the law

47 Ibid., pp 1–3.
48 Fiat: (Latin: 'let it be done') a brief order of a judge compelling some action.
49 John Magee (1750–1809) and his family continued to pursue governmental abuses in the next generation, when Daniel O'Connell led the defence. See P.M. Geoghegan, *King Dan: the rise of Daniel O'Connell, 1775–1829*, pp 125–40 (2008).

reports of the time, with much timidity and hesitation. We find it confined to a few instances only, in which very gross bodily injuries had been inflicted; and even then the bail demanded was exceedingly small.[50]

Despite the efforts of his counsel, Magee was found liable for £200 damages and 6 pence costs.[51] This verdict, however, was not the end of the legal issues of fiats, and George Ponsonby and Arthur Browne brought the question of judicial illegality before the House of Commons in the next session.

Before proceeding to his attack on fiats, Arthur Browne attempted to raise the question about the procedure for safeguarding records of trials, because of an erasure and alteration of the trial record in John Magee's case, an issue he had raised in 1790 in court, but which had not been fully investigated, leaving the issue unresolved.[52] Browne's efforts in 1791 to refer the question to a committee of the House were resisted by the attorney general (Arthur Wolfe), but a hearing before the House produced a witness to the alteration in Higgins' house; the issue was finally dropped after a major effort to surpress it by Dublin Castle through the solicitor general, chief secretary and the attorney general.[53]

Arthur Browne effectively re-tried *Daly v. Magee* on the issue of an unconstitutional use of the fiat, beginning with English law:

Mr Arthur Browne said, that by the common law, no person could be arrested, except for forcible injuries. By various statutes, the capias was introduced in actions, even for injuries unaccompanied with force; but still special bail was only demandable where the damages were certain and ascertained. Where the damages were precarious, and to be afterwards assessed by a jury, there was no special bail demandable of course; but if the damages, although precarious, had certainly happened, and were flagrant, it was thought, in course of time, an evil that the party should not be held to some bail; and hence a practice was introduced in such cases, of granting a judge's order, now usually called a fiat. This practice is scarcely, if at all heard of, till the reign of Charles the Second, and then was introduced by the judges, as appears from the law reports of the time, with much timidity and hesitation, and confined to a few instances, and those of very gross injuries, and the bail demanded was very small and trifling ...

Now, Sir, for this country. This power, thus innoxious in England, has been by degrees advancing itself in this country, until at length it has arisen to a height so dangerous and alarming, as to call aloud for the interposition of the legislature. Here it has been applied to acts where there has been no certainty of damage – where the party did not show when or how he had been damaged; – it had been applied particularly to slander; – and fiats have been granted for very large sums. Till of very late years, however, the evil was

50 Fitzpatrick, *Ireland before the union*, pp 3–6 (1867).
51 Inglis, *The freedom of the press in Ireland*, p. 78 (1954).   52 10 *Parliamentary Register*, p. 382.
53 11 *Parliamentary Register*, pp 57–60 (1 Feb. 1791).

moderate; but of late, I must say, particularly since a certain learned judge came upon the bench, [Lord Clonmell] it has grown to an enormous height. Sir, under the auspices of that particular judge, these doctrines have been advanced. That any man may, at his pleasure, without impunity, and without danger, deprive any other of his liberty; that any man may, upon his naked affidavit, swearing he has suffered damage, or he believes he has suffered damage, to any fancied amount, without showing when or how, hold another to bail without stint or boundary; that his fancy, or his perjury, is to be the guide of the judge's discretion, and the bail is to be accommodated to the ideal wrongs, to the fancied injuries, to the angry passions, or the wanton perjury of a wicked, or enraged prosecutor.

What is the necessary consequence? No man, however free from debt, or unconscious of crime, shall walk in security in the public streets. In vain shall the merchant state and settle his accounts – in vain shall the citizen watch his conduct, he is still at the mercy of passion and perjury, he is still liable to arrest, for any amount; and if he seeks to punish the accuser, he finds no spot on which to lay his hand. How can he indict the accuser for perjury? He only swore a general affirmative, that he had been damaged; – who can prove a general negative that he had not? He only swore to the belief of damage. Who can arraign his fancy? Who can convict him of mental perjury? If he had sworn to a particular instance, that his arm had been broken; that in consequence of scandal he had lost the setting of a house, or the customers that used to resort to his shop, I might prove the falsehood of the assertion by evidence. But upon a general charge, nothing remains but submission and a prison, and burning indignation against the abuse of the laws, and secret murmur against the ministers of justice, and: the humble, but fervent cry, to the supreme and healing legislature.

He then showed instances of the atrocious use of this power, with respect to the mercantile interest, how it might at once throw a man in gaol and destroy his credit. He mentioned the instance of Mr Dick, an eminent merchant of Dublin, who had been not long since arrested in the street, under a fiat of £16,000 on a mere uncertain charge, for which he could not be prepared, and of which he could have no foreknowledge. Mr Jameson of Cork, in the same manner of £2,000. on a charge which afterwards appeared to be groundless, by a verdict in his favour. Several gentlemen in the country, in the farming line, arrested under fiats, through the private malice of wicked neighbours; but this power had been particularly directed against printers.

Whoever presumed to print or publish with the leave, or not under the directions of Francis Higgins [the Sham Squire, a castle informer], was in great danger of a fiat; numbers of printers had been run down by fiats whom the public never heard of. John Magee was more sturdy, and therefore his sufferings made more noise. He then dwelt on those sufferings and showed how our fiats issued against him in June, to the amount of £7,800 – that he was kept in prison from June till the end of November, before the question (whether the bail should be reduced) was decided – that the plaintiff has now, by the practice of the courts, (which gives a plaintiff three terms before he need try his action) power to keep him in prison till November next, so that he may lie in prison 19 months for want of bail, before the action be tried, perhaps afterwards have a verdict in his favour, or only eight-pence damages given against him; and he reminded gentlemen, that each of the bail must swear himself worth twice the sum for which he was security; i.e. £30,000. And more in this case. What gentlemen in the kingdom almost could find such bail? – it amounted to perpetual imprisonment.

He said that the name, the terrific name of fiat, a name which threatens to be as formidable as general warrants, or lettres de cachet, has but recently assumed its terrors; it was not till of late year, that the innocent and peaceful citizen discovered, and felt that there was a power in this country, which, while he was unconscious of crime, and unembarrassed with debt, could seize him in the public streets, on the way home to his expecting family, and drag him with insult and ignominy, to slavery and a prison; a power which could at pleasure destroy the credit of the merchant, and tear the farmer from his labours; a complaisant power, which by placing an implicit confidence in any absurd or villainous accuser, might be ready to become the instrument of malice, and the origin of ruin. If the merchant can be dragged from his compter, not to answer his bond debts, sums certain and ascertained; not to obey the drafts of commerce, for which he knows to be prepared, but to enter into security, whose measure is fixed and appointed by the modest standard of passion, anger, or wickedness, or of perjury. If supposed injuries to the meanest of mankind should demand enormous bail; if the charge of scandal, yet unproved, on a woman of the town, or a bravo of a brothel, ever should require bail to the amount of a thousand pounds, a supposed libel on a libelous printer of £2,000 or an affront to a player of £4,000. If, without slating any particular instance of loss sustained, the affidavit of affronted vanity, or swollen malice, boldly swearing to the belief of damage, without showing when or how, can abolish at pleasure the rights of personal security; – we may talk of independence, but liberty is no more – the security of our boasted emancipation is a name, for we had nothing to secure.

Why, Sir, is it necessary to do more than state this, in order to convince the mind of man? Is it necessary to do more than appeal to your reason? If it be, the appeal is vain, for the reason must be subdued to some superior power, which hath not ears for the plain voice of truth. Do not be intimidated by being told, this is a legal question; questions of property are complex, and require study; but, thank Heaven! questions of liberty are simple, for Heaven, which intended it the lot of all men, has made it intelligible to all. It speaks by feeling, not by study. It speaks to the heart as much as to the understanding, and nature never sets us wrong. You may read the law of liberty in your souls; it plays about the heart, it vibrates in every nerve; it flows in the warm tide of your blood; you will meet it every where. Do not look abroad for it to the cold hearts or warm harangues of crown and prerogative lawyers. Look first at home, if you do not find it there, look for it no where, for you will not find it.

Do that justice, that honour to your constitution, to believe it does not contain principles manifestly wrong. See what an instrument this doctrine might be in the hands of private malice, or public oppression. Suppose a man willing to wreak his vengeance upon his foe, and for that purpose recommending himself to the favour of the bench. – Suppose a bad man, in possession of the ear of a judge, instilling his position into it, and willing to make it the conduit, through which to wreak his vengeance on his foe; suppose him to recommend himself by every wicked and base act, (for I must suppose him a bad man) to a wicked judge. and such may be conceived. Suppose him the mignion of that judge, requiring a little mutual favour, for his multiplied services, and asking the debasement of the law bench, as the price or former aid in the elevation of the judge. Suppose him seeking a monopoly of abuse, as Mr Daly has done of the theatre, and enraged at a rival in the dirty trade. – and suppose the slanderous assassin, seeking for a fiat against a far less criminal than himself, and fixing the sum, which he thinks sufficient to throw his neighbour into eternal bondage, is it not possible that his friendly judge may listen to his argument, in memory of old festivity, now forsworn, and grant him a fiat even to his heart's content, although, by doing so, your courts of law, instead of being the sacred deposits of justice, should become the channels of malevolence. They saw, that if ever an angry judge should blend his passions with his judgment; having been abused himself, should chuse to retort that abuse tenfold; having been reviled, should revile again; should make the bench ridiculous, by laughable defences of himself, and abuse of others; and administer justice, not in mercy, but in anger, that a fiat might become the instrument of vindictive oppression, instead of salutary caution.

Gentlemen had defended fiats, by its being a practice. So were general warrants, and ship money, practices; but what a horrid doctrine did they advance; the liberty of the subject to depend on practice. But if they would resort to practice, let them go to England, not look in this country, for alas! her practice had been oppression. Let them not object to novelty here, for here every thing favourable to liberty must be novel. He desired them to show a single instance in the report books of England, of a fiat granted on an affidavit like Mr Daly's, swearing no particular damage; and where fiats were granted, it was for small sums, in all the instances he could find in their books, £3 or £400 usually much less, some of which he proceeded to recount. [...]

If, then, this practice was not founded in reason or nature – in the example of England – in the laws – or in any judicial authority, where did it take its rise? Was it in the breast of corruption and revenge? No, he would not say that. Whether it was corruption or error, must be left to every one to judge. But he would say, that if a practice was evidently wrong, it was not the arguments of learned and ingenious gentlemen in the House, nor of young adulating barristers out of the House, though thank Heaven, that was not much the fashion of the younger Bar; nor the good nature of brother judges, which some people had termed cullability, wishing to throw out a plank to a sinking judge, that could excuse or justify such a practice, or make it palatable to the public.

He then adverted to the attacks upon Magee's character, which had been made a palliation for these fiats. He understood his character as a husband, a father, and a man, had been a good one, until goaded into madness by persecution, he might possibly be a little outrageous; but what had his character to say to the question? It was not so that England considered public questions … the public only considered the precedent, and the oppression.

It had been said, the courts would be undone. It was an idle fear. Integrity would defend itself; and if there was an unclean or unhallowed thing in the courts, it ought not be defended. How were they to support the judicial power? Not by turning away the eye from its pollutions, but by removing whatever was polluted. He knew much manly virtue, much sacred integrity there, which feared no enquiry. No man upon earth was more anxious than he, to support the authority of the bench; but that authority was not to be supported, by blinking inquiry, and avoiding scrutiny; it must be supported by the bench itself, the greater part of whose possessors he respected to a degree of veneration. – There was a stern and invincible virtue upon one of those benches. There was a conscious integrity, in a milder garb, upon another. There was a manly, intelligent, and honest mind upon a third, that did not think it a crime to have differed from him, but only recollected, whether in that difference, the contest had been honourable. None of these feared scrutiny. To none of these was the public voice raised, except to praise.

He concluded by observing, that if the wretched victims of this assumed power, did not find redress here, they knew not where to fly for refuge; on that House depended the fate of all who are, or may be subject to this tyranny; if they did not find relief here, they must be lost, but they would be lost in the wreck of the national character; and he conjured the House to exercise the healing and salutary power of the grand committee of justice, in remedying the greatest evil and mischief which had ever come before them.

In the course of his speech, he observed, what an instrument such power might be in the hands of a bad government. What an instrument it might be against the liberty of the press. How any printer who presumed to open his mouth against government, might be run down by it. And he noticed how careful in the Bill of Rights they were to guard against such evils, for although in the preamble they mentioned only excessive bail in criminal cases, the only evil they then knew, yet in the enacting clauses, they say generally excessive bail ought not to be demanded, as if foreseeing the possibility of the present evil. It is true the preamble is the key to a statute; but here they seem to make a marked distinction; they corrected the evil of their time; do you correct the evil of yours?[54]

54 11 *Parliamentary Register*, pp 368–74. Arthur Browne's speeches in king's bench and the Commons

After this 1791 exposure of the abuses by the judiciary of the fiat, the issue disappeared as no further fiats were used to control the press;[55] in fact, opposition to government became muted in the press and disappeared entirely during the rebellion of 1798 and the subsequent repression. It was not until the conflict over the union in the years 1799 and 1800 that opposition to government became a feature of the daily press, a situation that continued until long after the union went into effect in 1801.

In England the power of the jury to render a general verdict on all aspects of the case instead of the narrow issue of publication was enacted in May 1792 – a proposal of Charles James Fox and the Whigs, with Pitt's concurrence, despite the opposition of the lord chancellor.[56] Similar legislation was enacted in Ireland in 1793.[57]

Despite strong advocacy for the freedom of the press in Ireland in 1791, by 1798 Browne feared the example of revolutionary France where the press became 'the early propagator of blasphemy, of massacre, of anarchy', citing the example of Robespierre and the Jacobin press, which insisted that 'nothing should be published except their own new-fangled doctrines' that 'tended to unhinge all civilized society'.

> Would I therefore be an enemy to the press altogether? Surely not; we must take it with all its possible evils, to annihilate it would be to lose a certainty of much good, from an apprehension of possible mischief; it is an excellent antidote to tyranny, while it preserves itself from licentiousness, but a licentious press is necessarily the victim of arbitrary powers, by furnishing protests for its extirpation; a prudent controul of its exercise without affecting its liberty, must in every country be wise; further than that we should let it take its course. But what I mean to urge is, that the press without morals will not preserve civilization, and that immorality would make it the vehicle of barbarism.

He predicted that an age of barbarism would succeed 'the present state of illumination and refinement', because the art of printing 'may become exclusively the engine of wickedness, of vice, of folly, of irreligion'.[58] Freedom of press became a constitutional right in the United States in 1791.[59]

---

were printed in pamphlet form in 1790. Wolfe Tone's first pamphlet, *A review of the conduct of administration during the seventh session of Parliament, addressed to the constitutional electors ...* (March 1790), reviewed the trial of *Higgins v. Magee* for libel before Lord Clonmell and the parliamentary review of the case.

55 Inglis, *The freedom of the press in Ireland*, p. 79 (1954).

56 32 Geo. 3 c. 60. Ehrman traces Pitt's unexpected approval to the experiences of his father. J. Ehrman, *The younger Pitt: the years of acclaim*, p. 81 (1969).

57 33 Geo. 3 c. 43, An Act to Remove Doubts Respecting the Function of Juries in Cases of Libel.

58 Quotations from the essay, 'Whether the world will ever relapse into barbarism' in Browne, *Miscellaneous sketches*, pp 48–52 (1798).

59 In 1789 the first Congress amended the 1787 constitution with twelve amendments, the first of which is arguably the most important, 'Congress shall make no law ... abridging the freedom of

III. THE POLICE BILL

Medieval Dublin was organized for administrative purposes along the lines of the parish boundaries of the established church, and the vestrymen of each parish were responsible for the selection and employment of watchmen and a constable to safeguard the properties within the parish.[60] It was undoubtedly a disagreeable task, like the additional responsibility to care for the widows, orphans and the indigent in the parish workhouse. These civic responsibilities might barely have been within the competence of the parish organization in a village, but were hopelessly overwhelming in a city of about 150,000 people.

In 1784 the perceived need for a force of armed men to protect the city carried another rationale: a force of men to counteract the Volunteers. This accounts for the urgency of Prime Minister Pitt and the viceroy (Rutland) in pushing a Dublin police bill, based on legislation designed for London and favoured by Pitt at Westminster in 1783. The London bill was withdrawn because of opposition, but the Dublin bill went from introduction to third reading in eight days, despite efforts of the Patriot Party minority to delay enactment.[61] Dreams of extensive patronage (at least 500 new jobs) for hungry Castle politicians were a further spur to urgency. In 1787, the Dublin Police Act was successfully applied in part to areas beyond Dublin, in the provinces, despite efforts of Arthur Browne and Henry Grattan to amend it.[62] The police statutes allowed the Castle to appoint for Dublin 400 watchmen, 80 constables, 4 chief constables, 3 magistrates and a high commissioner, paid by the city taxpayers and controlled by the Castle.[63] Outside of Dublin, four counties (Cork, Kerry, Kilkenny and Tipperary) were divided into a number of districts with a chief constable and 16 constables, paid by the county and controlled by the Castle.[64] This new central police gave the Castle a substantial force of loyal adherents, instantly available to overawe the people and suppress the Volunteers.

speech or of the press.' These amendments applied only to the federal government (Barron v. Baltimore, 32 US (7 Pet.) 243 (1833)). After the Civil War, Amendment XIV (1868) created a new constitution, 'No state shall make or enforce any law which shall abridge the privileges and immunities of citizens of the United States nor shall any state deprive any person of life, liberty or property, without due process of law nor deny to any person within its jurisdiction the equal protection of the laws.' Prior censorship of the press by the states was prohibited in Near v. Minnesota, 283 US 697 (1931) but state laws dealing with defamation and privacy were not made subject to the first amendment until New York Times v. Sullivan, 376 US 254 (1964) and Time v. Hill, 385 US 374 (1967).

60 McDowell, *Ireland in the age of imperialism and revolution*, pp 67–70 (1979).

61 G. O'Brien, *Anglo-Irish politics in the age of Grattan and Pitt*, pp 106–16 (1987). See 26 Geo. 3 c.24.

62 McDowell, *Ireland in the age of imperialism and revolution*, pp 67–8 (1979). See 27 Geo. 3 c.38.

63 Ibid., p. 69. Whig suspicions of this legislation were undoubtedly encouraged by the fact that Attorney General John FitzGibbon was the Castle official supervising it. By the time of Browne's attack, FitzGibbon had become lord chancellor and Arthur Wolfe (the future Lord Kilwarden) was attorney general.

64 Ibid., p. 68.

By 1790 it was already too late to stop the centralized police function, so the target of Browne's attack was the excessive patronage reserved to the crown (i.e. Dublin Castle), depriving local citizens of any say in the choice of their guardians; this issue was raised in a discussion of the cost of policing, where Browne scorned the loss of civic pride in the military appearance of police:

> Mr Arthur Browne said he could not bear to see this question frittered away by both sides of the House, as it usually was, by confining the question to the expense. Its expense and inutility were loudly proclaimed by the city, but he had a much stronger objection than to the management in practice, viz. to the principle of the bill itself – a principle that went to give the crown directly and immediately the power of appointing the petty executive officers of free cities, was more dangerous and extensive in its consequences, than even some of the enemies of the police seemed to apprehend. All executive power is derived from the crown, but the crown has been used to delegate much of that power to faithful and trusty servants – to faithful and ancient corporations, for contributions made, and services conferred. It ought to do so. It ought to act through mediums, and by interventions. It is the genius of a free state.
>
> The supreme executive ought not to intermeddle immediately in inferior departments. When the majesty of the crown blends itself with inferior magistracy, when it comes to operate directly upon the people, when it makes the petty officer look directly up to itself, when the hand that holds the sceptre catches at the constable's staff, it may improve patronage, it may improve influence, it may increase power, but it will not cherish liberty. The constitution is wise, it illumes and subtilizes the electrical spark, that insensibility given it health and vigour; but when this bungling system draws down at once the lightning from clouded majesty, it is like the lighting of nature, not only of a dangerous, but of a sceptic quality, it scorches, it consumes, and it corrupts.
>
> Those who talk of all executive power being derived from the crown, and apply it to this system, either do not know the constitution, or they chuse to forget it – it is a sophism.
>
> All executive power is derived from the crown, but does it therefore follow that the executive officer ought to be appointed by the crown? Does it follow that the crown's representative ought to appoint three commissioners of police? That the approbation of the viceroy should be necessary to the appointment of four chief constables, and one high constable? That he should appoint divisional magistrates? The very contrary is the principle of the constitution. Wherever the liberty of the subject could in any degree be concerned, the officer was to be appointed by the people, though when appointed, he derived his authority from the crown. The sheriff, the coroner, verderor of the forest, were all appointed by the people, and looked up to the people. And when some of these ceased to be appointed in counties, where their cessation could not be of so much consequence to liberty, on account

of their great extent, and the numerous and spirited gentry they contained, they remained in corporations the boards of liberty, the nests from whence its life has been so often regenerated, the strong opponents of illegal power, which has so often given the alarm to the landed interest, and barred the designs of power and with fear of change, have perplexed and staid incroaching monarchs.

Such was the intention of the constitution. The genius of the police institution was directly the contrary: it looked to the crown alone; it was dressed in military array; it was armed with extraordinary powers; its first object was to corrupt one part of the city, and to bully the other. No one objects to a strong town watch; but that watch should be the servants and not the masters of the people, otherwise it degenerates into a little petty tyranny. The town is more secure. But if I am to pay for security from the robber, by being exposed to the violence and outrage of the guard, what have I gained? [...]

When it makes crimes of the little sports and gaieties of the common people; it is a Star Chamber, composed of whom? Not as in the last century, of men of science and knowledge, but of men, ignorant, indolent, conceited and vulgar; men corrupted to intimidate and break that spirit which had been so characteristic of free corporations and great cities. Whence this spirit, this vigour? Because they saw the crown only through the medium of their charter, its rays were transmitted clear and strong, but mild. While the kingdom at large was clothed with the great charter, they, wrapped in a little inferior circle of privilege, were doubly armed. The power of inferior police came ultimately from the crown, but the name of the monarch was not heard. [...]

More magnificent but less dangerous, it struck without destruction, it did not sour the spirit that was in the vessel. Any defect of energy was amply compensated by freedom of spirit. I love the irregularities of freemen, rather than the order of slaves. The crown did not love them. The ebullitions of spirit were wrong, but the spirit was generally right, and when well conducted it produced that jealousy on the part of the crown, which bad administration has ever dreaded, and warred against free corporations which has particularly hated the metropolis, the beacon of the kingdom, and by open war and covert wile, externally attacked its privileges.

In the last century it sought by *quo warrantos*. Strength, prerogative, power was its weapon. It has been so in this, where influence could not operate, witness the American charters, witness the charter of New York in 1766. But where influence could operate, that less, but more subtle way, has been adopted. The times of force are over, and now we are to be wheedled; rights are not plundered, but betrayed, and our attention is divided between the artful debaucher and the ready prostitute. The man who wishes to recover the city of Dublin from bondage, cannot flatter the inthralled whom he witness to set free – I mean the governing part of the city, for the great body of the city sufficiently reprobated the idea. The corporation meanly surrendered, in effect its charter; a kind of eunuch corporation, deprived of its virtue, confessing its own impotency, and forming an unnatural alliance, and justly drawing down upon itself the contempt of its own spouse, the administration.

He next considered the measure as an anti-reform, tending to corrupt the metropolis, and to set an example for corrupting every free borough in the kingdom, while we were talking with out effect of reforming rotten ones. He then considered it as debasing the spirit of the city, as making the pliant alderman an awkward imitator of the vices of the castle, but no longer the friend of the public, nor the honest representative of the people, nor the mild and good magistrate, nor the merciful yet just executor of the laws.

I object to the system, as giving your watch too much of a military spirit. A badge of distinction might be necessary, but did it follow it should be a military badge. – Was a military uniform necessary, was a loaded musket necessary. They instantly caught the spirit – they caught the name. The Act spoke only of constables, they called themselves captains. They were arrayed – they had their field days – they had their musters – they their roll call. The constable's staff became a truncheon, and the constable stared to hear himself saluted captain. The peaceful alderman preserved the peace with all the honours of war. What must be the consequence? Is there any thing civil in this? To forget that they are citizens, to get the manner of thinking they are soldiers, to get the military insolence without military discipline. These must be the points, and the event has answered. No, it may seem, a paradox; but I had rather see your city well guarded at once by the real military powers. I object to it as a confusion of the civil with the military powers. The military power should ever be kept distinct. We then see it, we know it by its proper name, we are on our guard, but when a power of a similar kind intrudes itself upon us, under the name of a civil power, the wolf in sheep's clothing deceives and endangers us. [...]

Has not the thing happened, has not the policeman been guilty of more insolence and outrage than ever the soldier was, but with this difference, that if you complain of the soldier, he was punished, if you complain of the policeman, they did not know how to punish him. We can do nothing, said they, but turn him off, and thereby lose an able man, unless we admit military discipline which we heartily wish. It was useless, they owned, because imperfect, and its perfection was, what? military discipline. In a peace establishment, these seeds of disorder would not be laid, in a military discipline they would be punished. Riots are the effects, military discipline is the remedy. By their own confession, this mongrel institution will not do. *Fatentem habetis reum.*

Mr Browne then drew a picture of the insolence and outrage of the police, an insolence which had laid the city under a kind of contribution, it was a compound of military contribution, and inquisitorial scrutiny. Money was raised upon every pretext, and to find the pretexts, a watch was set upon even the most trifling action of individuals or families. This insolence had reached even to the doors of the House of Commons; he had been stopt himself at the door of the House, and desired to give an account of himself. The earl of Ormond, when stopt in the same manner, offered to make his way by the sword; he would not mention himself in the same period with the earl of Ormond, except in point of feeling; but he had learned high feelings in another country, where he had known an assembly refuse to proceed to business, because a cannon happened, perhaps accidentally, to be posted near their doors. [This happened at Boston in 1769.] Swift says, speaking of England, they seem to think of us as one of their petty colonies. How would he stare to see the change, they were in 1769 petty colonies, but their senates had more spirit than yours. He then proceeded to speak of the inutility of the [police] institution and its expence; its inutility had been proclaimed by all the parishes of the city, though their peaceable meetings, for the purpose of so declaring, had been branded with. [...]

Take it then in all its parts, view its expense and its prodigality, view its insolences, its outrages, view its corruption, and its influence, view its military spirit, abhorrent to a free state, view it as an enemy to reform, view it as the debaser of free and generous spirit, view it as the instrument of a corrupt and arbitrary government, and pass your judgment on that government which patronises such a system; they will tell you it is trifling, nothing is trifling in a free country; they will tell you it is a local circumstance, but from that circumstance they will deduce a principle; they will tell you it is no part of the system, I say it is a part of a system which goes, in all its parts, to increase the influence of the crown, to corrupt its representation, and to debase the spirit of the people. Liberty is jealous to a degree, it ought to be so. In the reign of Edward VI, an attempt to make convicts work in chains set the whole kingdom in a flame, and now that they have adopted, it is carefully regulated and guarded, and still is unpopular. In the reign of King William, an attempt to register seamen, though apparently useful, was resisted and dropped for the same reason, and this very police in the city of London, the minister durst not urge; but it is the misfortune of this country to take all these insults which England would spurn. Imitate her spirit, and check in the bud, a system which wars against your constitution, and is more dangerous in its consequences than even its adversaries seem to apprehend.[65]

Despite Browne's lengthy oration and the assistance of other Patriot Party members, the effort to amend and reduce the police appropriation failed on a vote of 94 to 140.

Browne returned to an attack on the police budget in 1793 in a discussion of the promise by the government to reform the police among a list of reforms promised for the session.

---

65 10 *Parliamentary Register*, pp 307–12.

A repeal of the Police Act had been promised; its faults were admitted; amendment and correction was promised; the moment it comes to the point they retract: such, he now expected, would be their conduct in every instance; they had forgot all they said in the beginning of the session about reform: they would, if they could in the same manner bury it in silence, whiffle away every other article of their implied faith, and express covenants ...

He said, he abhorred the police system from the beginning; – he had been an eye-witness of instances of cruelty, oppression, and negligences, in that body: he had walked the length of the town without meeting a single police-man. He said, it was easy to raise a cry, that the town was mighty well guarded; and fashion and folly, which never think at all, re-echo it in the mouths of a number of silly boys, the dupes or the instruments of cunning men. So the town was well lighted for two years; it had been infamously lighted ever since, yet fashion still cried, that the town was brilliantly illuminated: such was the cry in favour of the police. He bowed not to fashion; he denied that the town was better guarded than in the time of the old watch. Never were outrages and robberies more frequent than since the police establishment. – When was a gentleman known not to be shot in the streets before they existed?

He said the right honourable gentleman [Mr Hobart, chief secretary], declared that patronage was no object; why then did he oppose the present bill? He did not deny the police wanted amendment; why then not go into the committee? Let them defend their conduct on any footing of consistency or common sense.[66]

This effort also failed, and it was not until the brief Whig administration in 1795 of Earl Fitzwilliam that changes were made in the administration of the Dublin police to vest control of the police in civic officials.[67]

66 13 *Parliamentary Register*, pp 460–2.
67 McDowell, *Ireland in the age of imperialism and revolution*, p. 70 (1979). See 35 Geo. 3 c.36.

CHAPTER TEN

The Catholic question, evangelism and the Trinity Defence Corps (1793–7)

I. THE CATHOLIC QUESTION

ON 20 FEBRUARY 1792, in Parliament, Arthur Browne said:

> [I] had never seen a Roman Catholic until [I] was seventeen years old, and [I] then considered him a prodigy ; but [I] had since by interviews with many respectable men of that sect got rid of [my] prejudices.[1]

In studying the Catholic question it will be necessary to distinguish Protestant Ascendancy attitudes to individual relatives, friends, companions or business associates who were Roman Catholics from the attitude to the majority Catholic population as a whole, seen as a hostile army prepared to subvert the Protestant constitution and the Hanoverian succession while betraying the Irish nation to the French enemy.

Political actions of the popes in the past were at the heart of Protestant fears: the power to excommunicate and depose Christian rulers, as had occurred to Elizabeth I at the hands of Pius V on 25 February 1570. It was also believed that Catholics were absolved from obligations of truth or honesty when dealing with Protestant heretics, and, even more fancifully, that they were obliged to kill heretics. Another legend was the belief that Catholics, unlike Protestants, were unable to resist the political opinions of their priests.[2]

By the eighteenth century, papal armies and Spanish armadas had become imaginary. Papal military force could not be taken seriously during a period of retrenchment in Rome. The eight popes of the eighteenth century continually struggled with the conflicting demands of Habsburgs and Bourbons while dealing

---

1   11 *Parliamentary Register*, pp 189–90. Grattan had said concerning British control of Ireland, 'The remedy was that Protestant Ascendancy should be strengthened by adopting the Catholic people.' 11 *Parliamentary Register*, p. 169 (18 Feb. 1792). This debate concerned a petition of the Catholic Committee for the right to vote. See, generally, J.R. Hill, *Popery and Protestantism: civil and religious liberty: the disputed lesson of Irish history, 1698–1812* (1988) and T. Bartlett, *The fall and rise of the Irish nation: the Catholic question, 1690–1830* (1992).

2   These elements of popular belief were denounced by the Catholic Committee in a declaration on 17 Mar. 1792. See R.B. McDowell, *Ireland in the age of imperialism and revolution, 1760–1801*, p. 405 (1979).

with and suppressing powerful internal forces: the Jansenists, the Freemasons and the Jesuits. It was the perpetual enmity of France's Catholic kings that terrorized Irish Protestant opinion. As the French Revolution became anticlerical and anti-Catholic after 1790, Protestant fears of French Catholicism lessened, but could not disappear in view of the historical confiscations of Catholic-owned lands by Protestants.

The underground Catholic church, with a pilgrim or peripatetic priesthood, unsupervised by non-resident bishops, did not have to deal with the openly licentious society that the established church confronted (and largely ignored). By 1775, the immediate problem was an abundance of badly prepared clergy – men who had not studied in France, Spain or Italy but had undergone a type of on-the-job training from older priests, followed by covert ordinations. The remedy was to limit the number of ordinations to the priesthood by each bishop.[3] A second problem, emerging from the first, was clerical misconduct of an intemperate or sexual nature, never reported to a non-resident bishop.[4] The third problem was the survival of pagan or evil practices, especially among rural people: clandestine and consanguineous marriages, incestuous relations, riotous and drunken wakes and funerals.[5] Lastly, as wealthy farmers and merchants emerged, there were disputes over fees and properties between regular (monastic) and secular clergy and even between religious orders.[6]

Due to the nature of political power in Ireland, legal emancipation and economic liberty could not be achieved for Catholics by their own actions. Protestant help was essential. Protestant help came from an unusual source in 1774: the bishop of Derry,[7] who pushed the Lords and then the Commons for a new oath of allegiance for Catholics, 'desirous to testify their loyalty and allegiance', as well as 'their abhorrence of certain doctrines imputed to them'. Bishop Hervey (not yet earl of Bristol) had begun his efforts in 1770 for a new oath of allegiance that distinguished papal temporal jurisdiction from spiritual leadership; Hervey did this in Rome in discussions with friendly cardinals and even Pope Clement XIV. The Romans did not recognize the distinction, but Hervey was not deterred. His new oath did not require Catholics to abjure their religious faith while swearing allegiance to George III and the Hanoverian Succession (13 & 14 Geo. 3 c. 35).

3 S. McBride, *Eighteenth-century Ireland: the isle of slaves*, pp 250–2 (2009).
4 Ibid., pp 254–8. See also E. Larkin, *The pastoral role of the Roman Catholic Church in pre-Famine Ireland, 1750–1850*, pp 4, 7, 62–88, 196–208 (2006).
5 McBride, *Eighteenth-century Ireland*, pp 258–63 (2009).
6 Ibid., p. 252; Larkin, *The pastoral role of the Roman Catholic Church*, pp 23–30, 33–42, 193–6 (2006).
7 Frederick Augustus Hervey (1730–1803), chaplain to his elder brother, the viceroy, became bishop of Cloyne (1766), translated to Derry (1768). He had adopted Ireland and her people before the deaths of his elder brothers, becoming 4th earl of Bristol in 1779. He was colonel of the Derry Volunteers, an opponent of tithes and supporter of equal treatment of Catholics and dissenters. See B. Fothergill, *The mitred earl: Frederick Hervey, earl of Bristol and bishop of Derry*, pp 31–7, 54–9, 71–3 (1974).

By 1775, there had been ninety years of official suppression, but the Roman Catholic church was still the faith of the majority, emerging from obscurity to assert traditional supervision over its adherents. To encourage Protestant sympathizers it was important that there be a Catholic voice telling Protestants they had nothing to fear. The first Catholic Association of 1756 tried to do this. It was made up of antiquarians and wealthy men. Its organizers in Dublin were Charles O'Conor, Dr John Curry and Thomas Wyse, supported by aristocratic land owners who had been able to avoid the penal laws and hold on to family lands by maintaining public devotion to the House of Hanover and no connections to the Stuarts. The modest and polite efforts to redress grievances did not risk Protestant vengeance, but were ineffective.

A change in the attitudes of Protestants to the penal laws occurred in the last quarter of the eighteenth century, the product of a number of factors: the development of a wealthy Catholic merchant class; the defeat of British imperial power at the hands of American revolutionaries; the indifference of the enlightened to religious issues; and the independence, after 1783, of the Protestant Parliament (although it included many fanatical anti-Catholics). The dramatic change to full citizenship of the Catholic populations of Ireland, England and Scotland actually required almost a half century to accomplish, but the removal of legal controls began very gradually in 1778, possibly because of a need to recruit Catholic soldiers for foreign wars. The Catholic question never ceased to be considered in those fifty years, but it is most convenient to consider four episodes during Arthur Browne's lifetime: 1778, 1782, 1792–3 and 1795.

1778–80

In February 1778, France became an ally of the Americans and resumed war with Britain. As a war measure, Dublin Castle pushed concessions to Catholics in 1778 and Presbyterians in 1780. This succeeded despite the bishops of the established church. First, the restrictions on Catholic land ownership and most of the anti-popery laws were repealed; Catholics became eligible to lease lands for 999 years; division of estates among all children and the law conferring title to the entire estate on a son conforming to the established church were eliminated; the criminal penalties on clergy for celebrating the marriage of a Protestant to a Catholic were also repealed.[8] The legislation, put forward by Luke Gardiner, MP for County Dublin, passed the Commons by vote of 127 in favour and 84 opposed. Second, in 1780, the elimination of the Test Act to permit dissenters (Presbyterians) to hold office was approved.[9] These bills were subject to Poynings' Law and required British cabinet approval before enactment in Ireland, but London encouraged and

8   17 and 18 Geo. 3 c. 49. See Bartlett, *The fall and rise of the Irish nation*, pp 82–92 (1992); R. Foster, *Modern Ireland, 1600–1972*, pp 206–7 (1988) and G. Tuathaigh, *Ireland before the Famine, 1798–1848*, pp 42–4 (1972).

9   R. Burns, 'The Catholic Relief Act in Ireland, 1778', 22 *Church History*, 181–207 (1962), as cited in Bartlett, *The fall and rise of the Irish nation* (1992). See also 19 and 20 Geo. 3 c. 6.

approved the loosening of anti-Catholic restrictions for political reasons. These first steps probably benefitted wealthy Catholic landowners only.

As later Irish parliaments approached the question of altering the penal laws to relieve the statutory oppression on Roman Catholics, they can hardly have ignored the Gordon riots of June 1780 in London. The English House of Lords was considering a reform measure to open the right to vote to all men, including Catholics, when Lord George Gordon, accompanied by a large mob on 2 June 1780, sought to petition Parliament to repeal the 1778 legislation ameliorating the restrictions on Catholics. Frustrated by its inability to storm the House of Commons, the mob became unruly as gentlemen retired and the lowest classes took over, screaming 'No popery!' and set off to burn Catholic chapels and homes. Taverns and distilleries were pillaged for the next six days while the mob controlled large parts of the city and Westminster, and burned embassy chapels, Newgate prison and whatever homes of judges or magistrates could be identified, looting and setting fire to them. Other jails were attacked and 1,600 prisoners freed. The Bank of England was endangered, as well as the persons and homes of the powerful. Nevertheless, the Commons refused to consider the petition. The army was summoned to confront the drunken mob, but the threat of force did not slow the mob until the soldiers began to shoot rioters, eventually killing at least 850. By 8 June the riot was controlled with 15,000 troops, and order restored to a frightened people.[10] William Pitt, the future prime minister, was a 21-year-old student at Lincoln's Inn when the quadrangle became an armed camp to hold the rioters at bay. He surely appreciated the power of militant bigots, but when he came to power three years later he determined to push the English and Irish parliaments to remove the legal disabilities of Britain's Roman Catholics, despite the possibility of renewed mob violence.[11] (He did not anticipate the royal obstinacy on Catholic emancipation that ended his government in 1801).

There was no strong Catholic voice in Irish government before the period of Grattan's Parliament (1783–1800), but this period witnessed increases in the numbers and wealth of Catholic merchants in urban centres, especially Dublin, who were unafraid to assert their rights to full citizenship. This change of the political outlook occurred as Arthur Browne took his seat in Parliament.

1782

In 1782, Luke Gardiner moved a second Catholic Relief Act, whereby Catholics obtained the right to deal with lands held in fee simple in the same way as Protestants – that is, the right to buy, sell, enjoy and bequeath property in land.[12]

---

10 C. Hibbert, *King Mob: Lord George Gordon and the riots of 1780*, pp 125–43 (1958).
11 J. Ehrman, *The younger Pitt: the years of acclaim*, pp 20–4 (1969). In 1781, English Roman Catholics were freed from most civil disabilities in legislation supported by Pitt, Burke and Fox, 31 Geo. 3 c. 32.
12 Bartlett, *The fall and rise of the Irish nation*, pp 100–2 (1992). M. O'Connell, *Irish politics and soial conflict in the age of the American Revolution*, pp 349–62 (1965). See 21 and 22 Geo. 3 c. 24.

Petty annoyances prohibiting members of religious orders and requiring registration of secular clergy were repealed, but the state still controlled the architecture of new Catholic churches by forbidding steeples with crosses. (Crosses had been removed from the established church in the Puritan reforms.)

It appeared that the last inhibitions on full Catholic citizenship would disappear after the Parliament, elected in 1783, freed from Poynings' Law, had convened; certainly Grattan knew that Irish Protestants could never be free until Irish Catholics had ceased to be slaves. It did not happen. What prevented further altruistic concessions to Catholics was Protestant fear that seventeenth-century confiscations of Catholic lands would be undone by increased political power in Catholic hands. Catholic challenges to the status quo were postponed while the Protestant nation dealt with its relations to Great Britain in the regency crisis and disputes over trade.

1792–3

France declared war on Austria, homeland of Queen Marie Antoinette, on 20 April 1792, but the war started badly and Austria, joined by its Prussian ally, began an invasion of France from Austrian Belgium. In Paris, mobs stormed the Tuileries Palace on 10 August 1792, and the king fled to the National Assembly for protection. The Assembly first suspended the king from office and then declared France a Republic on 21 September 1792. The trial and condemnation of the former king followed, as did his execution on 21 January 1793, to commemorate the death of Charles I on 21 January 1649. British condemnation at the judicial murder of the French king resulted in a French declaration of war on Great Britain on 1 February 1793. Thereafter, the Pitt administration's first task was to win the new war with France, which would continue until 1815.

Pitt clearly intended that there be Catholic participation in the defence of Great Britain and Ireland, encouraged by removal of the last restrictions on Catholics in England and Ireland. He saw no difficulties in England, which had a very small Catholic population, but Irish Protestants could prevent the collapse of their wealth and power in Parliament. Restrictions on Catholic education and the practice of law were removed, but Ascendancy fears were aroused when Grattan introduced a bill (from the Catholic Committee) for complete emancipation of Ireland's Catholics. This bill essentially would have meant that Roman Catholics could vote and sit as members of Parliament. It was rejected on 20 February 1792 by a vote of 208 to 25.[13] Arthur Browne was one of the twenty-five in favour of abstract justice for Catholics, but was troubled by the idea of an electorate of impoverished peasants following the demands of wealthy landlords.

13 Bartlett, *The fall and rise of the Irish nation*, pp 142–5 (1992). The awkward position urged by Browne was approval of Catholic franchise as the privilege of individuals, but rejection of the Catholic Committee petition representing organized Catholicism. See 11 *Parliamentary Register*, p. 190. Positive legislation for Catholic relief was approved in 32 Geo. 3 c. 21 and 22, and 33 Geo. 3 c. 21.

Rejection of the February bill produced a new vigor in the Catholic community, and especially in the Catholic Committee, with its wealthy merchant leader, John Keogh, and its new secretary, Wolfe Tone, a Protestant barrister and accomplished writer, not yet a committed revolutionary. The Catholic community had gained a wise and fearless opponent of French ideas in church and state in the archbishop of Dublin, John Thomas Troy. Arguably the rejection of the bill unleashed sectarian conflict in the Catholic Defenders and the Protestant Orange Order after 1795.

The most radical idea of the Catholic Committee was to demonstrate the nationwide voice for full citizenship by public meetings. Heads of families in each parish were to meet outside the church building (in the presence of the priests) to choose representatives on a county basis, and representatives based in Dublin, as a type of permanent information bureau.[14] The elected delegates were scheduled to assemble in Dublin as the 'Catholic convention' at the beginning of December 1792. The viceroy and Protestant political leaders were concerned, but believed they lacked legal authority to prohibit the meeting; their fears were aroused by the example of the Dungannon Convention of Volunteers in 1782, as well as the democratic process of election, which was more like that of the American states or France than of Ireland or England, with their rotten boroughs.

The Catholic Committee expected more than 200 to attend the convention and sought the Rotunda on the north side of Dublin at Rutland Square (now Parnell Square), but this was not permitted, and the meetings were held in the hall of the Tailors' Guild on Back Lane on the south side. About 230 prominent men attended the sessions 4–8 December, and produced a humble petition to the king, asking that Catholics be admitted to all rights of the constitution. A delegation of five, led by John Keogh, took the petition to London, where they were presented to King George on 2 January 1793. The king received the delegation with his usual warm and friendly greetings. Nothing further would be heard of it after the new war with France began on 1 February 1793. The Irish government was alarmed by these democratic elements and determined that there be no repetition. Accordingly, the new session of Parliament approved the Conventions Act (33 Geo. 3 c. 29), opposed by Grattan but approved 128 to 27, making illegal 'an assembly purporting to represent the people or any section of the people with intention to alter matters established by law in church or state'. This statute would confront O'Connell, the Young Irelanders and the Fenians until it was repealed in 1877 (42 & 43 Vict. c. 28).

After war broke out, a new Catholic relief bill (also proposed by the Catholic Committee), favoured by the viceroy (earl of Westmorland) but drafted by the chief secretary, Robert Hobart, was presented on 4 February 1793.[15] The House met as a committee of the whole: George Knox of TCD proposed to eliminate all restrictions on Catholics. This was opposed by a strong anti-Catholic group and

14 McDowell, *Ireland in the age of imperialism and revolution*, pp 405–13 (1979).
15 Ibid., pp 159–72.

lost by vote of 163 to 69.[16] While George Ponsonby supported Knox, Arthur Browne and his former colleague, Lawrence Parsons, opposed Knox. These committee discussions produced remarks by seventy-two of the members because they feared that uneducated farmers would be easily bought by politicians. It was the extension of the vote to forty-shilling freeholders – possibly the poor tenant farmers too easily influenced by landlords – that created a problem for Browne.

With the obvious support of Dublin Castle, and at least two-thirds of the votes in the committee of the whole, the relief bill, laden with delicate compromises, went through its three readings without a division in the House of Commons (April 1793).[17] Catholics were given the vote for Parliament as 'forty-shilling freeholders', both as to county and open borough elections; granted the right to bear arms; admitted to the grand jury and minor political offices; allowed commissions in the army up to the rank of colonel; and admitted to Trinity College. The proposal for a Catholic seminary to train priests in Ireland, rather than in France or Spain, was postponed, but would be approved in 1795. Nevertheless, Catholics could still not sit as members of the Irish Parliament. After enactment, the Catholic Committee voted its own dissolution under the threat of the new Conventions Act.[18]

The senior fellows of Trinity were opposed to the 1793 concessions. They prepared a petition to Parliament opposing the legislation, and required all fellows to sign it, but George Miller drew up a counter-petition signed by eleven junior fellows, at which the senior fellows withdrew their petition. The student body was strongly in favour of Catholic emancipation.

1795

The Catholic bishops, rather than the dissolved Catholic Committee, were the impetus for the proposal to erect and endow a Catholic seminary at Maynooth. Henry Grattan, speaking for the new viceroy, Earl Fitzwilliam, presented the bill to Parliament in January 1795. Final enactment did not occur until June, long after Fitzwilliam's recall, but Earl Camden did not abandon the idea. The institution, St Patrick's College, was not to be exclusively Catholic although it was to educate Roman Catholic clergy and lay people by academic officers selected by the twenty-one-member board of trustees, consisting of bishops, clergy, peers, gentlemen and senior judges. Financial support began with an annual grant of £8,000 for construction on lands made available by the duke of Leinster, whose family castle adjoined the site.

Another component of the programme of Grattan and Fitzwilliam was the emancipation bill to remove the restriction on Catholic membership in the Irish

16 Ibid., p. 163.
17 33 Geo. 3 c. 21. See also T. Bartlett, *The fall and rise of the Irish nation*, pp 166–8 (1992).
18 McDowell, *Ireland in the age of imperialism and revolution*, p. 421 (1979), 25 Apr. 1793, thereby enabling Tone to pursue other schemes with the United Irishmen.
19 Bartlett, *The fall and rise of the Irish nation*, pp 202–5 (1992).

Parliament. Browne supported Grattan's bill,[19] as he felt that Catholics must be seated in Parliament as an inevitable consequence of extending the vote, although his overriding concern was the preservation of the constitution of 1782.

> Dr Browne said, that he should have been glad, on a subject of such magnitude, to have been guided by the sentiments of his constituents; but having tried, upon a former occasion to obtain them on a similar subject, he found so great a diversity of opinion, that he was forced at last, as he knew he should in this case be obliged, to rest on his own judgment.
>
> He said, upon this subject he did not expect to please either party, because he should, as he always had done, follow his own opinions, without sacrificing to the prejudices of either. He had always been guided in that House by two principles, the one a wish to preserve the people from the encroachment of government, the other to preserve the establishment and the constitution from the violence of the people. An attempt to reconcile these two great principles will always, to party men, make their owner appear inconsistent, but to himself he will appear uniform. With these principles, he had always thought that any application from any great and respectable body of people ought to be treated with respect, and therefore, upon all applications from the Catholics, instead of talking as some did of scouting and affronting them, had voted for receiving and listening to them at least. On the same principles he had wished for every coalition with them, which everybody must see would contribute so much to the strength of the country, which was consistent with the safety and welfare of the whole empire; but he had always thought that such coalition should advance by very slow and cautious steps, and so as never to endanger the church or the Protestant interest, or instead of coalition set up one Ascendency in the room of another.
>
> He had therefore been used to think that we were proceeding too rapidly—that we were not wise for so rapid a conjunction. That notwithstanding all our flattering speeches to each other, there was still much heat, much ancient enmity, much ignorant bigotry to be overcome, before we were ready for a cordial union. Government had sometimes appeared to think so too, and sometimes the reverse, until by the strangest system of obstinacy and concession – of rejecting one day with haughtiness, and granting the next day with humility – of weak, and fluctuating, and inconsistent councils for twenty years past, that had brought matters to such a state, that it little signified what any man thought, or had thought; he was to determine how to act as well as he could in the actual state of affairs. In this view of things he had asked himself, not in order to determine on the present question, not what ought to have been done, but what is to be done now; and it really appeared to him that matters were come to that crisis, that it was just as impossible to prevent the Catholics from coming into Parliament, as to stop any of the natural laws of gravity. The weight which had been given them, by admitting them to the right of voting for members, must, by its natural

impulse, force their way into Parliament; he had voted against giving them votes at elections, (favouring £10 qualification instead of the 40 shilling freehold) but he knew not after that had been done, upon what principle of consistency government could oppose their admission into the House.

Some of their opponents in that House stood upon consistent ground; the objections to their tolerant religion, and their alleged disaffection; but the administrations of the country had deserted these grounds, and now talked of nothing but the constitution and the coronation oath. He would make but one observation, did not the constitution and coronation then stand equally in the way?

Thinking therefore, as he did, that this measure could not now be prevented but by a union or a military government, and that after having put a weapon in a man's hand, it was not wise to provoke him; and thinking also that the opposition to it was not in most men to the measure itself, but to throw a censure on a great person who lately governed the country, and whom he loved and revered, [Fitzwilliam] he would vote for the committal of the bill; at the same time here was perhaps the only part of it to which he assented.

He saw many clauses in it, which went, in his opinion, though he was sure not intended, to overturn the establishment; and supposing it to go into a committee; unless those clauses were totally expunged, he would vote against the bill on a third reading. He was of opinion that the establishment should be fenced and guarded by all possible means; but to prevent a communication of political power seemed to him now impossible, and the attempt to lead only to eternal dissension.[20]

Protestant fury at the risings in Wexford and Mayo (see chapter 12), viewed as a repetition by Catholics of the religious wars of the seventeenth century, made it unlikely that the Irish Protestant Parliament would ever allow Catholics to become members of that body. To fasten Catholics to the House of Hanover through emancipation or membership in Parliament required a new Parliament based in an enlightened country devoted to the preservation of religion and property: the United Kingdom of Great Britain and Ireland. This explains the attitude of Pitt, Cornwallis, Castlereagh and the Catholic bishops to the union (see chapter 13), although the Catholic bishops refrained from openly interfering in the political question. While Cornwallis and Castlereagh were ordered to dissociate Catholic emancipation from the union, there was an expectation in Dublin that the union Parliament would deal favourably with Catholic issues: membership in Parliament, financial support of the clergy and elimination of tithe. Nevertheless, King George was adamant that there would be no further concessions to Catholics in his lifetime because of his coronation oath to support the Protestant religion. Cornwallis resigned in April 1801 after Prime Minister Pitt resigned on 3 February 1801.

20 15 *Parliamentary Register*, pp 515–17 (4 May 1795). Grattan's emancipation bill was defeated on a vote of 86 in favour to 157 opposed.

(The resignation of Cornwallis may have been compelled, although Cornwallis always enjoyed the king's favour.)

During Arthur Browne's seventeen years in Parliament, the penal laws were repealed except for the right to sit in Parliament. Because of the dubious advice given to a senile monarch by the lord chancellors of England (Alexander Wedderburn, 1st Baron Loughborough) and Ireland (John FitzGibbon, earl of Clare) that allowing Catholics to sit in the Parliament of the United Kingdom was a breach of his coronation oath to support the Protestant religion that step could not be taken. Pitt and his successors could not raise this issue again in the life of the mad king despite the constant efforts of Henry Grattan, and Catholic emancipation finally succeeded as the indolent heir was dying in 1829 after the election of Daniel O'Connell, who could not take the seat for which the Clare voters had chosen him but whose persistence forced resolution of the issue.

II. EVANGELISM

The last years of the eighteenth century in England, Ireland and America witnessed an evangelical fervor in Protestantism generally. It affected the narrow ritualism of the established churches,[21] but there was another aspect to this fervor – the civic organization to reform the morals of all classes, in the expectation that social ills would disappear in a community of purified citizens.

Educated men and women in the Enlightenment recognized the evils that surrounded them, but there was no loud voice demanding repentance and reform in public. One of the evils, symptomatic of other evils, was the slave trade pursued by British businessmen to benefit the Caribbean sugar plantations; an early reform voice was that of John Newton, who became a parish priest for forty-three years after serving on slave ships for nine years. In his circle of influence was a recent college graduate, William Wilberforce, whose life became consecrated to the end of the slave trade[22] and the abolition of slavery in British colonies.[23]

Along with his commitment to the end of the slave trade, Wilberforce had been appalled by the public vice, infidelity and immorality of the London streets. George III had issued the customary proclamation on his accession in 1760 for the encouragement of piety and virtue and the prevention of vices, profaneness and immorality, and Wilberforce believed that a reissue in 1787 of the 1760

---

21 In this context, ritualism does not mean the ecclesiastical rituals of the Victorian era encouraged by the Oxford movement of Newman, Keble and Pusey, but the rigid adherence to the services of the Book of Common Prayer, anathema to the Calvinists, Baptists and Quakers of Browne's Newport youth.

22 47 Geo. 3. c. 36. In 1807, the vote in the Commons was 283 to 16. Wilberforce's first bill had been defeated in 1791 by vote of 163 to 88. This bill was sponsored by Charles James Fox in the Commons.

23 3 and 4 Will. 4 c. 73. Wilberforce died 29 July 1833. The bill to end slavery on 1 Aug. 1834 passed the Lords on 29 Aug. 1833.

proclamation would encourage private actions to defeat vice and immorality. Wilberforce worked quietly through a family friend, Bishop Beilby Porteus, as well as Prime Minister William Pitt and Queen Charlotte. The king eagerly agreed, possibly because of the debaucheries of his son, the prince of Wales. The proclamation was published 1 June 1787. It produced merciless satires in cartoons by Thomas Rowlandson, James Gilray and Isaac Cruikshank of the king's prudery and the wanton and lascivious conduct of the royal princes.

In the next week, Wilberforce began the search for high members of the nobility to form a private society to enforce the goals of the proclamation. He had to proceed cautiously lest he attract nobles whose concealed but fashionable immorality and infidelity would procure hypocritical endorsements. He also had to avoid the smothering embrace of the state church. Thus, for many reasons, his new society needed rigid controls on membership.

Almost six months after the reissue of the proclamation, Wilberforce and his supporters were ready to commence operations; the first meeting took place in London on 28 November 1787. A list of fifty names – dukes, peers, bishops, clergy and men of substance – was circulated before the first open meeting of the society on 28 February 1788 at the London house of the duke of Montagu.

Within four years the Proclamation Society was operating throughout Great Britain and its good works were known in Ireland. On 6 October 1792, three founding members – two clergy, Dr John O'Connor, fellow of Trinity College and Revd Singleton Harpur of St Mary's, Dublin, and one layman, William Watson, a seller of religious books – held the first Dublin meeting of the Association for Discountenancing Vice and Promoting the Practice of Virtue and Religion.[24] The influence of Willberforce and his circle was present in the person of Hannah More, who before her evangelical conversion had attended Dr Johnson's Literary Club; it is interesting how many Monks of the Screw and other veterans of liberal clubs of the 1770s were now, in the 1790s, involved in evangelical works.

Arthur Browne may have been describing the later growth of the Association for Discountenancing Vice in his 1798 meditation on religion:

> Sacred name of religion how have I known thee abused! Attacked and supported by the worst of men for the worst of purposes. When the infidels of France with gigantic impiety assaulted heaven, I rejoiced to see our governors at home with true and sincere impressions of thy dignity, guided by the great and illustrious and uniform example of the throne, strive to recall the minds of men to seriousness, to piety, and to God; but how many men did I see verbally join in their meritorious endeavors not with the same feelings, who had always scoffed at religion till worldly power and profit were attacked; who scarce knew what the inside of a church was made of, till they thought its roof a cover for their interests; and who with mouths full of

24 K. Milne, *APCK: the early decades*, p. 71 (1992).

infidelity and irreligious debauchery from their childhood, became the sudden and bitter inveighers against impiety and vice.[25]

Trinity College fellows were involved in the association's operation from the beginning, and by the time of the annual sermon on 25 April 1794, there were 300 members enrolled and more than £334 had been received for the association's purposes, of which £241 was paid to printers for Bibles, tracts and support of a school for children of soldiers. There was also a contribution to SPCK in England. Of the first members, the four archbishops, three bishops, 179 ordained clergy and 113 laymen were enrolled. Of the clergy, eleven were fellows of Trinity College, and several were members of Parliament.[26]

By 1795 Earl Fitzwilliam, the viceroy, and the countess, together with prominent Whigs including Arthur Browne, Thomas Newenham, Barry Yelverton, the duke of Leinster and the provost and thirteen fellows of TCD were members. Arthur Browne and the Trinity fellows' devotion to the association grew and strengthened thereafter, but its concern with individual piety did not include such goals as the ecumenism or social gospel of the twentieth century.

In the nineteenth century, organizations like this one became involved in Protestant proselytism (called 'souperism') and the struggle over denominational education, but this does not seem to be true of the eighteenth-century founders.[27] Reformation of manners through religious education and observance was the goal, 'to stem the baneful torrent' of infidelity and immorality, 'and to restore the belief and practice of religion and virtue' while not contradicting 'the doctrine and discipline of the established church'. The last phrase was to appease the fears of the bishops at the success of the Wesleyan Methodists and enthusiastic evangelicals among their own ranks.

Religious tracts, Bibles and prayer books were distributed in large quantities; it was claimed that 40,000 had been distributed in the first three years. Other activities involved the enforcement of closing hours in pubs and the discouragement of frivolous entertainments and commercial operations on Sundays and Good Friday.

In the closing days of the Irish Parliament, the Association for Discountenancing Vice and Promoting the Practice of Virtue and Religion was incorporated and was awarded a grant of £300 for its work under a new name, the Association for the Promotion of Christian knowledge (APCK), which is still flourishing after more than 200 years. Although the Association was top-heavy with prelates of the established church, it was not then sectarian, and was one of the few organizations – like the Masons or the Royal Irish Society – where all denominations could mingle.

---

25 Browne, *Miscellaneous sketches*, p. 254 (1798).   26 Milne, *APCK* (1992).
27 D. Akenson, *The Irish education experiment*, pp 80–3 (1978). See 40 Geo. 3 c. 66.

III. THE TRINITY DEFENCE CORPS

The Whig viceroy, Lord Fitzwilliam, whose brief tenure lasted merely from his arrival in Dublin on 4 January 1795 until his departure on 25 March 1795, was responsible for the new yeomanry, a military force to augment the professional army and the organized militia. This force was a wartime measure, justified by the war with France that began on 1 February 1793. Fitzwilliam would have united Catholics, Protestants and Presbyterians in the new yeomanry to protect property against Catholic Defenders and Peep O'Day Protestants. The measure was urged by Robert Stewart, Viscount Castlereagh, who would become chief secretary to Cornwallis in 1798. The legislation[28] was finally enacted and approved under Fitzwilliam's successor, Lord Camden. Despite Fitzwilliam's intention for the yeomanry, it soon became known as a Protestant organization under Lord Camden, and would be accused of religious atrocities in the Revolution of 1798.

The organization of the Defence Corps at Trinity College was a consequence of the official yeomanry and was described by H.A. Hinkson:

> Rumors of a French invasion to be expected at any moment were rife, and towards the end of 1796 a private meeting was held in college, at which resolutions were passed expressing a desire on the part of some students to arm in defense of their country. They promised that their academic duties should not be interfered with by their military avocations. When these resolutions were laid before the chancellor of the university he refused his consent, holding that by such a proceeding the literary pursuits of the students would be interrupted. On the 26th of December a second application was made for permission to arm; and on the 9th of January 1797, the college corps received their arms from the government. They chose four captains and eight lieutenants, all of the former and two of the latter being fellows of the college, and they selected for their uniform scarlet faced with blue, without any lace, and plain gilt buttons, white Kerseymere waistcoat and breeches, with black leggings.[29]

Arthur Browne described the circumstances of the organization of the Trinity Defence Corps without any mention of the reasons he was chosen as corps commandant.

> The extraordinary circumstances of the times, and the arrival of a French fleet in Bantry Bay induced the government of Ireland in January, 1797, to authorize the gentlemen of the University of Dublin, to form themselves

---

28 37 Geo. 3 c. 2 (1796). See H. McAnally, *The Irish militia, 1793–1816: a social and military study*, pp 94–8 (1949). See also P. Smyth, 'The Volunteers and Parliament, 1779–84' in T. Bartlett and D. Hayton (eds), *Penal era and golden age* (1979).

29 H.A. Hinkson, *Student life in Trinity College Dublin*, p. 58 (1892).

into a corps to the number of 300, of which the author had the honour to be appointed captain-commandant. The martial appearance, the spirit, the alacrity, and what is most extraordinary the discipline, order and obedience of the corps, supereminently distinguished and attracted the admiration of all the kingdom …[30]

The choice of Arthur Browne as corps commander is somewhat mysterious. Was it his position as senior fellow or his popularity as lecturer or military experience gained in the Volunteers?[31] His selection was unanimous. Despite its obvious patriotic purpose, the proposed Trinity Defence Corps was still controversial. Some thought it might be abused by Dublin Castle as a tool to crush the people. Others thought its existence would humiliate the military forces or that it would encourage idleness and a lack of discipline in the student body. Nevertheless, the students were armed and Arthur Browne became commander of the corps and began to study and teach military organization, strategy and tactics, although he always described himself as an amateur and not a soldier.[32] Most important, however, he had to convince the authorities of the loyalty and preparedness of Trinity students in a national emergency.

In describing Harvard College in his *Miscellaneous sketches*, Browne had written, 'A college military corps existed at Cambridge before I led it [the Trinity Corps].'[33] The Harvard students had organized a patriotic defensive corps in support of the province's Patriotic Party before Browne sought admission to Harvard. It was named the Marti-Mercurians after the Roman gods Mars and Mercury in the 1769–70 school year.[34]

Student defence corps on the Harvard model were organized at Rhode Island College (now Brown University) in 1774 and at Yale in 1775. Revd Miles Cooper, the loyalist president of New York's King's College (now Columbia University), refused to permit such activities in the college, but in 1775 students met secretly to organize a military corps, the Corsicans, of which Alexander Hamilton was a leader.[35]

Firearms had been forbidden in Trinity College in 1739 to suppress duelling, and many officials, including Lord Chancellor FitzGibbon, were strongly opposed to the presence of firearms in the college for fear of duelling and other abuses when

---

30 Browne, *Miscellaneous sketches*, p. 319 (1798).
31 Although no list of the members of the lawyers' corps has yet surfaced, there is indirect evidence that Arthur Browne was a member of the lawyers' corps in 1783. A patriotic history of Ireland by Rev. William Crawford, chaplain of the First Tyrone Regiment of Volunteers, dedicated to the earl of Charlemont, general of Volunteers, contains a list of subscribers, among whom is 'Arthur Browne, J.F.T.C.D. ditto'. The 'ditto' follows the names of 'Billings, esq. Lawyers Corps, and Ball, esq. Ditto'.
32 Browne, *Miscellaneous sketches* (1798).   33 Ibid., p. 208.
34 S.E. Morison, *Three centuries of Harvard*, pp 136–44, 214–15 (1936), and J.F. Roche, *The colonial colleges in the war for American independence*, pp 61–2 (1984).
35 R. Chernow, *Alexander Hamilton*, pp 62–7 (2004).

students were under the influence of liquor. Precept and example became the principal responsibilities of the leadership of the armed students. The captains, in addition to Arthur Browne, were Francis Hodgkinson, Robert Phipps and Whitley Stokes. The fellows' common room was assigned to them as headquarters. After the failed French effort at Bantry Bay in December 1796, the corps was assigned to guard the bridges over the Grand Canal. During the risings of May, June and July 1798, they were also assigned to patrol the Wicklow and Kildare mountains.

The members proudly and publicly wore distinctive uniforms: coats of scarlet cloth with blue facings and gold buttons, white waistcoats and breeches and black leggings and boots. They were armed with rifles. The archives of TCD contain one official letter from Arthur Browne as captain-commandant.[36]

Constantia E. Maxwell's *History of Trinity College* recounts some experiences of a student member of the Defence Corps from the journals of William Blacker of Armagh, who had been an officer in the yeomanry in Ulster:

I repaired to Dublin for the October [1797] examination and remained there carrying on the war in literature and politicks as usual. I joined the third company of the college corps which had that year been formed. This was somewhat of a come down from the captain to a full private, but it was necessary for every man who could pull a trigger to be ready to do his duty wherever he might be. I have seen four hundred firelocks in our parade in the courts borne by as determined a set of lads as ever were in scarlet. This corps possessed one striking advantage over most others in Dublin – they were to all intent and purposes in barracks and could turn out at once. The college too from its isolated position formed a strong military post – perhaps I might say the strongest in Dublin, having in fact a hollow square of solid mason work, the windows of which being properly manned, it would have kept an immense force at bay. Few persons took greater pleasure in the college corps than old Dr Barrett did in his own way. He used to watch the drilling of the different squads from the windows of the library and never failed to acquaint us at dinner of the movements the different cohorts had performed and how they formed one 'grait lay-gion just like Julius Say-zairs, do ye see, only Say-zairs men had no guns, the like not being invented in those days'.

Blacker also recounted a bloodless confrontation with United Irishmen for which he was reprimanded by the board for 'intoxication'. He attended the visitation of the college by the lord chancellor (Clare) and Paddy Duigenan, as was required, 'under pain of expulsion':

36 'To the Reverend Dr Elrington, bursar of Trinity College Dublin. July 9th 1798. Sir, I am desired by the members of the college corps in pursuance of their unanimous [*sic*] vote, to present to you their warmest thanks, for indefatigable exertions and kindness towards the corps and for your zeal in promoting its interests and enabling them by every seasonable aid to promote the public service; in obeying their commands I have the most sensible pleasure. Your humble servant, Arthur Browne Capn Commt.'

I remained in college from that period [April 1798] until the breaking out of the rebellion [23 May]. We had sundry alarms prior to it and the college corps on every occasion evinced superior alacrity. At length arrived the memorable 23rd May and so little was there suspected of any outbreak that I accompanied Lady E. Matthew, daughter of the earl of Landaff, to the theatre. I left it a little before ten o'clock and on reaching college found to my great surprise the corps on parade in the courts and a general exclamation from the third company to which I belonged on the subject of my unwonted lateness on parade on such an occasion – it must be remembered however that not a drum was heard in the way of alarm.

I soon got into my harness and away we marched to the north side of Stephen's Green where we remained under arms all night. I slept soundly as did many others, sitting on the steps of a hall door with my firelock on my knees. There was a regiment, I believe the Cork City, and some guns on our left towards Baggot Street and another on our right but whether of yeomanry or of more regular troops I know not, so little do men or officers in the ranks tell of the general 'goings on' in the field.

After this I mounted guard for six or seven successive nights without feeling the least fatigued. We generally occupied one of the canal bridges on the south side of Dublin, and except once never saw the face of anything like a foe. One night a man on horseback approached the bridge at the end of Leeson Street, where I and another were sentinels, in a full gallop and being challenged instantly whirled round and made off. We both fired at him but without effect – it was evidently a trial of our alertness. Thus passed the time all night on guard and all day reading the bulletins of the 'goings on' in the country and hearing the news of those who were daily arriving from it to seek shelter in Dublin. A substantial supper of cold meat was provided nightly by the board with plenty of October [ale] and on the whole it was as [illegible] a time as I ever spent …

He then recounted the winter season following the repression of the rebellion:

Dublin was unusually gay during the winter succeeding the rebellion – in addition to its ordinary quota of inhabitant gentry there were numbers who had flocked in from various parts of the country and did not wish at least to make a return until the ensuing spring. Indeed there were many who could not do so either from their residences having been much injured or in some instances totally destroyed by the rebels and not a few found it by no means inconvenient to permit their houses to be occupied as barracks, the government paying them a good round consideration for the same …

The students of TCD and I among the rest had then full share in all that was going on in the way of gaiety and dissipation, within and without the walls and gave full scope to our inclinations. My father authorised one Ferns, a wine merchant, to let me 'have a little wine now and then'. The theatre was greatly the rage among us at this time and we generally occupied a couple of rows in the middle gallery. [...]

A sad drawback upon the amusements of the students was the closing of the college gates at twelve o'clock after which hour none could gain admittance. Many were the attempts made to obviate this, by ladders, screw bars and such other contrivances. One fine young man, eldest son of Mr Wade of Clonabreny, Co. Meath, lost his life in attempting to get in. He walked along the provost's wall to get through a window on the south flank of the college, missed a foot and was literally impaled on the railing below. Many a time and oft have I trod the same path and entered by the same window which was purposely left open for me by the occupant of the apartments it belonged to ...[37]

Blacker's experiences were similar to those of Daniel O'Connell, who was a member of the Dublin lawyers' artillery corps patrolling Dublin streets in 1798.[38]

37 C. Maxwell, *A history of Trinity College Dublin, 1591–1892*, pp 257–74 (1946).
38 P.M. Geoghegan, *King Dan*, pp 43–52 (2008).

CHAPTER ELEVEN

Disappointment and humiliation (1798)

I. QUEST FOR THE PROVOST'S OFFICE (1794 AND 1799)

THE POWERFUL OFFICE OF PROVOST, the operational head of the new college, was established in the charter of 3 March 1591 by Elizabeth I, to be chosen by the fellows, but the 5 June 1636 charter of Charles I vested the office in the crown – normally the lord lieutenant or viceroy.[1] By the end of the eighteenth century, the office had a number of attractions that made it suitable as a reward for political services (past or future) from the London ministry, in the same way that high ecclesiastical or judicial offices were used. These attractions included a salary of £2000 per annum (similar to that of a bishop in a small diocese) and one of the finest houses in Dublin – a Palladian-style stone mansion built between 1759 and 1761 and copied from a London design of Lord Burlington.[2] Administrative duties, often required by statute, were an unpleasant but necessary part of the job, but there were also indeterminate powers derived from custom and the potential to change the intellectual climate to encourage scholarship and scientific research.

Seventeenth-century provosts were mostly elderly senior fellows in holy orders in the style of Richard Baldwin[3] (1667–1758), who held the office from 1717 to 1758, a former senior fellow and vice provost who satisfied the Whig aristocracy in Dublin and London by the application of rigorous standards of academic performance and civilized behaviour to rowdy students and lazy faculty. Baldwin, however, was followed by two political lawyers, not in holy orders and devoid of scholarly credentials. Francis Andrews (1758–74) was a great builder and did not discourage faculty scholarship, but John Hely-Hutchinson (1774–94) was a combative personality who sought to enrich himself and his family, and aggrandize the office. His years were very turbulent; he frequently struggled with faculty and students. The senior fellows began to conspire against the appointment of another politician provost. They had apparently stressed the importance of choosing a man in holy orders as well as a fellow of the college. The holy orders argument lingered in Pitt's mind while the fellowship argument disappeared.

The need for political patronage meant that the office of provost was not one to which a parliamentary Whig like Arthur Browne could aspire during Pitt's

---

1 J.V. Luce, *Trinity College Dublin: the first 400 years*, pp 3, 17–19 (1992). McDowell and Webb, *Trinity College Dublin, 1592–1952*, pp 3–4, 37–40, 53–8.
2 Luce, *Trinity College Dublin*, pp 52–7 (1992).
3 Richard Baldwin (1667–1758), ibid., pp 37–41, 49–50.

administration, even though Whig principles had dominated the college since Baldwin. But then things changed very suddenly. The division among the Whig opposition caused by Edmund Burke's denunciation of revolution in France gave Prime Minister Pitt the opportunity to cripple Charles James Fox and his followers permanently by reaching out and incorporating the old Whigs who followed Burke.[4] Pitt's decision to embrace former enemies required him to provide patronage, something he had denied to Whigs for the past dozen years. The possibility of Earl Fitzwilliam,[5] a prominent Whig aristocrat, as lord lieutenant (viceroy) of Ireland was being seriously discussed when Hely-Hutchinson suddenly died on 10 September 1794. The senior fellows immediately sought openly to forestall another unordained political lawyer as provost, sending a representative to London to raise their concerns about use of the provost's office for patronage purposes. They were shocked when their demand for a provost in holy orders raised the possibility of a careerist English clergyman, William Bennett, recently consecrated bishop of Cloyne, becoming provost while continuing as bishop of a distant diocese.

In 1794 Arthur Browne was a viable candidate for the office of provost of Trinity College as member of Parliament, professor of civil law and junior fellow, undoubtedly encouraged by students and younger faculty who had supported him in Parliament. In fact his candidacy was noted by Theophilus Swift in his review of the sorry state of the college in 1794.[6]

Arthur Browne began a campaign of self-promotion to influential politicians, including Earl Fitzwilliam.[7] However, Edmund Burke, a well-known alumnus of TCD, passed over his Whig colleague, Browne, and strongly argued for the choice

4   J. Ehrman, 2 *The younger Pitt: the reluctant transition*, pp 402–40 (1983). The 'old Whigs' received 5 places in the 13-member cabinet.
5   William Fitzwilliam (1748–1833), born at the family estate, Milton House at Peterborough (Cambridgeshire), he succeeded at age 8 to the title earl on the death of his father. He was educated at Eton. After the Grand Tour of Europe (1765–9), he entered the House of Lords in 1769 and married Lady Charlotte Ponsonby in 1770. As the nephew and heir of Lord Rockingham, leader of the Whigs after the death of the elder Pitt, Fitzwilliam acquired great estates in England (Yorkshire) and Ireland (Wicklow) on the death of Rockingham in 1782 but he did not succeed to leadership of the Whigs. Having joined the Pitt administration to be viceroy of Ireland, he held that office briefly (4 Jan. to 25 Mar. 1795) but was recalled because Pitt believed that Fitzwilliam had violated cabinet instructions regarding Catholic emancipation. See generally, E.A. Smith, *Whig principles and party politics: Earl Fitzwilliam and the Whig Party, 1748–1833* (1975) and B. Hilton, *A mad, bad and dangerous people? England 1783–1848*, pp 77–80 (2006). See also C.C. O'Brien, *The great melody: a thematic biography and commented anthology of Edmund Burke*, pp 511–17 (1992) and D. Wilkinson, 'The Fitzwilliam episode, 1795: a reinterpretation of the role of the duke of Portland', 29 *Irish Historical Studies*, 315–29 (1995).
6   In his diatribe against married fellows, Theophilus Swift made this aside: 'Dr Browne now aspires to be pope over two and twenty cardinals, whose conclave have hung out the broom and would confine the election to their own family', *Animadversions*, p. 182 (1794).
7   Browne had joined a petition against a lay provost on rumours that Hely-Hutchinson would soon resign, but by a letter to Dr Thomas Elrington of 4 Nov. 1793, he limited his objections to an *alien* lay provost (TCD: MUN/P/1/1063). A year later he wrote again to Elrington (3 Nov. 1794) about

to be made from senior fellows in holy orders.[8] The elderly Richard Murray was chosen.[9] Murray was professor of mathematics and vice provost, who was unlikely to change any of the pleasant prerogatives of the fellows. Murray was installed as provost on 29 January 1795 by Earl Fitzwilliam, about to be recalled by Pitt because of his proposed measures to accommodate Catholics.

Browne was possibly mollified by election as senior fellow, appointment by Fitzwilliam[10] to the status of king's counsel and selection by William Newcome, the new archbishop of Armagh (selected by Fitzwilliam), as manager of the properties of the established church.[11] The Whigs knew how to reward their champions, but Trinity lost the intellectual rigour and devotion to scholarship that Arthur Browne might have brought during the very difficult years ahead.

On 20 June 1799, Provost Murray died, one year after the end of the rebellion, during the period of Protestant vengeance. Arthur Browne was again a viable candidate for the office of provost.[12] He was now senior fellow, still a member of Parliament, professor of Greek in addition to professor of law and former captain-commandant of the Trinity Defence Corps during the rising, but he had already cast his vote in Parliament against the union of the kingdoms in January 1799. (He later changed his mind and voted in favour of the union in February 1800.)[13] The 1799 vote may have been fatal to his hopes. His new letter-writing campaign was not helpful, and his lack of holy orders provided the justification for the selection of Revd John Kearney,[14] the vice provost, who was appointed by Lord Cornwallis

the negotiations for the provostship (MUN/8/1/1109). Browne's letter of 9 Aug. 1794 to Earl Fitzwilliam announcing his candidacy for the position of provost is in the Sheffield Archives Fitzwilliam Collection WWM/F/27/2. Fitzwilliam's careful response of 25 Aug. 1794 (draft) is WWM/F/29/2. Browne restated his qualifications and attempted to finesse his lack of holy orders, even suggesting his willingness to submit to the priestly regimen, in an undated letter to Earl Fitzwilliam in December 1794 or early January 1795 (WWM/F/27/75).

8 Edmund Burke (AB 1748) had received the honourary degree LLD in 1793. Browne had no doubt that Burke had prevented his selection as provost. While praising 'that great man', Browne wrote, 'I consider him as one of the chief obstacles to my having attained a very considerable rank in my life.' A. Browne, *Miscellaneous sketches*, p. 222 (1798).

9 Richard Murray (1726–99), born in County Down, entered TCD as a sizar but became a scholar in 1745, AB 1747, Fellow in 1750. He became professor of mathematics in 1764 after publication in 1759 of his widely used textbook on logic. As vice provost in 1794, he was the unanimous choice of the senior fellows.

10 D.A. Fleming and A.P.W. Malcomson, *'A volley of execrations': the letters and papers of John FitzGibbon, earl of Clare, 1772–1802*, pp 206–8 (2005).

11 Browne's letter to Fitzwilliam concerning the appointment as agent for the Church, of 8 Jan. 1795, is in WWM/F/29/19.

12 Browne's letter (on the day after Murray's death) to Earl Fitzwilliam renewing his candidacy for the provost position is in WWM/F/30/121 (21 June 1799). It was followed in several days by another to inform Earl Fitzwilliam that Lord Cornwallis had selected Vice Provost Kearney, WWM/F/30/122 (25 June 1799). After Fitzwilliam's return to England, Arthur Browne kept him informed of the dangerous conditions in Ireland, see WWM/F/30/111 (30 Sept. 1798) and WWM/F/30/112 (30 Sept. 1798).

13 See chapter 13, n. 36.

14 Revd John Kearney (1741–1813), born in Dublin, entered TCD in 1757, scholar 1760. He received

in July 1799, during his campaign to reverse opposition to the union. Kearney, along with a majority of the fellows and students, remained opposed to the union in January 1799 and at the time of the February 1800 vote approving the union, but unlike Browne's vote, Kearney's opposition was not public. In the atmosphere of Pitt's policy of punishments, peerages, perquisites, promotions and bribery, it was Kearney's good fortune to have been outside Parliament when the crucial votes were taken, and he served as provost until February 1806.

II. THE VISITATION OR PURGE OF TRINITY COLLEGE (1798)

Arthur Browne's smooth and untroubled path in professional life was disrupted and nearly ended by the violence of the Irish Ascendancy reaction to the 1798 revolt of the United Irishmen, first in the purge of faculty and students of Trinity College in 1798. Another consequence of the revolt was the destruction of the independent Irish Parliament in 1801, creating the union of Ireland and Great Britain, in which Browne lost his seat in Parliament.

Present in both professional crises was John FitzGibbon, earl of Clare, lord chancellor of Ireland and vice chancellor of Trinity College.[15] For many nationalists, FitzGibbon was the evil genius of the Irish Ascendancy, whose heavy hand was always at the service of the British connection and inimical to the interests of Ireland and Irish people.[16]

The immediate cause of the visitation or purge of Trinity College was the threat of armed revolution under the United Irishmen. After the Trinity purge, armed revolution broke out in the Presbyterian counties of Antrim and Down, and continued in the Catholic counties of Wexford and Waterford.[17] Risings planned by the United Irishmen in Dublin, Wicklow and Arklow never began, because of preventive action by the government, the arrest of the United Irish executive committee.[18]

Protection of the realm from treason and revolution was entrusted to the lord chancellor of Ireland, John FitzGibbon. FitzGibbon was from a family group

---

an AB in 1762, became a fellow in 1764 and was awarded a DD in 1777. He became professor of oratory in 1781 and served as vice provost until he was appointed provost in 1799. He resigned as provost in 1806 upon consecration as bishop of Ossory.

15 John FitzGibbon (1747–1802). See Ann C. Kavanaugh, *John FitzGibbon, earl of Clare: Protestant reaction and English authority in late eighteenth-century Ireland* (1997). Cf. review by J. Kelly, 31 *Irish. Hist. St*, 129 (May 1998). See also C.L. Falkiner, *Studies in Irish history and biography* (1902); Elliot FitzGibbon, *The earl of Clare, mainspring of the union* (1960); and J.R. O'Flanagan, 2 *Lives of the lord chancellors of Ireland*, p. 162 (1870).

16 Jonah Barrington, 1 *Personal sketches of his own time*, p. 359 (1832). McDowell and Webb, *Trinity College Dublin*, pp 76–8 (1982).

17 T. Pakenham, *The year of liberty: the story of the great Irish rebellion of 1798*, pp 137–69 (1969).

18 M. Elliot, *Wolfe Tone: prophet of Irish independence* (1989); M. Elliot, *Partners in revolution: the United Irishmen and France* (1982).

known as the 'Old English' of Norman descent. Originally remaining aloof from the native Irish and staying 'within the Pale', they continued to be loyal to the crown of England in matters of politics and religion through the reign of Henry VIII. However, during the Elizabethan Reformation of the churches of England and Ireland and the succession of the Stuarts, the Old English rejected Irish Protestantism, and continued a firm attachment to the old Catholic faith.[19]

After a resurgence of Irish Catholic support for the Catholic King James II, the victorious Irish Protestants began the application of the penal laws (after 1695) to impoverish Irish Catholics. It is uncertain exactly where the FitzGibbon ancestors fitted in this ancient aristocracy, but this was the context in which the father of John FitzGibbon, also named John FitzGibbon (1708–80), a poor and landless youth, renounced his Roman Catholic faith and conformed to the established church in 1731.[20] This action permitted his legal education at the Middle Temple and his call to the Bar at Hilary term 1731. The senior John FitzGibbon succeeded brilliantly as a lawyer, acquired great wealth and purchased a landed estate, Mount Shannon, near Castleconnel in County Limerick.[21] It was in these comfortable circumstances that the younger John FitzGibbon was born; he became the lawyer who would bring his family into the peerage as earl of Clare, lord chancellor of Ireland.

The historian Lecky attempted a judicious portrait of FitzGibbon, but it is still grim: 'arrogant and domineering; he delighted in insulting language and in despotic measures, and he had a supreme contempt for the majority of his fellow countrymen, but he was wholly free from the taint of personal cruelty'.[22] The younger John FitzGibbon received his education at Trinity (AB 1766), Oxford (AM 1769) and the Middle Temple, where he was called to the Bar in 1772.[23] At age 30, in 1778, he became one of the two representatives of Trinity College in the Irish Parliament; but his loyalty to Pitt and the king during the regency crisis made his fortune.

Arthur Browne was elected member for the University of Dublin at age 27, in 1783, replacing FitzGibbon. It is uncertain whether FitzGibbon harboured personal resentment against Browne for the actions of the Trinity electors.

FitzGibbon's strong support of Pitt's English Tory government in the Irish Parliament caused Pitt to become greatly indebted to him, and at the restoration of the king's powers, John FitzGibbon at age 42 became lord chancellor of Ireland, an office that had been denied to native Irish in favour of Englishmen. It was partly

19 A. Clarke, *The Old English in Ireland, 1625–42*, pp 171–219 (1966).
20 A. Kavanaugh, *John FitzGibbon, earl of Clare: Protestant reaction and English authority in late eighteenth-century Ireland*, p. 10, n. 1 (1997). Conformity to the established church for economic or professional reasons is analyzed in T. Power, 'Conversions among the legal profession in Ireland in the eighteenth century' in D. Hogan and W.N. Osborough (eds), *Brehons, serjeants and attorneys*, pp 153–74 (1990).
21 Ibid., p. 11.   22 W.E.H. Lecky, 5 *A history of Ireland in the eighteenth century*, p. 17 (1892).
23 Browne and Parsons replaced FitzGibbon and the late Hussey Burgh.

judicial and partly political because it involved judicial selections as well as management of the House of Lords.

The Trinity College visitation was conducted in the dining hall of the college on 19, 20 and 21 April 1798 in the presence of the provost, the board and the entire student body. The proceedings were recorded in paraphrase with some apparently verbatim quotations by Revd Dr Matthew Young, fellow of TCD and professor of natural philosophy.[24] Aiding FitzGibbon was Dr Duigenan,[25] representing the archbishop of Dublin. Reading through FitzGibbon's cross-examinations of Trinity personnel it is interesting to note his concerns with the influence of the French Revolution, deism, atheism, the works of Tom Paine and the newer secret society, the Orange Order (founded in 1795), as well as the now secret United Irishmen.

FitzGibbon explained the visitation to Prime Minister Pitt five days after its conclusion, in the following letter:

> In consequence of certain information that the treason of the Irish brotherhood had extended to Trinity College, I thought it indispensably necessary to hold a visitation there as vice-chancellor of the university, the result of which has been the expulsion of nineteen of the most leading and active members of the association.[26]

The letter goes on to suggest the existence of a committee for assassinations and the preparation of arms for a rising at half an hour's notice, and concludes that the names of the expelled students will be forwarded to all British universities and professional societies to prevent their attendance or professional advancement.[27]

The United Irishmen, founded by Wolfe Tone in Belfast in 1791,[28] were officially suppressed by the Irish government on 23 May 1794,[29] but continued surreptitiously as a society whose members were sworn to secrecy. Discussions

---

24 M. Young, 'A contemporary account of the TCD visitation' in Fleming and Malcomson, '*A volley of execrations*', pp 298–333 (2005).

25 Patrick Duigenan (1735–1816), born a Roman Catholic in Derry, entered TCD as a sizar in 1753, scholar in 1756, AB 1757, AM 1761, LLB 1762, then to the Middle Temple, LLD 1765. He was fellow from 1771 to 1776, resigned on appointment to chair of feudal and English law. He was a violent opponent of provost Hely-Hutchinson, and composed a bitter attack, 'Lachrymae Academicae' (1777). He acted as deputy for the college visitor, the archbishop of Dublin. He had previously served in the Irish House of Commons, from Old Leighlin (1791–7), as king's advocate in admiralty and judge of the prerogative court (1792–1800). He served in the last Irish Parliament as member for Armagh and for the same constituency in the union Parliament at Westminster. Despite (or because of) a first Roman Catholic wife, he always hated 'popery' and spoke violently against it, becoming secretary of the Orange Lodge in 1801.

26 Letter of 26 Apr. 1798 (No. 383), Fleming and Malcomson, '*A volley of execrations*', p. 333 (2005).

27 Ibid. See also statement of FitzGibbon, pp 298–9.

28 Elliot, *Wolfe Tone*, pp 124–6, 130–42 (1989).

29 Ibid., pp 232–45. See also N. Curtin, 'The transformation of the Society of United Irishmen into a mass-based revolutionary organization, 1794–6', 24 *Irish Historical Studies*, 463–92 (1985).

with the revolutionary French government, the Directory, and later the first consul, Napoleon, concerning the possibility of French assistance to an Irish rising had occurred and were, of course, treasonable, as France had been at war with Great Britain since 1793. Many sworn members were government informers so that FitzGibbon already possessed lists of members and suspected members.[30] There were supposedly four separate groups of United Irishmen among the students of TCD in 1798.

It is likely that Browne became a target of FitzGibbon because of the informer Francis Higgins, the Sham Squire, who had written a false and malicious letter to Dublin Castle (10 April 1795):

> after the students of the university had presented their address to Mr Grattan, they went in numbers to [the Roman Catholic] Francis Street chapel vestry where their secretary, a Mr Moore (who lodges at Mr Cole's Trinity Street) declared that they were ready to join IN ANY ACT with the Catholics, damning the present administration and calling out 'Fitzwilliam and Grattan for ever!' And last night parties of them went through the streets vociferating the same. Dr Browne and others of the fellows are avowedly their encouragers ...[31]

Arthur Browne was well known to FitzGibbon, although he was about eight years younger. They had served simultaneously in the Irish House of Commons for six years, and had engaged in disputes. Browne's political allies were usually opposed to FitzGibbon and his allies. Further, FitzGibbon must have resented the award of silk in 1795 to Arthur Browne and seven others known to be Whig sympathizers. These appointments were at the insistence of the new lord lieutenant, Fitzwilliam.[32]

John FitzGibbon was greatly concerned about radical activities among the students in early 1798, at the same time as the administration was rounding up suspected leaders of the United Irishmen in Dublin. A 'commotion' in the college had occurred on 22 February 1798 when pro-French and republican songs were openly sung by drunken undergraduates. But the printed word, even more than shouts and singing, alarmed FitzGibbon and the Castle. An inflammatory publication, *Letter to the students of Trinity College*, was printed. Signed 'A. Sophister', it encouraged the students:

> '... to catch fire from the pages of Demosthenes', 'and ... raise Ireland to that rank in the climax of nations from which she is fallen'. Students' hearts

30 O. Knox, *Rebels and informers: stirrings of Irish independence*, pp 219–29, 246–7 (1997).
31 T. Bartlett (ed.), *Revolutionary Dublin, 1795–1801: the letters of Francis Higgins to Dublin Castle*, p. 76 (2004).
32 G. O'Brien, *Anglo-Irish politics in the age of Grattan and Pitt*, pp 160–5 (1987). See Fleming and Malcomson, '*A volley of execrations*', p. 209 (2005).

must not be hardened by '… those mercenary prefects sent hither as to a province devoted to rapine and desolation', for the sake of '… our afflicted country! How long will her green plains be dyed with the gore of butchery, and obscured with the ashes of conflagrations!'

This was apparently the work of Robert Emmet, who was about to be expelled, referring to the savage repressions by the army and yeomanry in Ulster and the judicial murder of United Irishmen.

The secretly printed pamphlet encouraging armed revolution against the British crown and disparaging the administration of Trinity College had been widely circulated in the college and in the city, supposedly by 'the independent scholars of the college'. It provoked FitzGibbon's most strenuous efforts to trace 'this most infamous libel to its authors', presumably not students but faculty.

Student David Power, a sophomore (entered 1796), and graduate Arthur Ardagh (AB 1797), who was serving as a postgraduate scholar, were expelled by the board of the college for a clamour implying revolutionary sympathies. Arthur Browne clearly sought to protect Ardagh, whose offence was that a public toast was offered by someone unnamed in his rooms, 'The French fleet on our coasts and arms in the hands of the Irish'.[33] The Board's action would be reviewed in the visitation.

As the roll of students was called at the visitation, each was required to subscribe an oath to inform the visitors of treasonable activities. FitzGibbon then went directly to the previous expulsions, asking the provost and vice provost whether any member of the board had 'expressed disapprobation of the proceedings?'[34] Both answered, 'Dr Browne'.[35] FitzGibbon targeted Browne 'because I do not think that such a degree of [student] insubordination could have taken place in this college without some encouragement by those whose duty it is to enforce discipline'. Prof. Duigenan attempted to distract FitzGibbon's attack by asking whether Browne had voted for any punishments in these two cases. The vice provost's response was that Browne voted for 'public admonition and rustication for a year', rather than expulsions that would 'excite disturbances'.[36] FitzGibbon now saw Browne as the source of student disaffection.

Arthur Browne had then been a member of Parliament for sixteen years, was a member of the English and Irish bars, had been a professor of law for thirteen years and a professor of Greek for five years, was the recipient of four Trinity degrees and was captain-commandant of the defence corps, but, most important, he was a consistent political opponent of FitzGibbon. Browne appeared three times before the visitors. In his first appearance, he explained that he had not been able

---

33 Fleming and Malcomson, '*A volley of execrations*', p. 308 (2005).
34 Ibid., p. 299.
35 Ibid.
36 Ibid. Two other members of the board opposed expulsion. J.W. Stubbs, *History of the Universtiy of Dublin from its foundation*, p. 297.

to remain for the entire board meeting after the vote on expulsions of Power and Ardagh, because of legal business and that on his way out he was questioned by a student about the proceedings. 'I told him how I had voted. I said I feared that the measures of the board would rather contribute to excite the disturbances which we all wished to extinguish.'³⁷ FitzGibbon responded:

> Consider, Dr Browne, what use has been made of your thus publishing your disapprobation. Do you not see that the students were impressed with the idea that you would not by your presence countenance the decision of the board? Do you not see that the same use has been made of your expressions, as if they had actually gone to the full extent of what has been alleged?³⁸

Browne interjected that he had done nothing wrong in disapproving the expulsions.³⁹ FitzGibbon then expressed his view – in a soliloquy on his love for the college – that Browne's indiscretion amounted to degeneracy:⁴⁰

> Dr Browne, I will set you right. If you had been expelled by the provost and senior fellows for this act of indiscretion as tending to excite sedition in this college, such a sentence would have been justifiable under the statue which I have read to you. I was educated in this college. I love it. I have here received the rudiments of that education which has enabled me to obtain my present station. When I reflect upon the days that I have spent here, it is with pain and anguish that I see the spirit which has now broken out. When I compare the present rebellious spirit of some of the junior members of this house [Trinity College] with that subordination and respect for the statutes and the governors of the college which prevailed when I first knew it, your degeneracy afflicts me with heartfelt anguish, and it is with peculiar regret that I observe the indiscreet conduct of one of the members of the board, by which a spirit of resistance to the legitimate authority certainly has been considerably encouraged – a spirit which I fear will compel us before this visitation is concluded to expel many of the members of this house …

FitzGibbon then turned to cross-examine Whitley Stokes,⁴¹ a lecturer in science and fellow of TCD who was a captain in Browne's Trinity Defence Corps and who had clearly been a member of the United Irishmen at its foundation. A number of Stokes' students were examined, concluding the first day.

At the beginning of the second day, Browne asked to enter a defence to FitzGibbon's condemnation of the previous day:

37 Fleming and Malcomson, *'A volley of execrations'*, pp 300–1 (2005).
38 Ibid., p. 301.   39 Ibid.   40 Ibid.
41 Whitley Stokes (1763–1845) was appointed fellow in 1788. Ibid., pp 301–3, 316–21. His fellowship was suspended for three years. In 1799 he published, *Projects for re-establishing the internal peace and tranquility of Ireland*. He returned to TCD and became senior fellow in 1805 at the death of Arthur Browne. He was professor of the practice of medicine (1798–1811).

Since the censure which your Lordships passed on me yesterday, I have been in a state of actual fever. My enemies indeed have had a complete triumph over me. My days are embittered. I have been twenty-one years a fellow of this college, sixteen of which I have had the honor of representing it in Parliament, and in that time mine enemies have discovered a single indiscretion; and for this I have incurred your serious reprimand. The authority which I should have over the younger members appears annihilated. I am degraded from the respectable situation which I held among them. I hope, my Lords, you will grant my earnest request that a strict enquiry may be made into my conduct. I have been not less diligent in my studies than my brother fellows; my moral character will I trust not be found inferior. But I request the inquiry made, in order that I may be able to obviate the misrepresentations which will be given of what your Lordships said yesterday.[42]

The request was promptly and curtly denied by FitzGibbon because of the commotion that had followed the Board's earlier decision:

See what has been the consequence. A libel with defiance had been hurled at me; at your provost. A riot has taken place in your courts [the student residences]. The public prints have teemed with libels against the governors of the college, and of the students against each other …[43]

Professor Duigenan added, 'I acquit Dr Browne of all criminality, but entirely agree with the lord chancellor that he was guilty of an act of indiscretion.'[44]

Thomas Moore was called on the second day.[45] He initially refused to take the oath required of all students, because, 'I have no fear, my lord, that anything I might say would criminate myself, but it might tend to affect others.' FitzGibbon knew Moore was not a United Irishman, but still hoped to turn him into an informer. Moore finally took the oath, reserving a right to refuse to answer. Explaining his earlier refusal, Moore said, 'it was the first oath I ever took, and it was, I think, a very natural hesitation'. Moore's answers were commended by Stokes and then followed by other students who were not United Irishmen. Moore's biographer has explained, 'So many others followed Moore's contumacious example that it proved impossible to dismiss so large a portion of the student body; and the result was that less than a score were expelled.'

42 Ibid., p. 308–9.   43 Ibid., p. 309.   44 Ibid.
45 Thomas Moore (1779–1853), born in Dublin, was the son of a wine merchant. He entered TCD as a pensioner in 1794 and was examined by the earl of Clare and released in the 1798 visitation. He received his AB in 1798 and proceeded to London to qualify for the Bar in 1799. His first poetic work, *Anacreon*, was published in 1800. Many of Moore's finest songs celebrate the friends who were killed or exiled in the 1798 and 1803 uprisings: 'She is far from the land'; 'Silent, O Moyle'; 'Oh! Breathe not his name'; 'When he, who adores thee'; 'Let Erin remember'; 'Through the last glimpse of Erin'; 'The tear, and the smile'; 'Avenging and bright'; and 'The minstrel boy'. See H.M. Jones, *The harp that once*, pp 27–43 (1937).

On the third day, Browne returned to ask the visitors whether duelling was an expellable offence.[46] The board had been divided on the question. Browne's inquiry really concerned the college defence corps. The epidemic of duelling was the curse of the Age of Enlightenment throughout Western Europe, and had even spread to the New World. There would have been no deadly duels among students if they had had no deadly weapons, but at the creation of the college defence corps in 1796 to fight the French, the student members were armed, and the ominous occurrence of student riots and political confrontations presented a clear and present danger.

FitzGibbon declared his opposition to allowing the students to be armed, especially in view of the recent turmoil, but his opinion was countered by the archbishop, a college visitor. However, at the end of the present emergency FitzGibbon will enforce the statutes against duelling.[47]

Just before announcing the sentence of expulsion, FitzGibbon partially withdrew his condemnation of Arthur Browne:

> I wish to state distinctly that Dr Browne does not appear to us to have had the most remote bad intent in what he said at the expulsion of Power and Ardagh. I know him too well to suppose any such thing, and I owe it to the friendship I have for him to state that I am persuaded it did not proceed from any disrespect for the board.[48]

Could this mitigate the accusation of degeneracy and indiscretion? The poet Thomas Moore never forgot his own inquisition by FitzGibbon, a 'monster of blustering arrogance' and 'domineering insolence and cruelty'.[49]

Whether a new vision of FitzGibbon will change the historical appreciation of the visitation, contemporaries had no doubts about it. An obituary of Arthur Browne gave a clear picture of the public perception of what had happened. The *Hibernian Magazine* said:

> Nor were his [Browne's] principles contained within the walls of Parliament; he avowed them out-of-doors, and his ingenious avowal soon roused the suspicious and petulant indignation of Lord Chancellor Clare, who when he visited the university in 1798, thought proper to direct insinuations against the character of Dr Browne. But the fair fame of a just senator was not tarnished by the aspersions of a statesman who libeled everyone that chanced to hold an opinion different from his own; it was too strong to break at the feeble blast of black inquisitor, and it happily survived his utmost

---

46 Fleming and Malcomson, '*A volley of execrations*', p. 327 (2005).
47 Ibid., pp 327–8.
48 Ibid., p. 333. Similar denunciations followed by partial exculpations had occurred in 1794, when FitzGibbon denounced lawyers Simon Butler and Wolfe Tone as disgraces to the profession (as members of the United Irishmen), but then said he meant no disrespect to either man and that he entertained a very high opinion of Tone. See O. Knox, *Rebels and informers*, p. 66 (1997).
49 Jones, *The harp that once*, p. 31 (1937).

malevolence. He was a professed enemy to the abuse of power, and always stood forward the champion of the poor when measures were proposed in the House of Commons, which he conceived injurious to their rights or prejudicial to their interests.[50]

The end result of the visitation was the humiliation of Arthur Browne, the degradation of two fellows and the expulsion of nineteen undergraduates: eight had refused to appear, nine had refused to take the oath and two were allegedly members or associates of United Irishmen. Revolution was in the air and in the next months would break out in Antrim and Wexford with great loss of life.[51]

50 *Hibernian Magazine*, Oct. 1805, p. 599.
51 R.B. McDowell, *Ireland in the age of imperialism and revolution, 1760–1801*, pp 594–651 (1979).

CHAPTER TWELVE

Revolution and retribution (1798–9)

I

THE IRISH REVOLUTION OF 1798 now seems to have been inevitable. Unlike the political revolution of England in 1688 or America in 1776, Ireland more closely resembled the social condition of France, where the revolution begun in 1789 consumed the old nobility. In contrast to these predecessors though, revolution failed completely in Ireland and produced a backlash that endured for several generations.

The context of the 1798 Rising was the virtual world war between England and France, begun in 1793 and lasting until 1815. France had readily grasped the idea that England could be defeated through French control of Ireland. The British electorate gave Prime Minister Pitt unbeatable majorities in Parliament that allowed his government to concentrate its attention on the war and to suppress any form of radical opposition at home.

In Ireland the disaffection that became revolution is usually considered to have begun after the six-week viceroyalty of Earl Fitzwilliam in early 1795. The riot that accompanied the arrival of the replacement viceroy, Earl Camden, on 1 April 1795 was an obvious warning of popular violence. FitzGibbon was nearly killed when his carriage was stoned. This violence was accompanied by the advices of informers that the suppressed Society of United Irishmen was being turned into a revolutionary army assisted by agrarian criminals in a massive conspiracy that cut across all classes and religious denominations. Thus, from March 1795 to December 1796 a series of war measures was carried in the Irish Parliament to empower the government to use deadly force to combat disaffection as well as actual insurrection. The Insurrection Act condemned the oaths of secret societies, authorized searches without probable cause and imposed 9 p.m. to 6.a.m. curfews in areas proclaimed by the viceroy as disturbed.[1] It also allowed the enlistment of a loyal yeomanry.

1   36 Geo. 3 c. 20 and 31. The membership of the Dublin branch of the United Irishmen, before its suppression in 1794, included at least 360 men, of whom 130 were identifiably Protestant and 140 identifiably Roman Catholic. The professions were represented with 30 solicitors, 26 barristers and 16 physicians. The remainder were manufacturers, wholesalers and retailers, of which the largest groups were 67 cloth merchants, 31 textile manufacturers, 14 printers and booksellers, 15 grocers and apothecaries, 6 jewellers, 6 iron mongers and 32 general merchants. R.B. McDowell, 'The personnel of the Dublin Society of United Irishmen, 1791–1794' in 2 *Irish Hist. Studies*, 12–15

The Insurrection Act was accompanied by the first of several Indemnity Acts[2] that would protect magistrates and law officers from the legal consequences of illegal acts to crush insurrection and maintain the peace that could not be legally justified. A further necessary element was the suspension of *habeas corpus*, something that Pitt had achieved in 1794 in Britain.

One of the important actions of the Parliament of 1782 was the Irish Habeas Corpus Act (21 and 22 Geo. 3 c. 11). The law permitted suspension for 'actual invasion or rebellion'. It was the government's overwhelming success in the suspension of the Habeas Corpus Act by a vote of 133 to 7 that drove Browne out of Parliament temporarily at the beginning of the 1796 session:

> Mr Browne, of the college, expressed himself much astonished at the indecent hurry used in pressing the bill thro' the House. He was aware that an insidious and mischievous party in this country would destroy, if they could, the constitution: but it was his duty as a member of Parliament to oppose violence, whether on the part of the government or the people, and danger from the encroachments of government. However, if the danger, as it was asserted, existed, why was not proof adduced? He thought the existing laws strong enough – adequate to all emergencies. Since the bill was urged forward with such improper rapidity, he begged leave to withdraw himself from voting – not because he arrogated consequence to himself, but because he wished to maintain the consequence of that house. Mr Browne left the House.[3]

Unlike many discouraged Whigs, Arthur Browne did not abandon Parliament altogether even though he knew his voice would not be heard. On 25 February 1796, he tried to moderate the government's hysterical fear of the Irish peasantry, about to be codified in the Insurrection Act:

> Mr A. Browne, (college) said he so far agreed with government, that he thought it an imprudent language to be continually telling the peasantry they were the most miserable and distressed peasantry upon Earth – but it was not peculiar to any gentleman – it had been the mode of talking of gentlemen, both in and out of the House, as long as he had known the country, he always thought it was unfounded: – in fact, he was well acquainted with the cottages of England, and knew in counties (not manufacturing), such as parts of Suffolk and Essex, it was a miserable habitation, and not preferable to the Irish cabin, less smoky, but less warm; nor did he conceive that abominable hard cheese and small beer, was so much

(1940) and N.J. Curtin, *The United Irishmen: popular politics in Ulster and Dublin, 1791–1798* (1994).

2   36 Geo. 3 c. 33; 37 Geo. 3 c.39; 38 Geo. 3 c. 19; 39 Geo. 3 c. 3 and 50.

3   *Report of debates in the House of Commons of Ireland, 1796–7*, p. 71. See 37 Geo. 3 c.3; 38 Geo. 3 c.14 and 40 Geo. 3 c.18.

better food, than potatoes and milk; he should prefer the latter – He had not
the same opportunities of observing the cottager in remote counties, with
country gentlemen and did not doubt that in many parts, there was great
distress – but where he could observe, at a wake, a fair, a funeral, an assize,
he saw a number of warmly clothed, strong, able, healthy men, the
handsomest peasantry in the world, as every officer who wanted to raise a
regiment would confess: he was told these were small farmers, not cottagers
– he could only say then, that the class of small farmers must consist of
hundreds of thousands – and there was so far at least, one great part of the
lower orders exempted from extreme distress. – The first remedy therefore
he should propose for the disturbances, would be to shew the people they
were not so comparatively miserable, as they supposed themselves to be –
and the next, to make them understand that the amelioration of their
condition (for that it could be much better he would not deny) could not be
produced precipitately, but must be the work of time – of the gradual
progress of the country – and that it was every day improving: – for instance,
the price of labour is considerably rising, though by degrees, in each step
almost insensible in most parts of the kingdom – so far he agreed with the
government.

– Nay, he would go farther, and declare that he thought the original cause
of the discontent of the peasantry, which was afterwards operated on by
wicked and designing men, was not in government, but in the gentry of the
country, living beyond their Incomes, and striving to make up the deficiency,
by refusing tenants, that due protection of the fruits of the grounds which
every writer on political economy, agrees they ought to have. He was aware
of the boldness of a man of no landed property, speaking thus of the great
landholders, but truth exorted it from him, and as a member of that House,
he had a right to speak his sentiments boldly, when the times made it
necessary, nor did he mean to arraign partially, the conduct of gentlemen at
present; it had been the usage of the country from time immemorial, and he
feared could not be corrected by any law, but would gradually mend itself, by
the wisdom, of the landlord, co-operating with the increasing illumination
of the peasant, and it was doing so; if men would wait. The peasant, though
he never would allow he was so distressed as represented, when well, had no
resource when sick, nor could he save or lay by, and therefore had no spring
of action, no source of ambition, and therefore was unhappy.

These were the remedies he would propose; a committee to enquire into
their grievances, if any – to enlighten them as to their real degree – and only
remedies in language of kindness, as well as a language of authority; – Bills
such as he had the honour of bringing in, for the encouragement of Friendly
Societies, to aid them in sickness and distress, education – raising the price
of labour, and such like – But what does this bill? It speaks merely the
language of terror, without one word of conciliation. The committee
preceding it enquired only what was the remedy of the disturbances, not
what was the cause. He did not mean the proximate cause in that discontent

of the lower orders, which afforded the subject matter for wicked men to
work upon, and which had shewn itself incessantly in some part or other of
that kingdom for 40 years past. – Surely there must be some cause for it,
more than sedition. This bill was only a system of terror, if it went to legalize
all those dreadful violations of the constitution, which had taken place in the
course of the summer, and thereby to continue a kind of struggle, which
should be most violent, which most outrageous, which most unconstitutional, the governors or the governed: that was not the way to command the
respect of the people, or to teach them to obey the laws.

Browne's analysis of disaffection denied the idea of a war between rich and poor:

As a system of terror, it was a puny one – but as a system of irritation, it was
a formidable one. – Robespierre's was a system of terror. – Oliver Cromwell,
going through the country with fire and sword, was a system of terror.
Nobody would approve such system; but this without intimidation would
irritate; witness the late outrages in the very verge of the capital, and under
the very brow of government. – Did that shew, intimidation? If the great
body of the common people of the county was disaffected, which he did not
say, but as gentlemen connected with the government seemed to represent
them – history, experience, reason told him, force would never subdue that
spirit, though it might be quelled for a time; and were we to go on for ever
with that spirit lurking in the country, and formed, as it would be by the
restless spirit of a foreign republic; whether at peace or at war, it was a short
sighted and dangerous policy, and went upon the principle that the common
people never could be reconciled; and thereby went directly to create that
eternal war and breach between the poor and the rich, of which an hon.
friend of his had spoken; he was therefore for a policy that went further, and
sought to subdue, not only the body, but the mind, and could not remind the
House that a scheme of transporting, exactly similar to one part of this bill,
(which seemed to legalize pressing not only of seamen, but of all men) had
been adopted within these five years, by General Dalton in the Low
Countries, and had actually lost those countries to the [Austrian] emperor. –
Nor could he compare this bill with an English bill, which related to poor
common vagabonds, and not to powerful insurgents. – Nor did he think any
such exportation of the guilty would have effect, unless they were prepared
to export half the country, like the Morescoes of old, out of Spain, and obtain
peace by depopulation.

He considered the bill, as a bill of passion, and as he was sure no private
man would act wisely in a passion; so he was much more sure, that no
legislature when angry, would make wise or salutary laws, – The country
gentlemen were angry – he did not wonder at it. If he lived in a county where
he could not tell whether he or those most dear to him, would be secure for
a single night, he would be most angry. As it was, from hearsay and report of
the shocking outrages committed, he felt himself enraged, and therefore he

was on his guard against them; – the more so, because there was nothing so cruel, so violent, so illegal, so unconstitutional, which he had not heard proposed and approved of in private society, by those naturally indignant at the scenes they had witnessed, and forgetting in their indignation, every principle but that of resentment. Individuals might be angry – the mob might be outrageous – but the senate should be ever calm, nor depart from the known principles of the constitution, but from extreme necessity, if such could exist, which he did not believe it could, because he verily believed the existing laws properly understood and exercised, provided for every evil, and it was only a symptom of weak government to be for ever looking for new criminal laws.[4]

The House of Commons approved the Insurrection Act without a division because of the absence of significant opposition.

The government's alarm was real after the French invasion force arrived but failed to land at Bantry in December 1796. Information was received from numerous informers that recruitment into the United Irishmen continued and had not been halted by official suppression.[5]

Events in Britain in May and June 1797, well known to Dublin Castle, but officially unknown to the public, were the naval mutinies at Spithead (between Portsmouth and the Isle of Wight) and the Nore (at the Thames' mouth) in the middle of the intense naval war with revolutionary France. The build-up of unacknowledged grievances in a fleet filled with impressed civilians paralyzed the navy as 50,000 men and 113 ships were idle.

The April–May 1797 Spithead mutiny began as a labour dispute about low wages, poor-quality provisions and the absence of shore leave. Word of the mutiny soon spread to the blockading fleets off Cadiz, Spain and Holland. Recognizing that the 1797 seaman's wage was the same as that of the seaman in Charles II's reign 130 years earlier, the admiralty commissioners negotiated with delegates of mutineers and settled the Spithead mutiny on 15 May 1797 without taking vengeance.

Delay in meeting the Spithead accords encouraged revolutionary leaders to come forward in the June mutiny at the Nore. They threatened to sail the fleet to France and surrender it to the French democracy. This did not involve a nameless union, as at Spithead, but a radical pro-French directorate led by Richard Parker, a dismissed naval officer. Their complaints included the sadistic brutality or flogging and the harsh life at sea. The government used military force to suppress the Nore Mutiny and Parker and twelve leaders were hanged at yardarms.[6]

---

4   *Report of debates in the House of Commons of Ireland, 1796–97*, pp 140–3.
5   See N. Curtin, 'The transformation of the Society of United Irishmen into a mass-based revolutionary organization 1794–96', 24 *Irish Hist. Studies*, 463–92 (1984–5).
6   See generally, J. Dugan, *The great mutiny* (1965); G.E. Manwaring and B. Dubree, *The floating republic: an account of the mutinies at Spithead and the Nore in 1797* (1935); C. Gill, *The naval*

Administrations in London and Dublin were terrified at the example of violence provided for the Irish Catholic majority by the mutinies, especially when Irishmen were discovered among the mutineers.[7]

Arthur Browne did not remain absent from the House as the Whig leaders Henry Grattan, John P. Curran, the Fitzgeralds and George Ponsonby did. In mid-April 1797 he questioned the forces available to protect Ireland from a new French invasion. He was responding to the chancellor of the exchequer, who had said:

> In his mind it was highly absurd to suppose for a moment that the government of Great Britain was indifferent to the safety of Ireland – if Ireland was lost to the empire, England herself must fall. It was unnatural to suppose she would be indifferent to her own safety, and she well knew the shortest road to her own ruin would be to abandon Ireland; if therefore Ireland had no other security for the protection of Great Britain, she had the strongest of all others, self-interest and self-love; and if England had no other motive to protect Ireland; the consciousness of her own salvation at stake would be a sufficient stimulus – and our gracious sovereign, the common father of both realms, was equally solicitous for each, because convinced that the loss of either must be the ruin of both. He moved the order of the day.
>
> Dr Browne (of the college) differed from the right hon. bart. who spoke last, with respect to the earnest solicitude of the British ministry for the safety of Ireland, and he appealed to the late uninterrupted attempt of the enemy at Bantry Bay, where not a single ship of England had even appeared, to molest or impede their hostile purposes. Had there been even three British ships of the line stationed in Cork harbour at the time, they might have taken the whole of the French vessels in that expedition; and the proof was, that the *Doris*, and another of Admiral Kingsmill's cruisers who sailed out of Cork harbour, were nearly able to keep up with the enemy till they reached Brest, and notwithstanding what had been said on a former night by an hon. gent. almost the only professional seaman in the House (Capt. Packenham), as to the zeal of the British admiralty for the protection of Ireland, and the destruction of the enemy's fleet, the notoriety of that fleet having been 17 days in our harbours unmolested, had set the public belief in opposition to the authority of that hon. gentleman.

mutinies of 1797 (1913). The status of research on the mutinies is reviewed in N.A.M. Rodgers, 'Mutiny or subversion? Spithead and the Nore' in T. Bartlett et al. (eds), *1798: a bicentennial perspective*, pp 549–54 (2003); further treatment of mutinies may be found in D. Pope, *The black ship* (1963).

7 Prof. McDowell has shown that the percentages of Irish were probably small, although accurate statistics do not exist. This was despite impressment at sea and the custom of judges to send unruly young men 'to the fleet'. See R.B. McDowell, *Ireland in the age of imperialism and revolution*, pp 493–6 (1979). By 1798 the leaders of the United Irishmen learned of the Spithead and Nore mutinies and sought to infiltrate and create risings in the royal navy – especially in HMS *Caesar*,

Here Dr Browne was called to order by Mr M. Beresford, who appealed to the chair, whether it was orderly or candid for the hon. member to allude to what had passed on a former debate, and more especially to what had then fallen from an hon. Gentleman, who was not now in his place to defend himself.

Dr Browne apologized for having alluded to a former debate, but observed, it was much the custom, when any member spoke in that House to arraign the measures of administration, for that hon. Member to endeavour to put him down by calling him to order.

Mr Beresford said he did not understand what the hon. gentleman meant to insinuate; he called the hon. gentleman to order when he was grossly irregular, and the hon. gentleman gets up and attributes to him, he might say falsely, motives which he dismissed.

Dr Browne said he would not press upon the House, a matter which appeared disagreeable to them, but if any gentleman said he had asserted anything falsely; he gave that gentleman the lie. The speaker instantly ordered the gallery to be cleared of strangers.[8]

Amid suspicions that the United Irishmen were arming and organizing, landlords in Ulster became further alarmed at the sight of squads of labourers brought in to reap the 1796 fall harvest. The viceroy's proclamation of 13 March 1797 that County Down was disturbed was followed by proclamations affecting portions of other Ulster counties. Accordingly, in spring 1797 General Lake and the army was ordered to disarm Ulster, the signal for a military terror of destructive searches, house burnings, at least 400 arrests and many floggings to produce some 10,000 firearms.[9] Nevertheless, disarmed Ulster rose in June 1798 at the call of the United Irishmen, allied with Catholic Defenders.[10]

II

On 15 January 1798 Arthur Browne responded in Parliament to a government programme to stamp out insurrection when he used a prescient expression that still resounds in British, Irish and American constitutional law: 'Martial law cannot be exercised in time of peace when the king's courts are open.'[11] Ten months later

HMS *Defiance*, HMS *Glory* and HMS *Marlborough*. Some Irish were implicated but most remained loyal and even informed. Vengeance was swift and violent, with at least 44 hanged from yardarms and 8 receiving from 300 to 500 lashes apiece. Dugan, *The great mutiny*, pp 420–7 (1965).

8   13 *Parliamentary Register*, p. 407.
9   McDowell, *Ireland in the age of imperialism and revolution*, pp 572–8 (1979). W.H. Lecky, 4 *History of Ireland in the eighteenth century*, pp 18–29, 35–49 (1892).
10 See T. Bartlett, 'Defenders and defenderism in 1795', 24 *Irish Hist. Stud.*, 373–94 (1984–5).
11 *Dublin Evening Post*, 16 Jan. 1798. See also W.N. Osborough, 'Legal aspects of the 1798 Rising, its suppression and the aftermath' in T. Bartlett et al. (eds), *1798: a bicentenary perspective*, pp 437, 446–9 (2003).

this powerful expression appeared in the words of Lord Chief Justice Kilwarden's grant of the writ of *habeas corpus* on 12 November 1798 in the court martial of Wolfe Tone, and forced the government to attempt to rectify its error by legislation.[12]

Arthur Browne, his former TCD colleague Laurence Parsons and a handful of others were the only voices opposed to violent suppression of potential disaffection. They held that the completion of Catholic freedoms and reform of Parliament to undo official influence was the proper solution to disaffection. Defeat in the Commons of peaceful conciliation in March 1798 resulted from a lopsided vote of 19 in favour, 144 opposed; the Lords, on a similar proposal, voted 9 in favour and 44 opposed.[13] Thus *habeas corpus* was suspended and the 1796 Insurrection Act was renewed.[14] By that Act, the lord lieutenant could 'proclaim' a county or portion thereof to be disturbed, so that curfews could be imposed, warrantless searches for arms conducted and distribution of seditious literature penalized. As the United Irishmen had been bound together by oaths,[15] much of the Act dealt with 'unlawful oaths' – making it illegal, for example, to obey the orders of an unlawful (suppressed) committee and refuse to testify against a fellow member. One who took such an oath committed a felony, and one who administered it could be sentenced to death.

Parliamentary defeats and the prolonged absences of allies disheartened the few Whig Club members, who could not resurrect their society while the secret order of revolutionaries the United Irishmen seemed to be thriving; there was no room for moderate reform. Without vigorous opposition in Parliament, the government proceeded to silence the Dublin press.[16]

Fully aware of the progress of plans for a rising because of the capture of one of the United Irishmen's leaders, Arthur O'Connor, in England on his way to France in February 1798, the government decided to raid the United Irishmen's headquarters, seize their papers and detain their leadership. The business premises

---

12 Suppression of Rebellion Act, 25 Mar. 1799, 39 Geo. 3 c. 11. See McDowell, *Ireland in the age of imperialism and revolution*, pp 666–8 (1979).

13 McDowell, *Ireland in the age of imperialism and revolution*, pp 596–7 (1979).

14 In the earlier debate Arthur Browne had denied the need for new legislation since existing laws were adequate if properly enforced. J.A. Froude, 2 *The English in Ireland in the eighteenth century*, 479 (1880).

15 A typical oath of the United Irishmen in 1798: 'In the awful presence of God, I do voluntarily declare that I will persevere in endeavoring to form a brotherhood of affection among Irishmen of every religious persuasion; and that I will also persevere in my endeavors to obtain an equal, full and adequate representation of all the people of Ireland. I do further declare that neither hopes, fears, rewards or punishments, not even death, shall ever induce me, directly or indirectly, to inform or give evidence against any member or members of this or similar societies; for any Act or expression of theirs done or made collectively or individually in or out of this society, in pursuance of this obligation. So help me God.' See T. Pakenham, *The year of liberty*, p. 225 (1969). Wexford oath ordered by Bagenal Harvey.

16 B. Inglis, *The freedom of the press in Ireland, 1784–1841* (1954) and McDowell, *Ireland in the age of imperialism and revolution*, pp 597–8 (1979).

of Oliver Bond, a wool merchant already suspect because of his support of the French Revolution, were serving as the meeting place of the United Irishmen's 'directory'. Bond's offices were on Bridge Street, near the ancient Brazen Head Tavern and a short walk across the Liffey from the new Four Courts. Army Major Sirr and revenue officers were used for the morning raid on 12 March 1798.[17] Papers were seized, although they were not directly incriminating, and twelve men were detained in the new (1792) Kilmainham Gaol. Among those detained were Oliver Bond and John McCann. They were later joined by William MacNeven, Henry Jackson and Thomas Addis Emmet. The anticipated rising was temporarily leaderless. It was about this time that the inflammatory sheet composed by Robert Emmet to inflame Trinity students was circulated, the basis for the lord chancellor's April visitation or purge of Trinity College.

III. REVOLUTION

Three months after Lord Chancellor FitzGibbon's 21–3 April 1798 visitation, the revolution of 1798 had been crushed and harsh retribution began to be applied by the Irish army and its allied yeomanry. It is almost impossible to measure the size of rebel forces in the entire nation in 1798. By some estimates 30,000 rebels and disaffected persons were slaughtered by the crown forces. (Other estimates range from 15,000 to 70,000.) The military forces available to the government are well known, so it is clear that Irish rebel forces were consistently outnumbered. The regular British army posted in Ireland (augmented by veterans of the American war) amounted to 32,281, to which must be added the Irish militia created in 1793,[18] amounting to 26,634 and the Irish yeomanry created in 1796,[19] amounting to 51,274 – for a total of 110,189. To this were added additional troops from England sent over in 1798 and artillerymen at the fortified posts, amounting to 32,281 – a grand total of 142,470. Crown forces lost an estimated 1,600 men.

Revolutionary actions of the United Irishmen occurred simultaneously in three areas, and the French invaded in a fourth area. It will be more convenient to summarize events in each area separately.

17 Pakenham, *The year of liberty*, pp 43–6 (1969) and McDowell, *Ireland in the age of imperialism and revolution*, pp 599–603 (1979).
18 33 Geo. 3 c. 22 (1793, frequently amended). In Cornwallis' view, the militia were contemptible and licentious. To General Ralph Abercromby there was in the army 'a state of licentiousness which must render it formidable to every one but the enemy'. See H.W. McAnally, *The Irish militia, 1793–1816*, pp 133–41, 282, 323 (1949). Militia had some military training and discipline.
19 37 Geo. 3 c.2. (1796). Militia companies contained large numbers of Catholics and were regarded, wrongly, as unreliable. The yeomanry were exclusively Protestant and landlord. Militia and yeomanry were used indiscriminately to support the army in suppression of the rebellion, ibid., pp 92–3. 126–49. See also T. Bartlett, 'Defence, counter-insurgency and rebellion: Ireland, 1793–1803' in T. Bartlett and K. Jeffrey, *A military history of Ireland*, pp 247, 249 (1996).

A. The Dublin vicinity (Meath, Kildare and Wicklow)

The Dublin leaders of the United Irishmen were arrested 12 March 1798 but their substitutes and subordinates met on 17 May and ordered the rising to begin Wednesday 23 May 1798. Lord Edward Fitzgerald,[20] military leader of the rising, was in hiding in various safehouses in and around Dublin until his capture on 19 May, and the Sheares brothers were captured on 20 May;[21] the last of the original leaders, Samuel Neilson,[22] was arrested on 23 May. The Dublin rising was leaderless, and coordinated military actions ceased to be possible.

The strategic thinking of the United Irishmen consistently presumed that French help in some form was necessary to overcome British military strength in view of the disarmed state of the Irish Catholic people. It was not unreasonable for the United Irishmen to expect a second invasion after the Directory had sent a force of 15,000 men and seventeen warships to Bantry Bay in December 1796;[23] that second invasion in great foce never occurred. The United Irish leaders, however, failed to appreciate the effects of the death of the Bantry commander,

20 Edward Fitzgerald (1763–98), fifth son (and twelfth child) of James Fitzgerald, the earl of Leinster and Kildare, a great Whig potentate and descendant of an ancient Norman house. Lord Edward, now a major, returned to Ireland, where he became a member of the Irish Parliament for Athy as a Whig follower of his English cousin, Charles James Fox. In 1792 he married Pamela and attended the victory celebration for the defeat of the Prussians at Valmy by the French general, Kellermann (20 Sept. 1792). Lord Edward renounced his hereditary title and toasted, 'The speedy abolition of all hereditary titles and feudal distinctions.' This indiscretion was soon reported by the press and Lord Edward was dismissed from the army. Returning to Ireland and committed to an Irish rising, Lord Edward joined the suppressed United Irishmen in 1796. He was not found in the 12 March raid and a reward of £1,000 was offered. Lord Edward was shot during his arrest at Thomas Street, Dublin, and died sixteen days later on 4 June 1798. He was buried in St Werburgh's, Dublin. See S. Tillyard, Citizen lord: the life of Edward Fitzgerald, Irish revolutionary (1991), and J. Lindsey, The shining life and death of Lord Edward Fitzgerald (1947).
21 Henry Sheares (1755–98) and his younger brother, John Sheares (1767–98), from Cork were both educated at Trinity College, and were members of the United Irishmen in 1793. They were tried for high treason and hanged on 14 July 1798. Their heads were displayed on pikes before their burial at St Michan's, Dublin.
22 Samuel Neilson (1761–1803), an Ulster Presbyterian from County Down, was a Volunteer. In 1791 in Belfast he founded the United Irishmen with Henry Joy McCracken, Wolfe Tone and Napper Tandy. In 1792 he began the radical newspaper Northern Star in Belfast. When the newspaper was suppressed in September 1796, he was arrested and imprisoned in Dublin. He was released in February 1798 and remained in Dublin as part of the directory of the United Irishmen to plan the rising. After his arrest and confinement in Kilmainham Gaol, he refused to plea or employ counsel at his trial with the Sheares brothers, Bond and McCann. This default saved his life, as the co-defendants were convicted and hanged. Before the resumption of his trial, Neilson joined the Kilmainham Treaty of August, whereby the remaining leaders agreed to provide evidence of the rising in exchange for exile. See W.A. Maguire (ed.), Up in arms: the 1798 rebellion in Ireland, pp 91–2. On the Kilmainham Treaty, See J. Quinn, 'The Kilmainham Treaty of 1798' in T. Bartlett, D. Dickenson, D. Keogh and K. Whelan (eds), 1798, pp 423–36.
23 The Bantry fleet escaped the British blockade of Brest in a windstorm on 16 Dec., but on arrival at Bantry on 22 Dec., the dispersed fleet was unable to land. J. Murphy (ed.), The French are in the bay: the expedition to Bantry Bay, 1796 (1997).

General Hoche, on 19 September 1797,[24] and the new authority of General Bonaparte, who readily abandoned a major effort in Ireland in favour of the occupation of Egypt. The French forces that might have supported the United Irish were missing in May 1798 because they were being ferried across the Mediterranean to defeat Britain's Egyptian allies in the Battle of the Pyramids on 21 July.

Strategy and tactics came together in the rebels' decision to isolate Dublin Castle from the rest of the country by intercepting the mail coaches, the sources of intelligence and means of directing government countermeasures. It was assumed that the Dublin rising would overcome the Castle defenders and imprison the viceroy and his government.[25]

The rising began on 24 May with the seizure of two mail coaches to Naas and Santry, but three others were not disturbed. The viceroy proclaimed Leinster disturbed 24 May and an 8 p.m. curfew was imposed. Dublin City remained quiet.[26] Word of rebel assemblies in counties Meath, Kildare and Wicklow reached the Castle and the viceroy, Earl Camden,[27] no longer confused by events, proclaimed insurrection nationwide and gave the military authority 'to punish all persons acting, aiding, or in any manner assisting in the rebellion ... according to martial law, either by death or otherwise'.[28]

Although rebels were gathered in strength at the ancient Hill of Tara (Meath), Knockallen (Kildare) and Blackmoor (Wicklow), they accomplished little before being dispersed. They surrendered to the military, which massacred unarmed prisoners from Knockallen at Gibbetrath in Kildare.[29]

Tight military control, accompanied by a strict curfew and the absence of leadership prevented any Dublin rising. In fact Dubliners rushed to surrender themselves and their few weapons; between 29 June (after the arrival of Cornwallis) and 9 September 1798, 1,069 alleged Dublin rebels surrendered to the Castle in exchange for pardons.[30]

24 General Lazare Hoche (1768–1797) climbed rapidly from sergeant to general in five years after surviving arrest under Robespierre's reign of terror. He was a rival of Napoleon and sought the Irish expedition. He died from tuberculosis at age 29.

25 McDowell, *Ireland in the age of imperialism and revolution*, pp 488–507 (1979), and Pakenham, *The year of liberty*, pp 28–44 (1969).

26 D. Gahan, 'The rebellion of 1798 in South Leinster' in T. Bartlett, D. Dickson, D. Keogh and K. Whelan (eds), *1798*, pp 104–21 (2003).

27 John J. Pratt, 2nd earl of Camden, 1st marquis of Camden (1759–1840), was the son of a famous father, Charles Pratt (1714–94), who was former attorney general, chief justice of common pleas and lord chancellor. John was selected by Pitt to replace the very popular Earl Fitzwilliam, but Camden could not handle the 1798 Rising and requested to be relieved in May 1798, at which point Pitt decided to combine the offices of military commander and viceroy in the person of Lord Cornwallis.

28 17 *Journals of the House of Commons, 1796–1800*, pt. 2, p. dccccxi, as cited in W.N. Osborough, 'Legal aspects of the 1798 Rising, its suppression and the aftermath' in T. Bartlett et al. (eds), *1798: a bicentennial perspective*, p. 437 (2003).

29 Pakenham, *The year of liberty*, pp 160–1 (1969) and D. Gahan, *Rebellion: Ireland in 1798*, pp 45–50 (1993). See Lecky, 4 *History of Ireland in the eighteenth century*, pp 338–42 (1892).

30 T. Bartlett (ed.), *Revolutionary Dublin, 1795–1801: the letters of Francis Higgins to Dublin Castle*,

B. Wexford and the Southeast

This region was the scene of carnage and destruction on both sides, beginning on 27 May, when the rebel camp at Oulart overwhelmed an army attack.[31] A larger rebel force was assembled outside Enniscorthy at the Vinegar Hill camp beginning 29 May.[32] The rebel force captured the town of Wexford on 30 May, under the command of Bagenal Harvey.[33] Rebel efforts to capture New Ross failed on 6 June.[34] In the meantime, troops from England began to arrive in mid-June, providing General Lake,[35] the commander-in-chief, sufficient force to commence suppression of Wexford in strength on 19 June, effortlessly capturing rebel camps at Gorey, Oulart and other depots.[36] On 20 June, General John Moore[37] fought a bloody but successful battle at Goff's Bridge outside Wexford, while in the town a massacre of about 100 Protestants by the rebels occurred at Wexford Bridge,[38] a

pp 347–73 (2004). Of the 1,068 men and 1 woman, 407 were engaged in the textile industries, 22 in the print industry, 20 publicans, 28 servants and 136 labourers. Religious preference was not recorded. The vast majority resided in the Liberties and areas west of Dublin Castle.

31 See Gahan, *Rebellion*, pp 104–21 (1993). See also Osborough, 'Legal aspects of the 1798 Rising, its suppression and the aftermath' (2003); Pakenham, *The year of liberty*, pp 136–51, 173–93, 245–75 (1969); and McDowell, *Ireland in the age of imperialism and revolution*, pp 462–79, 625–33 (1979).

32 The camp at Vinegar Hill raised the issue of the participation of Roman Catholic clergy: John Murphy, Michael Murphy, Moses Kearns and Edward Redmond. It is apparent that the hierarchy and most of the parish clergy opposed the rising; see Pakenham, *The year of liberty*; Lecky, 4 *History of Ireland in the eighteenth century*, pp 355–64 (1892). D.W. Miller, 'Irish Christianity and revolution' in J. Smyth, *Revolution, counter-revolution and union*, pp 195–202 (2000). D. Keogh, *'The French disease': the Catholic church and Irish radicalism, 1790–1800*, p. 159 (1993). Some Irish neighborhoods in America once had Vinegar Hills to commemorate the rising of 1798.

33 Beauchamp Bagenal Harvey (1754–98) entered TCD a pensioner in 1771, AB 1775, was a wealthy Protestant landowner and became a United Irishman in 1792. Elected commander of the Wexford forces for the unsuccessful attempt to besiege New Ross, he returned to become president of the Wexford council. He later resigned and fled but was captured, tried by court martial and hanged at Wexford Bridge. His head was displayed at the courthouse and his estate became escheat to the crown as a result of a bill of attainder. Lecky, 4 *History of Ireland in the eighteenth century*, pp 366–72, 466–72 (1892).

34 Pakenham, *The year of liberty*, pp 194–214 (1969).

35 Gerard Lake (1744–1808) began a military career at age 14 in Germany (1760–2) and the American Revolution. In 1794 he was promoted lieutenant general and sent to disarm Ulster. Renowned for brutality in carrying out his orders, his victory at Vinegar Hill was followed by mass executions. He had a brilliantly successful military career in India 1800–5 and became first Viscount Lake in 1807.

36 Pakenham, *The year of liberty*, pp 247–70 (1969) and McDowell, *Ireland in the age of imperialism and revolution*, pp 627–47 (1979). See also J. Kelly, 'We were all to have been massacred: Irish Protestants and the experience of rebellion' in Bartlett et al. (eds), *1798: a bicentennial perspective*, pp 299–311 (2003).

37 John Moore (1761–1809) was born in Glasgow, served in the American war (1779–83), in Corsica (1794), under General Lake in Ireland (1798) and in Spain in the Peninsular War, 1808. His death after victory at La Coruna was famously commemorated by Charles Wolfe's poem 'The burial of Sir John Moore' (1817).

38 Pakenham, *The year of liberty*, pp 253–6 (1969). Sectarian violence had not been apparent before

repeat of the 5 June barn burning at Scullabogue that killed about 100 Protestant and Catholic people.[39] On 21 June, General Lake successfully attacked the rebel camp at Vinegar Hill, but some of the rebels escaped and fled into Wexford Town. General Lake pursued, quickly overcame the town defences and began the speedy executions of captured rebels for the next week.[40] Isolated rebel groups gradually reassembled in northern Wexford and southern Wicklow, hoping to join up with the Ulster rebels (already defeated) but they were beaten and scattered on 14 July at Knightstown in County Louth.[41] Thereafter, rebel units ceased to exist and individuals sought shelter in the mountains of Wexford, Kildare and Wicklow.

C. Ulster

Ulster's slow response to the planned rising did not diminish the violence there. Henry Joy McCracken[42] began operations successfully in early June in County Antrim at Ballymena, Larne and Randalstown,[43] but the attack on 7 June at Antrim town failed and McCracken's army dissolved.[44] In County Down the rebels captured Newtownards and Saintfield on 9 June, but failed at Portaferry on Strangford Lough.[45] The next day, 10 June, the rebels took Bangor and Donaghadee, but Belfast remained quiet and under government control.[46]

Wexford Bridge, but it became prominent on both sides, notoriously on the part of the militia and yeomen after the Mayo invasion.

39 Ibid., pp 194–9; McDowell, *Ireland in the age of imperialism and revolution*, pp 630 (1979).

40 Pakenham, *The year of liberty*, pp 265–70 (1969). The rebels had used pikes to kill the Protestants at Wexford Bridge. The army used the bridge to hang the rebels.

41 L. Chambers, 'The 1798 rebellion in North Leinster' in Bartlett et al. (eds), *1798: a bicentennial perspective*, pp 122–36 (2003); and Gahan, *Rebellion*, pp 102–3 (1993).

42 Henry Joy McCracken (1767–98), son of a wealthy Belfast Presbyterian shipowner in Belfast, was an early and vigorous member of the United Irishmen. He was arrested in October 1796 and sent to Kilmainham Gaol in Dublin, where he was confined with his brother William for more than a year and then released in December 1797 when bail was allowed. Henry McCracken became one of the directors of the Belfast Society of United Irishmen. He returned to Belfast to find his colleagues unprepared for the rising and assumed command of the Antrim rebel forces. See E. Fitzhenry, *Henry Joy McCracken* (1936), and A.T.Q. Stewart, *The summer soldiers: the 1798 rebellion in Antrim and Down*, pp 54–9, 65–85, 102–21, 159–162, 240–6 (1995). See also T. Bartlett, 'Informers, informants and information: the secret history of the 1790s reconsidered' in Bartlett et al. (eds), *1798*, pp 406–22 (2003).

43 Pakenham, *The year of liberty*, pp 219–27 (1969). See also B. McDonald, 'South Ulster in the age of the United Irishmen' in Bartlett et al. (eds), *1798: a bicentennial perspective*, pp 226–42 (2003).

44 Stewart, *The summer soldiers*, pp 102–21 (1995).

45 Pakenham, *The year of liberty*, pp 223–31 (1969). See also T. McCavery 'As the plague of locusts came in Egypt: rebel motivation in North Down' in Bartlett et al., *1798*, pp 212–25 (2003). The United Irishmen leader in Down was a Presbyterian minister, William Steel Dickson DD of Portaferry, but he was detained before the expected rising and replaced by Henry Munro or Monroe (1758–98), a linen merchant and former Volunteer, who was elected by acclamation. Munro was betrayed, tried by court martial and hanged on 16 July. His head was subsequently exhibited. See also N. Curtin, 'The United Irish organization in Ulster, 1795–8' in D. Dickson, D. Keogh and K. Whelan, *The United Irishmen: republicanism and rebellion*, pp 209–21 (1993).

46 Stewart, *The summer soldiers*, pp 222–9 (1995).

General Nugent[47] attacked the Down rebels' camp at Ballynahinch, slaughtering hundreds of rebels on 13 June, concluding rebel operations in Ulster.[48] McCracken was captured on 8 July and hanged on 17 July, bringing an end to the revolution in eastern Ireland.[49]

IV. CORNWALLIS

In May 1798, the viceroy, Lord Camden, was unnerved by rebellion and the promise of bloodshed and in a panic sought to resign and return to England. Having already clashed with the military commanders, he recommended that his successor be both viceroy and supreme commander of the military. Pitt and the king agreed, since the choice of such a man was obvious. Charles Cornwallis[50] had already served as governor general and commander-in-chief in India from 1786 to 1793 and had returned in triumph.

The order to join the two offices and appoint Cornwallis was made on 13 June 1798. Cornwallis travelled by commercial packet and arrived in Dublin on 20 June. Camden left on 23 June. As a widower with a spartan lifestyle, Cornwallis avoided Dublin Castle and its pomp and formality as much as possible; he lived and worked at the Viceregal Lodge in Phoenix Park (built in 1751, now Áras an Uachtaráin or the Presidential Residence). He soon discovered that the job had certain built-in enemies, especially those whom Fitzwilliam had sought to remove: Beresford, Cooke and Lord Chancellor FitzGibbon, who demanded the severest measures of repression of all Catholics. Cornwallis arrived just as violent revolution was being crushed in Ulster and Wexford, but victory was not yet apparent to Pitt or even to Lord Camden. Cornwallis' experience in British politics had already made him suspicious of Protestant landlords who sought bloody vengeance to eliminate agriculture and the Catholic peasantry from their estates, in favour of cattle grazing. Cornwallis' job was to pacify Ireland and unify the British empire – contradictory goals that could only be achieved by the projected union of the kingdoms to enfranchise Catholics in a Protestant-majority empire and reduce the power of Irish (absentee) landlords in the Parliament at Westminster.

47 Lt Gen. George Nugent (1757–1849), illegitimate son of an army colonel, joined the army at age 14, served in the American Revolutionary War (1777–83). In 1798, he was in command of the forces in Ulster and directed the battle of Ballynahinch on 11 July after the successful defence of Antrim on 7 July. He served as adjutant general to Cornwallis. His career was capped by promotion to general and field marshal.

48 Nugent used artillery at Ballynahinch to terrify the lightly armed rebel forces in the town, where rebel pike contended with bayonet and rifle fire, killing possibly 500 of the rebel force; as rebel attacks failed, their forces did not reform but fled in disarray. See McDowell, *Ireland in the age of imperialism and revolution*, pp 640–4 (1979); Pakenham, *The year of liberty*, pp 219–31 (1969).

49 Stewart, *The summer soldiers* (1995). See Lecky, 4 *History of Ireland in the eighteenth century*, pp 413–24 (1892).

50 Charles Cornwallis (1738–1805). After he surrendered his army to Washington and Rochambeau (19 Oct. 1781), he returned to England on parole, thereby refusing any military appointments in

After hearing the gleeful reports of indiscriminate vengeance on Catholics, especially priests, by court martial, Cornwallis required that all records of courts martial be reviewed at his military headquarters and that death sentences must be approved by him.[51] Thereafter, many death sentences were commuted to 'transportation',[52] exile or imprisonment for a term of years. Sentences including flogging virtually ceased. Respecting death sentences from the royal courts, Cornwallis usually sought the advice of a group of crown lawyers: the lord chancellor, the solicitor general and the attorney general as well as Lord Castlereagh. This may account for the Kilmainham Treaty of 29 July 1798, which saved the lives of seventy-eight jailed leaders of the United Irishmen, including Arthur O'Connor, Thomas Emmet, Oliver Bond, Samuel Neilson and William MacNeven. Following their written confession – in reality a plea in avoidance – these state prisoners were transported to Fort George at Inverness, in northern Scotland, to spend four or five miserable years in exile, or awaiting deportation to America or Australia.[53]

Protestant Ireland did not approve of the lenient sentences, amnesty and conciliation of Cornwallis, and the persistent criticism of his performance contributed to his misery and desire to return to England or even India even before

the wars against America, France, Spain and Holland. He was promoted to lieutenant general and sent to India in 1786 as commander-in-chief and governor general. His attempted reforms in India were important, but he became known more for his suppression of the rebellion of Tipu Sahib, sultan of Mysore, and his victory in the battle of Seringapatam in 1792. In 1793 he was promoted to general and elevated to marquis at his return to England. He resigned as viceroy of Ireland in 1801. He negotiated the short peace of Amiens in 1802. He died in India on his return as viceroy in 1805. See F. and M. Wickwire, *Cornwallis: the imperial years* (1980).

51 Cornwallis Order, 15 July 1798; see P. Power, *The courts martial of 1798–99*, pp 14–15, 30–2 (1997) and M. Durey, 'Marquis Cornwallis and the fate of Irish rebel prisoners in the aftermath of the 1798 Rebellion' in J. Smyth (ed.), *Revolution, counter-revolution and union: Ireland in the 1790s*, pp 128–45 (2000). For the General Pardon Act and its many exceptions, see 38 Geo. 3 c. 55. Of 400 cases reviewed, 131 death sentences were approved but only 81 were actually executed.

52 The American colony of Georgia was used as a destination for transported convicts from 1733 to 1776. Discovery and exploration of the Australian continent by Captain James Cook in 1770 directed attention to possible transportation of convicts as a means of colonization, beginning with the first fleet in 1788 and continuing through 1830. Transportation to Botany Bay in New South Wales merely moved revolution from Europe to the South Seas, where Irish convicts were involved in risings beginning in 1804. See R. Hughes, *The fatal shore*, pp 183–95 (1987) and Lecky, 5 *History of Ireland in the eighteenth century*, pp 101–2 (1892).

53 See J. Quinn, 'The Kilmainham Treaty of 1798' in Bartlett et al., *1798: a bicentennial perspective*, pp 423–36 (2003). Cornwallis' rationale for the 'treaty' has been explained by James Quinn: 'Much of the evidence they had against them was vague and came from informers who were anxious to retain their anonymity, and the Castle had seen in the past how skillful defence counsel could tear reluctant or vague witnesses to pieces … The agreement, therefore, offered the Castle a convenient means of getting rid of a large number of troublesome agitators who otherwise would have to be detained indefinitely without charge.' The expression 'Kilmainham Treaty' reemerged in the career of Parnell, referring to his imprisonment and release at the hands of Gladstone in April 1882, during the struggle over Irish land reform. See F.S.L. Lyons, *Charles Stewart Parnell*, pp 196–207 (1977).

he encountered the odious politics of the union. Lord Chancellor FitzGibbon freely criticized the Cornwallis policy to London politicians:

> [Cornwallis] seems to be impressed with an opinion that the minds of gentlemen with whom he must act in his government, are so heated and warped by passion and prejudice, that their opinions are not the safest by which he can act; and therefore, his determination is made to act solely from himself. I fear also that he much mistakes the nature of the people, in supposing that they are to be brought back to submission by a system nearly of indiscriminate impunity for the most enormous offences.[54]

V. FRENCH INVASION AT MAYO

The United Irishmen's pleas for French assistance in the promised nationwide rising were finally heard at the end of July 1798, just as the actual rising was suppressed.[55] On 1 August 1798 General Humbert sailed from Rochefort with three vessels and about a thousand men, hardly an invasion force, but carrying arms and ammunition for the rebel army that was supposed to be waiting.[56] Three weeks later the French arrived at Killala on the northwest coast of County Mayo. The anti-Catholic French army announced their arrival to liberate Ireland under the protection of the Blessed Virgin.[57] Two other French forces were planned to coordinate operations with the (non-existent) rebel army: an army of about 3,000 under General Hardy and a squadron of seven warships under Admiral Bompard – gathering at Brest.[58] The problem for French potential invaders since the failure to land at Bantry in 1796 was the persistent blockade of the French Atlantic coast by squadrons of British vessels.

General Humbert landed at Killala on 22 August and occupied the town, using the episcopal palace of Bishop Joseph Stock as headquarters.[59] Gradually, a limited

54 Lord Clare to Lord Auckland, 26 Nov. 1798; D.W. Fleming and A.P.W. Malcomson, *'A volley of execrations': the letters and papers of John FitzGibbon, earl of Clare*, p. 359 (2005). Pardons had been authorized by 38 Geo. 3 c. 35 (1798).

55 See M. Elliott, *Partners in revolution: the United Irishmen and France* (1982); J. Hayter-Haines, *Arthur O'Connor* (2001); and McDowell, *Ireland in the age of imperialism and revolution*, pp 501–18 (1979).

56 H. Murtagh, 'General Humbert's futile campaign' in Bartlett et al., *1798: a bicentennial perspective*, pp 174–183 (2003), and Pakenham, *The year of liberty*, pp 294–328 (1969). The numbers of French invaders were: 35 officers, 888 infantry, 42 artillerymen, 12 naval gunners and 57 cavalry. The number of Irish varied throughout the campaign but was never more than 500.

57 Pakenham, *The year of liberty*, p. 306 (1969). Bishop Stock (*infra* n. 59) speculated that the official French attitudes to the pope (Pius VI, a prisoner of the French) and their ridicule of the religious beliefs of the Irish would soon cause a breakdown of relations, but this French army behaved correctly toward the churches and civilians.

58 McDowell, *Ireland in the age of imperialism and revolution*, pp 645–6 (1979).

59 Joseph Stock (1741–1813) entered TCD as pensioner in 1756, scholar 1759, AB 1761, fellow of TCD 1763, BD 1771, DD 1774, professor of classics and Old Testament. The bishop was held in

number of Catholic Defenders and United Irishmen joined the French, but there never was a rising.[60] Two weeks later Humbert announced the provisional government of Free Connaught, with a young lawyer, John Moore, as president.[61] The transport vessels then withdrew, so Humbert's future depended on victory or the French forces still at Brest.

Mayo was largely undefended by Irish government forces; Humbert easily took the nearby town of Ballina on 25 August and marched southwest to the most important and largest market town, Castlebar. In the meanwhile, General Lake, conqueror of the Wexford rebels, rushed towards Mayo with whatever forces could be patched together. The result was a great victory for Humbert and his French forces over Lake's forces on 27 August 1798, known as 'the Castlebar Races' because of the flight of government forces.[62]

The new viceroy, General Cornwallis, crossed Ireland by canal and river, arriving at Tuam two days after Lake was humiliated at Castlebar. Cornwallis then had an army of 8,000, made up largely of reinforcements from England, to attack Humbert's reassembled group of French troops and untrained Irish recruits.

Faced with Cornwallis' larger force and without news of an invasion by the French General Hardy, Humbert quickly abandoned Castlebar on 4 September and headed for Donegal, where Hardy was expected,[63] avoiding the defences of fortified Sligo by a march southeast along the Shannon River. After a successful defence at Collooney, Humbert camped at Ballinamuck in County Longford on 7 September. The next day, Humbert's forces had been surrounded by Cornwallis' superior army, and, after a brief skirmish, Humbert surrendered his forces to Cornwallis.[64] Because of the declared war between France and England, Humbert

the Castle while his son was forced to accompany the French as a hostage. In 1800 Stock published *Narrative of what passed at Killala during the French invasion of 1798*. His subsequent denunciation of the mass executions angered his flock and the hierarchy but he was translated to Waterford in 1810. His *Narrative* was an important component of Thomas Flanagan's novel, *The year of the French* (1979), which was made into a film in 1982.

60 Pakenham, *The year of liberty*, pp 304–9 (1969). Murtagh, 'General Humbert's futile campaign', pp 179–82 (2003).

61 John Moore (1767–98), son of a wealthy Catholic family, was schooled in France and trained at the Middle Temple. He was a Whig but not a United Irishman. John Moore claimed he only sought to preserve the property and lives of all the residents. He died in prison at Castlebar before he could be released on a writ of habeas corpus. George Moore (1852–1933), novelist, playwright, poet and member of the Celtic revival with Yeats and Martyn, was a great grandson of John Moore. See A. Frazier, *George Moore*, pp 6–8 (2000).

62 Lake's defeat at Castlebar was blamed on the militia's disorganized flight from a smaller force of French troops without Irish rebel assistance. It was estimated that 1,700 militia fled on the approach of 700 French regulars.

63 Joseph Amable Humbert (1767–1823) was part of the Bantry Bay attempt in 1796. Humbert's intelligence sources in 1798 were inaccurate, as there was no popular rising for the munitions he carried and Hardy had not embarked to invade Derry. After Humbert's return to France, his army career stalled and he was sent to the West Indies. He emigrated to the United States and fought in the War of 1812.

64 Ballinamuck was hardly a battle; the French forces were exhausted, having abandoned their gear

and his officers and men became prisoners of war. They were marched to Dublin and subsequently exchanged for British captives.[65] The fate of the untrained and uneducated farmers and labourers captured at Ballinamuck was grim; they were slaughtered after surrender in batches selected randomly for death, without accusation, defence, finding or sentence,[66] a method of deterrence allegedly used by Cornwallis and Tarleton in the American South in 1780–1 and a forerunner of fascist and communist extermination techniques; possibly 2,000 Irish were exterminated.

Sectarian violence, as in Wexford, was not apparent in Mayo; in fact, Professor Beckett has estimated that there were more Catholics on the government side than on the French side because of the use of militia.[67] A violent exception was the hanging by yeomen on 8 June 1799 of Fr Manus Sweeney (1763–99) of Achill Island. Sweeney was probably trained and ordained at the Irish College in Paris. He was curate of Burrishole, County Mayo, and he served as an interpreter and possibly a recruiter for the French army.[68]

Matthew Tone, who had accompanied Humbert from France, and the Catholic radical Bartholomew Teeling, were tried by court martial at Dublin and hanged on 24 September 1798.[69] The first French invasion since the Normans had lasted only seventeen days, but it fed the frenzy of Irish Protestants to seek vengeance on the Catholic majority, even though Cornwallis had prevented any reignition of the rising by his prompt actions.

While the Trinity Defensive Force guarded the bridges and patrolled the Wicklow Mountains, their elders in the college turned savagely against anyone suspected of sympathy to members of the United Irishmen. These were labelled traitors, accounting for the removal of Henry Grattan's portrait from the Trinity examination hall in September 1798 over the strong objections of Arthur Browne, who still honoured the father of the 1782 constitution, despite the false accusations that the absent Grattan had aided and abetted traitors.[70]

and heavy guns on the march. Unwilling to sacrifice his troops, Humbert surrendered after a few shots were exchanged.

65 Customary international law (before the Geneva Conventions of 1929, 1949 and 1977) had developed a number of protections of prisoners of war, including humane treatment and prisoner exchange instead of slavery and ransom. Exchange of officers was usually much faster than exchange of enlisted personnel. The French had a central POW camp at Orleans.

66 W.H. Lecky, 5 *History of Ireland in the eighteenth century*, p. 63 (1892). Citing Tarleton's account of the American campaign, FitzGibbon urged, 'a severe lesson to the people … to feel that the consequences [of rebellion] will be extremely unpleasant to them'. D.W. Fleming and A.P.W. Malcomson, *'A volley of execrations': the letters and papers of John FitzGibbon, earl of Clare 1772–1801*, p. 360 (2005).

67 J.C. Beckett, *The making of modern Ireland, 1603–1923*, p. 265 (1983).

68 G. Moran (ed.), *Radical Irish priests, 1660–1970*, pp 79–90 (1998).

69 Matthew Tone (1771–98). His legal challenge to the jurisdiction of the court martial was overruled and he was hanged on 24 Sept. 1798. The legendary explanation for the suicide of Wolfe Tone on 12 Nov. is that Matthew had secreted the razor in the same cell used to confine his brother.

70 R.B. McDowell, *Grattan: a life*, p.164 (2001).

One week after the surrender of General Humbert, the French fleet under Admiral Bompard sailed from Brest, eluding the British blockade, and headed for Donegal. Almost one month later, the French fleet entered Lough Swilly. Admiral Bompard had one 74-gun warship, the *Hoche*, and eight smaller frigates, while Commodore Warren[71] had three superior warships of 74 guns or more and five frigates. In the action of 12 October 1798, after several broadsides, the *Hoche* could no longer be maneuvered, and Admiral Bompard surrendered his flagship and three of his eight frigates. Three of these French frigates were subsequently captured and two escaped to return to Brest. The surrender of the flagship *Hoche* resulted in the capture of Wolfe Tone[72] – who was onboard, wearing a French military uniform – and the end of the revolution of 1798.

Tone was recognized and brought to Dublin, where he was tried by court martial at the Royal Barracks before General Loftus and six officers on 10 November, convicted of treason and sentenced to be hanged, drawn and quartered, despite his plea for a soldier's death before a firing squad; Cornwallis remitted the gruesome details, but ordered a public execution outside Newgate on 12 November at 1 p.m.

The outcome of Tone's court martial was never in doubt, as he readily admitted guilt, and he was found guilty of high treason against the English king, but was the court martial legal?

71 John Borlase Warren (1753–1822), born in Stapleford (Nottinghamshire), entered Emmanuel College (Cambridge) in 1769 but left to join the navy as a seaman in 1771, was elected to Parliament from Great Marlow in 1774 and created baronet in 1775. He rejoined the navy in 1777, holding his parliamentary seat until 1784. He received his first command in 1779 and led a squadron of frigates after 1794 on blockade duty. He became KCB and PC after defeat of the French in Lough Swilly in 1798, returned to Parliament for Nottingham 1797–1800, 1801–6. He was commander-in-chief of the North American station 1807–10 as admiral and returned during the American war, 1813–14, where he participated in the invasion of Maryland.

72 Theobald Wolfe Tone (1763–98). In his early years as a barrister, he served as secretary to the Catholic Committee. In 1794, Tone's activities brought official scrutiny, and his correspondence with the French spy William Jackson put him in serious danger that he avoided by accepting voluntary exile to America with his family. They sailed from Belfast 13 June 1795, arriving in Wilmington, Delaware, on 1 Aug. The Tone family settled outside Princeton, New Jersey, where he acquired 180 acres. Tone's United Irish colleagues persuaded him to become the agent for Irish independence to the French Directory, and with the aid of the French minister, he left his family in America and sailed to France on 1 Jan. 1796. The Directory gave Tone an army commission with the rank of adjutant general, joining the staff of General Hoche at Brest to plan the invasion at Bantry Bay, expecting that an Irish peasant army would collaborate to defeat any crown forces. Tone accompanied the 45-ship expedition, arriving at Bantry Bay on 22 Dec. where ferocious storms prevented the landing. Tone's wife, Matilda, remained in France until her second marriage in 1816 to Thomas Wilson. They eventually settled in Georgetown, DC, where Matilda died at age 80 in 1849, having received a French government pension since 1804. Two of Tone's children died in France from tuberculosis, but the second son, William, survived to serve in Napoleon's army and then emigrate to America, where he studied law and served as a lawyer in the war department until his death in 1828. Matilda Tone was buried in Greenwood Cemetery, Brooklyn, NY; the memorial headstone was restored and rededicated by Irish societies in the presence of President Mary Robinson on 8 Oct. 1996. See generally: M. Elliot, *Wolfe Tone* (1989); M. Elliot, *Partners in*

On the morning of Tone's scheduled execution, his defence counsel, John P. Curran, moved for a writ of *habeas corpus* for Tone in the king's bench at 11 a.m. before the lord chief justice, Lord Kilwarden.[73] Noting Tone's civilian status as not a member of the British military yet subject to martial law before a court martial while the king's courts remained open, the justice stated his intent to grant a writ, but Tone's custodian refused to comply. Accordingly, Justice Kilwarden issued a writ directing the sheriff to take custody of Tone, his jailer and the provost marshal.

Tone's executioners, however, discovered that he had slit his own throat to cheat the hangman. Since he was too weak to stand, FitzGibbon supposedly suggested hanging Tone seated. FitzGibbon thought the court martial preposterous; Tone should have been hanged on the shore of Lough Swilly. Tone's desperate act had only severed his wind pipe and he died one week later from the accompanying infection.[74]

The *habeas corpus* proceeding for Wolfe Tone raised a question of law that could have undone hundreds of court-martial convictions and unexecuted death sentences, but Tone's death terminated the proceeding without judgment. The issue of the military proceedings over civilians while the ordinary courts remain open is still with us.[75]

revolution: the United Irishmen and France (1982); H. Boylan, *Wolfe Tone* (1981); S. O'Faolain (ed.), *The autobiography of Wolfe Tone* (1937); and F. McDermott, *Theobald Wolfe Tone* (1939).

73 Lord Kilwarden (Arthur Wolfe, 1739–1803) of the Wolfes of Kildare in the vicinity of Clondalkin, was distantly related to Wolfe Tone's father. Arthur Wolfe entered TCD as pensioner in 1755, scholar 1759, AB 1760, called to the Bar 1766 after the Middle Temple. His diligent progress in the Bar, consistent support of the establishment and the Beresfords' Castle connections resulted in his appointment as solicitor general in 1787 and attorney general in 1789. He was appointed lord chief justice as Baron Kilwarden in 1798. Known as a fair and careful judge, he supported the union in 1799 and 1800 and was made Viscount Kilwarden. He was taken from his coach and murdered with his nephew on Thomas Street, Dublin, on 23 July 1803 by followers of Robert Emmet.

74 27 State Trials 625. See M. Elliot, *Wolfe Tone*, pp 390–402; Fleming and Malcomson, *'A volley of execrations'*, pp 358–60 (2005), in two letters to Lord Auckland, 15 and 26 Nov. 1798.

75 In Ex Parte Milligan, 71 US (4 Wall.) 2 (1866) the United States Supreme Court said, 'Martial rule can never exist where the courts are open, and in the proper and unobstructed exercise of their jurisdiction' (71 US at 127), a unanimous grant of habeas corpus in the case of a death sentence imposed by a military commission on an Indiana lawyer and politician who was an outspoken opponent of the union cause and a Southern sympathizer. Lambdin P. Milligan was accused of conspiracy to overthrow the federal government. The trial had occurred during the war (21 Oct. 1864), probably 400 miles from the nearest war zone, but the Supreme Court did not publish its decision until twenty months after the end of the war (10 Dec. 1866). During the Second World War, eight Nazi saboteurs, landed by submarine in civilian clothes were tried by military commission in Washington, DC during July 1942. The Supreme Court reviewed the denial of habeas corpus petition during the military trial, effectively creating a total war exception to Milligan; six of the saboteurs were executed on 8 Aug. 1942 (Ex Parte Quirin, 317 US 1 (1942)). The Supreme Court refused to apply the Quirin exception to the proposed military commission of an Afghan war detainee being held at the US naval base at Guantanamo Bay, Cuba, in Hamdan v. Rumsfeld, 548 US 557 (2006).

VI

The exact number of Irish who were killed in battle or murdered after surrender is uncertain, although the fate of gentlemen members of the United Irishmen is known and recorded. Lecky estimated more than a hundred years ago that by March 1799 there had been 400 trials resulting in 131 death sentences, of which 81 had been carried out, but that 418 people had been transported to penal colonies.[76] About ninety years later, Professor McDowell concluded:

> it is impossible to say with anything approaching precision how many persons were convicted and sentenced for insurrectionary activities in the eighteen months following the outbreak of the insurrection in May 1798. The available figures suggest at least 1,450, a number reflecting a policy of measured severity.[77]

Because of deliberately careless record-keeping, and record destruction, it is unlikely that these numbers can be changed.

VII. EXPORTING RADICALS

British proposals to send Irish revolutionaries to the United States in 1799 were firmly rejected by President Adams' administration during an undeclared war with France. Surely Adams' concern was exacerbated by the presence of large numbers of Irish radicals with French sympathies in Philadelphia, then the national capital.[78] This was conveyed to the British government by the American minister, Rufus King,[79] backed by Secretary of State Timothy Pickering and President Adams.

76 Lecky, 5 *A history of Ireland in the eighteenth century*, p.105 (1892). Estimates of the number of deaths of peasant farmers vary between 15,000 and 50,000; 30,000 seems to be a compromise figure. Lecky relied on Castlereagh's February 1799 estimates.

77 McDowell, *Ireland in the age of imperialism and revolution*, p. 677 (1979). Osborough, 'Legal aspects of the 1798 Rising' (2003), reviews the available evidence of legal actions taken by government as to prosecutions, and the post-rebellion legislation to exonerate zealous officials and compensate owners of properties destroyed by rebels in the conflict. British compensation of American loyalists in the 1780s was the example for this compensation. See T. Bartlett, 'Clemency and compensation: the treatment of defeated rebels and suffering loyalists after the 1798 Rebellion' in Smyth, *Revolution, counter-revolution and union*, pp 99, 119 (2000).

78 Lecky, 5 *A history of Ireland in the eighteenth century*, pp 98–9 (1892). For the attitudinal change in America towards Irish revolutionaries, see W. Walsh, 'Religion, ethnicity and history' in R. Bayor and T. Meagher, *The New York Irish*, pp 48–69 (1996) and T. Keneally, *The great shame and the triumph of the Irish in the English-speaking world*, pp 36–52 (1998). For Philadelphia, see M. Bric, *Ireland, Philadelphia and the reinvention of America, 1760–1820*, pp 216–91 (2008). See generally, M. Durey, *Transatlantic radicals and the early American republic*, pp 80–133, 144–57, 151–71 (1997).

79 Rufus King (1755–1827), born in Scarborough, Maine, AB Harvard 1777, became a lawyer in Newburyport (1780) and a member of the Massachusetts legislature (1782). He served in the

In the United States, the declaration of war by France on Great Britain on 1 February 1793 produced the first political crisis of Washington's new administration, and developed into partisan conflict before organized political parties even existed. The United States 1778 treaty of alliance with King Louis XVI of France was still in force, as was the 1783 treaty of peace with Great Britain. Despite their conflicting sympathies, President Washington's advisers – Alexander Hamilton and Thomas Jefferson – nevertheless urged American neutrality. Hamilton, secretary of the treasury, was sympathetic to English financial and commercial expertise as well as firm government. Jefferson, secretary of state, was sympathetic to the early days of the French Revolution and distrustful of English officials. Since Hamilton and Jefferson advised neutrality, President Washington issued a formal declaration warning Americans to avoid any hostility to either belligerent.[80] In the next year, Congress enacted the Neutrality Act,[81] prohibiting enlistment of American citizens in the service of a foreign power and the outfitting of foreign warships in the United States.

This neutrality of the United States was rejected by the French, who demanded American assistance in their European war. When the United States negotiated a new treaty with Great Britain (19 November 1794 – known as Jay's Treaty), the French Directory turned hostile to the United States as if it were an enemy, and refused to receive the new US minister, Charles Cotesworth Pinckney, when he arrived in Paris in December 1796.

The new president, John Adams, sent a commission to France to negotiate grievances and a new treaty of friendship, commerce and navigation, to escape the implications of the political alliance with the French king. The foreign minister, Talleyrand, demanded a bribe of 12 million livres (£50,000 or $240,000) to receive the commission. No bribe was paid and Talleyrand refused to receive the Commissioners. Talleyrand had implied that France was about to declare war on the United States, which threat was reported to President Adams and the Congress (3 April 1798 – the XYZ Affair).[82]

Congress then turned its attention to French sympathizers and republican radical refugees in the series of statutes known as the Alien and Sedition Acts.[83]

continental congress under the articles of confederation 1784–7, became a delegate from Massachusetts to the constitutional convention (1787) and its supporter in the ratification assembly (1788). On his marriage, he moved to New York City, where he was elected to the US Senate by the New York legislature (1789–96). Then President John Adams sent him to London as minister 1796–1803. He served in the same post under President John Quincy Adams, 1825–6. See *Rufus King: American federalist* (1968). See also M. Durey, *Transatlantic radicals and the early American republic* (1997).
80 Proclamation of 22 Apr. 1793.
81 Act of 5 June 1794, 1 Stat. 381.
82 P. Smith, 2 *John Adams*, pp 952–65 (1962); D. McCullough, *John Adams*, pp 495–503 (2001). J. Orieux, *Tallyrand: the art of survival*, pp 162–74 (1970, 1974).
83 1 Stat 5, 566, 570, 577. See also J.M. Smith, *Freedom's fetters: the Alien and Sedition Acts and American civil liberties* (1956).

The Naturalization Act of 18 June 1798[84] required a period of fourteen years (instead of five) for citizenship. The Alien Act of 25 June 1798[85] gave to the president authority to deport 'dangerous' aliens (a definition that included persons suspected of treasonable inclinations). The Alien Enemies Act of 6 July 1798[86] authorized the president to arrest, imprison or banish enemies in wartime. Congress then terminated the 1778 treaty of alliance with France on 7 July 1798[87] and on 14 July 1798 it enacted the Sedition Act, authorizing criminal penalties for the publication of any false, scandalous and malicious writing bringing into disrepute the United States government, president or Congress. The Supreme Court never reviewed these statutes, which were later repealed or expired.

During the fall and winter 1799–1800, nine individual actions were fought between American and French ships in the Caribbean,[88] but before further hostilities, the belligerent Directory was removed by Naploeon Bonaparte in the coup d'état of 18 Brumaire (9 November 1799) and President Adams then sent a new commission, headed by Chief Justice Oliver Ellsworth, which successfully concluded the Treaty of Môrtefontaine on 30 September 1800,[89] just before President Adams lost his bid for re-election. That treaty provided a mutually agreed termination to the 1778 treaty of alliance and ended the hostilities at sea.

Thus, the United States was in the grip of political hysteria and war (although undeclared), as the Irish Revolution, supported by revolutionary France, was fought and crushed. However, on 4 March 1801, Thomas Jefferson became president; he determined that the United States would again be an asylum for oppressed humanity, and refugees from the 1798 uprising – such as Thomas Addis Emmet, William Sampson, William James MacNeven and John Chambers – were welcomed to firm up the republican principles of Jefferson's party.[90]

VIII

For the next three generations, the Revolution of 1798 became Ireland's dirty little secret, not to be discussed in polite society, virtually ignored by scholars and concealed from the young; but the memory of the Revolution could not be suppressed in popular imagination, where it lived on in anonymous ballads like the 'Wearing of the green', the 'Shan Van Vocht', 'The croppy boy' and Thomas Moore's passionate 'Minstrel boy'.

Almost fifty years after the revolution, the memory was kept alive by a young Trinity student who scorned those who had shamed and forgotten the heroes of

---

84 1 Stat 566.   85 1 Stat 570.   86 1 Stat 577.   87 1 Stat 578.
88 A. de Conde, *The Quasi War: politics and diplomacy in the undeclared war with France, 1797–1801*, pp 89–130 (1966).   89 8 Stat 224.
90 C.G. Bowers, *Jefferson in power*, pp 362–4 (1936). See also D. Wilson, 'The United Irishmen and the reinvention of Irish America' in Bartlett et al. (eds), *1798: a bicentenary perspective*, pp 634–41 (2003).

'98. John Kells Ingram's[91] poem 'The memory of the dead' was published by Thomas Davis in the *Nation* on 1 April 1843 and preserved by generations of Irish nationalists:

> Who fears to speak of Ninety Eight?
> Who blushes at the name?
> When cowards mock the partriot's life
> Who hangs his head in shame?
> He's all a knave or half a slave
> who slights his country thus.
> But a true man like you, man will
> fill your glass with us.

Nationalist audiences in the time of Parnell supported the Irish National Drama Company in 1889 with the J.W. Whitbread plays 'Lord Edward' and 'Theobald Wolfe Tone', and J.B. Fagan's 'The Rebels'.[92] The events of 1798 were still too dangerous for Dublin Castle in 1898, but Yeats remembered them in *Cathleen ni Houlihan*, as did popular legends. Victor Herbert, the Irish-American composer, used the 1798 Revolution in his musical *Eileen*, which opened on Broadway in 1917, influenced by the 1916 Easter Rising.[93] The 1998 anniversary was accompanied by the Good Friday Agreement, ending civil war in Northern Ireland.

91 John Kells Ingram (1823–1907), son of a Donegal rector, entered TCD in 1837 as a sizar, scholar 1840, AB 1843, fellowship 1846, professor of oratory 1852, English 1855, Greek 1866, librarian 1879, senior lecturer 1886, vice provost 1898. See S.D. Barrett, *John Kells Ingram*, Trinity Economic Paper 99/9 (1998).
92 R.F. Foster, *Vivid faces: the revolutionary generation in Ireland, 1880–1923*, pp 79–83 (2014).
93 N. Gould, *Victor Herbert: a theatrical life*, pp 436–43 (2008).

CHAPTER THIRTEEN

The union of the kingdoms (1799–1801)

I

ARTHUR BROWNE'S REPUTATION as an Irish patriot suffered in the eyes of nationalist Ireland in the nineteenth century because, between January 1799 and February 1800, he changed his mind about the union of Ireland and Great Britain. The debate on the union was seen as the great watershed in the political history of the Irish people for the 150 years following the union. The scholarship of the last fifty years, however, has sought to reinterpret the union debate based on documentation unavailable to earlier historians.

In January 1799, with what was left of the Patriot Party, Browne successfully opposed the suppression of the Irish Parliament and the union of the Irish church and state with Great Britain. This plan of union was Prime Minister Pitt's mandatory resolution of Irish problems. Browne's colleagues at the Bar and in the university were similarly opposed to the union and remained so for several years after Browne changed his mind. The question is whether his 1800 vote broke a pledge to his constituents or was bought by the government in exchange for office, preferment or cash. Browne always denied the charges.

An anonymous colleague published a pamphlet in the year of the union (1800) *Some documents relative to the late parliamentary conduct of Doctor Browne, representative in Parliament for the University of Dublin*. It contains Browne's versions of his speeches and correspondence, and will be used here instead of the *Parliamentary Reports*, because it is a fuller account of Browne's remarks.

The union ordered by Prime Minister William Pitt[1] was hardly original to him. His unexamined enthusiasm for union may have been due to the advice of the viceroy (Westmorland) in 1792:

1 William Pitt, the younger never devoted much attention to Irish problems and relied on Ascendancy politicians not connected to the Whigs for advice, but the threat of an Irish regency for the prince of Wales in 1789 must have aroused his determination to prevent a repeat. Obviously, his fears of Irish intrigues were confirmed by the 1798 revolution. Westmorland's advice, 13 Nov. 1792, is cited in B. Hilton, *A mad bad and dangerous people: England, 1783–1846*, p. 79, n. 132 (2006). During the 1799 defeat in the Irish Commons, Pitt gave detailed explanations of his Irish policy in the British House of Commons on 23 and 31 Jan. 1799. After the 1800 victorious vote in Ireland, Pitt again gave a lengthy explanation to the House on 21 Apr. 1800. After the 1796 election he could regularly count on 250 votes, more or less, opposed by only ninety Whig votes, more or less. The opposition Whig party had shattered after the split between Edmund Burke and Charles James Fox over the French Revolution in 1791. Pitt served as prime minister for twenty-two of his

The Protestants frequently declare they will have a union rather than yield the franchise to the Catholics. The Catholics will cry out for union rather than submit to their present state of subjection, it is worth turning in your mind, how the violence of both parties might be turned on this occasion to the advantage of England.

Even before the union of the Kingdom of Scotland with the Kingdom of England (and Wales) in 1707[2] there had been suggestions of a unified imperial nation including Ireland,[3] but it did not come about until the Revolution of 1798 made major changes in Ireland necessary. The word 'union' itself is a euphemism for subordination following conquest. Any connection with England was perilous for the weaker party. Opponents of the union in 1799 saw it in that light, but proof of this assertion was not apparent until the Famine of 1845–50.

Many of the problems of unequal economies in the 1800 union with Ireland were present in the parliamentary union with Scotland in 1707.[4] The religious differences between Scotland and England had been downplayed in 1707 when the established Church of Scotland continued to be Presbyterian, but sharing the ecclesiastical establishment with Roman Catholics in 1800 remained impossible for Ireland by reason of King George's adherence to his coronation oath to support the Protestant religion.[5] The legal differences between English common law and Scots Roman-Dutch law were the substantial hurdle in 1707, but law was no serious problem in the Irish union because of the constant infiltration of English lawyers into Irish judicial offices.[6]

Subordination of both Scotland and Ireland to England was clearly apparent in the 'negotiated' numbers of members of the Commons and Lords from those nations. Equal representation of the three kingdoms at Westminster was never seriously considered. The result in 1707 was the addition of 16 Scottish members to the English House of Lords and 45 members to the Commons. In 1801, 100 Irish members were added to the Commons and 32 peers to the Lords. Over-representation of England in the union Parliament was the result.[7]

---

forty-seven years. See generally J. Ehrman, *The younger Pitt* i: *The years of acclaim* (1969), ii: *The reluctant transition* (1983), iii: *The consuming struggle* (1996); K. Feiling, *The second Tory Party, 1714–1832*, pp 184–230 (1959); G. O'Brien, *Anglo-Irish politics in the age of Grattan and Pitt*, pp 484–96, 501–3 (1987); and W. Hague, *William Pitt the younger*, pp 159–70, 383–400 (2005).

2 See 6 Anne c. 6 (1707).

3 R.B. McDowell, *Ireland in the age of imperialism and revolution*, pp 678–9 (1979). See also, J. Kelly, *Prelude to union: Anglo-Irish politics in the 1780s* (1982).

4 J. Livesey, 'Acts of union and disunion: Ireland in Atlantic and European contexts' in D. Keogh and K. Whelan, *Acts of union*, p. 95 (2001).

5 The coronation oath 'to support the Protestant religion' was imposed by Parliament in 1689 for the joint coronation of William and Mary. See 2 Will. and Mary c. 6 (1689).

6 English lawyers were consistently appointed to high judicial office in Ireland as English clergymen were appointed to Irish bishoprics. These offices were available for English politicians whether Whig or Tory.

7 The estimated population of England and Wales was 10.5 million and of Scotland, 1.5 million.

II. THE IRISH PARLIAMENTARY STRUGGLE

The Parliament elected in 1797, before the Revolution, sat from 8 January 1798 until 1 October 1798 during the horrors of rebellion and repression. It continued to sit during the union debates of 1799 and 1800. That fact alone was a devastating assault on the primitive parliamentary democracy of Ireland in that a major constitutional change was accomplished without an election.[8]

While the 1798 session insisted on vengeance against the Catholic majority, despite Cornwallis' efforts to ameliorate the disaffected elements of society, suggestions of a parliamentary union aroused opposition in Parliament before any formal proposal by government was introduced. During the Revolution, Lord Chancellor John FitzGibbon assessed the question of union:

> The main difficulty which it strikes me you will have to encounter at the outset of the very important business to which your last letter alludes, is our strong national love of jobbing, which must receive a fatal blow in the ultimate success of the measure … The landed interest is in favour of the measure, and when the advantages of it in a commercial point of view are understood, I should suppose the commercial interest of the country would also be generally and strongly for it. The Catholics will, I make no doubt, oppose it with violence, as will northern republicans, and therefore before the measure is avowed, it will be essentially necessary to have a strong British military force here, nor in my opinion will it be prudent to avow it until Great Britain is at peace with her foreign enemies. The speaker will, I believe, be against the measure, and I know the archbishop of Cashel will oppose it vehemently. Lord Shannon, I think, sees the necessity which presses for it; and I am pretty confident that the general feeling of the House of Lords is in favour of it. Our proprietors of boroughs which would not be represented, will demand compensation; and if this should be practicable, I make no doubt a great majority of them will acquiesce.[9]

England had 491 members after 1801; there were also 45 from Scotland, 24 from Wales and 100 from Ireland, making a total membership of 660. The number 100 for Irish members could not have reflected population size, but may have reflected some other criterion such as wealth or political importance. In the time of Parnell (1875–90), the 100 Irish members had a decisive impact when British Tories and Liberals were approximately equal.

8 J. Barrington quoted Frederick Trench, MP for Portarlington, that the union was premature until the wishes of the people were known because Parliament has no right to make a radical change in the constitution. P.M. Geoghegan, *Irish Act of Union: a study in high politics*, p. 62 (1999). The classic mode of changing the unwritten constitution appeared in the reform of the House of Lords in 1910 following an election and the threat of the king to appoint additional peers to force the Lords to consent to their loss of power to block legislation permanently. See D. Keir, *The constitutional history of modern Britain, 1485–1951*, pp 491–3 (6th ed. 1951). Threats to appoint additional peers were used in 1712 (Anne), 1832 (William IV) and 1910 (George V).

9 D.A. Fleming and A.P.W. Malcomson, *'A volley of execrations': the letters and papers of John*

The Dublin Bar,[10] Irish manufacturers, urban merchants and Catholic lay people joined the remnants of the Patriot Party to oppose the closing of the Dublin Parliament even though that organization had never been a protector of their liberties or commercial interests, and the Orange Order also opposed the union to preserve its power in Ulster.[11]

Government could rely on the great landowners, the established church and even the Catholic hierarchy to support the parliamentary union as the only way to conserve the status quo.

The parliamentary struggle lasted a little more than sixteen months, during which time there must have been considerable uncertainty and speculation about the future of Ireland and its capital city. The 1799 session witnessed a brief resurgence of the 1782 Patriot Party and a temporary victory but the outcome of the 1800 session was predictably a victory for Pitt and the Irish government, who were determined on union regardless of the length of time required and regardless of the number of pensions, peerages, promotions and perquisites needed.[12]

A. The 1799 session

The first step in the government strategy was enforcing support by dismissing known opponents from government jobs as a threat to members holding public office. John Parnell, chancellor of the exchequer, James Fitzgerald, prime serjeant and John Foster Jnr, son of Speaker Foster, were dismissed before Parliament reconvened 22 January 1799 – a cheaper form of pressure than the traditional 'influence'.[13] These dismissals were a clear sign that there would be no government favours in the future for those who opposed the union. The floor manager of the union, Viscount Castlereagh, member for County Down and chief secretary for Ireland, attempted to make the case before a hostile audience including the speaker of the House of Commons, John Foster.[14] Despite some political experience, Castlereagh was not known for subtle persuasion, companionable character or convincing oratory; his icy logic and abrupt treatment of others may have been a symptom of the melancholia that later destroyed him.

    FitzGibbon, earl of Clare (1772–1802), p. 345 (2005), letter of 3 July 1798 to Lord Auckland. P.M. Geoghegan, *Irish Act of Union: a study in high politics*, pp 50–4 (1999).

10 The Dublin Bar debated a possible union and rejected it by a vote of 166 to 32. *Report of debate of the Irish Bar, Sunday 5 December 1798*.

11 A. Jackson, *Ireland 1798–1998: politics and war*, pp 24–5 (1999); but see G.C. Bolton, *The passing of the Irish Act of Union*, pp 77–84 (1966) and P.M. Geoghegan, *The Irish Act of Union: a study in high politics*, pp 51–3 (1999).

12 G.C. Bolton, *The passing of the Irish Act of Union*, pp 74–6 (1966); J. Quinn, 'Dublin Castle and the Act of Union' in M. Brown, P.M. Geoghegan and J. Kelly (eds), *The Irish Act of Union*, p. 95 (2003).

13 G.C Bolton, *The passing of the Irish Act of Union*, p. 103 (1966).

14 FitzGibbon explained the problems of Speaker Foster's attitude to the union: 'The struggle has been arduous and severe, principally if not altogether from the part taken by Foster, our speaker, who has strained every nerve to defeat us, not only by violent opposition in and out of Parliament,

The speech from the throne did not propose union, but merely to 'improve a connection essential to their common security' and consolidate 'as far as possible into one firm and lasting fabric the strength, the power and the resources of the British empire'.[15]

Traditionally, the speech from the throne required an answer, invariably thanks for the gracious speech, offered as a motion on this occasion by Henry de la Poer, Lord Tyrone, but immediately amended by George Ponsonby, pledging the maintenance of, 'The undoubted birthright of the people of Ireland to have a free and independent legislature.'[16] The struggle began on Ponsonby's amendment to the address of thanks, but was lost by one vote, after more than twenty hours of speeches varying between dull endorsements of government and inflammatory rhetoric reminiscent of the recent rebellion, and including a lengthy defence of union by Castlereagh.[17]

Arthur Browne joined the Ponsonbys and Speaker Foster in opposition to the union at that time and place, but unlike his colleagues he was not prepared for eternal opposition:

> Though I at present vote against the union, I wish to treat the arguments for it with all possible respect. I agree with the noble lord [Castlereagh] in thinking that no motion can go to all futurity, though I do not therefore think the present motion [Lord Corry's] unnecessary.
>
> I am one of those, who, shocked with the distractions of the nation, have been inclined to listen to any rational resource, and was at first disposed to receive the propositions for an union at least into consideration, if it be shewn that Parliament is competent so to do. [...]
>
> I commend the motion of the noble lord as cautiously worded as to futurity; I should have objected to it, if it went to bind me for ever; at all events I cannot foresee any possible circumstances which can incline me to an union, except it were necessary to prevent the country from becoming a French province; but not being able to foresee all possible circumstances, I did, even at my election into Parliament, boldly refuse to make any such unnecessary declaration.[18]

but by all the intrigue of which he is so perfect a master.' Fleming and Malcomson, '*A volley of execrations*', p. 399 (2005), letter of 9 Mar. 1800 to Lord Wellesley.

15 See *A report on the debate in the House of Commons in Ireland on 22 and 23 January 1799*, p. 3 (1799). See also W.H. Lecky, 5 *A history of Ireland in the eighteenth century*, pp 219–21 (1892). Pitt had prescribed that the speech from the throne be identical in Dublin and London.

16 *Report, supra* n. 15, p. 13; Lecky, n. 15, p. 220.

17 *Report, supra* n. 15, pp 150–65, 220–1. The vote was 105 for the Ponsonby motion, 106 opposed (ibid., p. 91).

18 *Some documents relative to the late parliamentary conduct of Doctor Browne representative in Parliament for the University of Dublin*, pp 1–2 (1800). The parliamentary report merely stated that Dr A. Browne, in a very neat and concise manner, condemned the measure of a union and declared himself an enemy of it (p. 69).

These words would come to haunt him as some constituents believed that their members had sworn eternal opposition to the union at the time of the last parliamentary election in 1797.

As expected, the Lords voted the motion of unamended thanks by 51 to 19, but the single-vote government victory (106 against 105) in the Commons was surely a pyrrhic triumph. Overnight, the government and the opposition rallied their forces and the struggle resumed on 24 January 1799 when another issue emerged on the address of thanks for the gracious speech. This time the question was to delete even the viceroy's veiled references to union. The government lost by a vote of 109 in favour of deletion against 104 opposed.[19] This five vote victory was the high point of the defence of the Irish Parliament.

FitzGibbon's account of the government's defeat sought to coat the bitter pill with a wish:

> government were beat, I understand, by a majority of three [*sic*]. I cannot conceive how they could have been so grossly deceived as to their strength. Ely [Charles Tottenham Loftus, earl and marquis of Ely] played them foul, certainly, as did many individuals. But allowing for the villainy and treachery which might have been expected, I always understood there were a certain majority of thirty in support of government. Mr George Ponsonby wished to follow up his victory, and proposed a resolution to pledge the House against the measure of a union; but he was obliged to with draw it, several country gentlemen who had voted with him for expunging the paragraph in the address, declaring that they would oppose any such resolution; so that this malignant knave has been in the event, the best friend of government …

In London, Parliament had returned on 23 January 1799 and Pitt had no difficulty with the union proposal, despite the oratory of Richard Brinsley Sheridan in opposition. Pitt's London majority on 31 January was 140 to 15.[20] The lesson of the Irish 1799 vote to Pitt was that neither rational argument nor irrational fears of French invasion or agrarian violence had produced the union, therefore, traditional methods based on greed must be employed.

B. The 1800 session

The Irish Parliament stood adjourned from 1 June 1799 to 15 January 1800. This time was used by Dublin Castle to buy the union from corruptible members at great cost. Of course, there were members who changed their votes from negative or abstention to approval without the incentives available from the administration, but the odour of political corruption has permeated the union debates of 1800 in the Irish Parliament for more than 200 years, despite revisionist efforts to launder

---

19 Fleming and Malcomson, '*A volley of execrations*', p. 365 (2005), letter of 25 Jan. 1799 to Lord Auckland. *Report, supra* n. 15, p. 91; Lecky, *supra* n. 15, pp 222–7.
20 J. Ehrman, *The younger Pitt: the consuming struggle*, p.185 (1996).

the process. Undoubtedly the viceroy, Lord Cornwallis, contributed to the negative impression:

> My occupation is now of the most unpleasant nature, negotiating and jobbing with the most corrupt people under heaven. I despise and hate myself every hour for engaging in such dirty work, and am supported only by the reflection that without an union the British empire must be dissolved. When it is impossible to gratify the unreasonable demands of our politicians, I often think of two lines of Swift, speaking of the lord lieutenant and the system of corruption –
>
> > And then at Beelzebub's great hall
> > Complains his budget is too small.[21]

Without giving details. Cornwallis had earlier informed the same correspondent, 'With the concurrence and advice of the king's confidential servants, I am prepared to employ every exertion in my power to bring it [the union] to a successful issue.'[22] Cornwallis delegated much of the 'dirty work' to an Irishman, Robert Stewart,[23] usually called Lord Castlereagh, chief secretary to the viceroy, who described his task, 'to buy out and secure to the crown for ever the fee simple of Irish corruption.'[24]

Pitt had determined that the only way to prevent a recurrence of rebellion in Ireland was the union of the kingdoms and the suppression of the Irish Parliament. To carry out this policy, Cornwallis was instructed to press the matter until it carried, no matter how often defeated; thus, the proposal's defeat in January 1799 was merely the first skirmish in a long campaign.

Pitt's only difficulty in achieving the union would come from the corruptible Irish House of Commons, which was expected to be bought off in the traditional manner (with titles, jobs and honours). To unify the kingdoms, it was well known that forty-eight peerages, along with government jobs, military appointments, ecclesiastical promotions and a public cash outlay of £1,260,000 (to compensate

---

21 Cornwallis' letter to Maj. Gen. Ross, 8 June 1799, as quoted in J. Killen (ed.), *The decade of the United Irishmen: contemporary accounts*, p. 175 (1997).

22 Ibid. Cornwallis letter to Maj. Gen. Ross, 24 May 1799.

23 Robert Stewart (1769–1822), known as Viscount Castlereagh from 1796 to 1821, was born in Dublin, the son of Baron Londonderry (1739–1821), possessor of great estates in Ulster. Robert attended the Royal School in Armagh and Cambridge (St John's, 1786–9). In 1790, he contested a seat for County Down at the enormous cost of £60,000 to defeat the nominee of Lord Downshire. He entered the Dublin Parliament as a reforming Whig but was always a supporter of the younger Pitt. He represented County Down in Dublin from 1790 to 1801 and at Westminster from 1801 until his death. See J. Derry, *Castlereagh*, pp 26–99 (1976); I. Leigh, *Castlereagh*, pp 111–38 (1951); P.M. Geoghegan, *Lord Castlereagh*, pp 18–43 (2003); and J. Bew, *Castelereagh: a life* (2012).

24 Castlereagh's letter to his uncle, former Viceroy Camden, 24 July 1799, cited in Geoghegan, *Lord Castlereagh*, p. 30 (2002).

the owners of pocket boroughs) were used. Until recently, it was not clear how much bribe money also secretly changed hands to guarantee the outcome.

In his 1966 work, Geoffrey Bolton wrote that the change of mind of the Irish Commons was not, however, a simple matter of massive bribery. One-fifth of the membership of the House of Commons had changed in the intervening year, and the disorganized Irish Whigs had no hope that the entrenched Tory ministry in London could be replaced in the foreseeable future by the English Whig party, which was fractured by war and revolution. Although nineteenth-century nationalist Ireland chose to believe that only massive corruption could have persuaded the Irish Parliament to agree to its final dissolution, twentieth-century scholars view the efforts of Viscount Castlereagh as a simple continuation of the methods traditionally used to control the fractious and disputatious Parliament. Bolton wrote:

> The anti-unionists then failed to sustain their [1799] victory because they were unable to agree on any constructive alternative to union, owing to the conflicting elements on their side. This failure, and not corruption, ensured the government's eventual victory ... The government's majority in 1800 was principally secured from interests which had hitherto stood neutral.[25]

Following discovery of the secret services' accounts at Kew revealing that £32,556 had been paid by the king to strengthen and confirm the government majority in Dublin, and the deeper involvement of the Catholic question, Patrick Geoghegan concluded, in his 1999 work:[26]

> For the opponents of union the Irish Parliament, enshrined by the constitution of 1782, had represented the Irish nation. It had symbolized an ideal, and it was a humiliating experience to find it so easily dismantled and destroyed. Worse, it had been bought out of existence, willingly sold by people they dismissed as misguided or corrupt. Even with the full resources of the king's government arrayed against them it had never appeared inevitable that the union would pass. Ultimately, their prejudiced refusal to include the Irish Catholics within their group doomed their struggle to failure. For the proponents of union, how the measure was passed was

25 G.C. Bolton, *The passing of the Irish Act of Union*, pp 218–19 (1966). See also J. Kelly, 'The historiography of the Act of Union' in M. Brown, P.M. Geoghegan and J. Kelly, *The Irish Act of Union: bicentennial essays*, p. 5 (2003). The nationalist view before the Anglo-Irish War is found in J.S. MacNeill, *The Irish Act of Union and how it was carried* (1912). Sanitized accounts supportive of the union were published in the nineteenth century: C. Coote, *History of the legislative union between Great Britain and Ireland (1802)* and T. Ingram, *A history of legislative union of Great Britain and Ireland* (1887), the latter during Gladstone's struggle for home rule.
26 P.M. Geoghegan, *The Irish Act of Union: a study in high politics*, p. 87 (1999). See also D. Wilkinson, 'How did they pass the union? Secret service expenditure in Ireland, 1799–1804', 82:266 *History Ireland*, 223–51 (1997).

immaterial, it merely reinforced their belief in the essentially corrupt nature of the Irish Parliament.[27]

Long before the work of Bolton and Geoghegan, Lecky had accurately said, 'everything in the gift of the crown in Ireland; in the church, the army, the law, the revenue was devoted to the single object of carrying the union'.[28] However, Pitt's biographer, John Ehrman, has downplayed the role of bribery and fraud:

> Vacant places, and pensions, went to unionist supporters, not 'converted opponents'; a practice familiar and normal in itself … Compensation to borough owners was likewise tolerable in principle: it was or could be held to be in aid of a reforming as well as a tactical exercise … The peerages for their part did not go to avowed early opponents – few of whom indeed changed their minds throughout – but, as was usual, to friendly or uncommitted patrons and members for services rendered. Such practices, therefore, it has been argued, were perfectly defensible. Their scale may have been distasteful, but in principal they did not transgress accepted norms. […]
>
> Patronage, 'not by itself by definition corrupt' – in fact the only way of doing things – was moved by an ethos; and Irish practices were agreed to be traditionally laxer than English … Bearing this in mind, it may be hard to maintain that Cornwallis and Castlereagh broke the conventions. We might well say rather that in the terms of place and terms they strained them to the limits.[29]

This may well be true of peerages, pensions and promotions, and may account for Arthur Browne's benign interpretation. It does not explain cash transactions.

Browne's respect and admiration for Lord Cornwallis and Viscount Castlereagh was such that he could not believe the rumours of wholesale bribery in the 1800 vote for union; he could not have known Pitt's relentless orders nor the true feelings of Cornwallis and Castlereagh. In his last political pamphlet, he supported his unbribed vote:

> I come in the last place to consider the undue means by which this measure is said to have been carried, and the settlement of 1782, which has been set up against it as a bar. I am one, and I am confident, one of many, who can boldly say, if such means have been used, we know not of them. The charge

---

27 Geoghegan, *The Irish Act of Union*, p. 117 (1999). See also P.M. Geoghegan, 'The making of the union' in D. Keogh and K. Whelan (eds), *Acts of union: the causes, contexts and consequences of the Act of Union*, p. 34 (2001). Dr Geoghegan puts the total of secret government funds available to purchase the union at £63,650 (ibid., p. 43).

28 Lecky, *supra* n. 15, pp 302–3. Government expected to compensate owners of rotten boroughs at £7,500 to £15,000 per seat. It was rumoured that votes could be bought for £4,000 from ordinary members while members of the Bar demanded 4,000 guineas (£1 plus 1 shilling – customary fees at the Bar).

29 J. Ehrman, 3 *The younger Pitt: the consuming struggle*, pp 188–9 (1996).

in a case where proof must have been eagerly sought, rests entirely on the assertion of those who make it. The character of the chief governor, whose name contrary to every rule of Parliament and every principle of decorum, has been so often introduced in the House of Commons, is above their censure and above my praise. The character of the minister, has with great courtesy of manners too great an intermixture of virtue and proper pride to suffer any man to refuse the acknowledgments that he is utterly incapable of, and infinitely above such debasing and unworthy arts. May we not conclude then that these suspicions are the offspring of spleen. But if the charge were true, what would follow? That it would be an argument for the union. If the Parliament were capable of being packed and corrupted, a packed and corrupted Parliament ought not to exist.[30]

The session began on 15 January 1800. To avoid an early confrontation there was no mention of the union in the speech from the throne.[31] Nevertheless, Lawerence Parsons, now member for King's County and formerly Arthur Browne's colleague from TCD, began a direct assault on the union, proposing to amend the routine address of thanks for the speech from the throne by the statement that the House of Commons was determined to maintain a free and independent Parliament.[32] Again, the oratory continued without stop through the night and into the next day, when the prematurely aged and infirm Grattan, dressed in a Volunteers uniform but unable to stand, delivered a two-hour oration from his seat in praise of 'the body that restored your liberties', and in condemnation of ministerial corruption to buy the vote for union.[33] Grattan said that Ireland would be under-represented at Westminster and that the proposed union was merely a merger of parliaments and not a unification of interests and identities. Union had no benefits for Ireland and its people.

Grattan's conclusion, thought to be treason by Castlereagh, was the incitement for Irish nationalism during the next century:

> Though in her tomb she lies helpless and motionless, still there is on her lips a spirit of life and on her cheek a glow of beauty ... While a plank of the vessel [Ireland] sticks together I will not leave her ... I will remain anchored here, with fidelity to the fortunes of my country, faithful to her freedom, faithful to her fall.

---

30 A. Browne, *Remarks on the terms of the union*, p. 23 (1800).
31 See *A report of the debate in the House of Commons in Ireland on 15 January 1800*, pp 1–6 (1800).
32 Lecky, *supra* n. 15, pp 344–8; pp 19–23. Castlereagh responded immediately.
33 *Report, supra* n. 31, pp 116–36, pp 348–50. The report noted, 'an indescribable emotion seized the House and gallery and every heart heaved in tributary pulsation to the name, the victors and the return to Parliament of the founder of the constitution of 1782' (p. 115). Grattan's followers had purchased a seat for him to enable him to return to Parliament after an absence of three years.

How greatly this differed from his triumphal cry of 1782, 'Ireland is now a nation!' But Arthur Browne could no longer support Grattan's romantic vision, which did not then exist, if it ever had. In a speech he likely gave on 16 Jan. 1800, he said he thought the union must at least be considered:

Doctor Browne, (College.) Real change of opinion after twelve months reflection, respect for the sentiments, of no considerable part of the nation, attention to his Majesty's repeated declarations that he thought union essential to the interests of the empire, might be adequate causes of men's now voting, at least to hear the propositions; indignation at the measures which were pursued after the rejection of the union last year, not by the chief governor [Corwallis], (whose conduct and character I have always admired and revered, and whose coming into this country I consider a blessing to it) but by Parliament, was the special cause which made me declare both in and out of the House, and write to several of my political friends last summer, that if ever propositions of union were brought on again, I would vote to hear what they were, as I thought our situation could scarcely be worse, and any report that hope, promise or inducement of any kind was held out to me to influence my vote, is inconsistent with my parliamentary conduct for seventeen years, and absolutely false and groundless. My vote this night leaves me as much at liberty to reject the propositions in toto, i.e. to vote against an union as ever I was in my life.

I always as I conceive have left myself unconfined as to considering this important subject, as I think every rational man should do: I am sure I have always intended to do so, and accordingly at the last general election, being the first interrogated upon the subject, I refused to bind myself, saying that I could not foresee all possible cases, but I did not conceive any probable, in which I could be brought to assent to such a measure. My present colleague [Knox], being next asked, put the case of preference to an union with France. I am positive that he first mentioned this as one instance, but I do not recollect in the least, nor do I believe that he or any of the candidates confined himself to that single possible case, and I am sure it is not conformable to the constant modes of thinking and resolutions which I have had upon the subject, nor did I ever hear it asserted that I had limited myself in any such manner till about two hours before the House met, nor ever dream of any person asserting or thinking so; if any words were written down, why were not the candidates furnished with a copy? And if it was so, how it happened, that no person ever reminded me of it; and in pursuance of the same principle, I did positively in Parliament, on the third day of the last session, when an attempt was made to exclude the question for ever, refuse to assent; and if my constituents thought I had bound myself, what occasion to address me on the subject, or why not remind me of this in the address.

Allegations of pledged hostility to union pursued Browne relentlessly:

Inconsistency of conduct is objected to me on three grounds: 1st, as to what passed at the election, to which I have answered: 2nd, as to my vote last year, to which I answer, that my speech at the time shews it was founded upon reasons and arguments adapted only to that time and occasion, except as to the competency of Parliament, on which I had serious doubts, which however I conceive must have been unfounded, as not a single man supported me in them: 3rd, as to the amendment last year proposed by the opponents of the union, going to bar it *in perpetuum* as much as that of this year, I do not conceive that it did. It is avowed to have that meaning at present. It was not so understood last year by me or by the Parliament, for they distinguished it from the resolution proposed on the third night of the Session, to which as being final, they refused to assent, and so did I in express words.

To a union in the abstract I am no friend; if I ever agreed to it, it would only be as to a lesser evil. I have ever wished to preserve the constitution of 1782, but I have ever thought that an union with England was preferable to some situations in which we have been. Not any union, but union upon great and comprehensive terms, made acceptable to all and every part of the nation. After the scenes which I beheld in this country during the rebellion and for some time after, I expressly declared to some very respectable and dignified friends who well remember it, that I thought such an union, under the then existing circumstances, desirable, and I never did at any time shew that heat and fury upon the subject which other men have done. The disposition of the college in general is against it, but so far from being universal, that nearly half of the governing part of the society favour it; and some leading members of it have said they would never vote for the man who opposed the union.

It doth not seem to me a good method of [preventing] the union, to persecute every man with calumny and abuse, who says that he thinks we ought to hear what England proposes, even though he rests that opinion merely on his notion of its propriety; if opposition to the union proceeds from love of the nation I respect it; if from regard to individual power or personal aggrandizement, I concern not myself about it.

One word to an insinuation, not very liberal, that I have lived on the bounty of a country to which I am ungrateful. Both parts of the assertion I deny. The fellow of a college who obtains his situation by hard labour and industry, purchases it, and no more lives on bounty than the lawyer or the rector. I am not so humble as to think that I could not obtain a competency in any country, nor did I come into this without one. Seventeen years disinterested service have not been ingratitude, though in some quarters they have met with it.

34 *Some documents, supra* n. 18, pp 1–5; *Report, supra* n. 31, pp 85–7.

I should be more affected by this kind of attack, if it did not proceed from
a gentleman notoriously a candidate for the college [W.C. Plunket], who
communicates with those of my constituents whose great industry is to
supplant me.[34]

It was at this point that Arthur Browne based his change of mind on the
Parliament's bloodthirsty vengeance on Catholic subjects and the failure of
Parliament to complete the emancipation of Catholics by repeal of the statutes that
prevented Catholics from sitting in Parliament:

Had I seen, after the rejection of the union last year, any measures brought
forward to conciliate the people, or to heal the distractions of the country;
had I seen any reviviscence of that spirit which produced the constitution of
1782, coming forward to preserve it; I should not have listened to proposals
of union, nor would you have again heard its name. But for gentlemen to
suppose that if Parliament doth not support itself, that it can be supported;
to suppose that without domestic virtue, the nation will trouble itself about
its existence, is absurd; the truth is, apathy is gone through the nation upon
the subject; the thing is evident; in 1782, the idea of union could not have
been brought forward; in 1785, it could not have been brought forward; why
can it now? Because then the Parliament had the warm affections of the
nation, and now it has not.

The remainder of his remarks were anticlimactic, having indicated the trend of
his thinking, after denouncing Parliament's indemnification of abusers of law and
order:

This language from me at least is not inconsistent; I have never said with one
side of the House, at one time that the Parliament was the most virtuous, at
another time the most vicious assembly upon earth; nor with the other, after
abusing it during my parliamentary life, hold it up as a paragon of virtue; I
have never been ready at one time to hang my friend [Grattan], or pull down
his picture, at another to hold him up as being from heaven; my mind is
more equable, and I have ever said, that if there was not renovation in the
Parliament, it must perish.

The method of preventing union was not by rebellion, nor by Orange
systems; not by looking for republics, nor by holding up every man as a
rebel, who disapproved of particular measures; it would have been by regular
obedience to the laws, and constitutional parliamentary opposition to any
improper measures.

He then indicted Parliament for its vengeance against the innocent:

The measures of last session, to which I have already alluded particularly, are
the rebellion bill and the Fitzgerald bill; the first, which I know was rather
forced upon the government than fought for by it, and which therefore is not

imputable to the executive power, enables any petty officer to take up any person on the vague charge of assisting the rebellion on his mere suspicion, founded on any foolish word or indiscreet trifling action, try him and execute him, without the possibility of appeal to any other tribunal. This law still exists – why do we not feel it? Why do we not know it? Why are we ignorant that we live under such power? Because the wisdom, the prudence, the temper, the humanity, the goodness of the chief governor prevent it; but can I forget that we live under such law; can I forget that the Parliament, while it contended against the ademption of its rights, voluntarily relinquished them all, or that to-morrow a hot or imprudent or weak successor might make us feel this unbounded power in its excess?

The other, which I call the Fitzgerald bill [to compensate a sheriff accused of atrocities], made for a particular instance, has, as it was thought it would, screened the greatest outrage upon private innocence that ever was known: give me leave to say to my certain knowledge no measure ever so much promoted the union, nor made so many converts among the dispassionate viewers of our conduct in England; and of that country permit me to say, the abuse upon this occasion neither tends to peace, nor is true – for I have found in it, and so I said a year ago to my constituents, more coolness, more kind disposition to Ireland, than among the sons of Ireland; and to represent it as always hostile to us evidently tends to separation.

Let me know before I reject union what is to follow: is it the old system? Is it the colonial system? Are we to see the chief governor with all his might holding in the reins of government to prevent absurd fury from plunging it again in scenes of blood and horror, which I do verily and in my conscience believe it would be at this moment, were it not for his prudence, wisdom and temper? On the other hand, let me wait to hear what are the terms of the union; is the Church of Ireland sufficiently protected? That being done, are all safe privileges given to all other his Majesty's subjects? If the city of Dublin is injured, are any measures taken to make it compensation? If the poor and peasantry of Ireland are to be injured by increase of absentees, is any additional provision made for them? Let me hear all this, and then determine, but not determine madly and unhearing. Doth the contrary conduct favour of private views or public affections? For my part, I will use my judgment coolly, regardless of abuse, if I justify myself to rational and dispassionate men. […]

If I have been guilty of any crime or any folly, it has been that of not following throughout my original sentiments, (which were in favour of an union, as I could shew by appeal to the first and purest men in the nation, ever since the rebellion broke out) and in suffering false complaisance to an ungrateful portion of my constituents, and foolish hopes of a renovation in the Parliament, to give me in the last session an appearance and in some measure the reality of holding for the time a different sentiment.[35]

35 *Some documents, supra* n. 18, pp 5–8.

The division was taken just before noon after the all-night session, resulting in a government victory by 138 negative votes against 96 votes for the motion. The opposition had lost and gained some votes: a difference of 10 from 1799, but the government had gained 33 votes from 1799. One of twelve 1799 opponents who changed his vote was Arthur Browne. (Not voting, however, were 62 members.)[36] The reason for Arthur Browne's change of mind was the failure of Parliament to address the hopes and needs of the nation. Not only did the Parliament make no effort to remedy any of the grievances of the majority of the population, it was willing to substitute martial law and military government for civil liberties. Thus, Arthur Browne came to believe that the Irish Parliament had forfeited the confidence of the people.[37]

Browne's subsequent appointments to the board of accounts in 1801 and the office of prime serjeant in 1802 were tainted with the scandal of the final corruption of the Irish Parliament. Yet these offices, although not paltry, hardly compare with the lavish rewards made by the government to change the votes of uncertain and uncommitted members. Arthur Browne's preeminence at the Bar and in teaching, together with his wide circle of friends, classmates and former students, would surely have guaranteed the few honours he received in the last years of his life. More importantly, Browne was deprived of his most valuable clients in 1800, losing his position as property agent for the bishops of the established church, surely not a sign of government favour.

Somerville and Ross absolve Browne of corruption in their biography of Charles Bushe:

William Conyngham [Plunket] began by falling upon the apostasy of Dr Arthur Browne, an American, member for the Dublin University, who having been a violent anti-unionist, had recently been moved … by sincere conviction to change his opinion. Having demolished the unhappy Browne with a completeness worthy of Attila the Scourge of God, Plunket proceeded to lay bare the past history of … the wicked plot of the union.[38]

In his first 1800 speech on the union, Browne was echoing the thought of Lord Cornwallis on his arrival in Dublin in June 1798:

---

36 *Report, supra* n. 15, p. 142.

37 See also, D. Mansergh, 'The union and the importance of public opinion' in D. Keogh and K. Whelan, *Acts of union*, p. 126 (2001).

38 E. Somerville and M. Ross, *An incorruptible Irishman: the life of Charles Bushe*, p. 122 (1932). Lord Chief Justice Bushe was an ancestor of both Edith Somerville and Violet Martin (alias Ross). Martin died in 1915, so much of this work was the product of 'automatic writing' and spiritualist seances rather than deep archival research. Charles Kendal Bushe (1767–1843) from Kilmurry (Kilkenny) entered TCD 1782, scholar 1784, AB 1788, Irish Bar 1790, MP for Callan 1796–9, Dongela 1799–1800, third serjeant 1805, solicitor general 1805–22, lord chief justice, king's bench 1822–41.

The principal persons of this country, and the members of both houses of Parliament are in general averse to all acts of clemency and would pursue measures that could only terminate in the extermination of the greater number of the inhabitants.[39]

Nevertheless, within a week of his delivery of the quoted speech, Browne received a letter signed by 45 constituents (of about 90 to 100 electors) – 9 junior fellows and 36 scholars – in which they complained that his speech and vote were not in accordance with a solemn promise at election time. The demand was clear: 'Determined as we are to reject as long as possible the suspicion that you are capable of acting in a manner so disgraceful to your character', they called on him to provide, 'mainly opposition to the measure of a legislative union with Great Britain'.[40]

Arthur Browne responded immediately. He denied the charge that he had promised to oppose union – 'though repeatedly applied to, I refuse[d] absolutely to bind myself on the subject, saying that I could not foresee all possible cases' – mentioning the names of electors who would support his recollection of the election meeting and members of Parliament who would recall that he had refused to bind himself in 1799 to perpetual opposition. He concluded that he would always attend to the wishes of all constituents, but that opposition to the union was not uniform in the college. He also noted that some of the signatures to the letter were not in the college at the time of the last election.[41]

Pursuant to the government plan to exclude the union from the viceroy's speech and devote a session entirely to it, Parliament reconvened on 5 February 1800 to consider the union; this time 50 of the January absentees attended. Another marathon debate followed Viscount Castlereagh's explanation of the treaty between Great Britain and Ireland to accomplish the union.[42] The speech was greeted sullenly by opponents, who were now helpless. The division in favour of the union was by 161 votes to 117.[43] (Five of those present did not vote.) Thomas Goold[44]

39 Letter from Cornwallis to the earl of Portland, 8 July 1798, as quoted in Bolton, *The passing of the Irish Act of Union*, p. 58 (1966).
40 *Some documents, supra* n. 18, pp 23–4.
41 Ibid., pp 25–9.
42 See *A report of the debate in the House of Commons in Ireland on 5 and 6 February 1800*, pp 15–37 (1800). The proposed treaty language is at pp 29–37. Beyond parliamentary union, the treaty dealt with union of the established churches (Article 5), customs union (Article 6) and the national debt (Article 7). The treaty enacted by the Irish Parliament is 40 Geo. 3 c. 38.
43 Ibid., p. 88.
44 Thomas Goold (1766–1846), from Cork, entered TCD as senior commoner in 1781, AB 1786, AM 1791, called to the Irish Bar in 1791. A political follower of Grattan, he travelled to revolutionary Paris and published *In defence of Burke's reflections on the French Revolution*. He was renowned as a great wit and a flamboyant orator. He influenced the resolution of the Dublin Bar against the union on 9 Dec. 1798 and published, *An address to the people of Ireland on the subject of the proposal projected union*. His anti-union colleagues purchased the borough seat of Kilbeggan for him and he entered Parliament in February 1800 to vote against the union (and confront Browne).

challenged Browne as a foreigner waging a war of words against the liberties of Ireland. (The 'foreign charge' had also been made by W.C. Plunket seeking Browne's seat for TCD.) Goold said he had been an eyewitness when Browne had 'entered into the most solemn engagement' with his constituents three years earlier to oppose the union. Doctor Duigenan denied that parliamentary representatives were bound by the instructions of their constituents. Goold returned to the attack on Browne, despite calls for order, to silence him. Goold concluded:

> I will proceed undismayed and unintimidated by any man or set of men, when the rights of the people are at issue; and I do say that he who derelicts from a solemn test, not only violates the duty of a representative, but also the laws which are obligatory on a man of honor.

Fighting to preserve his honour and reputation from the allegations that he had pledged to vote against the union, Browne offered the testimony of a senior barrister, Robert French,[45] who was present at the 1797 election, that Browne did not bind himself for or against the union:

> Mr Browne appealed to the House, if he had not studiously avoided all species of personality; besides that he trusted that such a conduct was foreign to the natural bent of his mind, he felt himself delicately circumstanced with respect to the consequences which might result without the walls of that House. He denied that he had ever subscribed to any test, or had pledged himself to his constituents as to any line of parliamentary conduct. At the time of his election the idea of a union was considered ridiculous; but even so he would not suffer his freedom of opinion and judgment to be fettered. To establish this he read a letter from Counsellor French of Kildare Street, who had been professionally engaged in the election [by the provost]. He acknowledged that a numerical majority of his constituents were adverse to an union, but he averred that the most important portion, and those the most deeply interested, the governing members [senior fellows] were all, except one, decided friends to the measure. As to the personality against him, which an hon. gentleman was pleased to indulge in, he would pass it by with the same indifference that he would the babbling of a parrot.

Following the 5 February government victory, other efforts to defeat the union failed by similar substantial majorities, and the threat of mob violence also receded because of displays of the British military. As the government could depend on at least fifty votes more than the opposition, the treaty proceeded through the Commons at an easier pace. Even emotional issues, such as the temporary unseating of the speaker (John Foster, a committed opponent of union), and

---

45 Robert French (1745–?), from County Roscommon, entered TCD as pensioner 1759, scholar 1762, AB 1764, called to the Bar from the Inner Temple in 1767. He had an extensive practice in wills and estates from chambers on Kildare Street.

adjournment to prevent presentation of anti-union petitions, could not break government's fifty-member majority.[46]

After the government's success, when surely Browne must have suspected the massive expenditures in cash, as well as promotions and perquisites, to which previous speakers had alluded, he attempted to marshal arguments in favour of the union including prospective Catholic emancipation by the Westminster Parliament, on 18 February 1800:

> Doctor Browne, (College.) Said that he persisted in his opinion that Parliament should go through the consideration of all the propositions, though, until they came out of the mill and it was seen how they might be modified by Parliament, it was impossible for any man to say whether he would ultimately approve the mass; but in this his mind was now settled, that under the existing circumstances, union, if upon good terms, was desirable as a refuge from ruin, and therefore he must wish and hope that the terms should come out such as might be advantageous and acceptable to the nation. He never had disguised the great foundation of his opinion, however un-polite or unpalatable it might be; it rested on long observation of the state of the country and of the state of Parliament, and particularly of what happened in the last session.
>
> Ever since I sat in this house, [I have] condemned the system of Parliament; [the rotten boroughs] I said it must end in its extinction. I did, when the rebellion broke out, though I abhorred and shuddered at the atrocities of the rebels, think that many things were done in and after its suppression more founded in resentment and rage than in cool and sound policy; but even supposing those severities necessary, I do not wish to see them repeated: it may be necessary to cut off an arm or a leg, but I do not wish to see the operation; and these two abuses, the corruptions of Parliament and the scenes of the rebellion, have given to my mind this bias to an union.

He again condemned parliamentary vengeance on the innocent:

> When the present chief governor [Cornwallis] came over, and wished to appease those evils, I naturally approved his measures, and I became warmly attached to his person; his candour, his goodness and his wisdom attached me, and no other motive. I did then think that union was necessary, and I said so to many respectable persons who well remember it: when the measure actually came on, I thought the nation was taken unawares and had not proper time; I had doubts of the competency of Parliament; I felt a temporary hope that experience would teach us the absolute necessity of altering the system of Parliament, and departing from the system of violence if we wished to preserve the Parliament; and perhaps false complaisance to a

---

46 *Report of the debate in the House of Commons in Ireland on 14 February 1800*, p. 83.

portion of my constituents had some effect in counteracting my real opinion; the Parliament instantly afterwards returned to its old systems; violence and bills of violence were redoubled with multiplying force; most of the opponents of union were as ready to agree in them as any other men; an absolute military government was established, under which we still live, though happily so administered that we do not feel it; every thing returned to its former state, and I returned to my former opinion; in so doing I do not think I have been inconsistent; I do not differ in opinion from other gentlemen who have condemned the systems of Parliament; we differ only in inference; they think it will be better, I am convinced it never will, and therefore act accordingly.

He derided the opponents of union in 1800:

But as to the greater part of the gentlemen who oppose the union, hear what their language is; we are in opposition only on this one measure; we do not oppose it to save the people from taxation: no, there is no quantity of taxation and contribution which they are not willing to give; is it to save the people from power? No, there is no power which they are not willing to part with, even the very whole power of the Parliament and all its control to the executive; is it to save the people from the scourge? No, they are ready and will re-enact all the laws of the last session in the present: ask for a window tax, calculate it at what you please, let it produce five times as much, we have no objection; ask for unlimited powers, you need not ask for them, we would force them on you; do you complain of the Parliament having the power of war and peace? We engage never to exert it; do you complain of its having power to appoint a regent? We will disclaim it; all the properties of a free and independent Parliament we will give up, but leave us the name: are these arguments to be addressed to the people of Ireland? What doth it all come to? 'Leave us to our power and individual importance, let us recur to the old colonial method of governing or rather grinding the country, and we do not care what you do.' When I saw and when I heard these things, is it wonderful that I did not find myself much attached to an opposition to union upon such principles; no men have been more effective in bringing us to the necessity of union by mistaken and severe modes of government than these very gentlemen.

It has been said that I pass a libel on the Parliament; I do not mean to do so; if I did, this should not be the place; I am not ambitious of being sent to prison, or of kneeling at your bar; but every one must laugh at the encomiums passed on the Parliament out of doors, by those who for twenty years have been representing it as the great nuisance and grievance of the nation, and who now speak of it as the paragon of virtue, as the quintessence of excellence, as the paradise of disinterestedness; I know not what epithet of Oriental hyperbole they would not bestow upon it; *timeo Danaos [et dona ferentes]*; give me leave to suspect these praises; they want the Parliament, not because they love it, but as a theatre for future machinations and dangerous designs.

He then had to confront the reputation of the English Parliament and speculate on the union Parliament:

> But it is said is the English Parliament better? I believe it is infinitely; but if it were not, what would that argument go to; it might go to the extinction of parliaments altogether. I cannot help it, said the good Bishop Butler, when arguing for the immortality of the soul he was told, why this will prove dogs and horses to be immortal; I cannot help it, if the argument be a good one, it must remain so, I say if I were writing an Utopia, I would say if ever the time came that Parliament served as a stalking horse under which to shoot the arrows of the executive, as a name under which the executive might do what it would not dare to without its influenced sanction, or, as a circus, in which to combat for the destruction of the constitution, I should think the existence of that Parliament of little consequence; this is not the case of the English Parliament; I do not presume to say that it is of any other.
>
> But would the English united Parliament be kinder to this country? No man seems to dare to answer the question; I will answer it – I believe in my heart and soul it would – the reason is plain, because it would not be actuated by those passions, those resentments, that thirst for revenge, that rooted memory of injuries which exists here. We have heard it this night lamented, that persons who are said to have been in rebellion were suffered to open their mouths; we hear it every day in conversation lamented that they are suffered to open their mouths; we hear it every day in conversation lamented that they are suffered to exist; what! Was there to be no amnesty, no pardon, no oblivion, no termination to these distractions? Yet this is natural, it is incident to human nature; and therefore I say, men at a distance, more cool, less impassioned, will think more kindly of the gross of the inhabitants of this country, and I do assert that in all my intercourse with the English I have found them more reasonable, more compassionate, more kindly disposed to the people and the peasantry of this country than are its own gentry.
>
> England is perpetually spoken of as a foreign, nay as an hostile country; does this lead to peace? Is it wise? Is it true? The policy of England to us was false for 600 years! It was; but has she not for a long time past acknowledged her error, retracted her claims and altered her system; and what is the wisdom of perpetually reminding a sincere friend of old bickerings and ancient errors; in commercial concerns there may be some jealousy of England, let this be well watched in the articles of union; but in all other respects I cannot conceive why England should possibly entertain any sentiments hostile to us, and every man conversant in England knows the contrary to be the fact.
>
> But of all the charges against England, the most audacious as most false is in my opinion that of her causing or fomenting the disturbances and

distractions of this country; let any man lay his hand upon his heart and say that he really believes this: Good heaven, Sir, have we occasion to look abroad for the causes of our dissentions? – do we not know and see every moment the bitter animosities of Catholic to Protestant and Protestant to Catholic, of ancient inhabitants to modern settlers, of old claimants to new possessors, of tenants who think themselves oppressed and landlords who complain of murder and massacre, of rebels to loyalists, and loyalists to rebels? What has England to say to all this? Did England create Catholics? Did England create Orange men? Did England create men's hearts or their passions? No, England is endeavouring to do all she can to allay and prevent these distractions; and the passions, the prejudices and the fury of the Parliament, the gentry and the people of Ireland, stand in her way.

See how just is this accusation; she sends over a chief governor here on purpose to cool and moderate and quiet and allay those furious animosities, and for that very reason a party is made against him by the very men who complain of England's fomenting our disorders; had that great man yielded to the violence of such advisers, perhaps he would not have found so many opponents to an union.

He must hear the voice of the Irish nation on Parliament or union:

Foolish and deluded people of Ireland, I cannot help exclaiming! I know your virtues, I know your spirit, but surely a more versatile people never was seen upon the face of the earth! You seem in love with oppression, and when a power comes here which endeavors to extricate you from it, you long to return to those scourgings and whippings and burnings which first disgusted me into the support of union, and like a Russian wife seem to like those best who beat you most, and surely you will find them among its opponents.

I think therefore in favouring an union I am a friend to the people; but if they are of a contrary opinion, if they wish, as the king of Prussia said of the people of Neuschâtel, to be damned to all eternity, I cannot help it, and should be sorry that they were forced or made by violence even to be happy; but let me first hear the voice of the nation: I hear the voice of violence, I hear the voice of party, I hear the voice of lawyers bawling because their [market] will be gone and of politicians because their personal importance will be lessened, but I cannot hear the cool, sober voice of the nation at large.

I must next avert to the inflammatory language heard in this place; men admit the competency of Parliament, and yet say they will not obey it; they say Parliament is wise and good, and yet the next moment they will not submit to it! But, say they, it is influenced and packed; this is not very consistent, but if this be so it ought to be reformed or to be extinguished; say they, it is not free: there are different modes of affecting its freedom, it may be influenced by government or intimidated by mobs, seats may be filled by administration or bought up by the purse of a party; a man's freedom is not a little affected, if following his own sentiments is to be followed by calumniating his character or knocking him on the head. And here give me leave to say, that the vile calumny, the monstrous abuse, the lying slander cast upon every man who is friendly to an union, is one reason which gives me a strong bias to it; that cause is not good which requires such supports.

Another thing which has been truly observed gives me a strong bias to an union; it is that, however loyal men disagree upon the subject, the disaffected have no difference; it was said they would be delighted with the measure as leading to separation; I have not found it – on the contrary they are outrageous against it: must not I think that measure a guard against separation which the friends of separation so vehemently detest.

But the details of the union must be carefully examined and negotiated:

As to the propositions of union themselves in detail, there are some things which I dislike, and many which I would wish to see modified; I wish the peers were not to be elected for life; I wish the boroughs were not to be bought, or if it must be so, that it had been a private transaction, and I even think it would have been wise in England to have done it with her own money, not to give pretence for discontent at the burthen in this country; I have some doubts whether our quota or proportion of taxation of two seventeenths may not be too much, and I am extremely anxious that something very considerable indeed should be done for the city of Dublin: I wish the city would point out itself what it thinks most for its advantage, and I think the Parliament should be most liberal and go [to] great lengths indeed in making compensation to it, if it is likely to suffer [by the end of the Irish Parliament].

Union would be the answer to the disaffection of the majority. He could not foresee the intransigence of the mad king.

I have the honour of being descended from a long series of clergymen of the Church of England and must naturally be attached to it, but I do not see what mischief could ensue, if after an union the Catholics were put on the same footing with any other dissenters from the established church; at present, if admitted into Parliament, they might acquire too much weight in this isolated kingdom and danger might ensue, but then they would have exactly the proportionable weight in the whole empire which they ought to have, neither more nor less; they would have no pretext for complaint, but be exactly on a footing with all other his majesty's subjects: why then is not this done? I verily believe because an Irish Parliament would not suffer it; in the united one it is open to be done: no, says one honourable gentleman, this excludes the Catholics for ever; no, says another, my objection is that this doth not exclude them for ever. These are contrary objections, but I think the latter assertion is evidently true, and therefore I hope and think that the united Parliament will do that with safety which the Irish Parliament always has refused to do as dangerous.

And now, Sir, with all these objections, give me leave to ask, if union be rejected what system is to be pursued? I may object to parts of the proposals, but I must wish on the whole that they should be acceptable, because otherwise what follows? Says an honourable friend of mine, an union must be followed by a completely military government, I hope not; but what will the rejection of union be followed by? An infinitely more military government fought for and approved by most of those men who oppose the union, by the re-enaction and continuation of all the severe laws of former years, by all the ancient severity, by the old colonial system, probably by a revival of all the horrors and distractions which we have not long since escaped.

As I fear this city may be injured, though not in the degree which wild imagination represents, I own the apprehension lest I should by my vote injure one tradesman or his family in the city of Dublin affects my mind more than all the declamations which could be made for years about the free and independent Parliament which I never saw and never shall see, and about the pride of the nation opposed to its felicity: but are not the poor of Dublin as wretched now as they can be; I know much about them, I have felt much for them, according to my ability have endeavoured to shew it; can an union make them worse? I hope not, I hope it may bring in that capital and those manufacturers which are wanted to make their condition better; at all events, how can they be worse off than now without an union; we may talk of union, but the ladies of Dublin might, by adopting a single fashion, by not flying to foreign manufacturers, by wearing the really beautiful dresses of their own country, do more for the poor of Dublin in a year than an union could effect against them in ten; there is one of our misfortunes, it is absolutely wicked, and I never see the present dresses of the female sex without melancholy and sorrow.

He does not fear Catholic emancipation in a United Kingdom:

One word more as to the Catholics; I am a sincere Protestant, not like many, a merely political but a religious Protestant, with opinions founded on reason, study and reflection; but I wish that every privilege should be granted to the Catholics consistent with the safety of the establishment, for to the establishment also on much reflexion I am a steady friend.

Every body says we cannot go on as we have done, yet no new plan is proposed by the opposers of union; in fact they never could agree upon one: the major part are of opinion that union is not necessary, that if they had been let alone they would have kept down the country with a strong hand as has been done for one hundred years past, and that nothing was wanting but not to have stopt them in the career of whipping, scourging, shooting and burning, and refusal of all amnesty, to bring matters to their old footing, they, therefore, will wish to return to their old measures; the rest will be for redress of grievances, and the old question of Catholic emancipation will instantly be revived; in truth I think it follows inevitably that we must incorporate with the Catholics: to give them a liberty of getting into Parliament while the boroughs continue as they are would be trifling and mockery; they therefore must wish for reform. Thus all the old questions will be revived, all the old distractions; and after three, or four, or six years misery, the whole property of the nation, or at least the Protestant part of it, will recur back to union as the only resource.

Such is the picture which I form to myself of future events in case this measure be rejected, and under these impressions, as I have said, though I may disapprove of parts of the detail, I must necessarily wish that the whole may be so modified as to meet the wishes of the nation and pass into stability.[47]

After the decisive February votes, Arthur Browne revealed his thoughts about the distractions of Ireland in 4 March 1800 business correspondence for the college, to an unnamed addressee:

Dear Sir,
I beg leave to inform you, by direction of the board, in answer to the first part of your letter, that the whole sum to be paid for renewing your lease is £1996 3s. 10½d. i.e. within four pounds of two thousand pounds and ten years of the lease have expired. One of our tenants, Mr Gunn of Henly [?] has let his lease run out, & we have to advertise the lands, I never knew such a case before. As to the other part, my dear sir, give me leave to heartily congratulate myself, that you agree in opinion with me as to the union. I have always thought it the only thing for Ireland, & if I have a little disguised my sentiments, it was from false and foolish compliance to my constituents. I think it is the best thing under the existing circumstances for Ireland, & particularly for the Protestants of Ireland, & I am convinced everybody will think by and by. I cannot bring myself to praise and flatter Parliament, after we have so long & so long firstly abused it.

I am sorry they are taking the good men from your regiment, which was a very fine one, yet I own I am not partial to the system of militia, & particularly of the Irish militia. I prefer troops of the line, but perhaps I am wrong.

I shall always, dear sir, be extremely eager to retain your good opinion. Indeed I do not find that I have lost that of my old friends, tho I differ from them in sentiment, & the heat of the times is immoderate. I have the honor [*sic*] to be

47 *Some documents, supra* n. 18, pp 9–21; *Report, supra* n. 42, pp 74–80. The government's majority on the motion was 46 (161 against, 115 in favour). *Report,* p. 83.

With great respect
Your obliged and obedient servant

Arthur Browne.

The House resolved into committee of the whole to deal with details of the relations between Ireland and Great Britain under the union, and government continued to prevail by even larger margins as opponents became absentees. Arthur Browne's conversion to the union did not change his opposition to Protestant vengeance on Catholics, as he continued to oppose immunity (38 Geo. 3 c.74 and 39 Geo. 3 c.55) for Fitzgerald, the sadistic sheriff of Tipperary in April 1800.

The completed union bill was given its first reading on 21 May 1800, resulting in an easy victory by vote of 160 in favour to 100 opposed. It was at this time that Browne made his last parliamentary speech, denying that his vote for the union had been purchased by the government after an insinuation to that effect by John Ball,[48] member for Drogheda, and a strong opponent of the union. Browne reviewed his parliamentary career since the Revolution of 1798:

> Dr Browne said it was not his intention to have trespassed upon the attention of the House, but an honourable gentleman [Mr Ball] had made some observations so personal to him that he could not avoid saying a few words. The honourable and learned gentleman had stated that he [Dr Browne] before he supported the measure of union had made a bargain with government; he begged leave flatly to deny the assertion; he sincerely wished that every thing that had passed between government and him was known to all the world, and he was sure his character would not suffer, nor the motives which led him to support this measure be questioned after such a disclosure, which would do honour to both parties. The attack which the honourable gentleman had made upon him was of a nature more calculated to excite his laughter than any other sensation; sometimes he was represented as being desirous of being a bishop, sometimes a judge, and sometimes a provost; he confessed he never had any objection to the dignities which the gentleman so liberally conferred, if they were attainable with honour, but he solemnly denied that he had made any thing like terms with government, or was actuated by any such unworthy motive in the support he gave to this measure. He believed he might without impropriety state the only conversation he had with the noble lord [Castlereagh] previous to the introduction of this subject; the noble lord, with a proper respect to the members of that House, enquired the sentiments of every gentleman upon

48 John Ball (1754–?) entered TCD as pensioner in 1771, scholar 1774, was called to the Irish Bar in 1778. He practised at the Bar in Dublin. He was sometimes a follower and sometimes an opponent of Speaker Foster, representing County Louth. He won a by-election for Drogheda in 1796. He denounced the union as 'an absolute subjection to the will and uncontrolled dominion of a superior'.

the important question of the union with England; upon that occasion he did declare his sentiments to the noble lord to be decidedly in favour of the measure; he confessed that afterwards, in compliance with the wishes of his constituents, he had foolishly opposed his own opinion by voting against the discussion of union; he was not afraid to state the whole of his conduct upon this subject to the House and the world.

He disputed the interpretation given to his remarks fifteen years previously:

> The honourable and learned gentleman had alluded to the language which he held upon the propositions in the year 1785; he was ready to avow every word he had said upon that occasion; he did oppose them, because he considered them as an attack upon the freedom of the Irish legislature; but what similarity was there between that measure and the present; nothing but a complete confusion of ideas could lead any man to confound them together. He was willing to confess that he was no friend to union in the abstract, and that he was convinced if good councils had been adopted the measure would not have been necessary; but on the termination of the late rebellion he was convinced of the necessity of an union. He knew the sentiments he was delivering would not be pleasing to either side of the House, but he was at that time convinced that the extremities and violence to which some of the Orangemen went, together with the excesses of the rebels, endangered the existence of the country; the name of Orangeman had been abused; in the true original sense of the word he was proud to state himself an Orangeman [a supporter of King William in 1689]. When the question was brought forward, he had, as he before stated, voted in compliance with the sentiments of his constituents against the measure; but when he saw of what discordant materials the opposition was formed, when he saw that all its new assistants only opposed the union because they thought it would diminish their own power, he determined never to act with them again. Though he differed from many gentlemen in this country in his opinion upon this subject, he was happy to find that he agreed with persons of the greatest eminence in England, with whom he was always proud to concur in sentiment – he alluded particularly to Earl Moira and Earl Fitzwilliam, who appeared to him to object not to the principle but to the time.

He then challenged the major assertion of the opposition:

> He begged now to take notice of an assertion made by the gentlemen on the other side of the House, and which they had repeated so often that they really seemed to believe it themselves, viz. that the people of this country were decidedly against the measure; he had never heard any other proof of this circumstance than the assertion of the gentlemen themselves: indeed, there was every reason to believe that the very reverse was the fact, for if the

country had been as decidedly hostile to measure as it had been represented, it would not be so tranquil as it now is; was it not supposed that on the last circuit the country would have been worked up into a state of agitation against the union? And yet the most perfect tranquility had prevailed. In the year 1780, when Ireland demanded a free trade, it was the voice of the whole people, and it was irresistible; in 1782, when she demanded the repeal of the 6th Geo. 1st [the Poyning's Law enforcement] it was also the voice of the whole people, and was consequently irresistible; and if the union with England was as contrary to the sentiments of the people as had been represented, no minister, whatever his power in Parliament might be, could possibly carry it; if the people were not in favour of the union, at least they were indifferent to it.

The gentlemen on the other side were very fond of appealing to the people, and language was frequently used of the most inflammatory tendency. He remembered, when some time ago he opposed the measures of Lord Westmorland and Lord Camden, some of the gentlemen now in opposition applied very strong epithets to him, but by their conduct upon this occasion they had shewn that it was only some kind of rebellion to which they were averse.

Gentlemen professed to appeal to the people; he would willingly appeal to any peasant of common understanding upon this question, and would ask him what he most feared as the consequence of an union – an increase of his tythes, his rent, or his taxes? With respect to his tythes he would not be put in a worse state by a union, and the late bill would place him even in a better situation. As to rent, perhaps he differed from many gentlemen upon this subject, but one of his strongest reasons for supporting this measure was that he thought it would have the effect of reducing the rents in Ireland, and this he thought would be of advantage to the country, because at present the rents bore no proportion to the profits of the land; he was persuaded that after an union rent would decrease, because hitherto land was the only commodity at market; but the increase of manufactures and of capital would lower the revenue and increase the value of the land. With regard to taxes, he should be glad to know what tax the people of this country were ever saved from by the Parliament except only the absentee tax.

He had but one observation more to make; gentleman were much in the habit of wishing to make personal attacks upon him; he was not ashamed to say that he feared God; if not the scriptures had told him that at the last day heaven would be ashamed of him; he was not afraid to observe that from his peculiar situation, as senior fellow of a college, decorum made it particularly incumbent upon him not to seek for quarrels; nor was he forgetful that the knowledge that a duel might deprive him of £700 a year made adventuring adversaries particularly courageous in seeking for so unequal a combat; he spoke boldly because he felt he was no coward, and he believed every man felt it; but while at the same time he was conscious that there were situations arising accidentally and involuntarily between gentlemen which are much to be lamented, and to real spirit difficult to be resisted; he was free to own, that if any man vented his cool blooded, interested, and premeditated malice upon him, and much more if he was the poor instrument of the malice of others, he would treat his impotent assault with silent contempt.[49]

In this pathetic end to his parliamentary career Browne spoke of his contempt of those who accused him of accepting government bribery, and offered the opportunity for the ritual challenge to his word 'liar', even though his position in the college prevented him from being the challenger.

Browne had referred to the recent duel, in February, between Henry Grattan and Isaac Corry, newly become chancellor of the exchequer, replacing the ousted Parnell, after a long career in opposition. Corry had implied that Grattan was a confidante of United Irishmen, and therefore a traitor. Grattan responded that Corry had sold out like a parasite or panderer. At that time this reckless verbal exchange in Parliament could only be resolved on the 'field of honour'. In the duel by pistols, Corry missed, but Grattan's shot hit Corry in the arm; a second round did no damage and the affair concluded with an insincere reconciliation of the former friends.[50] No member challenged Arthur Browne.

Inflammatory oratory and delaying motions by opponents of union marked the second reading on 26 May. The third reading on 7 June was anticlimactic as opposition members fled from the House in such numbers that the measure was declared adopted without a division.[51]

The king gave the royal assent on 1 July, and the Irish Parliament closed on 1 August 1800. The new nation of the United Kingdom of Great Britain and Ireland came into existence on 1 January 1801, and the Kingdom of Ireland and its Parliament ceased to exist. No celebrations accompanied the national humiliation. No new election was held to select the 100 Irish members for the Westminster Parliament; a complex lottery scheme was devised to create the Irish delegation; where the district's representation was reduced to one member, a drawing was held to select the single member. No election was held until July 1802.[52]

In 1800 Browne published a twenty-four-page pamphlet, *Remarks on the terms of the union*. He sought to prove that his assent to the terms of the union was not 'blindly implicit or servilely universal'. He was not alarmed by the paucity of representatives in the Westminster Commons (100 Irish members) so long as there

49 *Some documents, supra* n. 18, pp 17–23.
50 R.B. McDowell, *Grattan: a life*, pp 166–7 (2001). Barrington, Castlereagh, Clonmell, Curran, Duigenan, FitzGibbon, Flood, Hely-Hutchinson and many members of Parliament fought duels. See J. Kelly, *That damned thing called honour: duelling in Ireland, 1570–1860*, pp 191–212 (1995). Duelling was always popular, but had declined in the last decade of the eighteenth century. Dr Kelly analyzed 113 reported duels: 45 occurred in Dublin and 29 in Munster; of the participants, 70 were gentlemen, 46 military officers and 14 lawyers; 24 of the duels resulted in fatalities, mostly by pistols (pp 213–14).
51 40 Geo. 3 c. 38. Geoghegan, *The Irish Act of Union*, pp 107–111 (1999).
52 40 Geo. 3 c. 38, §VIII. Lecky, *supra* n. 15, p. 410.

were 'men acquainted with the local interests of each county or great town in Ireland, and empowered to communicate them to Parliament at large', because 'the general advantage of the empire' rather than local interests will be considered.

Catholics would be admitted 'to a full participation of political advantages' without peril to the whole empire where 'they then might safely share in that due proportion of weight which their numbers in the ordinary course of things would possess'. His greatest anxiety was for the city of Dublin, 'dispeopled' and impoverished in those miserable habitations, which 'makes my heart bleed', but he foresaw the development of the port, canals and manufacturers to which government was pledged. Concerning finances, he challenged the idea that 'separate interests, exchequers, debts and revenues require separate Parliaments', by comparison to the operation of the Scottish exchequer and commissioners of revenue – these institutions that will remain separate in Ireland.

He ended with the thought that although the constitution of 1782 was to be eternal, no one could forsee that further alterations might be required by future contingencies. He noted the musings of an American commercial friend (whose Constitution was a mere eleven years old), who could not understand why Irishmen would reject the blessings of union, saying, 'You have sacrificed riches and comfort for pride.'

III. AFTERMATH OF UNION

The union of the kingdom of Ireland with the kingdom of Great Britain in 1801 was intended to bring an end to rebellion and disaffection in Ireland. It did not; it eventually produced famine, poverty, emigration and war.

The world situation was bleak in 1801, as the new United Kingdom of Great Britain and Ireland began. The (second) coalition of France's enemies – Russia, Great Britain, Austria, the Two Sicilies, Portugal and Turkey – had come apart, and Britain alone faced a powerful France. Britain's struggle with France had become an unwinnable war, with conflicts occurring almost simultaneously in the North Atlantic, the Baltic, Holland, Switzerland, Italy, the western Mediterranean, Egypt, South Africa, India and the Caribbean.[53] On the home front, prosecutions of the London Corresponding Society members for high treason had previously failed, but now succeeded.[54] Continued fear of a French invasion required a

---

53 Ehrman, 3 *The younger Pitt*, pp 363–411 (1996). P. Mackesy, *War without victory: the downfall of Pitt, 1799–1802* (1984).

54 Ehrman, 3 *The younger Pitt*, pp 116–17, 304–6 (1996). W. Hague, *William Pitt the younger*, pp 297–9 (2005). Prosecutions of radical leaders Thomas Hardy, Horne Tooke and John Thewall resulted in acquittals in 1794 by London juries, after which nine further prosecutions were abandoned. In 1798, the 'Margate Five' were prosecuted for treason; James Coigley was convicted and hanged, but four were acquitted. See C. Emsley, 'Repression "terror" and the rule of law in England during the decade of the French Revolution', 100 *Eng. Hist. Rev.*, 801–25 (1985).

defensive force of about 250,000 men – army, militias and irregulars – to be on duty in England.[55]

One of the immediate consequences of the union was the loss of office of William Pitt, architect and engineer of the union, after seventeen years in power – eight as war leader in the struggle with French revolutionaries. While there are other explanations for Pitt's resignation – physical debility, the need for peace with France and mistrust of George III and his unconstitutional actions – there is no question that the actual precipitating factor was Irish Catholic emancipation (i.e. the right to sit in Parliament).[56] Before the introduction of the measure in Parliament, King George III had expressed violent disapproval of the measure in public – 'I shall look on every man as my personal enemy who proposes that question to me.'[57] Pitt had become unalterably fixed on Catholic emancipation after the success of the union, and he resigned 5 February 1801.

Pitt asked to be relieved of the burdens of office if the king's objections to Catholic emancipation could not be removed or diminished. George III happily accepted Pitt's suggestion and had already decided on Henry Addington, speaker of the House of Commons and an opponent of Catholic emancipation, as Pitt's chosen successor, just before a brief return of the madness of 1788–9. By 14 March 1801, the king had recovered his sanity and Pitt left office.[58] Resignations by Cornwallis (27 April), Castlereagh and other ministers followed.

There is no question that Arthur Browne received two lucrative appointments from Dublin Castle after the union, for both of which he was well qualified: member of the board of accounts (1801), which he surrendered to be appointed prime serjeant at the beginning of 1802. It is in the sense of the loss of his parliamentary seat and his legal qualifications that the viceroy justified his appointment as 'satisfying the engagement to Dr Browne in his own profession'.[59]

Political opposition to the union was not eternal. Former borough owners – both those in favour and those opposed to union – eagerly accepted their compensation of £7,500 to £15,000 each. Within a short time, the most vociferous opponents were accepting offices from the crown: Charles Bushe became attorney general and later chief justice of Ireland; John Philpot Curran became master of the rolls; William Plunket became solicitor general, attorney general, chief justice and lord

55 Ehrman, 3 *The younger Pitt*, pp 115–26 (1996). Hilton, *A mad, bad, and dangerous people?*, pp 91–8 (2006).

56 Ehrman, 3 *The younger Pitt*, pp 495–533 (1996). See also R. Willis, 'William Pitt's resignation in 1801: re-examination and document', 44 *Bulletin Inst. Hist. Research*, 239–57 (1971).

57 The king used the same expression ('personal enemy') with respect to Charles James Fox in 1783 concerning the proposed India bill. See J. Derry, *Charles James Fox*, p. 186 (1972).

58 Ehrman, *The younger Pitt*, pp 508–23 (1999). Henry Addington (1757–1844), son of a famous London physician, was educated at Oxford (Brasenose), AB 1778, entered Parliament from a pocket borough in 1784, speaker 1789–1801. See P. Ziegler, *Addington* (1965).

59 Letter from Lord Hardwicke to the secretary of state, 26 Dec. 1801, Hardwicke Papers, British Library, Add. MS 35, 732, f. 12, as cited in A. Hart, *A history of the king's serjeants at law in Ireland*, pp 104–5 (2000).

chancellor; John Foster became chancellor of the Irish exchequer; and George Ponsonby became lord chancellor of Ireland. At Westminster in 1801, 46 of the 100 Irish members had voted against the union in 1800.

Jonah Barrington,[60] sometimes admiralty judge, gossip and raconteur of the eighteenth-century foibles to a righteous nineteenth-century audience, had lists of those members of Parliament who could be bought (and their price), and those who could not be bought. He viewed Browne's change of vote as 'one of the most unexpected and flagitious acts of public corruption'. The modern historians of Trinity College, however, take a different view. Professors McDowell and Webb say:

> On the question of the union he [Arthur Browne] hesitated for some time, but at the final vote, although he realized that most of his constituents took a contrary view, he came down in favour of it from a conviction that it gave the best promises of peaceful progress for Ireland.

They concluded that the only thing Arthur Browne received for his affirmative vote for the union was the loss of his seat in Parliament.[61]

60 Jonah Barrington (see chapter 14, n. 24).
61 McDowell and Webb, *Trinity College Dublin, 1592–1952*, p. 81. The obituary in *Fowler's Dublin Journal* (June 1805) said: 'Upon the great question of union, he thought (as he always thought for himself) that it was the only measure which promised security to the constitution in church and state and tranquility to the country, despite the calumny, by an active and malignant party, he gave to the measure of union, the full support of his vote and his talent.'

CHAPTER FOURTEEN

Last honours and death (1801–5)

WHEN THE UNION GOVERNMENT began on 1 January 1801, Arthur Browne was no longer a member of Parliament. In the 1797 election, he had been re-elected, and a new and popular young colleague, George Knox, who was connected to the duke of Abercorn, also had been elected. Browne and Knox originally opposed the union in 1799, but in 1800 Browne voted in favour of the union while Knox abstained. The union reduced the Dublin University representation to one member, and there was no new election for the single seat.[1] It is unclear whether they cast lots for the seat as was done in some cases, or whether Browne simply declined to be a candidate for a costly exile in London. The electors certainly still felt betrayed by Browne's changed vote in 1800. George Knox went to Westminster, rather than Arthur Browne.

There was, however, in the union campaign, the provision for compensation for lost perquisites, which was the reason for payments to borough owners who lost their parliamentary seats and office holders whose functions ceased to exist when the Irish Parliament disappeared. The new Parliament of the United Kingdom of Great Britain and Ireland had only 100 Irish members of its House of Commons (62 county members, 37 borough members, 1 from Trinity) instead of the 300 members of the Dublin House of Commons. The membership of the House of Lords was reduced to 32 from the 85 in Dublin, of whom four were bishops of the established church serving in rotation, and 28 were elected for life by their fellows. To the eighteenth-century mind, parliamentary seats and governmental offices were regarded as personal property. This principle of compensation for loss of office combined with outright bribery of members to produce the extraordinary financial transactions to purchase the union. Thus, the appointment to the board of accounts for Arthur Browne was arguably not for the purchase of his vote for the union, but might even be considered compensation for the loss of his parliamentary seat.[2] Within a short time he would be prime serjeant, an important

1 McDowell and Webb, *Trinity College Dublin, 1592–1952*, p. 522. In addition to Browne, Elrington, Fitzgerald, Graves and Prior supported the union, but the provost, Dr John Kearney, and a majority of the fellows, were opposed to the union. Student opinion did not then favour the union.

2 G.C. Bolton, *The passing of the Irish Act of Union: a study in parliamentary politics*, pp 161–9, 181–98 (1966). After publication of Bolton's book, the discovery of Secret Service payment records at the Public Records Office in Kew provided clearer evidence of the transfer of more than £30,000 in Secret Service funds to Ireland for the union campaign because the price of union votes had increased over earlier estimates. See P. Geoghegan, *The Irish Act of Union: a study in high politics, 1798–1801*, pp 85–97 (1999).

legal office, for which he received a short note from Lord Chancellor FitzGibbon, who had been seriously injured in London.[3]

Four months later Browne sought a judicial appointment from the new viceroy,[4] the earl of Hardwicke.[5] Lord Chancellor FitzGibbon, tormentor of Browne at the 1798 visitation of Trinity College, wrote to the viceroy on Browne's qualifications, after warning Browne of his opinions 'honestly and conscientiously' stated:

> I have been applied to on this subject [judgeships] by the solicitor general and Mr Arthur Browne of Trinity College. With respect to the first of these gentlemen, I believe him to be a man of very considerable talents, but he has so very impracticable a temper that I cannot think he would acquit himself well in a judicial situation. Mr Browne has certainly not the same disadvantage of temper but I must say that there are so many gentlemen at the Bar of superior professional pretensions.[6]

Of course, FitzGibbon sat in chancery and it is not apparent that Browne ever practised there, so FitzGibbon's ranking may have been based on his political confrontation with Browne at the visitation and the earlier dispute about Provost Hely-Hutcheson, Browne's efforts to obtain the office of provost of Trinity in 1794 and 1799 or simply Browne's history as an American Whig.

In the court system, the ancient office of the king's serjeants at law had a monopoly on government business in the courts.[7] After the union, the prime serjeant, St George Daly, MP for Galway, a strong supporter of the union, was given a judgeship as baron of the exchequer. Edmund Stanley, MP for Lanesborough, another supporter of the union, had been third serjeant, and was appointed prime serjeant.[8]

The volume of government business – as plaintiff or defendant – had increased to the point where the prime serjeant and his two assistants were required to be

3 'My dear Browne ... I presume you will not hesitate to accept the situation which for the present is within your reach ... it is melancholy to see that intrigues should flourish as vigorously as ever in Trinity College.' D.A. Fleming and A.P.W. Malcomson, *'A valley of execrations': the letters and papers of John FitzGibbon, earl of Clare*, p. 430, 25 May 1801 (2005).

4 Browne's application is in the Colchester Papers (Chief Secretary Charles Abbot) PRO 30/9/106, National Archives. FitzGibbon's note to Browne (21 Sept. 1801), ibid., p. 447.

5 Philip Yorke, 3rd earl of Hardwicke (1775–1834), was appointed lord lieutenant of Ireland after Pitt left office and served from March 1801 to May 1806. During Hardwicke's time, the rising of Robert Emmet (23 July 1803) occurred and his non-activity at that time was criticized because he was engaged in a bureaucratic power struggle with the commander of the military.

6 Fleming and Malcomson, *'A valley of execrations'*, pp 447–8 (2005).

7 J.H. Baker, *The order of serjeants at law* (1984). A. Hart, *A history of the king's serjeants at law in Ireland* (2000). The word 'serjeant' was derived from a special group of Knights Templar, the *fratres servientes*, which was corrupted to 'serjeants' in English. Early on, judges came exclusively from the king's serjeants, but this monopoly was lost as the order of barristers developed.

8 Edmond Stanley (1760–1845) entered TCD 1774, scholar 1777, AB 1778, Inner Temple 1780, KC 1789, MP for Lanesborough 1790 and 1797. Hart, *A history of the king's serjeants*, pp 103–5 (2000).

present in Dublin during all sessions of the royal courts. This proved to be the undoing of Prime Serjeant Stanley, and the golden opportunity for Arthur Browne, because Stanley's unpaid debts had reached such a volume that sheriffs, constables and debt collectors were on his trail and debtors' prison was a serious possibility, so Stanley could not appear in Dublin. Stanley and Browne exchanged jobs with government's blessing. Edmund Stanley took Arthur Browne's place on the board of accounts, and Arthur Browne became prime serjeant from the end of 1801 until his death on 8 June 1805.[9] Browne also became a privy councillor at the same time.

The source of his financial ruin is now unclear, but the end result was the sale of Stanley's membership of the board of accounts for £5,000 in 1803.[10] To escape his debts he sought a career in the East India Company, and in 1807 he was knighted and appointed recorder of Prince of Wales Island (now Penang, Malaysia) at a salary of £3,000 per year.[11]

Among the functions of the prime serjeant was to advise government, both formally and informally, something Arthur Browne had already done for the bishops of the established church. Of course, Arthur Browne's service as prime serjeant would not have involved the preparation and argumentation of legislative proposals, unlike previous holders of the office, because the legislative function had shifted to the Westminster Parliament. Nevertheless, the closure of the Dublin Parliament and reorganization of church and state after 1801 must have involved intricate and delicate legal problems.

Another function of the prime serjeant was service as an assize judge on circuits outside Dublin, to take the place of a senior judge who had an excuse to avoid the arduous and even dangerous travel; this was a duty that was also well compensated (with an allowance of £200).[12] As to government business in court, the prestige of the prime serjeant's office resulted in the privilege of being heard first in court before members of the Bar and even before the solicitor general and attorney general.

There is little doubt that Arthur Browne's final years were very well compensated. Judge Hart estimates that the prime serjeant received between £1,200 and £1,300 per year.[13]

In addition to his office as prime serjeant, Arthur Browne's service at Trinity College remained substantial as Regius Professor of Civil Law (1785), lecturing on his specialties in admiralty, canon law, probate and matrimonial issues; in these last

9   Ibid., p. 104. '[Stanley] was dismissed in the closing days of 1801. Although Stanley and others were to attribute this purely to the enmity towards him of the lord chancellor, the earl of Clare [John FitzGibbon], the lord lieutenant took the view that, quite apart from the impropriety of his continuing in office when his affairs were in such a state, Stanley's absence from Dublin was impairing his ability to discharge his duties. The earl of Hardwicke appointed Arthur Browne prime serjeant in his place but softened the blow by giving Stanley Browne's place on the board of accounts …' See C.J. Smyth, *Chronicle of the law officers of Ireland*, pp 191, 261 (1839).
10   Hart, *A history of the king's serjeants*, p. 105 (2000).
11   Ibid., pp 181–2.   12   Ibid., pp 74–8.   13   Ibid., pp 78, 185–9.

years he was also Regius Professor of Greek (1792–5, 1797–99 and 1801–5), and, as senior fellow, was a member of the governing board of the college.[14] Even today his portrait, by the distinguished portraitist, Hugh Douglas Hamilton,[15] hangs in the provost's house of Trinity College.

In the years after Parliament, Arthur Browne devoted more attention to the *Proceedings* and *Transactions* of the Royal Irish Academy,[16] at the same time as his legal treatises were being revised for new editions. His publications in the *Transactions* dealt with Greek language,[17] Persian poetry,[18] old Spanish poetry and romances,[19] and archeological discoveries in Armagh.[20]

Browne was elected a bencher of King's Inns in 1804.[21] The ancient society of barristers, eventually known as King's Inns, was established in 1541. It occupied an area known as Blackfriars on the north bank of the Liffey for 250 years, but lost the site for the construction of the Four Courts, begun in 1776. Thus, Arthur

14 McDowell and Webb, *Trinity College Dublin*, pp 77–82 (1982). Senior fellows received an annual stipend of £100.

15 Hugh Douglas Hamilton (1734?–1808) was born and schooled in Dublin, went to London 1760–79, then to Florence and Rome for twelve years. After returning to London and Dublin in 1791, he enjoyed commissions to paint portraits of the leading men in both cities and the British royal family. His portrait of Arthur Browne was done in 1795 when Browne was elected senior fellow of Trinity College Dublin.

16 England's Royal Society emerged from the restoration of monarchy in 1662 to encourage research and publication in the sciences. The Royal Irish Academy began at a meeting at Trinity College on 5 Mar. 1785, in the presence of seven fellows: lawyers, physicians and politicians. A meeting of a greatly expanded group was called to approve a constitution at the Dublin house of the earl of Charlemont, who was chosen as president. The society began its publications in 1800 with its *Transactions*, to which Arthur Browne, an original member, submitted articles in the sections on polite literature and antiquities.

17 *Some observations on the Greek accents* (1800) was criticized as unscientific because it was based on conversations with modern Greek sea captains interviewed in Dingle harbour. This piece was reprinted in 7 *Transactions*, 359–80 (1800) and reviewed in 36 *Monthly Review*, 16 (1801). Noting the fierce controversies in the academic world, and Browne's conclusion that the accent governs the quantity of the syllable, the reviewer, however, faulted Browne's comparisons to the use of accent marks in other languages.

18 Hussein O'Dil, *Beauty and the heart: an allegory translated from the Persian language* (1801). A professor of Hebrew was first appointed in 1656 and has never ceased; professorships in Arabic, Persian and Sanskrit were not appointed until the mid-nineteenth century, but many Irish served in the East India Company and the Indian Civil Service and were familiar with Persian.

19 *Translations from various languages, mostly illustrative of the old Spanish poetry and romance* (1802). A professor of Spanish, Antonio Vieyra, served from 1776 to 1797 at Trinity College Dublin.

20 'Some accounts of the Vicar's Cairn in the Country of Armagh communicated to the Committee of Antiquities', 8 *Transactions*, 3 (1803), reviewed in 41 *Monthly Review*, 195 (1803); and 'An account of some ancient trumpets dug up in a bog near Armagh', 8 *Transactions*, 11 (1803), reviewed in 41 *Monthly Review*, 196 (1803). The Dublin Society, founded in 1731 to promote husbandry and other useful arts, had developed a committee on antiquities by 1772, predecessor of the Royal Irish Society. Browne's interest was generated on a business trip to Armagh for the church as property agent.

21 Honourable Society of King's Inns, *Entry of benchers, 1794–1864*. See also P. McCarthy, *A favourite study: building the King's Inns* (2006).

Browne's service as a bencher of King's Inns occurred while the society was building its present headquarters on Constitution Hill. The society decided in 1794 on the architect James Gandon, already famous for the Custom House and the Four Courts. A temporary structure next to the site of the present building was in use from 1798 to 1806, but the existing King's Inns was not ready for use before Arthur Browne's death in June 1805.

Browne's appointment to the office of prime serjeant and election as a bencher of King's Inns was surely a prelude to his appointment as a senior judge. This, however, was never to be, even though FitzGibbon was no longer around to hinder his advancement.

On 8 June 1805, Arthur Browne died in his home from a sudden illness in his fiftieth year.[22] The cause of death was described as 'dropsy', a catch-all term for edema, a swelling from fluid in tissues of the body. The term was often used to describe degenerative heart failure or kidney disease. It is unlikely that Jonah Barrington's mean-spirited diagnosis was correct. Barrington demonized all those who had voted for the union in 1800. In *Personal sketches*, Barrington described Arthur Browne as follows:

> He was by birth an American, of most gentlemanly manners, excellent character, and very considerable talents. He had by his learning become a senior fellow of the university, and was the law professor. From his entrance into Parliament he had been a steady, zealous and able supporter of the rights of Ireland – he had never deviated; he would accept no office; he had attached himself to Mr Ponsonby, and was supposed to be one of the truest and most unassailable supporters of Ireland.
>
> In the session of 1799 he had taken a most unequivocal, decisive, and ardent part against the union, and had spoken against it as a crime and as the ruin of the country: he was believed to be incorruptible. On this night he rose, crestfallen and absorbed at his own tergiversation; he recanted every word he had ever uttered – deserted from the country – supported the union – accepted a bribe from the minister – was afterwards placed in office, but

---

22 The obituary in a newspaper generally supportive of government is as follows: 'THE LATE ARTHUR BROWNE, ESQ. Died, in Saturday morning, at his house in Clare Street, deeply regretted by all who knew him, Arthur Browne, esq., his Majesty's sergeant and senior fellow in the University of Dublin. He was a man of refined taste, a highly cultivated understanding, and peculiarly mild and engaging manners. He had a deep sense of the truth of the Christian religion, and his conduct in the various relations of life evinced its prevailing influence on his heart. Even those who were seldom in his private society, and who may have differed most warmly from him on subjects connected with politics, respected and esteem him; by his more intimate acquaintances he was beloved. He has left a widow and five children bereaved of the protection and tenderness of husbands and fathers. 13 June 1805. On Tuesday, the remains of the lamented Dr Browne, were interred in the church yard of St Anne's parish. The funeral procession was attended by the fellows and students of the university in their academical dress, by a great number of the Bar, and a numerous concourse of gentlemen anxious to pay their last tribute of affection and esteem' (*Faulkner's Dublin Journal*, 11 June 1805).

shame haunted him – he hated himself: an amiable man fell a victim to corruption.[23]

In his list of rewards to barristers for support of the union, Barrington wrote, 'Mr Arthur Browne, commission of inspector 800 £ per annum'. That same list notes two rewards of £5,000 per annum; eight rewards of £3,300 per annum; one of £1,200 per annum; fifteen judgeships with rewards of £600 a piece per annum; two commissions of inspection (like that of Arthur Browne) at £800 per annum; an office in the chancery at £500; an office in the custom house at £500; and a secret pension at £400. Barrington piously claimed that he had been offered appointment as solicitor general by FitzGibbon for support of the union, but had declined; in view of his financial worries, this is unlikely.

The college historian W.B.S. Taylor echoed Jonah Barrington in his 1845 work:

> On the 24th of July, 1797, Arthur Browne, esq., LLD, and the Hon. George Knox, LLD, were returned to serve in the last national Parliament assembled in Ireland, and both these representatives of the university surrendered the trust reposed in them, and, unmindful of the solemn obligations which they had taken to uphold the independence of the Parliament of Ireland, thus aided in passing the Act of political union, and did not even preserve the college privilege in this affair, by which it was deprived of one of its representatives.
>
> In 1800, the Hon. George Knox, who had so acted towards his constituents, was rewarded by being appointed by the Act of Union, as sole representative of this college in the imperial Parliament; but his conduct had made him so unpopular, that, though a person of some rank and fortune, he was looked down upon, and scarcely tolerated among the respectable classes in Ireland. His late colleague, Arthur Browne, LLD, had been very popular in the college; his manners were mild and gentlemanly, and in private life he was kind and honourable; but, in an hour of weakness, he was prevailed on to sell that, which was strictly the property of others, but delegated in confidence to his guardianship, and for so voting he was made a privy counsellor and attorney-general; but *his* heart was not scared to evil deeds. In the sullen calm that succeeded the late political turmoil, Dr Browne had time for reflection. He found himself shunned by many, and looked down upon by others with whom he had long been in habits of friendship. This was too much for his sensitive mind; he fell into a lingering disorder, and died in

---

23 Barrington, *Personal sketches*, p. 460. In 1815, Barrington's efforts to avoid creditors, bailiffs and sheriffs forced him to go to France (before Waterloo), where he remained until his death. His downfall came from his conversion or misappropriation of the funds of parties in litigation over derelicts in 1805, 1806 and 1810. He was deprived of his judgeship in 1830 by Parliament. K. Costello, *The court of admiralty of Ireland, 1575–1893*, pp 165–72 (2011). See *Personal sketches of his own time* (1827–32), and *The rise and fall of the Irish nation* (1833).

about three years after voting for the union, leaving his widow and children in circumstances far from affluent.[24]

Ninety years after the events of the union, Trinity's greatest historian, W.E.H. Lecky, described the change of mind by Arthur Browne in dispassionate terms:

> George Knox and Arthur Browne, who were the members for the University, both spoke and voted against the union in 1799. In the following year Browne changed his side and supported it; but he acknowledged in the House of Commons that he was acting in opposition to the wishes of the majority of his constituents. He afterwards received some legal promotion, and he never again represented the university.[25]

Arthur Browne left a widow, Bridget Browne, and five children. No record of the probate or administration of his estate has been found. His passing was honoured by his college when, three days after his death, the faculty and students, gowned in their academic robes, accompanied his body from his home on Clare Street through the College Park, crossing Nassau Street to Dawson Street and St Ann's church where he was buried in the parish churchyard.[26]

CONCLUSION AND RETROSPECT

The short but active life of Arthur Browne occurred during a time of historic struggles in America, France and Ireland that even influence the structure of our twenty-first-century world. The United Kingdom and the Republic of Ireland now cooperate in the effort to resolve the problems created by the British surrender of 'home rule' in 1921 to an independent enclave in Northern Ireland.

Through the eyes of Arthur Browne, we have observed the dissolution of colonial status in America. We have traced his lonely way as an orphan to begin his preparations for a professional career at Trinity College Dublin. We have also seen the haphazard studies to prepare for the common law courts, contrasted with the rigorous studies of the classics for the admiralty and the other courts of civil law.

24 W.B.S. Taylor, *History of the University of Dublin*, pp 223–4 (1845). Despite the inaccuracies (George Knox abstained, Browne was not attorney general and died more than five years after the vote), there may be some truth in the penury of Browne's widow in view of the sale of his library after his death, but his last years were very well paid. The catalogues of his library are on file in the Trinity College Dublin library. The auction house, Vallance and Jones, Eustace Street, Dublin, sold the 'miscellaneous' catalogue of 2,009 works on 18 Nov. 1805; the 'legal' catalogue of 631 works was sold on 9 Dec. 1805.

25 W.E.H. Lecky, 5 *History of Ireland in the eighteenth century*, p. 325 (1892). It is a compilation drawn from his earlier (1878) *History of England*. Lecky describes the history of that revolutionary period as 'imperfectly written and usually under the influence of the most furious partisanship: there is hardly a page of it which is not darkened by the most violently contradictory statements'.

26 The parish of St Ann's, Dawson Street, was founded in 1707 in the reign of Queen Anne. The

Arthur Browne was an academic, an advocate and a politician who spoke his mind freely in defence of civil liberties and the constitutional changes of 1782. He was a strong supporter of the independent Irish Parliament until revolution and savage repression undermined it. It is difficult to disentangle his love of his Irish adopted country from his admiration for the English constitution – a democracy disguised as a monarchy. He also admired England's enlightened classes and its established church in which he was raised. Nevertheless, he was well aware of English intolerance of Irish people and Irish subservience to English economic interests that had been compelled by England. His love for America and its popular government continued, as did his disapproval of the chaotic and destructive popular government in France. But these controversies are now simply matters of history.

Arthur Browne's legacy to the modern world is his treatise, *A compendious view of the civil law and of the law of the admiralty*. It was the vehicle by which the jurisprudence of Rome and continental Europe was carried over to new American courts dealing with probate, testimonial disputes and marital controversies; it also became the principal authority for admiralty courts in the early republic because of its historical background, systematic analysis and clear exposition.[27] His scholarly lectures were the foundation of a tradition of academic rigour in the training of lawyers.

Completing these studies, I cannot forget the request of the 16-year-old orphan to his father's congregation to portray him to the Society for the Propagation of the Gospel, his late father's employers, as 'a lad of some merit, who, if properly encouraged, might turn out something'. How fortunate for us that the SPG sent his passage money.

present Georgian structure was finished in 1720, although the west façade is now marred by a Victorian Romanesque design (1868). The churchyard along Molesworth Street was sold to build offices for the European Union after Ireland's entry (1973). The churchyard was dug up and all the bones were reburied in a crypt of the church.

27 The treatise was cited more than 50 times (before the Civil War) in the United States Supreme Court and an additional 125 times in lower courts, although these figures are necessarily imprecise because early courts did not spell out the full names of authors and sources. Nevertheless, most of the citations use the text authoritatively. Dissenters occasionally cite the text to indicate a preference for settled law of an earlier day.

Bibliography

Abel-Smith, Brian & Robert Bocking Stevens, *Lawyers and the courts: a sociological study of the English legal system, 1750–1965* (London, 1967).

Acheson, Alan, *A history of the Church of Ireland, 1691–2001* (Dublin, 2002).

Addison, Daniel Dulany, *The life and times of Edward Bass, first bishop of Massachusetts* (Boston, 1897).

Akenson, Donald H., *The Church of Ireland: ecclesiastical reform and revolution, 1800–1885* (New Haven, CT, 1971).

Albion, Robert Greenhalgh, William A. Baker & Benjamin Woods Labaree, *New England and the sea* (Middletown, CT, 1972).

Alden, John Richard, *General Gage in America* (Baton Rouge, LA, 1948).

Allibone, S. Austin, *A critical dictionary of English literature and British and American authors* (Philadelphia, 1878).

Ammerman, David, *In the common cause: American response to the Coercive Acts of 1774* (Charlottesville, VA, 1974).

Andrews, John H., 'Anglo-American trade in the early eighteenth century', *Geographical Review*, 45 (1955), 99–110.

Anonymous, *Thoughts on the present state of the College of Dublin, addressed to the gentlemen of the university* (Dublin, 1782).

Anonymous, *Some documents relative to the late parliamentary conduct of Doctor Browne, representative in Parliament for the University of Dublin* (1800).

Ashburner, Walter (ed.), *Nomos Rodiōn Nautikos: the Rhodian sea-law* (Oxford, 1909).

Ashe, Geoffrey, *The Hell-Fire clubs: a history of anti-morality* (Stroud, UK, 2000).

Axtell, James, *The European and the Indian: essays on the ethnohistory of North America* (New York, 1981).

Ayling, Stanley, *George the Third* (New York, 1972).

Bailyn, Bernard, 'Communications and trade: the Atlantic in the seventeenth century', *Journal of Economic History*, 13 (1953), 378–87.

Bailyn, Bernard, *The ideological origins of the American Revolution* (Cambridge, MA, 1967).

Bailyn, Bernard, *The ordeal of Thomas Hutchinson: loyalism and the destruction of the first British empire* (Cambridge, MA, 1974).

Baker, John Hamilton,. *The Order of Serjeants at Law* (London, 1984).

Ballard, Lockett Ford, *Trinity Church in old Newport on Rhode Island* (1979).

Barnard, T.C., 'Protestants and the Irish language, c.1675–1725', *Journal of Ecclesiastical History*, 44 (1993), 243–72.

Barnard, T.C., 'Parishes, pews and parsons: lay people and the Church of Ireland, 1647–1780' in R. Gillespie & W.G. Neely (eds), *The laity and the Church of Ireland, 1000–2000* (Dublin, 2002), pp 70–103.

Barnard, T.C., *A new anatomy of Ireland: the Irish Protestants, 1649–1770* (New Haven, CT, 2003).

Barnard, T.C., *Making the grand figure: lives and possessions in Ireland, 1641–1770* (New Haven, CT, 2004).

Barnard, T.C. & W.G. Neely (eds), *The clergy of the Church of Ireland, 1000–2000* (Dublin, 2006).

Barrington, Jonah, *Personal sketches of his own times*, 3 vols (London, 1827–1832).

Barrington, Jonah, *Rise and fall of the Irish nation* (New York, 1833).

Barry, John M., *Roger Williams and the creation of the American soul: church state and the birth of liberty* (New York, 2012).

Bartlett, Thomas, 'Defenders and defenderism in 1795', *Irish Historical Studies*, 24 (1985), 373–94.

Bartlett, Thomas, *The fall and rise of the Irish nation: the Catholic question, 1690–1830* (Savage, MD, 1992).

Bartlett, Thomas, 'Clemency and compensation: the treatment of defeated rebels and suffering loyalists after the 1798 rebellion' in J. Smyth (ed.), *Revolution, counter-revolution and union: Ireland in the 1790s* (Cambridge, 2000), pp 99–127.

Bartlett, Thomas, 'Informers, informants and information: the secret history of the 1790s reconsidered' in T. Bartlett et al. (eds), *1798: a bicentenary perspective* (Dublin, 2003), pp 406–22.

Bartlett, Thomas (ed.), *Revolutionary Dublin, 1795–1801: the letters of Francis Higgins to Dublin Castle* (Dublin, 2004).

Bartlett, Thomas, David Dickson, Dáire Keogh & Kevin Whelan (eds), *1798: a bicentenary perspective* (Dublin, 2003).

Bartlett, Thomas & David W. Hayton (eds), *Penal era and golden age: essays in Irish history, 1690–1800* (Belfast, 1979).

Bate, Walter Jackson, *Samuel Johnson* (New York, 1977).

Beach, Stewart, *Samuel Adams: the fateful years, 1764–1776* (New York, 1965).

Beckett, James Camlin, *Protestant dissent in Ireland, 1685–1780* (London, 1946).

Beckett, James Camlin, *The making of modern Ireland, 1603–1923* (New York, 1983).

Bellamy, John, *Whig Club* (London, 1799).

Bemis, Samuel Flagg, *The diplomacy of the American Revolution* (London, 1935).

Benedict, Robert D., 'Historical position of the Rhodian law', *Yale Law Journal*, 18 (1909), 223–42.

Berkeley, George, 'On the prospect of planting arts and learning in America' in *A miscellany containing several tracts on various subjects* (Dublin, 1752).

Berman, David, *George Berkeley: idealism and the man* (Oxford, 1994).

Berman, Harold Joseph, 'The origins of Western legal science', *Harvard Law Review*, 90 (1977), 894–943.

Berresford Ellis, Peter, *The Boyne water: the battle of the Boyne, 1690* (London, 1976).

Bew, John, *Castlereagh: a life* (New York, 2012).

Black, Jeremy (ed.), *Britain in the age of Walpole* (Basingstoke, UK, 1984).

Black, Jeremy, *Pitt the elder* (Cambridge, 1992).

Blumin, Stuart M., *The emergence of the middle class: social experience in the American city, 1760–1900* (New York, 1989).

Bolton, Geoffrey Curgenven, *The passing of the Irish Act of Union: a study in parliamentary politics* (Oxford, 1966).

Bottigheimer, Karl S., *English money and Irish land: the adventurers in the Cromwellian settlement of Ireland* (Oxford, 1971).

Bourguignon, Henry J., *Sir William Scott, Lord Stowell, judge of the high court of admiralty, 1798–1828* (Cambridge, 1987).

Bowers, Claude Gernade, *Jefferson in power: the death struggle of the federalists* (Boston, 1936).

Boylan, Henry, *Theobald Wolfe Tone* (Dublin, 1981).

Bradford, Charles H., *The battle road: expedition to Lexington and Concord* (Philadelphia, 1988).

Bradford, William, *Of Plymouth Plantation, 1620–1647*, ed. S.E. Morison (New York, 1970).

Bradsher, Earl Lockridge, *Matthew Carey: editor, author, and publisher: a study in American literary development* (New York, 1912).

Brayton, Alice, *George Berkeley in Newport* (Newport, RI, 1954).

Brewer, John, 'The look of London, 1776' in K. Pearson & P. Connor (eds), *1776: the British story of the American Revolution* (London, 1976), pp 55–68.

Bric, Maurice J., *Ireland, Philadelphia and the re-invention of America, 1760–1820* (Dublin, 2008).

Bridenbaugh, Carl, *The colonial craftsman* (New York, 1950).

Bridenbaugh, Carl, *Cities in the wilderness: the first century of urban life in America, 1625–1742* (New York, 1955).

Bridenbaugh, Carl, *Cities in revolt: urban life in America, 1743–1776* (New York, 1955).

Bridenbaugh, Carl, *Mitre and sceptre: transatlantic faiths, ideas, personalities, and politics, 1689–1775* (New York, 1967).

Bridenbaugh, Carl, *Fat mutton and liberty of conscience: society in Rhode Island, 1636–1690* (Providence, RI, 1974).

Brockunier, Samuel Hugh, *The irrepressible democrat: Roger Williams* (New York, 1940).

Brooke, John, *King George III* (New York, 1972).

Brown, Michael & Seán Patrick Donlan, *The laws and other legalities of Ireland, 1689–1850* (Farnham, UK, 2011).

Brown, Michael, Patrick M. Geoghegan & James Kelly (eds), *The Irish Act of Union, 1800* (Dublin, 2003).

Brown, Richard D., *Revolutionary politics in Massachusetts: the Boston Committee of Correspondence and the towns, 1772–1774* (Cambridge, MA, 1970).

Brown, Wallace, *The king's friends: the composition and motives of the American loyalist claimants* (Providence, RI, 1966).

Browne, Arthur, *A brief review of the question: whether the Articles of Limerick have been violated?* (Dublin, 1788).

Browne, Arthur, *Miscellaneous sketches* (London, 1798).

Browne, Arthur, *A compendious view of the ecclesiastical law of Ireland* (Dublin, 1799).

Browne, Arthur, *Remarks of the terms of the union* (Dublin, 1800).

Browne, Arthur, 'Some observations upon the Greek accents', *Transactions of the Royal Irish Academy*, 7 (1800), 359–80.

Browne, Arthur, *Hussen O Dil: Beauty and the heart, an allegory* ... (Dublin, 1801).

Browne, Arthur, 'An account of some ancient trumpets, dug up in a bog near Armagh', *Transactions of the Royal Irish Academy*, 8 (1802), 11–12.

Browne, Arthur, *A compendious view of the civil law, and of the law of the admiralty* (2nd ed. London, 1802).

Browne, Arthur, 'Some accounts of the Vicars Cairn in the County of Armagh ...' *Transactions of the Royal Irish Academy*, 8 (1802), 3–9.

Browne, Arthur, *Translations from various languages, mostly illustrative of the old Spanish poetry and romance* (Dublin, 1802).

Browne, Revd Arthur, *Remarks on Dr Mayhew's incidental reflections* (Portsmouth, NH, 1763).

Browning, John Dudley (ed.), *Education in the 18th century* (New York, 1979).

Budd, Declan & Ross Hinds, *The Hist and Edmund Burke's Club* (Dublin, 1997).

Buglass, Leslie J., *Marine insurance and general average in the United States: an average adjuster's viewpoint* (3rd ed. Centreville, MD, 1991).

Bullion, John L., *A great and necessary measure: George Grenville and the genesis of the Stamp Act, 763–1765* (Columbia, MO, 1982).

Bumsted, John Michael, *The Pilgrims' progress: the ecclesiastical history of the old colony, 1620–1775* (New York, 1989).

Burns, Robert E., 'The Catholic Relief Act in Ireland, 1778', *Church History*, 32 (1963), 181–206.

Burke, William P., *Irish priests in penal times (1660–1760)* (Shannon, 1968).

Burrows, Edwin G. & Mike Wallace, *Gotham: a history of New York City to 1898* (New York, 1999).

Calhoon, Robert M., *The loyalists in revolutionary America, 1760–1781* (New York, 1973).

Callahan, North, *Henry Knox: George Washington's general* (Bronxville, NY, 1958).

Carp, Benjamin L., *Rebels rising: cities and the American Revolution* (New York, 2007).

Cash, Arthur H., *John Wilkes: the scandalous father of civil liberty* (New Haven, CT, 2006).

Cash, Philip, *Dr Benjamin Waterhouse: a life in medicine and public service, 1754–1846* (Sagamore Beach, MA, 2006).

Chambers, Liam, 'The 1798 rebellion in north Leinster' in T. Bartlett et al. (eds), *1798: a bicentenary perspective* (Dublin, 2003), pp 122–35.

Chandler, Alfred D. Jnr, *The visible hand: the managerial revolution in American business* (Cambridge, MA, 1978).

Channing, Edward, *A history of the United States: the American Revolution, 1761–1789* (New York, 1912).

Chernow, Ron, *Washington: a life* (New York, 2010).

Colombos, C. John, *The international law of the sea* (6th ed. London, 1967).

Conley, Patrick T., *Liberty and justice: a history of law and lawyers in Rhode Island, 1636–1998* (East Providence, RI, 1998).

Connolly, Sean J., *Priests and people in pre-Famine Ireland, 1780–1845* (Dublin, 1992).

Connolly, Sean J., *Religion, law, and power: the making of Protestant Ireland, 1660–1760* (Oxford, 1992).

Connolly, Sean J. (ed.), *Political ideas in eighteenth-century Ireland* (Dublin, 2000).

Coote, Charles, *History of the union of the kingdoms of Great Britain and Ireland* (London, 1802).

Costello, Kevin, *The court of admiralty of Ireland, 1575–1893* (Dublin, 2011).

Coughtry, Jay, *The notorious triangle: Rhode Island and the African slave trade* (Philadelphia, 1981).

Craig, Maurice James, *The Volunteer earl* (London, 1948).

Craig, Maurice James, *Dublin, 1660–1860: a social and architectural history* (Dublin, 1969).

Crane, Elaine Forman, *A dependent people: Newport, Rhode Island, in the revolutionary era* (New York, 1985).

Crawford, John, 'Retrenchment, renewal and disestablishment, 1840–77' in J. Crawford & R. Gillespie (eds), *St Patrick's Cathedral, Dublin: a history* (Dublin, 2009).

Crump, Helen Josephine, *Colonial admiralty jurisdiction in the seventeenth century* (London, 1931).

Cullen, Louis M., *The emergence of modern Ireland, 1600–1900* (New York, 1981).

Curry, John, *An historical and critical review of the civil wars in Ireland*, 2 vols (London, 1786).

Curtin, Nancy J., 'The transformation of the Society of United Irishmen into a mass-based revolutionary organisation, 1794–6', *Irish Historical Studies*, 24 (1985), 463–92.

Curtin, Nancy J., 'The United Irish Organisation in Ulster, 1795–8' in D. Dickson et al. (eds), *The United Irishmen: republicanism, radicalism, and rebellion* (Dublin, 1993), pp 209–21.

Curtin, Nancy J., *The United Irishmen: popular politics in Ulster and Dublin, 1791–1798* (Oxford, 1994).

Curtin, Nancy J., '"A perfect liberty": the rise and fall of the Irish Whigs, 1789–97' in D.G. Boyce et al. (eds), *Political discourse in seventeenth- and eighteenth-century Ireland* (Basingstoke, UK, 2001), pp 270–89.

Curtin, Philip D., *The Atlantic slave trade: a census* (Madison, WI, 1969).

Curtis, Edmund, *A history of mediaeval Ireland from 1110 to 1513* (Dublin, 1927).

Curtis, Edmund, *A history of Ireland* (6th ed. London, 1950).

Davis, Thomas, *The life of the Right Hon. J.P. Curran* (Dublin, 1846).

de Conde, Alexander, *The Quasi-War: politics and diplomacy in the undeclared war with France, 1797–1801* (New York, 1966).

Delany, V.T.H., 'The history of legal education in Ireland', *Journal of Legal Education*, 12 (1959–1960), 396–406.

Derry, John Wesley, *The regency crisis and the Whigs, 1788–9* (Cambridge, 1963).

Derry, John Wesley, *Charles James Fox* (New York, 1972).

Derry, John Wesley, *Castlereagh* (New York, 1976).

Derry, John Wesley, *Politics in the age of Fox, Pitt and Liverpool* (Basingstoke, rev. ed. 2001).

Dexter, Franklin Bowditch (ed.), *Extracts from the itineraries and other miscellanies of Ezra Stiles, D.D., LL.D., 1755–1794* (New Haven, CT, 1916).

Dickerson, Oliver Morton, 'Commissioners of customs and the "Boston Massacre"', *New England Quarterly*, 27 (1954), 307–25.

Dickerson, Oliver Morton, *Boston under military rule, 1768–1769* (Westport, CT, 1971).

Dickson, David, Dáire Keogh & Kevin Whelan (eds), *The United Irishmen: republicanism, radicalism, and rebellion* (Dublin, 1993).

Dixon, W. Macneile, *Trinity College Dublin* (London, 1902).

Donaldson, Alfred Gaston, *Some comparative aspects of Irish law* (Durham, NC, 1957).

Donlan, Seán Patrick, '"The debt is forgiven": a compendious view of Arthur Browne, c.1756–1805', *Electronic Journal of Comparative Law*, 13:3 (2009), http://www.ejcl.org/133/abs133-3.html, accessed 4 Feb. 2016.

Downing, Antoinette Forrester & Vincent Scully Jnr, *The architectural heritage of Newport, Rhode Island, 1640–1915* (Cambridge, MA, 1952).

Dugan, James, *The great mutiny* (New York, 1965).

Dunn, Richard S., *Sugar and slaves: the rise of the planter class in the English West Indies, 1624–1713* (Chapel Hill, NC, 1972).

Durey, Michael, *Transatlantic radicals and the early American republic* (Lawrence, KS, 1997).

Durey, Michael, 'Marquess Cornwallis and the fate of Irish rebel prisoners in the aftermath of the 1798 rebellion' in J. Smyth (ed.), *Revolution, counter-revolution, and union: Ireland in the 1790s* (Cambridge, 2000).

Duyckinck, Evert A. & George L. Duyckinck, *Cyclopædia of American literature*, 2 vols (Philadelphia, 1877).

Ehrman, John, *The younger Pitt*, i: *The years of acclaim* (London, 1969).

Ehrman, John, *The younger Pitt*, ii: *The reluctant transition* (London, 1983).

Ehrman, John, *The younger Pitt*, iii: *The consuming struggle* (London, 1996).

Elliott, Marianne, *Partners in revolution: the United Irishmen and France* (New Haven, CT, 1982).

Elliott, Marianne, *Wolfe Tone: prophet of Irish independence* (New Haven, CT, 1989).

Elliott, Maud Howe, *This was my Newport* (Cambridge, MA, 1944).

Elsbree, Oliver Wendell, *The rise of the missionary spirit in America, 1790–1815* (Philadelphia, 1980).

Emsley, Clive, 'Repression, "terror" and the rule of law in England during the decade of the French Revolution', *English Historical Review*, 100 (1985), 801–25.

Evans, Dorinda, *The genius of Gilbert Stuart* (Princeton, NJ, 1999).

Eyck, Erich, *Pitt versus Fox: father and son, 1735–1806*, trans. E. Northcott (London, 1950).

Falkiner, C. Litton, *Studies in Irish history and biography* (London, 1902).

Farrell, Brian (ed.), *The Irish parliamentary tradition* (Dublin, 1973).

Feiling, Keith, *The second Tory Party, 1714–1832* (London, 1959).

Ferguson, Kenneth, 'The Irish Bar in December 1798', *Dublin Historical Record*, 52 (1999), 32–60.

Ferling, John E., *Almost a miracle: the American victory in the War of Independence* (Oxford, 2007).

Ferriter, Diarmaid, *The transformation of Ireland, 1900–2000* (Woodstock, NY, 2004).

Fischer, David Hackett, *Paul Revere's ride* (New York, 1994).

Fitzgerald, Richard, 'Admiralty and prize jurisdiction in the British Commonwealth of Nations', *Juridical Review*, 60 (1948), 106–22.

FitzGibbon, Elliot, *Earl of Clare: mainspring of the union* (London, 1960).

Fitzhenry, Edna C., *Henry Joy McCracken* (Dublin, 1936).

Fitzpatrick, William John, *Ireland before the union* (Dublin, 1867).

Fleming, D.A. & A.P.W. Malcomson (eds), *'A volley of execrations': the letters and papers of John FitzGibbon, earl of Clare, 1772–1802* (Dublin, 2005).

Fleming, Thomas J., *Beat the drum: the siege of Yorktown, 1781* (New York, 1963).

Fleming, Thomas J., *The first stroke: Lexington, Concord, and the beginning of the American Revolution* (Washington, DC, 1977).

Flexner, James Thomas, *George Washington*, ii: *In the American Revolution, 1775–1783* (Boston, 1968).

Ford, Alan, *The Protestant Reformation in Ireland, 1590–1641* (Frankfurt am Main, 1985).

Ford, Alan, J.I. McGuire & Kenneth Milne, *As by law established: the Church of Ireland since the Reformation* (Dublin, 1995).

Foster, Roy, *Modern Ireland, 1600–1972* (New York, 1988).

Foster, Roy, *Luck and the Irish* (Oxford, 2006).

Foster, Roy, *Vivid faces: the revolutionary generation in Ireland, 1880–1923* (New York, 2014).

Fothergill, Brian, *The mitred earl* (London, 2010).

Fowler, William M., *William Ellery: a Rhode Island politico and lord of admiralty* (Metuchen, NJ, 1973).

Fraser, Antonia, *Royal Charles: Charles II and the Restoration* (New York, 1979).

Froude, James Anthony, *The English in Ireland in the eighteenth century*, 3 vols (New York, 1881).

Gahan, Daniel, *Rebellion! Ireland in 1798* (Dublin, 1997).

Galvin, John R., *The Minute Men: a compact history of the defenders of the American colonies, 1645–1775* (New York, 1967).

Gaustad, Edwin S., *George Berkeley in America* (New Haven, CT, 1979).

Geoghegan, Patrick M., *The Irish Act of Union: a study in high politics, 1798–1801* (Dublin, 1999).

Geoghegan, Patrick M., 'The making of the union' in D. Keogh and K. Whelan (eds), *Acts of union: the causes, contexts and consequences of the Act of Union* (Dublin, 2001), pp 35–45.

Geoghegan, Patrick M., *Lord Castlereagh* (Dundalk, 2002).

Geoghegan, Patrick M., *King Dan: the rise of Daniel O'Connell, 1775–1829* (Dublin, 2008).

Gibbons, Luke & Kiernan O'Connor (eds), *Charles O'Conor of Ballinagare: essays on his life and works* (Dublin, 2012).

Gilbert, John Thomas, *A history of the city of Dublin*, 3 vols (Dublin, 1854; repr. Shannon, 1972).

Gillespie, Raymond & W.G. Neely (eds), *The laity and the Church of Ireland, 1000–2000* (Dublin, 2002).

Gill, Conrad, *The naval mutinies of 1797* (Manchester, 1913).

Gilmore, Grant & Charles L. Black Jnr (eds), *The law of admiralty* (2nd ed. Mineola, NY, 1975).

Gold, Edgar, *Maritime transport: the evolution of international marine policy and shipping law* (Lexington, MA, 1981).

Gormley, W. Paul, 'The development of the Rhodian-Roman maritime law to 1681, with special emphasis on the problem of collision', *Inter-American Law Review*, 3 (1961), 317–46.

Grainger, John D., *The Battle of Yorktown, 1781: a reassessment* (Rochester, NY, 2005).

Greene, Jerome A., *The guns of independence: the siege of Yorktown, 1781* (New York, 2005).

Guinness, Desmond & Julius Trousdale Sadler, *Newport preserved: architecture of the 18th century* (New York, 1982).

Guttmacher, Manfred, *America's last king: an interpretation of the madness of King George III* (New York, 1941).

Hague, William, *William Pitt the younger* (New York, 2005).

Hague, William, *Wilberforce: the life of the great anti-slave-trade campaigner* (London, 2007).

Harrington, Matthew P., 'The legacy of the colonial vice admiralty courts (part I)', *Journal of Maritime Law and Commerce*, 26 (1995), 581–600.

Harrington, Matthew P., 'The legacy of the colonial vice admiralty courts (part II)', *Journal of Maritime Law and Commerce*, 27 (1996), 323–52.

Hart, Anthony R., *A history of the king's serjeants at law in Ireland* (Dublin, 2000).

Hattendorf, John B., *Semper eadem: a history of Trinity Church in Newport, 1698–2000* (Newport, RI, 2001).

Hawes, Alexander Boyd, *Off-soundings: aspects of the maritime history of Rhode Island* (Chevy Chase, MD, 1999).

Hayter-Hames, Jane, *Arthur O'Connor, United Irishman* (Cork, 2001).

Healy, Nicholas J. & Joseph C. Sweeney, *The law of marine collision* (Centreville, MD, 1998).

Henkin, Louis, *Foreign affairs and the constitution* (Mineola, NY, 1972).

Hibbert, Christopher, *King mob: the story of Lord George Gordon and the riots of 1780* (Cleveland, OH, 1958).

Hibbert, Christopher, *George IV: prince of wales, 1762–1811* (New York, 1972).

Hibbert, Christopher, *George IV: regent and king, 1811–1830* (New York, 1973).

Hibbert, Christopher, *George III: a personal history* (New York, 1998).

Hill, Jacqueline R., 'Popery and Protestantism, civil and religious liberty: the disputed lessons of Irish history, 1690–1812', *Past & Present*, 118 (1988), 96–129.

Hill, Jacqueline R., *From patriots to unionists: Dublin civic politics and Irish Protestant patriotism* (Oxford, 1997).

Hilton, Boyd, *A mad, bad, and dangerous people? England, 1783–1846* (Oxford, 2006).

Hinkson, Henry Albert, *Student life in Trinity College Dublin* (Dublin, 1892).

Hoffman, Ross John Swartz, *The marquis: a study of Lord Rockingham, 1730–1782* (New York, 1973).

Hoffman, Ross John Swartz & Paul Levack (eds), *Burke's politics: selected writings and speeches of Edmund Burke on reform, revolution, and war* (New York, 1949).

Hogan, Dáire, *The legal profession in Ireland, 1789–1922* (Dublin, 1986).

Hogan, Dáire & W.N. Osborough (eds), *Brehons, serjeants and attorneys* (Dublin, 1990).

Holdsworth, Sir William Searle, *A history of English law* (2nd ed. London, 1937).

Holmes, David L., 'The Episcopal church and the American Revolution', *Historical Magazine of the Protestant Episcopal Church*, 47 (1978), 261–91.

Holmes, Pauline, *A tercentenary history of the Boston Public Latin School, 1635–1935* (Cambridge, 1935).

Honoré, Tony, *Ulpian: pioneer of human rights* (Oxford, 2002).

Honourable Society of King's Inns, *Entry of benchers* (1794–1864).

Hume-Williams, William Ellis, *The Irish Parliament from the year 1782 to 1800* (London, 1879).

Hutchinson, Thomas, *The history of the colony and province of Massachusetts Bay* (Cambridge, 1936).

Inglis, Brian, *The freedom of the press in Ireland, 1784–1841* (London, 1954).

Ingram, T. Dunbar, *A history of the legislative union of Great Britain and Ireland* (London, 1887).

Isham, Norman Morrison, *Trinity Church in Newport, Rhode Island: a history of the fabric* (Boston, 1936).

Jackson, Alvin, *Ireland, 1798–1998: politics and war* (Oxford, 1999).

Jados, Stanley S. (trans.), *Consolate of the Sea and related documents* (Tuscaloosa, AL, 1975).

James, Francis Godwin, *Ireland in the empire, 1688–1770* (Cambridge, MA, 1973).

James, Francis Godwin, *Lords of the Ascendancy: the Irish House of Lords and its members, 1600–1800* (Washington, DC, 1995).

James, Sydney V., *Colonial Rhode Island: a history* (New York, 1975).

James, Sydney V., *The colonial metamorphoses in Rhode Island: a study of institutions in change* (Hanover, NH, 2000).

Jarrett, David, *Pitt the younger* (New York, 1974).

Jasanoff, Maya, *Liberty's exiles: American loyalists in a revolutionary world* (New York, 2011).

Jeffreys, C.P.B., *Newport, 1639–1976: an historical sketch* (Newport, RI, 1976).

Johnston, Edith M., 'Member of the Irish Parliament, 1784–7', *Proceedings of the Royal Irish Academy: Section C: Archaeology, Celtic Studies, History, Linguistics, Literature*, 71 (1971), 139–246.

Johnston, Henry Phelps, *The Yorktown campaign and surrender of Cornwallis, 1781* (New York, 1881).

Jones, Howard Mumford, *The harp that once* (New York, 1937).

Kavanaugh, Ann C., *John FitzGibbon, earl of Clare: Protestant reaction and English authority in late eighteenth-century Ireland* (Dublin, 1997).

Keeton, Page & William L. Prosser, *Prosser and Keeton on torts* (5th ed. St Paul, MN, 1984).

Keir, Sir David Lindsay, *The constitutional history of modern Britain since 1485* (6th ed. London, 1951).

Kelly, James, *Prelude to union: Anglo-Irish politics in the 1780s* (Cork, 1992).

Kelly, James, *The damn'd thing called honour: duelling in Ireland, 1570–1860* (Cork, 1995).

Kelly, James, '"A wild Capuchin of Cork": Arthur O'Leary (1729–1802)' in G. Moran (ed.), *Radical Irish priests, 1660–1970* (Dublin, 1998), pp 39–61.

Kelly, James, *Henry Flood: patriots and politics in eighteenth-century Ireland* (Notre Dame, IN, 1998).

Kelly, James, 'The rebellion of 1798 in south Leinster' in T. Bartlett et al. (eds), *1798: a bicentenary perspective* (Dublin, 2003), pp 104–21.

Kelly, James, '"We were all to have been massacred": Irish Protestants and the experience of rebellion' in T. Bartlett et al. (eds), *1798: a bicentenary perspective* (Dublin, 2003), pp 312–30.

Kelly, James, *Poynings' Law and the making of law in Ireland, 1660–1800* (Dublin, 2007).

Keneally, Thomas, *The great shame and the triumph of the Irish in the English-speaking world* (London, 1998).

Kennedy, Denis Robert, 'The Irish Whigs, 1782–1789' (MA, University of Kansas, 1961).

Kennedy, Denis Robert, 'The Irish Whigs, 1789–1793' (PhD, University of Toronto, 1969).

Kenny, Colum, *King's Inns and the kingdom of Ireland: the Irish 'inn of court', 1541–1800* (Dublin, 1992).

Kenny, Colum, 'The Four Courts at Christ Church, 1608–1796' in W.N. Osborough (ed.), *Explorations in law and history: Irish Legal History Society discourses, 1988–1994* (Blackrock, Ireland, 1995), 107–32.

Keogh, Dáire, 'Archbishop Troy, the Catholic church and Irish radicalism: 1791–3' in D. Dickson et al. (eds), *The United Irishmen: republicanism, radicalism, and rebellion* (Dublin, 1993), pp 124–34.

Keogh, Dáire, *The French disease: the Catholic church and Irish radicalism, 1790–1800* (Dublin, 1993).

Keogh, Dáire & Kevin Whelan (eds), *Acts of union: the causes, contexts and consequences of the Act of Union* (Dublin, 2001).

Ketchum, Richard M., *Victory at Yorktown: the campaign that won the revolution* (New York, 2004).

Killen, John (ed.), *The decade of the United Irishmen: contemporary accounts* (Belfast, 1997).

Kirafly, A.K.R. (ed.), *Potter's historical introduction to English law and its institutions* (4th ed. London, 1958).

Knox, Oliver, *Rebels and informers: stirrings of Irish independence* (New York, 1997).

Kronenberger, Louis, *The extraordinary Mr Wilkes: his life and times* (Garden City, NY, 1974).

Labaree, Benjamin Woods, *The Boston Tea Party* (New York, 1964).

Lamb, George Woodward, 'Clergymen licensed to the American colonies by the bishops of London, 1745–1781', *Historical Magazine of the Protestant Episcopal Church*, 13 (1944), 128–43.

Lambert, Frank, *Pedlar in divinity: George Whitefield and the transatlantic revivals, 1737–1770* (Princeton, NJ, 1993).

Langdon, George D. Jnr, *Pilgrim colony: a history of New Plymouth, 1620–1691* (New Haven, CT, 1966).

Larkin, Emmet J., *The pastoral role of the Roman Catholic church in the pre-Famine Ireland, 1750–1850* (Dublin, 2006).

Lauterpacht, Hersch, 'The Grotian tradition in international law', *British Year Book of International Law*, 23 (1946), 1–53.

Lawson, Frederick Henry, *A common lawyer looks at the civil law* (Ann Arbor, MI, 1953).

Lawson, Philip, *George Grenville: a political life* (Oxford, 1984).

Lecky, William Edward Hartpole, *A history of Ireland in the eighteenth century*, 5 vols (London, 1892).

Legg, Marie-Louise, 'The parish clergy of the Church of Ireland in the eighteenth century' in T.C. Barnard & W.G. Neely (eds), *The clergy of the church of Ireland, 1000–2000* (Dublin, 2006), pp 128–41.

Leigh, Ione, *Castlereagh* (London, 1951).

Lemmings, David, *Professors of the law: barristers and English legal culture in the eighteenth century* (Oxford, 2000).

Leslie, Anita, *Mrs Fitzherbert* (New York, 1960).

Leslie, Shane, *George the Fourth* (London, 1936).

Levy, Leonard W., *Emergence of a free press* (New York, 1985).

Lindsey, John, *The shining life and death of Lord Edward Fitzgerald* (London, 1947).

Livesey, James, 'Acts of union and disunion: Ireland in Atlantic and European contexts' in D. Keogh & K. Whelan (eds), *Acts of union: the causes, contexts and consequences of the Act of Union* (Dublin, 2001), pp 95–105.

Lobingier, Charles Sumner, 'The maritime law of Rome', *Juridical Review*, 47 (1935), 1–32.

Lord, Evelyn, *The Hellfire Clubs* (New Haven, CT, 2008).

Lovejoy, David S., *Rhode Island politics and the American Revolution, 1760–1776* (Providence, RI, 1958).

Lowther Clarke, William Kemp, *A history of the S.P.C.K.* (London, 1959).

Luce, Arthur Aston, *The life of George Berkeley, bishop of Cloyne* (New York, 1949).

Luce, John Victor, *Trinity College Dublin: the first 400 years* (Dublin, 1992).

Lyman, E.B., *A reminiscence of Newport before and during the Revolutionary War* (Newport, RI, 1906).

Macalpine, Ida & Richard Alfred Hunter, *George III and the mad-business* (London, 1969).

Mackesy, Piers, *The war for America, 1775–1783* (London, 1964).

Mackesy, Piers, *War without victory: the downfall of Pitt, 1799–1802* (Oxford, 1984).

MacNeill, John G.S., *The Irish Act of Union – how it was carried* (London, 1912).

MacNevin, Thomas, *The history of the Volunteers of 1782* (Dublin, 1882).

Magnus, Sir Philip, *Edmund Burke: a life* (London, 1939).

Maguire, W.A. (ed.), *Up in arms: the 1798 rebellion in Ireland* (Belfast, 1998).

Maier, Pauline, *From resistance to revolution: colonial radicals and the development of American opposition to Britain, 1765–1776* (New York, 1972).

Malcomson, Anthony P.W., *John Foster: the politics of Anglo-Irish Ascendency* (Oxford, 1978).

Malcomson, Anthony P.W., *Archbishop Charles Agar: churchmanship and politics in eighteenth-century Ireland, 1760–1810* (Dublin, 2002).

Maloney, Thomas H.D., *Edmund Burke and Ireland* (Cambridge, MA, 1960).

Mansergh, Daniel, 'The union and the importance of public opinion' in D. Keogh & K. Whelan (eds), *Acts of union: the causes, contexts and consequences of the Act of Union* (Dublin, 2001), pp 126–39.

Manwaring, George Earnest & Bonamy Dobrée, *The floating republic: an account of the mutinies at Spithead and the Nore* (New York, 1935).

Marshall, Dorothy, *Dr Johnson's London* (New York, 1968).

Mason, George C., *Annals of Trinity Church, Newport, Rhode Island, 1698–1821* (Newport, RI, 1890).

Mathiasen, Joanne, 'Some problems of admiralty jurisdiction in the 17th century', *American Journal of Legal History*, 2 (1958), 215–36.

Maxwell, Constantia Elizabeth, *A history of Trinity College Dublin, 1591–1892* (Dublin, 1946).

Maxwell, Constantia Elizabeth, *Dublin under the Georges, 1714–1830* (London, 1956).

McAnally, Henry W.W., *The Irish milita, 1793–1816: a social and military study* (Dublin, 1949).

McBride, Ian, *Eighteenth-century Ireland: the isle of slaves* (Dublin, 2009).

McCarthy, Michael (ed.), *Lord Charlemont and his circle: essays in honour of Michael Wynne* (Dublin, 2001).

McCarthy, Patricia, *A favourite study: building the King's Inns* (Dublin, 2006).

McCavery, Trevor, '"As the plague of locusts came in Egypt": rebel motivation in North Down' in T. Bartlett et al. (eds), *1798: a bicentenary perspective* (Dublin, 2003), pp 212–25.

McCracken, J.L., *The Irish Parliament in the eighteenth century* (Dundalk, 1971).

McCullough, David G., *John Adams* (New York, 2001).

McCullough, David G., *1776* (New York, 2005).

McDermott, Frank, *Theobald Wolfe Tone* (London, 1939).

McDonald, Brian, 'South Ulster in the age of the United Irishman' in T. Bartlett et al. (eds), *1798: a bicentenary perspective* (Dublin, 2003), pp 226–42.

McDowell, Robert Brendan, 'The personnel of the Dublin Society of the United Irishmen, 1791–4', *Irish Historical Studies*, 2 (1940–1941), 12–53.

McDowell, Robert Brendan, *Irish public opinion, 1750–1800* (London, 1944).

McDowell, Robert Brendan, *Ireland in the age of imperialism and revolution, 1760–1801* (Oxford, 1979).

McDowell, Robert Brendan, *Grattan: a life* (Dublin, 2001).

McDowell, Robert Brendan & David Allardice Webb, *Trinity College Dublin, 1592–1952: an academic history* (London, 1982).

McLoughlin, William G., *Rhode Island: a bicentennial history* (New York, 1978).

Metaxas, Eric, *Amazing grace: William Wilberforce and the heroic campaign to end slavery* (New York, 2007).

Midwinter, Edward, 'The Society for the Propagation of the Gospel and the Church in the American colonies', *Historical Magazine of the Protestant Episcopal Church*, 4 (1935), 67–82.

Miller, David W., 'Irish Christianity and revolution' in J. Smyth (ed.), *Revolution, counter-revolution and Union: Ireland in the 1790s* (Cambridge, 2000), pp 195–210.

Miller, John Chester, *Sam Adams: pioneer in propaganda* (Stanford, CA, 1936).

Milne, K., *APCK: the early decades* (Dublin, 1992).

Mitchell, Leslie George, *Charles James Fox and the disintegration of the Whig Party, 1782–1794* (London, 1971).

Moran, Gerard (ed.), *Radical Irish priests, 1660–1970* (Dublin, 1998).

Morgan, Edmund S., *Roger Williams: the church and the state* (New York, 1967).

Morgan, Edmund S. & Helen M. Morgan, *The Stamp Act crisis: prologue to revolution* (Chapel Hill, NC, 1953).

Morison, Elizabeth Forbes & Elting Elmore Morison, *New Hampshire: a bicentennial history* (New York, 1976).

Morison, Samuel Eliot, *Sources and documents illustrating the American Revolution, 1764–1788* (2nd ed. Oxford, 1929).

Morison, Samuel Eliot, *Three centuries of Harvard, 1636–1936* (Cambridge, MA, 1936).

Morison, Samuel Eliot, *The Oxford history of the American people* (New York, 1965).

Morison, Samuel Eliot, *The European discovery of America: the northern voyages* (New York, 1971).

Morley, Vincent, *Irish opinion and the American Revolution, 1760–1783* (New York, 2002).

Morris, Richard B., *The peacemakers: the great powers and American independence* (New York, 1965).

Morris, Richard B., *John Jay: the winning of the peace: unpublished papers, 1780–1784* (New York, 1980).

Morris, Richard B., *The forging of the union, 1781–1789* (New York, 1987).

Morrison, Wayne (ed.), *Blackstone's commentaries on the laws of England*, 4 vols (London, 2001).

Mount, Charles Merrill, *Gilbert Stuart: a biography* (New York, 1964).

Munson, James, *Maria Fitzherbert: the secret wife of George IV* (New York, 2001).

Murphy, David, *The Irish brigades, 1685–2006* (Dublin, 2007).

Murphy, John A. (ed.), *The French are in the bay: the expedition to Bantry Bay, 1796* (Dublin, 1997).

Murphy, Orville Theodore, *Charles Gravier, Comte de Vergennes: French diplomacy in the age of revolution, 1719–1787* (Albany, NY, 1982).

Murtagh, Harman, 'General Humbert's futile campaign' in T. Bartlett at al. (eds), *1798: a bicentenary perspective* (Dublin, 2003), pp 174–88.

Namier, Lewis Bernstein, *The structure of politics at the accession of George III* (revd ed. London, 1957).

Namier, Lewis Bernstein, *England in the age of the American Revolution* (2nd ed. London, 1963).

Nelson, William, E., *The common law in colonial America*, vol. 1 (New York, 2008).

Norris, John M., *Shelburne and reform* (New York, 1963).

Norton, Mary Beth, *The British-Americans: the loyalist exiles in England, 1774–1789* (Boston, 1972).

Ó Tuathaigh, Gearóid, *Ireland before the Famine, 1798–1848* (Dublin, 1972).

O'Brien, Conor Cruise, *The great melody: a thematic biography and commented anthology of Edmund Burke* (Chicago, 1992).

O'Brien, Gerard, *Anglo-Irish politics in the age of Grattan and Pitt* (Dublin, 1987).

O'Brien, Gerard & Tom Dunne (eds), *Catholic Ireland in the eighteenth century: collected essays of Maureen Wall* (Dublin, 1989).

O'Connell, Maurice R., *Irish political and social conflict in the age of the American Revolution* (Philadelphia, 1965).

O'Flanagan, J. Roderick, *The lives of the lord chancellors of Ireland and the keepers of the great seal of Ireland: from the earliest times to the reign of Queen Victoria* (London, 1870).

O'Gorman, Frank, *The rise of party in England: the Rockingham Whigs, 1760–1782* (London, 1975).

O'Higgins, Paul, 'Arthur Browne (1756–1805): an Irish civilian', *Northern Ireland Legal Quarterly*, 20 (1969), 255–73.

Ohlmeyer, Jane H., *Making Ireland English: the Irish aristocracy in the seventeenth century* (New Haven, CT, 2012).

O'Mahony, Charles Kingston, *The viceroys of Ireland* (London, 1912).

Orieux, Jean, *Talleyrand: the art of survival*, trans. P. Wolf (New York, 1974).

Osborough, W.N., 'Legal aspects of the 1798 Rising, its suppression and the aftermath' in T. Bartlett et al. (eds), *1798: a bicentenary perspective* (Dublin, 2003), pp 437–68.

Owen, David R., 'The origin and development of marine collision law', *Tulane Law Review*, 51 (1977), 759–819.

Owen, David R. & Michael Carlton Tolley, *Courts of admiralty in America: the Maryland experience, 1634–1776* (Durham, NC, 1995).

Pakenham, Thomas, *The year of liberty: the story of the great Irish rebellion* (Englewood Cliffs, NJ, 1969).

Pares, Richard, *George III and the politicians* (Oxford, 1953).

Pares, Richard, *Yankees and Creoles: the trade between North America and the West Indies before the American Revolution* (Cambridge, MA, 1956).

Parliamentary Register of Ireland, 1781–1797, 17 vols (Dublin, 1782–1801).

Pascoe, C.F., *Two hundred years of the S.P.G.: an historical account of the Society for the Propagation of the Gospel in Foreign Parts, 1701–1900* (London, 1901).

Pearson, Hesketh, *Merry monarch: the life and likeness of Charles II* (New York, 1960).

Pennington, Edgar Legare, *The Reverend Arthur Browne of Rhode Island and New Hampshire* (Hartford, CT, 1938).

Philbrick, Nathaniel, *Mayflower: a story of courage, community, and war* (New York, 2006).

Plucknett, Theodore, *A concise history of the common law* (5th ed. Boston, 1956).

Plumb, John Harold, *The first four Georges* (London, 1956).

Pollock, John Charles, *Wilberforce* (London, 1977).

Pope, Dudley, *The black ship* (London, 1963).

Pope-Hennessy, James, *Sins of the fathers: a study of the Atlantic slave traders, 1441–1807* (New York, 1968).

Power, Patrick C., *The courts martial of 1798–99* (Kilkenny, 1997).

Power, Thomas P., 'Conversions among the legal profession in Ireland in the eighteenth century' in D. Hogan & W.N. Osborough (eds), *Brehons, serjeants and attorneys* (Dublin, 1990), pp 153–74.

Puls, Mark, *Samuel Adams: father of the American Revolution* (New York, 2006).

Quinn, James, 'Dublin Castle and the Act of Union' in M. Brown et al. (eds), *The Irish Act of Union, 1800: bicentennial essays* (Dublin, 2003), pp 95–107.

Quinn, James, 'The Kilmainham treaty of 1798' in T. Bartlett et al. (eds), *1798: a bicentenary perspective* (Dublin, 2003), pp 423–36.

Rappleye, Charles, *Sons of providence: the Brown brothers, the slave trade, and the American Revolution* (New York, 2006).

Reid, John Phillip, 'In accordance with usage: the authority of custom, the Stamp Act debate, and the coming of the American Revolution', *Fordham Law Review*, 45 (1976), 335–68.

Reid, John Phillip, *In a defiant stance: the conditions of law in Massachusetts Bay, the Irish comparison, and the coming of the American Revolution* (University Park, PA, 1977).

Report of debates in the House of Commons of Ireland, session 1796–7 (Dublin, 1797).

Report of the debate in the House of Commons of Ireland, on Tuesday and Wednesday the 22nd and 23rd of January, 1799 (Dublin, 1799).

Report of the debate in the House of Commons of Ireland, on Wednesday and Thursday the 15th and 16th of January, 1800 (Dublin, 1800).

Rhoden, Nancy L., *Revolutionary Anglicanism: the colonial Church of England clergy during the American Revolution* (New York, 1999).

Richardson, Joanna, *George IV: a portrait* (London, 1966).

Ripley, George & Charles Anderson Dana, *The American cyclopedia: a popular dictionary of general knowledge* (New York, 1873).

Roche, John F., *The colonial colleges in the war for American independence* (Millwood, NY, 1986).

Rogers, Mary Cochrane, *Glimpses of an old social capital (Portsmouth, New Hampshire) as illustrated in the life of the Reverend Arthur Browne and his circle* (Boston, 1923).

Rogers, Patrick, *The Irish Volunteers and Catholic emancipation (1778–1793): a neglected phase of Ireland's history* (London, 1934).

Rudé, George F.E., *Wilkes and liberty: a social study of 1763–1774* (Oxford, 1962).

Ruggles, Thomas, *The barrister: or, strictures on the education proper for the Bar* (Dublin, 1792).

Sanborn, Frederic Rockwell, *Origins of the early English maritime and commercial law* (London, 1930).

Schecter, Barnet, *The battle for New York: the city at the heart of the American Revolution* (New York, 2002).

Schlesinger, Arthur Meier, *The colonial merchants and the American Revolution, 1763–1776* (New York, 1918).

Scott, Samuel Parsons (ed. and trans.), *The civil law* (Cincinnati, OH, 1932).

Senior, William, *Doctors' commons and the old court of admiralty: a short history of civilians in England* (London, 1922).

Simms, John Gerald, *The Williamite confiscation in Ireland, 1690–1703* (London, 1956).

Simms, John Gerald, *Jacobite Ireland, 1685–91* (London, 1969).

Smith, Earnest Anthony, *Whig principles and party politics: Earl Fitzwilliam and the Whig Party, 1748–1833* (Manchester, 1975).

Smith, James Morton, *Freedom's fetters: the alien and sedition laws and American civil liberties* (Ithaca, NY, 1956).

Smith, Page, *John Adams* (Garden City, NY, 1962).

Smith, Paul Hubert, 'The American loyalists: notes on their organization and numerical strength', *William and Mary Quarterly*, 25 (1968), 259–77.

Smith, Robert S., 'The Llibre del Consolat de Mar: a bibliography', *Law Library Journal*, 33 (1940), 387–95.

Smyth, Constantine J., *Chronicle of the law officers of Ireland* (Dublin, 1839).

Smyth, Jim (ed.), *Revolution, counter-revolution and union: Ireland in the 1790s* (Cambridge, 2000).

Smyth, P.D.H., 'The Volunteers and Parliament, 1779–84' in T. Bartlett & D.W. Hayton (eds), *Penal era and golden age: essays in Irish history, 1690–1800* (Belfast, 1979), pp 113–36.

Snell, Steven L., *Courts of admiralty and the common law: origins of the American experiment in concurrent jurisdiction* (Durham, NC, 2007).

Somerville, Edith Oenone & Martin Ross, *An incorruptible Irishman: being an account of chief justice Charles Bushe, and of his wife, Nancy Crampton, and their times, 1767–1843* (London, 1932).

Squibb, George Drewry, *Doctors' commons: a history of the College of Advocates and Doctors of Law* (Oxford, 1977).

Steiner, Bruce E., *Samuel Seabury, 1729–1769: a study in the High Church tradition* (Athens, OH, 1971).

Stensrud, Rockwell, *Newport: a lively experiment, 1639–1969* (Newport, RI, 2006).

Stewart, Anthony Terence Quincey, *The summer soldiers: the 1798 rebellion in Antrim and Down* (Belfast, 1995).

Stinson, J. Whitla, 'Admiralty and maritime jurisdiction of the courts of Great Britain, France and the United States', *Northwestern University Law Review*, 16 (1921), 1–22.

Stout, Neil R., *The royal navy in America, 1760–1775: a study of enforcement of British colonial policy in the era of the American Revolution* (Annapolis, MD, 1973).

Straub, Peter, *The Hellfire Club* (New York, 1995).

Stubbs, John Williams, *The history of the University of Dublin from its foundation to the end of the eighteenth century* (Dublin, 1889).

Sullivan, Francis Stoughton, *An historical treatise on the feudal law and the constitution and laws of England* (Dublin, 1772).

Sweeney, Joseph C., 'An overview of commercial salvage principles in the context of marine archaeology', *Journal of Maritime Law and Commerce*, 30 (1999), 185–204.

Sweeney, Joseph C., 'Limitation of shipowner liability: its American roots and some problems particular to collision', *Journal of Maritime Law and Commerce*, 32 (2001), 241–78.

Sweeney, Joseph C., 'The Silver Oar and other maces of the admiralty: admiralty jurisdiction in America and the British empire', *Journal of Maritime Law and Commerce*, 38 (2007), 159–76.

Sweeney, Joseph C., 'The just-war ethic in international law', *Fordham International Law Journal*, 27 (2008), 1865–1903.

Swift, Theophilus, *Animadversions on the fellows of Trinity College* (Dublin, 1794).

Tanner, Marcus, *Ireland's holy wars: the struggle for a nation's soul, 1500–2000* (New Haven, CT, 2001).

Taylor, William Benjamin Sarsfield, *History of the University of Dublin* (Dublin, 1846).

Thomas, Hugh, *The slave trade: the story of the Atlantic slave trade, 1440–1870* (New York, 1997).

Thomas, Peter D.G., *British politics and the Stamp Act crisis: the first phase of the American Revolution, 1763–1767* (Oxford, 1975).

Thomas, Peter D.G., *The Townshend Duties crisis: the second phase of the American Revolution, 1767–1773* (Oxford, 1987).

Thomas, Peter D.G., *Tea Party to independence: the third phase of the American Revolution, 1773–1776* (Oxford, 1991).

Thomas, Peter D.G., *John Wilkes: a friend to liberty* (New York, 1996).

Thompson, Henry Paget, *Into all lands: the history of the Society for the Propagation of the Gospel in Foreign Parts, 1701–1950* (London, 1951).

Tillyard, Stella K., *Citizen lord: the life of Edward Fitzgerald, Irish revolutionary* (New York, 1997).

Tone, Theobold Wolfe, *The autobiography of Theobold Wolfe Tone*, ed. S. O'Faoláin (New York, 1937).

Tourtellot, Arthur Bernon, *William Diamond's drum: the beginning of the war of the American Revolution* (Garden City, NY, 1959).

Towle, Dorothy S., *Records of the vice-admiralty court of Rhode Island, 1716–1752* (Washington, DC, 1936).

Trench, Charles, *Portrait of a patriot: a biography of John Wilkes* (Edinburgh, 1962).

Trench, Charles, *The royal malady* (London, 1964).

Trevelyan, George Macaulay, *England under the Stuarts* (London, 1904).

Trevelyan, George Otto, *George III and Charles Fox: the concluding part of the American Revolution*, 2 vols (London, 1912).

Tuchman, Barbara W., *The first salute: a view of the American Revolution* (New York, 1988).

Twiss, Travers, *Monumenta juridica: the black book of the admiralty*, 4 vols (London, 1871).

Tyler, John W., *Smugglers and patriots: Boston merchants and the advent of the American Revolution* (Boston, 1986).

Ubbelohde, Carl, *The vice-admiralty courts and the American Revolution* (Chapel Hill, NC, 1960).

Updike, Wilkins, *Memoirs of the Rhode Island Bar* (Boston, 1842).

Van Deventer, David E., *The emergence of provincial New Hampshire, 1623–1741* (Baltimore, 1976).

Wall, Maureen, *The penal laws, 1691–1760* (Dundalk, 1967).

Walsh, Walter J., 'Religion, ethnicity, and history: clues to the cultural construction of law' in R. Bayor & T. Meagher (eds), *The New York Irish* (Baltimore, 1996), pp 48–69.

Weintraub, Stanley, *Iron tears: America's battle for freedom, Britain's quagmire, 1775–1783* (New York, 2005).

Wendorf, Richard, *Sir Joshua Reynolds: the painter in society* (Cambridge, MA, 1996).

Weslager, Clinton Alfred, *The Stamp Act Congress, with an exact copy of the complete journal* (Newark, DE, 1976).

Whitridge, Arnold, *Rochambeau* (New York, 1965).

Wickwire, Franklin B. and Mary Wickwire, *Cornwallis: the American adventure* (Boston, 1970).

Wickwire, Franklin B. and Mary Wickwire, *Cornwallis: the imperial years* (Chapel Hill, NC, 1980).

Wiener, Frederick Bernays, 'Notes on the Rhode Island admiralty, 1727–1790', *Harvard Law Review*, 46 (1932), 44–90.

Wiener, Frederick Bernays, 'The Rhode Island merchants and the Sugar Act', *New England Quarterly*, 3 (1938), 464–500.

Wigmore, John Henry, *A panorama of the world's legal systems* (St Paul, MN, 1928).

Wild, John Daniel, *George Berkeley: a study of his life and philosophy* (New York, 1936).

Wilkinson, David, 'The Fitzwilliam episode, 1795: a reinterpretation of the role of the duke of Portland', *Irish Historical Studies*, 29 (1995), 315–39.

Wilkinson, David, '"How did they pass the union?" Secret Service expenditure in Ireland, 1799–1804', *History*, 82 (1997), 223–51.

Williams, Basil, *The Whig supremacy, 1714–1760* (2nd ed. Oxford, 1962).

Willis, R. Ellen, 'William Pitt's resignation in 1801: re-examination and document', *Bulletin of the Institute of Historical Research*, 44 (1971), 239–57.

Wilson, David, 'The United Irishmen and the re-invention of Irish America' in T. Bartlett et al. (eds), *1798: a bicentenary perspective* (Dublin, 2003), pp 634–41.

Wilson, D.J., J.H.S. Cooke & Richard Lowndes (eds), *Lowndes and Rudolf: the law of general average and the York-Antwerp rules* (11th ed. London, 1990).

Wiswall Jnr, F.L, *The development of admiralty jurisdiction and practice since 1800: an English study with American comparisons* (Cambridge, 1970).

Wolf, Nicholas M., *Irish-speaking island: state, religion, community, and the linguistic landscape in Ireland, 1770–1870* (Madison, WI, 2014).

Wood, Gordon S., *The creation of the American republic, 1776–1787* (Chapel Hill, NC, 1969).

Wood, Gordon S., *The radicalism of the American Revolution* (New York, 1992).

Wroth, L. Kinvin, 'The Massachusetts vice admiralty court and the federal admiralty jurisdiction', *American Journal of Legal History*, 6 (1962), 250–68.

Wroth, L. Kinvin & Hiller B. Zobel (eds), *Legal papers of John Adams*, 3 vols (Cambridge, MA, 1965).

Wyse, Thomas, *Historical sketch of the late Catholic Association of Ireland* (London, 1829).

York, Neil Longley, *Neither kingdom nor nation: the Irish quest for constitutional rights, 1698–1800* (Washington, DC, 1994).

Young, Arthur, *A tour in Ireland, 1776–1779* (Dublin, 1780, repr. Shannon, 1970).

Ziegler, Philip, *Addington: a life of Henry Addington, first viscount Sidmouth* (New York, 1965).

Zobel, Hiller B., *The Boston Massacre* (New York, 1970).

Index

Irish Legal History Society

Established in 1988 to encourage the study and advance the knowledge of the history of Irish law, especially by the publication of original documents and of works relating to the history of Irish law, including its institutions, doctrines and personalities, and reprinting or editing of works of sufficient rarity or importance.

PATRONS 2015–16

The Rt Hon. Sir Declan Morgan   The Hon. Mrs Justice Susan Denham
Lord Chief Justice of Northern Ireland   Chief Justice of Ireland

COUNCIL 2015–16

President
The Hon. Mr Justice Deeny

Vice-Presidents
Dr Patrick M. Geoghegan   John G. Gordon

Honorary Secretaries
Dr Thomas Mohr   Dr David Capper

Honorary Treasurers
R.D. Marshall   Kevin Neary

Website editor
Dr Niamh Howlin

Council Members
Ex officio: Robert D. Marshall, President 2012–15

Dr Kevin Costello   Dr Coleman Dennehy
Paul Egan   Dr Kenneth P. Ferguson BL
The Hon. Hugh Geoghegan   Dr Maebh Harding
Sir Anthony Hart   Dr Robin Hickey
Professor Colum Kenny BL   Felix M. Larkin
John Larkin QC   James I. McGuire MRIA
His Honour John Martin QC   Mark Orr QC
Dr Sean D. O'Reilly   Richard Sheilds BL

www.ilhs.eu